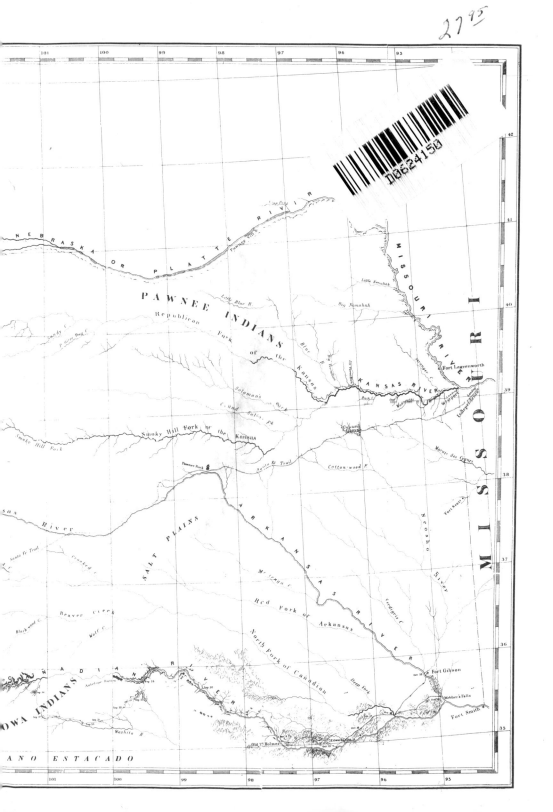

PAGE

THE
COLORADO
BOOK

George Elbert Burr, "Mount of the Holy Cross," n.d.

THE
COLORADO
BOOK

Edited by

Eleanor M. Gehres, Sandra Dallas, Maxine Benson and Stanley Cuba

FULCRUM PUBLISHING

Golden, Colorado

Cover image "Heart of the Rockies," photographed by William Henry Jackson;
image colorized by Detroit Publishing Company through color lithography.
Courtesy of the Denver Public Library, Western History Collection

Library of Congress Cataloging-in-Publication Data

The Colorado book / edited by Eleanor Gehres ... [et al.].
      p.   cm.
   Includes bibliographical references and index.
   ISBN 1-55591-116-1
     1. American literature—Colorado. 2. Colorado—Literary collections.
3. Colorado—Description and travel. I. Gehres, Eleanor M.
PS571.C6C59   1993
810.8'032788—dc20   92-53034
                                                                CIP

Printed in the United States of America

0 9 8 7 6 5 4 3 2 1

Fulcrum Publishing
350 Indiana Street, Suite 350
Golden, Colorado 80401-5093

TABLE OF CONTENTS

INTRODUCTION

ON A JULY DAY IN 1893, Katharine Lee Bates and a group of friends climbed into a covered wagon marked "Pikes Peak or Bust" and rode to the top of Colorado's most famous mountain. For Bates, a Wellesley College English instructor who had spent the summer teaching at Colorado College in Colorado Springs, the trip up Pikes Peak was a final outing before returning to Massachusetts.

When the travelers reached the 14,110-foot summit of Pikes Peak, Bates' friends scooped up snow and pelted each other with snowballs. The portly Bates, however, walked off by herself to gaze at the mountains and at the prairie below.

The trip was a hurried one, cut short because some of the party were stricken with altitude sickness. But it was a memorable journey for Bates—and for America. By the time the English teacher boarded the train for the East, Bates had scribbled four immortal lines:

> O beautiful for spacious skies,
> For amber waves of grain,
> For purple mountain majesties
> Above the fruited plain!

"America the Beautiful" was published in 1895 in *The Congregationalist.* Put to music several years later, it became one of America's most beloved songs—and surely the most famous bit of verse ever inspired by Colorado.

Bates was a better versifier than most of the state's visitors, but she was only one of thousands, perhaps millions, of writers who were inspired by Colorado. Spanish explorers and fur trappers, journalists and poets and immigrants "out to see the elephant," beetpickers and cowboys, bankers and beatniks—nearly everyone who came to Colorado, it seems, felt compelled to write about it.

With so many writers from which to choose, then, it's not an easy task to select the 150 who should be featured in an anthology of Colorado literature. There was no way, of course, to include everyone. A book that large would have to be carried around in a wheelbarrow. Not only did the editors have to choose the writers who represented best the rich variety of the state's literature, but they had to pick the most compelling example of each one's writing.

Work began on *The Colorado Book* in 1990, when Bob Baron of Fulcrum Publishing, inspired by *The Last Best Place: A Montana Anthology,* a gargantuan collection of Montana literary excerpts, decided to publish a Colorado literary anthology. He asked a committee of historians and writers to develop a similar, though less unwieldy, work on the Centennial State. Headed by Eleanor Gehres, manager of the Denver Public Library Western History Department, the group turned up a long list of writers, but the process showed that a large committee is no way to edit a book. So Eleanor and Maxine Benson, former Colorado state historian and coauthor of *A Colorado History,* took over the task.

They asked Stanley Cuba, independent curator and member of the Arvada Center's Gallery I Museum Committee, and Sandra Dallas, former *Business Week* Denver bureau chief and author of ten books on the West, to join them as editors. The four of us believed our complementary backgrounds made us familiar with both scholarly and popular works, and with a variety of other subjects as well.

In compiling *The Colorado Book,* we realized at the outset that we might be criticized for our choices. So instead of trying to please everybody, we decided to please ourselves. We first organized the state into various topics such as mountains, mining and women, then divided the subjects among ourselves. We each read everything we could find on our topics, then recommended excerpts for publication. The four of us generally were unanimous in selecting or rejecting the pieces. In fact, there was only one serious disagreement, and that was Katherine Anne Porter's *Pale Horse, Pale Rider.* The story probably was set at the *Rocky Mountain News* in Denver, where Porter once worked, but neither the paper nor Denver is mentioned in the short story. Eventually, we decided not to include it.

Some of our subject categories fell by the wayside, too. We decided that women, for instance, shouldn't be relegated to a single category but included in each of the groupings. We wanted variety, and that meant selecting not only the state's best writing but some of its most offbeat as well. Silver Dollar Tabor, for instance, is no literary icon, but she is too important to Colorado for us to overlook her funky writing. Still, we had our standards, and we rejected some popular topics because we could not find an author whose work was good enough to be included.

Guidelines developed as we went along. With only a few exceptions, we limited authors to one entry each. Wherever possible, we chose first-person accounts. We went back to the originals when possible, even though more modern editions were available. All excerpts had to have been published previously, so there are no newly discovered letters or journal excerpts included here. While many of our choices appeared in newspapers, we eliminated straight news accounts because this is a literary book, not a history. For the same reason, we generally opted for art instead of archival photographs.

There were some surprises. We had believed the radio serial "Our Gal Sunday" was loosely based on Lady Moon, the Greeley washerwoman who married an English lord. Each episode of the serial asks the question, "can this girl from a mining town in the West find happiness as the wife of a wealthy and titled Englishman?" We don't know how things turned out for Sunday, but the four of us were doomed to disappointment. We began hunting for an "Our Gal Sunday" radio script to include in this book, only to discover that the soap opera was based on the Broadway play, *Sunday,* which had nothing to do with the Moons.

Other discoveries were happier ones. While most western anthologies are heavy on historical work, we were pleased to find a wealth of post–World War II Colorado literature. Much of Jack Kerouac's *On the Road* , for instance, is set in the state. Folk singer Judy Collins grew up in Denver, so Colorado is prominent in her autobiography, *Trust Your Heart,* and is a source of inspiration for her songs. And Edgar Award winner Rex Burns, whose Hispanic detective, Gabe Wager, works Denver's gritty streets, is as contemporary as the porno houses of East Colfax Avenue.

We are Coloradans, and this is a book about Colorado. We hope you like our selections. We do, and that is why we chose them.

SECTION I

THE
CENTENNIAL STATE

THE LAND WHERE
THE COLUMBINES GROW

Arthur J. Fynn

(Adopted by the State Legislature as State Song, 1915)

Where the snowy peaks gleam in the moonlight,
 Above the dark forests of pine,
And the wild foaming waters dash onward
 Toward lands where the tropic stars shine;
Where the scream of the bold mountain eagle
 Responds to the notes of the dove,
Is the purple-robed West, the land that is best,
 The pioneer land that we love.

CHORUS

'Tis the land where the columbines grow,
Overlooking the plains far below,
While the cool summer breeze
In the evergreen trees
Softly sings where the columbines grow.

The bison is gone from the upland,
 The deer from the canyon has fled,
The home of the wolf is deserted,
 The antelope mourns for his dead,
The war-whoop re-echoes no longer,
 The Indian's only a name,
And the nymphs of the grove in their loneliness rove,
 But the columbine blooms just the same.

Let the violets brighten the brookside,
 In the sunlight of earlier spring,
Let the clover bedeck the green meadow,
 In days when the orioles sing,
Let the goldenrod herald the autumn,
 But, under the midsummer sky,
In its fair western home, may the columbine bloom
 Till our great mountain rivers run dry.

WHERE THE WEST BEGINS

Arthur Chapman

Out where the handclasp's a little stronger,
Out where a smile dwells a little longer,
    That's where the West begins;
Out where the sun is a little brighter,
Where the snows that fall are a trifle whiter,
Where the bonds of home are a wee bit tighter—
    That's where the West begins.

Out where the skies are a trifle bluer,
Out where friendship's a little truer,
    That's where the West begins;
Out where a fresher breeze is blowing,
Where there's laughter in every streamlet flowing,
Where there's more of reaping and less of sowing—
    That's where the West begins.

Out where the world is in the making,
Where fewer hearts with despair are aching—
    That's where the West begins;
Where there's more of singing and less of sighing,
Where there's more of giving and less of buying,
And a man makes friends without half trying—
    That's where the West begins.

DEDICATION TO
THOMAS HORNSBY FERRIL

"A man is as tall as his height
Plus the height of his home town.
I know a Denverite
Who measured from sea to crown,
Is one mile five feet ten.
And he swings a commensurate pen."

        (Robert Frost to Thomas Ferril in Thomas Ferril's copy
              of *Collected Poems of Robert Frost*)

STORIES OF THREE SUMMERS COLORADO 1776* 1876* 1976*

Thomas Hornsby Ferril

I.   1776

Two hundred years ago
In the dog days of that summer
    Of Life, Liberty and Pursuit of Happiness
Two friars scuffing golden rabbit-brush
For the glory of God
And the Holy King of Spain
Were goading their guides,
Their cattle, dreams and horses
Down the Dolores River
And over the Uncompaghre Mesa
Where Colorado was going to be.

    They needed guides to show them where to go
    As we do now.

The guides were Utes,
Young men and boys
Who knew the roads of rivers and old trees
Their fathers and their fathers
Had long traveled
Under the Goose-Going-Moon,
Under the Star-That-Never-Marches.

Admiring citron trees
And stalks of sarsaparilla,
Fray Silvestre Valez de Escalante
Smoked his cigars,
Stared at the constellations,
Knowing no more than a prong-horned antelope
Of how a leaden statue
Of King George the Third
Had been melted into bullets
In New York.

Nor did he know
He'd never reach
What he was yearning for ...
Those holy missions
Blessed by the vespers of the Western Sea
In far-off California.

> *We never know*
> *Until long afterward*
> *If even then.*

Francisco Atanasia Dominguez
Was sick with chills and fever
While Lord Cornwallis
Was prodding his red-coat musketeers
Toward Flatbush
But knew nothing of it.
Nor did he know
Foreshadowings of *Figaro*
Were lilting in the singing heart
Of Mozart.

> *We never know.*

II. 1876

Ten decades of manzanita berries
Come and go on the Uncompaghre Mesa,
The Fathers Escalante and Dominguez
Fade into waters naming the arroyos.

In Colorado Territory
Statehood long denied
Can be denied no longer.

Sagacious gentlemen in Oddfellows Hall
Puff out their waistcoats
Prouder than pouter pigeons,
Hitch up the galluses of their pantaloons
And slap each other on the back
To end their endless bickerings
Over a Constitution

For Beautiful Colorado
Most Glorious Jewel
In the Diadem of States.

Ladies in sunbonnets plant sweet peas
Under windy trellises of chickenwire.
Snowballs blossom,
Doves coo to their mates,
Taffeta girls and mandolin boys
Sing old sweet songs at twilight
On the jig-saw front piazza.

Sales are brisk for ladies' linen collars
And Mustang Liniment, the Foe of Pain,
Hand-hammered horseshoe nails
Are in abundance

    And rosewood coffins.

The sun comes up with a bang on the
Fourth of July!
Bells! Whistles!
Stove pokers beating dishpans!
Parades! Parades!
Proud horses nodding plumes!

    Miss Neoma Haggerty
    Is *The Spirit of Liberty.*

A shuffling boy of a Negro slave intrudes,
Parading down the street alone
In a tattered old Prince Albert coat,
The clapper of his hand-bell clangs
The *lost-child* clang of the mining camps,
He chants
    Loss Chile!
       Loss Chile!
         Loss Chile!

They reach the park,
They hear *Centennial Hymn*
By John Greenleaf Whittier of Haverhill,
They hear *Centennial*

A poem by Lawrence Greenleaf
Proprietor
Of the Toy-and-Stationery Store.

The poem starts
  O, day, aforetime, ominous
  and heralded with fears
Continues through
  Two thousand
        and eighty-one words
And ends
  Till Freedom with her halo-light
  pervades the world at last.

Tumult drowses down the morning star,
Trumpeters sleep late,
Husks of skyrockets
Tangle the tumbleweeds
And business of the grasshoppers
Goes on.

On August 1 Ulysses Simpson Grant
Takes pen in hand and signs a piece of paper.

Another State begins to be a State
And over the long blue echoings
Of plains against the ranges
Eagles fly,
Beavers build dams
And there is joy
In Growth
And Progress
And Prosperity.

III.   1976

Another hundred years …

Trails of pack-mules fade into vapor trails
To Elsewhere,
Any Elsewhere anywhere.

Here to Las Vegas
In two martinis flat!
Caesar's Palace!
Under the undulations of the desert
Trundling megatons
Kill yucca moths and prairie dogs
And mice,
Caesar's Palace trembles

And rolls dice.

We elbow through an opiate shadowland.

The air is foul,
The seas are sour,
Trees of the forest disappear,
Why do we cringe back home from blundering wars?
Why are too many people here?

We grin and grimace into apathy.

There is no laughter,
No delight,
If there be sunrise
Sunrise will be night.

I go out Washington Street to Washington Park,
Old men are fishing by the lake,
I say hello and ask one pensioner
        "Why do we call this *Washington* Park?"
        "Because we always did ..."
And the old man drifts
Like the bobber on his bait
Way back to when "they let us kids
        go swimmin' in Wash Park Lake
        before it made you sick."

Platoons of children trot around the lake
With placards on their backs
        Jogging for Jesus
I ask one straggler if he'd like to hear
Me tell a story about George Washington,

"Is that your dog's name?
"Does he bite?"

My beagle has a water-fight with a sprinkler,
The lake is rippling up the undersilver
Leaves of cottonwood and I pretend
I see the Washington Monument
Splitting the heavens
Like a whetstoned obelisk.

I make a rhyme:

> *The first stone came from Bunker Hill,*
> *The last stone came*
> *From the Emperor of Brazil ...*

The phallic obelisk takes off like a rocket
In a blaze of hatchets and cherry trees
Plugging a Washington's Birthday sale
Of sure deodorants
Or your money back.

I who tell those stories of three summers
Must not let allegory blunt
My plain intention
To interweave old tales of Colorado
With deeds of far-off patriots long ago
We try to celebrate
By mere coincidence
Of dates on calendars

Like saying *Happy Birthday*
To ourselves
As we click a stop-watch on oblivion.

Off to the west
Where my elm tree used to be
Before the beetles killed it
I see the Rocky Mountains
Trying to shoulder up
Above the violet-ochre smog
Of Jefferson County.

Jeffco we call it.

Jeffco, I ask,
How often do you think of Thomas Jefferson
In morning times and evening times?

The smog is drifting my way,
I can taste it.

I turn my car on Adams Street in Denver,
John Adams, do I hear your voice?
Yours, Abigail Adams,
Bride of a President,
Mother of a President?

I hear one sparrow chirp.

I make another turn at Franklin Street,
You, Benjamin Franklin?
You lewd outrageous fellow!
Would we put up with the likes of you today
Even in Washington?

Washington ...Washington ...
I repeat the word ... what does it mean!

At home I drowse in honeysuckle shadows,
Our heroes, where have *they* gone?
Where have *we* been?
What are *we* heading to?

There ought to be some moral
To my chronicles,
I am too old to break with my belief
The world is getting better

Yet ...

My garden wall is a lens through which I see
Tortures of war on every continent
And across the alley
Little Felicita before she became a nun
Jerking the legs off grasshoppers.

Eyes half closed
I watch a bumblebee in the honeysuckle
Buzzing the sandy dynasties of Egypt
From flower to flower,
I hear the warble of a rosy breasted finch
Over the wheezings of the snow-bound elephants
Of Hannibal,
I hear a squatting sorcerer in Denver
Talking shop with a con-man in Babylon.

Out of the time-slosh of the tides
We've learned to crawl
And race the stars so soon,
We can't remember who we were tomorrow,
We can't remember who it was
Back in those quaint old days
Who walked the moon.

Do I hear terror singing into laughter?
Do I hear torture gasping into love?
Dare I believe more dreams than I can prove?
We never never know until long after

If even then

For centuries are only flicks
Of dragonflies
Over the granite mountains.

THE COLORADO

Frank Waters

MOST RIVERS ARE CONFINED to the needs and histories of men. Like roads, they seem inconsequential without their travelers. The Colorado is an outlaw. It belongs only to the ancient, eternal earth. As no other, it is savage and unpredictable of mood, peculiarly American in character. It has for its background the haunting sweep of illimitable horizons, the immensities of unbroken wilderness. From perpetually snow-capped peaks to stifling deserts below sea level, it cuts the deepest and truest cross section through the continent.

As the Rocky Mountains are the backbone of physical North America, the Colorado is the vertebral tube carrying the spinal fluid of the continent. From this viscous, reddish flow the river derives its name. Despite a score of other names, it has become known at last simply by its one unchanging color—in Spanish the *Rio Colorado*, the great Red River of the West.

Its landscapes are never anywhere urban or commercial, not even pastoral. They are purely mystical in tone. There are the wind-swept rocky wastes high above timberline, the sunless gloom of deep gorges. When the river does rise to the surface again it is upon the face of an earth whose expressions are never twice the same.

The black volcanic picachos creep closer in the moonlight, baring their saw-tooth fangs. By day the crinkled desert hills diminish and recede, or merely float, bottomless, upon the horizon. More often than not the mountains are mirages. Glistening salt beds and alkali flats turn into seas; uncovered veins of legendary native gold into mere banks of micaceous gravel.

In this shifting realm of the fantastic unreal only the river is permanent. It is the one enduring mesmer from whose spectral spell no man who has once seen it is ever quite freed.

Those who love it best are those who fear it most. For like all things touched with the sublime it carries a lurking horror, and its mysteries wear the mask of the commonplace. To allude to it as something more than a river would sound like a literary affectation only to the literary. The illiterate might well comprehend most fully all that it expresses. As from a Navajo sand painting or ceremonial blanket he would read the river's cryptic meaning in the earth it threads.

The dreamlike vacuousness, wild beauty and barbaric boldness of design form but the pattern of the warp which underlies the subtle, inimical resistance of the woof. Old, ancient America! With its own great spirit of place; with the shadows of aboriginal ghosts still gliding across it; and with its own demons not yet appeased—the haunting promise of the far-off, its tormenting unrest.

It is still a wilderness. To understand it you must think in new dimensions. You must feel in terms of depth as well as space, of eternity and not of time.

WHERE THE SILVERY COLORADO WENDS ITS WAY

C. H. Scoggins

The twilight softly gathers 'round my home among the hills,
And all nature soon will settle down to rest,
While I sit and sadly ponder and my heart with longing fills,
As I often think of one that I loved best;
We were wedded in the June-time, and our hearts then knew no pain,
Fair nature seemed to smile on us that day;
Now she sleeps beneath the lilacs and she'll ne'er come back again,
Where the silv'ry Colorado wends its way.

REFRAIN

There's a sob on ev'ry breeze, and a sigh comes from the trees,
And the meadowlark now croons a sadder lay,
For the sunlight plays no more 'round my cheerless cabin door,
Where the silv'ry Colorado wends its way.

The silv'ry snow is gleaming on yon distant mountainside,
Where we often used to wander, Nell and I,
And the birds are gaily singing in the valley far below,
Where I long some day to lay me down and die;
Then our lives were gay and happy, in the shadow of the hills,
My heart beat fonder for her day by day;
And I feel her presence near me as I sit alone tonight,
Where the silv'ry Colorado wends its way.

INSIDE U.S.A.

John Gunther

COLORADO, THE MOST SPECTACULAR of the mountain states, lives on many things—scenery, beet sugar, gold, molybdenum, livestock, tourists, and tuberculosis. As to this last I heard an ungentle and tasteless Coloradan complain, "Some fiend in human form discovered that rest, not altitude, was the best cure for t.b., and so the tuberculosis cases don't come to Colorado so much any more, and the economy of

John Frederick Kensett, "In the Heart of the Rockies [Bergen Park]," 1870.

the state suffered terribly as a result, so I suppose you could say that t.b. is killing us, not the patients."

Very little in the world can compare to the scenery of Colorado. The vistas here stretch the eyes, enlighten the heart, and make the spirit humble. Colorado has more than 1,500 peaks—literally—more than 10,000 feet high, and of the sixty-five in the United States higher than 14,000 feet, it has not less than fifty-one. This is indeed the top of the nation. Colorado has the highest automobile road in the country, the highest automobile races, the highest ski courses, the highest astronomical laboratory and the highest railway tunnel and the highest lake and the highest yacht anchorage and the highest suspension bridge. It has two national parks and six national monuments, fourteen million acres of national forest and more than seven thousand miles of fishing streams. And no matter where you turn, up and down or left and right, the overwhelming variety and magnitude of the view makes you blink. But—the state has had to learn these past years that scenery alone, no matter how stupefyingly dramatic, does not pay the bills. Scenery alone is not enough.

Colorado, like Oregon among the western states, is distinctly on the conservative side. It is conservative politically, economically, financially. I do not mean reactionary. Just conservative—with the kind of conservativeness that does not budge an inch for anybody or anything unless pinched and pushed. For instance, one point among several, Colorado is the thirty-ninth state in amount of state aid to education. Or consider reconversion. Washington and California, as we know, worked hard and concretely on postwar planning, to ease the gap toward peace. Colorado did almost nothing—and was proud of it. It has ridden for year after year on its prestige, its reputation. Nothing better illustrates this than affairs in Denver, ...

But to return to scenery and tourist traffic for a moment. In a normal year tourists bring into the state something like sixty-five million dollars. This sum is not to be sneezed at, but it could be greater. I heard complaints generally that "Colorado has missed the boat on tourism." Scenery is to Colorado what sunshine is to California, but it makes nothing like California's effort to capitalize on this asset, dramatize and buttress it. There will be many, I grant, who will congratulate Colorado for its lack of organized booster spirit. But progressive Coloradans themselves worry about how the state is becoming a backwater. Until quite recently, for instance, it employed no director of public relations and the governor had no press advisor. This was mostly the result of negative influence by the *Denver Post*, which held that it, exclusively, provided enough publicity for Colorado; it vehemently opposed creation of any other agency. As a consequence the state paid comparatively small attention to roads, country hotels, and the like; it built no enterprises like Sun Valley, and the general mood was to give the visitor a quick glimpse of Pike's Peak, and then let him get out.

Colorado is divided down the middle by the sharp and impenetrable spine of the continental divide; its western and eastern sections differ considerably, though the cleavage is not so sharp as in Washington. The western slope faces Salt Lake City, the eastern Denver. The west, behind the divide, is mostly mining and livestock country; the east is irrigated and merges into the Great Plains. The western slope is dominated by two or three land-owning families; the eastern—including Denver—has one overriding magnate, Claude K. Boettcher. I use this somewhat old-fashioned word, "magnate," because Mr. Boettcher so precisely evokes its spirit. The word "tycoon" connotes a touch of the parvenu, the adventurous. Boettcher is no parvenu. He is solid like a plinth, adhesive, and pachydermous. If I were a casting director in Hollywood and wanted a type to play one of the railroad barons of the last century, I would hire Mr. Boettcher at once. This margrave of the sugar beets, this padishah of cement, potash, mining, what not, one of the richest men in America and one of the least known, is a magnate like the antique Astors and Vanderbilts.

But the chief element of difference between eastern and western Colorado is water. Touch water, and you touch everything; about water the state is as sensitive as a carbuncle. Water—as is true all over the West—is everybody's chief preoccupation. In the briefest kind of summary, the situation is that western Colorado has more water than it can use, eastern less than it needs. Hence the east must have irrigation and the problem—this is reminiscent of California—is to get the water over. This the west resents. It thinks it is being milked of water for the benefit of capitalists in Denver which, in many respects, is almost as "foreign" a city as Wilmington, Delaware or Brookline, Massachusetts. The east replies that the water is "spare" water and that the west wastes it anyway.

Water is blood in Colorado; only California among American states has a greater irrigated area.

& & &

Historically Colorado is of mixed origin; in whole or in part it has variously belonged to Spain, France, Mexico, and Texas. There is still a strong Spanish underlay in the southern tier of counties; all these bear Spanish names. Its modern annals begin with the discovery of gold in 1858, nine years after the California Gold Rush, and the mines at Leadville and Cripple Creek became a mud-and-canvas Mecca. It is an interesting revelation of the national character—James Truslow Adams makes a point of this—that California and the far West, though farther away, should have been settled *before* the states of the Rockies and Great Plains. It is as if a crazy impetuosity carried the first frontiersmen as far as they could possibly go geographically; they swooped straight across the continent without pause (of course this generalization is too broad); then later a second wave, less volatile, descended on the states between.

Coloradans are proud of being Coloradans, and the state has a large proportion of citizens born within its borders. This is in acute contrast to Oklahoma and Arizona, say. A very real cleavage, especially in Denver, is that between old-timers born locally and those who moved in from outside; I felt this more strongly in Colorado than anywhere else in the country, except possibly New England. This prompts one to a word about the Indians who, after all, were in Colorado even before the first families of Denver got there. Colorado is the only western state where I never once heard the word "Indian" spoken, which is the more interesting in that the Utes were the only Indian tribe in the United States—like the Araucanians in Chile—never conquered. Today they play no role in state life at all.

The total wealth of Colorado was estimated in 1937 at $3,434,000,000 and the foundation of the state's economy is not, as one would be apt to think, mining, but agriculture. Mining began to decline thirty years ago. The easy gold got scooped out; the easy money ended when it became necessary to use complex and expensive metallurgical processes to refine ore. People turned instead to sugar beets and livestock. Today, it is not gold or even comparatively rare metals like uranium and vanadium that are the heart of the mining industry that remains, but prosaic coal. Colorado is the first state in the union in coal reserves, with—in theory—enough deposits to last forever.

Colorado has more big game than any other American state, and Denver is the biggest manufactory of fishhooks in the world; Colorado Springs is the glisteningly suave "Newport of the West," and the greatest man the state ever produced was Judge Ben Lindsey, who was of course reviled by the city he worked so hard to improve. Once, when he sentenced a utilities executive to jail, the executive shouted in the courtroom, "This state has more sunshine and more bastards than any place on earth!"

ROTUNDA MURALS

Thomas Hornsby Ferril

Here is a land where life is written in water
the West is where the water was and is
Father and Son of old Mother and Daughter
Following Rivers up immensities
of Range and Desert thirsting the Sundown ever
Crossing a hill to climb a hill since Drier
Naming tonight a City by some River
a different Name from last night's Camping Fire.

Look to the Green within the Mountain Cup
Look to the Prairie parched for water lack
Look to the Sun that pulls the Ocean up
Look to the Cloud that gives the oceans back
Look to your Heart and may your Wisdom grow
to power of Lightning and peace of Snow.

ABOUT CENTENNIAL

James A. Michener

IN THE LATE SUMMER OF 1936 I left the eastern seaboard of the United States, where I had been educated in the smug conviction that the universe revolved about a Massachusetts-New York-Pennsylvania-Virginia axis, and moved to Colorado, where the empty prairie and the snow-capped Rockies knocked some sense into me.

I settled in the town of Greeley—I was teaching history in what was to become the University of Northern Colorado—where I had the good fortune to meet a remarkable man, Floyd Merrill. A decade older than I, he was a newspaper editor of great erudition, fierce partisanship and profound commitment to the best traditions of America.

He became my cicerone to Colorado. Together we explored the Indian caves and the highest trails of the Rockies, and time after time, the lonely reaches of the prairie. He was one of the early ecologists, although neither of us had then heard that word, and he was keen to share his enthusiasms with a younger man.

    ✿ ✿ ✿

At least three times each month Merrill and I went on excursions out of Greeley, sometimes to the intricate irrigation systems which made our part of the desert a garden of melons, sometimes to glens far above timberline, from which we would look down into valleys crowded with blue spruce and aspen, and quite often out onto the prairie east of town where majestic buttes rose starkly from the barren waste. I remember vividly two of these trips.

The first was to the rocky area at the foot of two splendid buttes, where men with forked sticks ran down rattlesnakes, pinioned them behind their triangular heads, deftly caught them by their rattling tails, and whipped them sharply in the air so that their heads popped off.

The second was more placid. It was a trip north of the Colorado-Wyoming border to an area in which wind erosion had cut into red rocks, creating grotesque statues. If the land had contained only these amazing monuments, forty and fifty feet high, the spot would have been memorable, but it contained also a scattering of low, very dark piñon pines, and the contrast of brick-red and dark-green, of high figures and low trees, was unforgettable.

But Merrill's chief contribution to my perception was his preoccupation with the river systems of the west. Far ahead of his contemporaries, he foresaw the day when water would determine the quality and even the extent of life in Colorado. We examined every facet of the South Platte River system, the dams, the irrigation ditches, and it was while we were on such a trip that he first expounded to me his concept of a gigantic tunnel that would start at the bottom of a lake high on the wet western side of the Continental Divide, run eighteen or twenty miles directly under the topmost peaks of the Rockies, then throw its much-needed water onto the dry eastern slope, where it would enter the Platte River and move out to the drylands, where it was needed by the irrigation ditches operating there.

Others before Merrill had conceived this ingenious plan, but none had tried to put it into effect. It was his contribution that he turned his newspaper over to this vast project and propagandized for it year after year, until he saw it come to fruition. In this campaign he was, of course, supported by the owner of the paper, but the philosophical persuasion came from Merrill. From him I learned what a river really was: a natural canal which could be used by clever men to move water where and when they wished. I remember well one summer day when Merrill and I saw the Platte bone-dry east of Greeley; all its water had been siphoned off to feed one ditch or another, and when I complained that men had killed a river, he laughed and said, 'No, the water's inland ... working ... where it ought to be.'

                          🐜 🐜 🐜

When I returned to the east and became a writer, Merrill kept in touch with me through some of the most fact-filled letters I've ever received, and whenever my path took me to Greeley, we would resume our discussions of the great problems: the recurring dust bowl, the increasing salinization of the water table, the merits of the Hereford bull as contrasted to the Black Angus, what a liberal college ought to be, the wrong decisions of the Supreme Court, and always the prairie and the mountains and the flowers.

He spoke with considerable insight about my writings and often asked why I had never done a novel on Colorado, but my work kept me confined to other areas and I never did get to write about the part of the world that I knew best. Yet during all those years, whenever a chance presented itself for me to revisit the prairie, I did so. I remained constantly fascinated by the great rolling emptiness of Wyoming. Those miles of nothingness west of Cheyenne became for me some of the most compelling land in America, and I still recall the spring day when I stopped my car at Hell's Half Acre and climbed down to the bottom of that jagged ravine. It was an exhilarating trip, and the climb up, hand over hand, was even more fun. But when I reached the top a rancher stood there, his face ashen. 'Son,' he said, 'you're either the bravest man on earth or the biggest fool.'

With sweaty bravado I said, 'It's not too hard to climb. The rock crumbles a bit, but if you ... '

'It's spring,' the rancher explained. 'The sun's out. And every crevice you stuck your hand into had its quota of rattlesnakes ready to come out of hibernation.'

With a long probe he gingerly explored a few of the ledges near at hand, and from them he lifted six or seven big dormant rattlers. 'If you had climbed down there tomorrow,' he said gravely, 'with one more day of sun to warm them up, all those snakes would have been awake. And you'd have been sure to be bitten.'

🐜 🐜 🐜

In 1970, when I started seriously planning to write my long-contemplated novel on the west, I had a final chance to spend some days with Merrill. He was an old man now, hard hit by various attacks, but his wit was as sharp as ever. We went to see the incredible Big Thompson Diversion, which he had championed for so long, and saw the clear, cold water rushing out from beneath the mountains. We went onto the prairie to see the flowers—millions of them, though the casual eye might see nothing but sere grass—and then to his study, where hundreds of books I had not seen before bespoke his continuing interests.

'I'm thinking about that novel,' I told him. He nodded, and one week later he was dead.

SECTION II

DISCOVERING COLORADO

THE DOMÍNGUEZ-ESCALANTE JOURNAL

Francisco Silvestre Vélez de Escalante

ON THE 1ST OF SEPTEMBER we set out, headed north from San Ramón, and after going three leagues through small narrow valleys of abundant pastures and thick clumps of scruboak we came upon eighty Yutas, all on good horses and most of them from the encampment to which we were going. They told us that they were going out to hunt, but we figured that they came together like this, either to show off their strength in numbers or to find out if any other Spanish people were coming behind us or if we came alone; for, since they knew from the night before that we were going to their encampment, it was unnatural for almost all of its men to come out at the very time that they knew we were to arrive, unless motivated by what we have just said.

We kept on going with only the Laguna, descended a very steep incline, and came into a very pleasant narrow valley, in which there was a small river and all along its bank a spreading grove of spruces, very tall and straight, among them certain poplars which seem to ape the erectness and height of the pines. Through this narrow valley we traveled eastward for a league and reached the encampment, which had numerous people and must have consisted of thirty tents. We stopped a mile down from it by the edge of the river mentioned, naming the site San Antonio Mártir. Today four leagues—199 [in all].

As soon as we halted, Padre Fray Francisco Atanasio went on to the encampment with Andrés the interpreter to see the chieftain and the others who had remained. He went into the chieftain's tent and, after greeting and embracing him and his children, asked him to gather there the people who were on hand. He did so, and when those of either sex who could attend had been assembled, he announced the Gospel to them through the interpreter. All listened with pleasure, and especially six Lagunas who were present, among whom our guide and another Laguna stood out. As soon as the padre began instructing them, the new guide mentioned interrupted them so as to predispose the Sabuaganas as well as his own fellow tribesmen "to believe whatever the padre was telling them because it all was true." In the same way, the other Laguna relayed the pleasure and eagerness with which he heard the news of his eternal salvation.

Among those listening there was one a bit deaf who, not grasping what was being treated, asked what it was the padre was saying. Then this Laguna said: "The padre says that this which he shows us"—it was the image of Christ crucified—"is the one Lord of all, who dwells in the highest part of the skies, and in order to please Him and go to Him one has to be baptized and must beg His forgiveness." He emphasized this idea by beating his breast with his hand—a surprising gesture on his part for his never having seen it made before, either by the padre or by the interpreter. When the padre saw the evident joy with which they heard him, he suggested to the chieftain now in charge of the encampment that if, after he had conferred with his people, they would accept Christianity we would come to instruct them and set them in a way of living that would lead to baptism. He replied that he would propose it to his people, but he did not return all afternoon to provide further cause whereon to base a likely hope of their accepting the proposal.

Filled with joy by the open declaration of the Lagunas mentioned, the padre asked how the latter one was called (the guide we had already named Silvestre), and on learning that they called him Red Bear he instructed them all by explaining to them the difference existing between men and brutes, the purpose for which either of them were created, and the wrong thing they did in naming themselves after wild beasts—thus placing themselves on a par with them, and even below them. Promptly he told the Laguna to call himself Francisco from then on. When the rest saw this, they began repeating this name, although with difficulty, the Laguna joyfully pleased for being so named.

It also happened that when the padre addressed as chief the one who, as already said, was in charge of the encampment, he replied that he was not it and that the real chief was a fine-looking youth who was present; and when the padre asked him if he [the youth] was married, he answered that he was and that he had two wives. This embarrassed the said youth (whom the other had done the honor of pointing out for his being the brother of a greatly revered chieftain among the Sabuaganas named Yamputzi), and he tried to make out that he had only one wife. From this it can be inferred that these barbarians are aware or cognizant of the repugnance inherent in having multiple wives at one and the same time. From here the padre grasped the opportunity to instruct them on this point, and to exhort them not to have more than one.

When this was all over, some jerked bison meat was bought from them, they being paid for it with white beads, and they were asked if they wanted to exchange some horses for other now hoofsore ones that we brought along. They replied that they would exchange them later in the afternoon. This done, the padre came back to the king's camp.

THE JOURNAL OF JACOB FOWLER

Jacob Fowler

13th novr 1821 tusday

WENT TO THE HIGHEST of the mounds near our Camp and took the bareing of the Soposed mountain Which Stud at north 80 West all So of the River Which is West. We then proceded on 2-1/2 miles to a Small Crick Crosed it and asended a gradual Rise for about three miles to the Highest ground in the nibourhood—Wheare We Head a full vew of the mountains this must be the place Whare Pike first discovered the mountains. Heare I took the bareing of two that Ware the Highest the longest South 71 W—the other Which appeered like a point South 75 West—nither of those are the mountain Seen this morning—on looking forward We Seen a Branch Puting in from the South Side Which We Sopose to be Pikes first forke and make for it—Crossed and Camped in a grove of Bushes and timber about two miles up it from the River We maid Eleven miles West this day—We Stoped Heare about one oclock and Sent back for one Hors that Was not able to keep up—We Heare found some grapes among the brush—While Some Ware Hunting and others Cooking Some Picking grapes a gun Was fyered off and the Cry of a White Bare Was Raised We Ware all armed in an Instent and Each man Run His own Cors to look for the desperet anemel—the Brush in Which We Camped Contained from 10 to 20 acors Into Which the Bare Head [bear had] Run for Shelter find[ing] Him Self Surrounded on all Sides— threw this Conl glann With four others atemted to Run But the Bare being In their Way and lay Close in the brush undiscovered till the Ware With in a few feet of it—When it Sprung up and Caught Lewis doson and Pulled Him down In an Instent Conl glanns gun mised fyer or He Wold Have Releved the man But a large Slut Which belongs to the Party atacted the Bare With such fury that it left the man and persued Her a few steps in Which time the man got up and Run a few steps but Was overtaken by the bare When the Conl maid a second atempt to shoot but His [gun] mised fyer again and the Slut as before Releved the man Who Run as before—but Was Son again in the grasp of the Bare Who Semed Intent on His distruction—the Conl again Run Close up and as before His gun Wold not go off the Slut makeing an other atack and Releveing the man—the Conl now be Came alarmed lest the Bare Wold pusue Him and Run up Stooping tree—and after Him the Wounded man and Was followed by the Bare and thus the Ware all three up one tree—but a tree standing in Rich [reach] the Conl steped on that and let the man and Bare pas till the Bare Caught Him [Dawson] by one leg and drew Him back wards down the tree. While this Was doing the Conl Sharpened His flint Primed His gun and Shot the Bare down While pulling the man by the leg be fore any of the party arived to Releve Him—but the Bare Soon Rose again but Was Shot by several other [men] Wo Head [who had] got up to the place of action—it Is to be Remarked that the other three men With Him Run off—and the Brush Was so thick that those on the out Side Ware Som time geting threw—

I Was my Self down the Crick below the brush and Heard the dredfull Screems of man in the Clutches of the Bare—the yelping of the Slut and the Hollowing of the men to Run in Run in the man Will be killed and noing the distance So grate that I Cold not get there in time to Save the man So that it Is much Easeer to Emagen my feellings than discribe them but before I got to the place of action the Bare Was killed and [I] met the Wounded man with Robert Fowler and one or two more asisting Him to Camp Where His Wounds Ware Examined—it appeers His Head Was In the Bares mouth at least twice—and that When the monster give the Crush that Was to mash the mans Head it being two large for the Span of His mouth the Head Sliped out only the teeth Cutting the Skin to the bone Where Ever the tuched it—so that the Skin of the Head Was Cut from about the Ears to the top in Several derections—all of Which Wounds Ware Sewed up as Well as Cold be don by men In our Situation Haveing no Surgen nor Surgical Instruments—the man Still Retained His under Standing but Said I am killed that I Heard my Skull Brake—but We Ware Willing to beleve He Was mistaken—as He Spoke Chearfully on the Subgect till In the after noon of the second day When He began to be Restless and Some What delereous—and on examening a Hole in the upper part of His Wright temple Which We beleved only Skin deep We found the Brains Workeing out—We then Soposed that He did Heare His Scull Brake He lived till a little before day on the third day after being Wounded—all Which time We lay at Camp and Buried Him as Well as our meens Wold admit Emedetely after the fatal axcident and Haveing done all We Cold for the Wounded man We turned our atention [to] Bare and found Him a large fatt anemel We Skined Him but found the Smell of a polcat so Strong that We Cold not Eat the meat—on examening His mouth We found that three of His teeth Ware broken off near the gums Which We Sopose Was the Caus of His not killing the man at the first Bite—and the one not Broke to be the Caus of the Hole in the Right [temple] Which killed the man at last—the Hunters killed two deer Cased the Skins for Baggs We dryed out the Bares oil and Caryed it with us the Skin Was all so taken Care of—

A JOURNEY TO THE ROCKY MOUNTAINS IN THE YEAR 1839

F. Adolphus Wislizenus

ON AUGUST 15TH, WE crossed the Green River, which winds its way among precipitous mountains, and at this point can still be easily forded, going slantingly down stream for two more days. The road was generally steep, and led through forests of pine and cedar. The river valley at first was narrow, but widened further on. The geological formation was still the primitive. On August 17th we reached Fort Crocket. It is situated close by the Green River on its left bank. The river valley here is broad, and has good pasturage and sufficient wood. The fort itself is the worst thing of the kind that we have seen on our journey. It is a low one-story building, constructed of wood and clay, with three connecting wings, and no enclosure. Instead of cows the fort had only some goats. In short, the whole establishment appeared somewhat poverty-stricken, for which reason it is also known to the trappers by the name of Fort Misery (*Fort de Misere*). The fort belongs to three Americans: Thompson, Gray and Sinclair. The latter was at the fort, and received us very kindly but regretted his inability to offer us any supplies. For our store of meat was exhausted, and we had hoped to supply ourselves here with new provisions. But the people at the fort seemed to be worse off than we were. The day before they had bought a lean dog from the Indians for five dollars, and considered its meat a delicacy. I, too, tried some of it, and found its taste not so bad.

In addition to some trappers and Indians, we found five Americans here, who had started in the spring with a larger party from Peoria, Illinois, to make a settlement on the Columbia River. They had arrived in Westport after our departure, and had journeyed first by the Santa Fe road, then up the Arkansas. But through several quarrels and mishaps, the company, consisting mainly of novices, was split up into several smaller groups. The party we here met had made most progress, and had not yet abandoned the plan of going to the Columbia. But the most difficult part of their journey lay before them. So two of them, Mr. Ogley and Mr. Wood, thought it best to avail themselves of the opportunity to return now offered them, and to join our party. Our party was thereby increased to seven. Among the people of the fort I had expected to meet an old friend of University days who had been roving through the mountains these six years, and who was supposed to be at this time at the fort. To note the metamorphosis from a jovial student at Jena into a trapper would be interesting enough in itself. The presence of S. would have afforded me a pleasure far beyond this, as we had not seen each other for ten years. Unfortunately, I learned that he had gone beaver-trapping and would not return before fall. So we left the fort the next day.

MATT FIELD ON THE SANTA FE TRAIL

Matt Field

THE MILK PEOPLE ARE A community residing in a mud fort on the Arkansas about four hundred miles this side of Santa Fé. They are composed of the dark skinned, half Spanish half Indian tribe, who inhabit Taos and the Department of Santa Fé, and there cannot exist in any nook or corner of the wide universe, a wilder, stranger, more remarkable collection of human beings for a civilized eye to look upon. The pencil of old romance would fly from forest cave and daring freebooters, and find here in real life a scene more full of all the best ingredients for its colors. A rude mud built fortification rises in the very center of a trackless wilderness hundreds of miles in extent, and a part of whose confines are even yet unknown, and here a knot of beings of so wild a race as to create in the beholder ideas of what men were long centuries ago, men

> Who look not like the inhabitants of earth,
> And yet are on it,

reside, unknown to the world, and seeming to claim neither knowledge or kindred with any tribe or nation in existence.

Milk Fort is so termed from the number of goats possessed by its tenants, and the quantity of milk so procured, which is always sure sustenance when buffalo or other game cannot be found. In case the fort should be besieged by the wandering hordes of Indians, these milk people could exist a far greater length of time than the marauders could be content to remain in one spot. But of this there is no danger, for the men are brave and daring as the Camanches themselves, of whose wild nature, indeed, they seem to partake, and they could sally forth and battle successfully with any war party of ordinary numbers. They possess the fleetest horses, and sit them as though they had been cradled in the saddle, and to say they were would perhaps be but a literal fact, for the writer saw once a Mexican woman making a little naked infant cling and balance itself on a horse's back, with its arms and legs, while the animal was walked about by the bridle. The poor little innocent creature could not yet walk, and its little fat fist grasped instinctively the horse's mane with ludicrous earnestness. The men of Milk Fort are also full as expert with the bow as the Indians, and, although provided with fire arms, they kill more buffalo with arrows than with ball.

How to describe this strange fort and its nondescript inhabitants is somewhat perplexing.—There are about thirty houses, of small dimensions, all built compactly together in an oblong square, leaving a large space in the center, and the houses themselves forming the wall of the fort, into which there is but one entrance, through a large and very strong gate. Some of these houses have an upper story, and the rooms are generally square, twelve feet from wall to wall, more or less, with the fire place in the corner, where it is found most convenient to construct the chimney up through the mud wall. These rooms are whitewashed and look enough like Christian apartments to surprise us, while we remember that they are constructed of mud, and, in the way of comfort, they are really desirable, being cool, like cellars, in warm weather, and in winter close and warm. The best way, perhaps, to convey an idea of the people will be just to describe our entrance through the great gate and the scene that then presented itself.

Half a dozen boys and men ran and took our horses, pulled off the saddles and head gear with swiftness that excited our wonder, and in an instant our animals were haltered and led into a corner of the fort, where a feast of corn shucks lay piled upon the ground before them. We looked around us, and the first thing that took our attention was the women suddenly appearing at every door and window in the place to look at the strangers. They were generally rather neat in their appearance, though the men, with scarcely an exception, exhibited the reverse.—Their dress consisted of just three articles, a common domestic undergarment, a coarse petticoat, and a long, narrow shawl thrown over the head. They were combed and seemed to take delight in showing off their raven hair to advantage. Most of them were blotched and disfigured with vermilion, their cheeks, nose, forehead, all horridly daubed with it, but some, who had taste enough to abstain from this vile Indian custom, were really pleasant looking females. They were all much taken with us, however, and crowded about us chattering Spanish in a manner most bewildering to American ears.

But the men held aloof from us, perhaps not liking the attention bestowed upon us by the women. They kept their eagle eyes bent upon us from under their dark brows, but did not rise from the ground, where they were chiefly lying outside the doors, smoking their clay and stone Indian made pipes. Dogs, goats, cats, tame coons, tame antelopes, tame buffalo calves, kids, and jack asses were about in all directions, and little children were on their backs kicking up their heels and playing with the animals. A stout little rascal near us was bellowing "Madre! Madre!" to come and punish a juvenile buffalo who had hit him a butt and knocked him against the wall.

The men generally had beards at full length, and long hair flowing over their shoulders, which, together with their dark skin and piercing eyes, gave them a truly wild and ferocious appearance. They were armed also, some with, some without pistols, but not one was without his large knife; and as they lounged about the ground they were employed filing up arrow heads from bits of sheet iron, cutting and trimming the long sticks and fixing the delicate feather at the end.

We remained one night in this fort, that we might note all its singularities, though not without experiencing some awkward sensations relative to the black-looking fellows who were around us. We had been told, however, at Fort William that these men were not to be feared, being of peaceable character, and living entirely by hunting and trading now and then with friendly Indians. Once or twice a year they travel to Santa Fé, sell skins, and buy necessaries. Just before night closed in a confusion was heard, and a man with a tremendous voice called out for the corral to be cleared. Instantly there was a rush among the women to catch up the children, and run with them into the houses, and the next moment the whole stock of horses and mules, "full of the pasture," the rich pasture of the prairie, was driven through the wide gates and into the center of the fort. Here was a scene! Before we knew it we were wedged in among the animals, and had no small work to extricate ourselves, for the stock completely filled the corral. The heavy gate was now strongly barred and fastened, and we found ourselves secured for the night within the walls of *Pueblo de Leche*.

A REPORT ON THE EXPLORATION OF THE COUNTRY LYING BETWEEN THE MISSOURI RIVER AND THE ROCKY MOUNTAINS

John Charles Frémont

JULY 9. [1842]—THIS morning we caught the first faint glimpse of the Rocky Mountains, about sixty miles distant. Though a tolerably bright day, there was a slight mist, and we were just able to discern the snowy summit of "Long's peak," (*"les deux oreilles"* of the Canadians,) showing like a small cloud near the horizon. I found it easily distinguishable, there being a perceptible difference in its appearance from the white clouds that were floating about the sky. I was pleased to find that among the traders and voyageurs the name of "Long's peak" had been adopted and become familiar in the country. In the ravines near this place, a light brown sandstone made its first appearance. About 8, we discerned several persons on horseback a mile or two ahead on the opposite side of the river. They turned in towards the river, and we rode down to meet them. We found them to be two white men, and a mulatto named Jim Beckwith, who had left St. Louis when a boy, and gone to live with the Crow Indians. He had distinguished himself among them by some acts of daring bravery, and had risen to the rank of a chief, but had now, for some years, left them. They were in search of a band of horses that had gone off from a camp some miles above, in charge of Mr. Chabonard. Two of them continued down the river, in search of the horses, and the American turned back with us, and we rode on towards the camp. About eight miles from our sleeping

John Casilear, "The Rockies from near Greeley, Colorado," 1881.

place we reached Bijou's fork [Bijou Creek], an affluent of the right bank. Where we crossed it, a short distance from the Platte, it has a sandy bed about four hundred yards broad; the water in various small streams, a few inches deep. Seven miles further brought us to a camp of some four or five whites, New Englanders, I believe, who had accompanied Captain Wyeth to the Columbia river, and were independent trappers. All had their squaws with them, and I was really surprised at the number of little fat buffalo-fed boys, that were tumbling about the camp, all apparently of the same age, about three or four years old. They were encamped on a rich bottom, covered with a profusion of fine grass, and had a large number of fine-looking horses and mules. We rested with them a few minutes, and in about two miles arrived at Chabonard's camp, on an island in the Platte. On the heights above, we met the first Spaniard I had seen in the country. Mr. Chabonard was in the service of Bent and St. Vrain's company, and had left their fort some forty or fifty miles above, in the spring, with boats laden with the furs of the last year's trade. He had met the same fortune as the voyageurs on the North fork, and finding it impossible to proceed, had taken up his summer's residence on this island, which he had named St. Helena. The river hills appeared to be composed entirely of sand, and the Platte had lost the muddy character of its waters, and here was tolerably clear. From the mouth of the South fork, I had found it occasionally broken up by small islands, and at the time of our journey, which was at a season of the year when the waters were at a favorable stage, it was not navigable for anything drawing six inches water. The current was very swift—the bed of the stream a coarse gravel.

From the place at which we had encountered the Arapahoes, the Platte had been tolerably well fringed with timber, and the island here had a fine grove of very large cottonwoods, under whose broad shade the tents were pitched. There was a large drove of horses in the opposite prairie bottom; smoke was rising from the scattered fires, and the encampment had quite a patriarchal air. Mr. C. received us hospitably. One of the people was sent to gather mint, with the aid of which he concocted very good julep; and some boiled buffalo tongue, and coffee with the luxury of sugar, were soon set before us. The people in his employ were generally Spaniards, and among them I saw a young Spanish woman from Taos, whom I found to be Beckwith's wife.

July 10.—We parted with our hospitable host after breakfast the next morning, and reached St. Vrain's fort, about forty-five miles from St. Helena, late in the evening. The post is situated on the South fork of the Platte, immediately under the mountains, about seventeen miles east of Long's peak. It is on the right bank, on the verge of the upland prairie, about forty feet above the river, of which the immediate valley is about six hundred yards wide. The stream is divided into various branches by small islands, among which it runs with a swift current. The bed of the river is sand and gravel, the water very clear, and here may be called a mountain stream. This region appears to be entirely free from the limestones and marls which give to the lower Platte its yellow and dirty color. The Black hills lie between the stream and the mountains, whose snowy peaks glitter a few miles beyond. At the fort we found Mr. St. Vrain, who received us with much kindness and hospitality. Maxwell had spent the last two or three years between this post and the village of Taos, and here he was at home and among his friends. Spaniards frequently came over in search of employment, and several came in shortly after our arrival. They usually obtain about six dollars a month, generally paid to them in goods. They are very useful in a camp in taking care of horses and mules, and I engaged one, who proved to be an active, laborious man, and was of very considerable service to me. The elevation of the Platte here is 5,400 feet above the sea. The neighboring mountains did not appear to enter far the region of perpetual snow, which was generally confined to the northern side of the peaks. On the southern I remarked very little. Here it appeared, so far as I could judge in the distance, to descend but a few hundred feet below the summits.

I regretted that time did not permit me to visit them; but the proper object of my survey lay among the mountains further north; and I looked forward to an exploration of their snowy recesses with great pleasure.

DOWN THE SANTA FE TRAIL AND INTO MEXICO

Susan Shelby Magoffin

BENT'S FORT, JULY 27, 1846. *Monday noon.* I have been rather negligent in my writing lately. The last I wrote was on Tuesday 21st, after our little ship-wreck. After this was over I supposed an Indian fracas would be our next adventure, for the day following we passed their sign, such as old *mockasins*, and a post set in the ground, with a fork at the other end, in which were a sword and bundle of fagots, *many in number*, representing, as I was told a sign to some other of their tribe passing after them, the army of the whites they were numerous: The sword was painted red, for the use they made with it, and it also had several notches cut in it to represent the number of days since they passed.

We met with no very strange adventure. I was careful enough at every little hill to get out and walk, for the last narrow escape we had is not out of my mind yet.

One evening we had an abundance of musquitoes and another slight thunder storm. It was not so fearful tho' as the other in more than one respect. We had the tent secured by ropes fastened to the top of the pole and to the carriage and *la cara* [*carro*—wagon] wheels.

The road has been very sandy and almost on the river bank, which are poorly timbered till some 120 miles from the crossing it is rather thicker for ten or 12 miles, and taller the trees, with more the appearance of the Mississippi banks. In some places the country is hilly and covered with large stones, but generally speaking it is perfectly level plain, destitute of every thing, even grass, the great reliever of the eye, and making it painful to the sight.

Saturday morning we saw in front of us and many miles distant, perhaps eighty, a mountain called I think James Peak.

In the evening we came on some five miles ahead of the wagons, to where Messrs Davie, Harmony and Hickman were encamped till we have permission to take a final start. Here we pitched our tent for the night and I believe for the forty-fifth time.

Sunday morning after getting the wagons up there and encamped, some fifteen miles from the fort, we came on ourselves.

Some four miles below the Fort we passed the soldiers encampment, another novel sight to me, perhaps there were fifty or more little tents stretched around in a ring with here and there a wagon, and a little shade made of tree limbs. The idle soldiers were stretched under these, others were out watering horses staked about the camp, some were drying clothes in the sun &c. &c.

At the outer edge of the encampment stood a sentinel, who with all the dignity and pomp, though by no means a Sampson in statue, of his office shouldered his musket marched up, and stoped us with the words "where go you"? We gave him our directions, he reported us to the sergeant at arms, and without farther ceremony we were permitted to pass on. In a little time we were in sight of the Fort and soon after, were in it.

And now for something of a description. Well the outside exactly fills my idea of an ancient castle. It is built of adobes, unburnt brick, and Mexican style so far. The walls are very high and very thick with rounding corners. There is but one entrance, this is to the East rather.

Inside is a large space some ninety or an hundred feet *square*, all around this and next the wall are rooms, some twenty-five in number. They have dirt floors—which are sprinkled with water several times during the day to prevent dust. Standing in the center of some of them is a large wooden post as a firmer prop to the ceiling which is made of logs. Some of these rooms are occupied by boarders as bed chambers. One is a dining-room—another a kitchen—a little store, a blacksmith's shop, a barber's do an ice house, which receives perhaps more customers than any other.

On the South side is an inclosure for stock in dangerous times and often at night. On one side of the top wall are rooms built in the same manner as below. We are occupying one of these, but of that anon.

They have a well inside, and fine water it is—especially with ice. At present they have quite a number of boarders. The traders and soldiers chiefly, with a few *lofers* from the States, come out because they can't live at home.

There is no place on Earth I believe where man lives and gambling in some form or other is not carried on. Here in the Fort, and who could have supposed such a thing, they have a *regularly established billiard room!* They have a regular race track. And I hear the cackling of chickens at such a rate some times I shall not be surprised to hear of a cock-pit.

Now for our room; it is quite roomy. Like the others it has a dirt floor, which I keep sprinkling constantly during the day; we have two windows one looking out on the plain, the other is on the *patio* or yard. We have our own furniture, such as bed, chairs, wash basin, table furniture, and we eat in our own room. It is keeping house regularly, but I beg leave not to be allowed *that* privilege much longer.

They have one large room as a parlor; there are no chairs but a cushion next the wall on two sides, so the company set all round in a circle. There is no other furniture than a table on which stands a bucket of water, free to all. Any water that may be left in the cup after drinking is unceremoniously tossed onto the floor.

When we came last evening, while they were fixing our room, I sat in the parlour with *las senoritas* [the ladies], the wife of Mr. George Bent and some others. One of them sat and combed her hair all the while notwithstanding the presence of Mr. Lightendoffer, whose lady (a Mexican) was present. After the combing she paid her devoirs to a crock of oil or greese of some kind, and it is not exaggeration to say it almost *driped* from her hair to the floor. If I had not seen her at it, I never would have believed it greese, but that she had been washing her head.

We had Cpt. Moore, of the U.S. dragoons, to call this P.M.; he promises me double protection, as an American citizen, and as a Kentuckian; he is from that noble state himself, and even claims a kinship! Both yesterday and this evening we have taken a walk up the River, such as we used to take last winter in N. Y. from Spring to Wall Street.

Tuesday 28th. The Dctr. has just left and I shall endeavour to write a little before dinner. I've been busy all the morning. Wrote a long letter to Mama, which Cpt. Moore says I can send by the Government express. The army affords me one convenience in this. Though I cannot hear from home, it is a gratification to know that I can send letters to those who will take pleasure in reading them.

Dctr. Mesure brought me more medicine, and advises *mi alma* to travel me through Europ. The advice is rather better to take than the medicine, anything though to restore my health. I never should have consented to take the trip on the plains had it not been with the view and a hope that it would prove beneficial; but so far my hopes have been blasted, for I am rather going down hill than up, and it is so bad to be sick and under a physician all the time. But cease my rebellious heart! How prone human nature is to grumble and to think his lot harder than any one of his fellow creatures, many of whom are an hundred times more diseased and poor in earthly assistance and still they endure all, and would endure more.

Had Capt. Waldo, of the Mo. Volunteers to call this P.M. *Mi alma* is paving his way to "protection" and polite treatment from all the chief men &c.

Wednesday 29th. The same routine today as yesterday, several gentlemen, among the traders and officers called and paid their respects to the "Madam." My health, though not good, is drank by them all, and some times a complimentary toast is ingeniously slipped in. The Fort is not such a bad place after all. There are some good people in and about it as well as in other places. I am not very much displeased with Col. Kearny for sending us here, but he has arrived himself this P.M. and gives the command to leave in three days. The idea of getting onto those rough, jolting roads, and they say this is rather worse, if anything, than the one we have passed, is truly sickening.

I have concluded that the Plains are not very beneficial to my health so far; for I am thinner by a good many lbs. than when I came out. The dear knows what is the cause!

Thursday July 30th. Well this is my nineteenth birthday! And what? Why I feel rather strange, not surprised at its coming, nor to think that I am growing rather older, for that is the way of the human family, but this is it, I am sick! strange sensations in my head, my back, and hips. I am obliged to lie down most of the time, and when I get up to hold my hand over my eyes.

There is the greatest possible noise in the *patio* [yard]. The shoeing of horses, neighing, and braying of mules, the crying of children, the scolding and fighting of men, are all enough to turn my head. And to add to the scene, like some of our neighbours we have our own private troubles. The servants are all quarreling and fighting among themselves, running to us to settle their difficulties; they are gambling off their cloths till some of them are next to nudity, and though each of them are in debt to *mi alma* for advancement of their wages, they are coming to him to get them out of their scrapes.

José, our principal Mexican about the camp, and my maid Jane, have had a cat and dog difficulty, he says he can't stand it and she puts on airs, does her business when and how she pleases, leaving a part of it for *me* to do, and here we have it, in addition to all this the Dctr. comes to tell how his men have treated him, therefore we have our own and our neighbours trials to encounter.

The Fort is crowded to overflowing. Col. Kearny has arrived and it seems the world is coming with him. Volunteers are under his command now only as he, on his arrival dispatched them under Capt. Moore ahead, for the purpose of repairing fifteen miles of the road called the Raton, a bed of rocks impassable for wagons, of which there are a goodly No. to pass.

Three Indian warriors came in today; they belong to a large war party of the Arrapaho Indians who are they say some sixty miles off. They are believed by the company to be spies, though they come rather with the appearance of trading.

With the intention of awing them a little Mr. Bent and others are about taking them down to the soldiers' encampment. They hesitate rather saying they have "two hearts on the subject; one of which says go! and the other says don't go"! They are cunning people, and no doubt 'twould be a rich treat to hear, on their returning to their tribe, their graphic account of the American Army "the white faced Warriors."

August. 1846. Thursday 6. The mysteries of a new world have been shown to me since last Thursday! In a few short months I should have been a happy mother and made the heart of a father glad, but the ruling hand of a mighty Providence has interposed and by an abortion deprived us of the hope, the fond hope of mortals! But with the affliction he does not leave us comfortless!

We have permission to "come unto him when our burden is grievous and heavy to be borne; we have permission to pray for more submission and reliance on his goodness, and in that petition we have an intercessor with the Father, Jesus Christ, who himself came into the world an infant, after the manner of man.

Friday morning 31st of July. My pains commenced and continued till 12 o'c. at night, when after much agony and severest of pains, which were relieved a little at times by medicine given by Dctr. Mesure, *all was over.* I sunk off into a king of lethargy, in *mi alma's* arms. Since that time I have been in my bed till yesterday a little while, and a part of today.

My situation was very different from that of an Indian woman in the room below me. She gave birth to a fine healthy baby, about the same time, *and in half an hour after she went to the River and bathed herself and it*, and this she has continued each day since. Never could I have believed such a thing, if I had not been here, and *mi alma's* own eyes had not seen her coming from the River. And some gentleman here tells him, he has often seen them immediately after the birth of a child go to the water and *break the ice* to bathe themselves!

It is truly astonishing to see what customs will do. No doubt many ladies in civilized life are ruined by too careful treatments during child-birth, for this custom of the hethen is not known to be disadvantageous, but it is a *"hethenish custom."*

EATING UP THE SANTA FE TRAIL

Sam'l P. Arnold

BUFFALO JERKY, OR CARNE SECA

AFTER A KILL, HUNTERS would traditionally feast upon the fresh, choice parts: the tongue; the "fleece"—a fatty meat strip on each side of the hump backbone area; the rib racks; liver; and kidneys. The balance of the meat was taken back to the nearest fort, if it was within a few hours' ride. Otherwise, the meat was cut in long, thin strips and hung out in the air to dry, or jerk, as they called it. Instead of spoiling, it became almost permanently preserved and could travel with the hunters.

Good buffalo jerky is delicious but hard to find. Whether you have buffalo, deermeat, elk, antelope, or beef, here's the procedure for making truly delicious jerky:

PREPARING CARNE SECA, OR JERKY

Jerky sticks are available at many bars, but the extruded ersatz jerky produced commercially in this country is not worthy of the name. Be sure you have real beef or buffalo slices that have been dried. You can easily do this yourself by having the butcher thinly slice a beef or buffalo rump. Some people dip it momentarily into lime or lemon juice and salt, then leave it hanging from a wire or over a string overnight. A bit of cheesecloth will keep away the insects, if you are finicky.

I make great jerky in my oven, but *without* any heat. Oil the racks or spray with a non-stick oil. Leave the meat strips hanging down over the metal racks. Don't let the pieces touch or overlap. You may sprinkle the pieces with salt, pepper, chile, or hot sauce if you like. Place a running electric fan on the open oven door and aim it into the oven overnight. REMEMBER ... NO HEAT in the oven—it changes the taste. In the morning, you'll have excellent air-dried jerked meat. Use it as is, fry it, or roast it a bit in a hot oven. Toasted jerky tastes a bit like bacon and may be used in many dishes.

BUFFALO TONGUE

"I, by good luck, had some buffalo tongue in my pocket, that added not a little to our rural repast" (*Abert's New Mexico Report,* 45).

Considered a holy meat by the Indians, buffalo tongue was thought by many to be the greatest gourmet delicacy of the American nineteenth century. The intense flavor and fine texture, somewhat like a fine pâté, are superb and far exceed that of beef tongue, which has a coarser quality. Buffalo tongue was served at such fine hostelries as the Maxwell House and famed Delmonico's in New York City, where President Ulysses S. Grant and singer Jenny Lind, the Swedish Nightingale, were reported to have feasted upon the delicacy. The demand for buffalo tongue was a major reason for the wholesale slaughter of the bison. Whole herds were killed for their hides and tongues, which were smoked, salted, or pickled, and sent east in fully loaded railroad cars. A green horn [newcomer] hunter who killed a buffalo was expected to bring the tongue back to camp as a trophy. Today, in limited numbers, buffalo tongues are once again gracing gourmet palates. Fortunately, few of the public know how good they are.

COOKING A BUFFALO TONGUE

Slowly boil buffalo tongues about 4 hours in water flavored with a few bay leaves, some black peppercorns, and minced onion. When soft, cool and peel away the skin with a knife. Cut one-half inch-thick slices and serve hot or cold. A nice but not historic sauce I favor consists of mayonnaise, capers, horseradish, and Worcestershire sauce, to taste. (Recipe collection of Sam Arnold.)

THE OREGON TRAIL

Francis Parkman

MEETING ARAPAHOES HERE on the Arkansas was a very different thing from meeting the same Indians among their native mountains. There was another circumstance in our favor. General Kearney had seen them a few weeks before, as he came up the river with his army, and, renewing his threats of the previous year, he told them that if they ever again touched the hair of a white man's head he would exterminate their nation. This placed them for the time in an admirable frame of mind, and the effect of his menaces had not yet disappeared. I wished to see the village and its inhabitants. We thought it also our best policy to visit them openly, as if unsuspicious of any hostile design; and Shaw and I, with Henry Chatillon, prepared to cross the river. The rest of the party meanwhile moved forward as fast as they could, in order to get as far as possible from our suspicious neighbors before night came on.

The Arkansas at this point, and for several hundred miles below, is nothing but a broad sand-bed, over which glide a few scanty threads of water, now and then expanding into wide shallows. At several places, during the autumn, the water sinks into the sand and disappears altogether. At this season, were it not for the numerous quicksands, the river might be forded almost anywhere without difficulty, though its channel is often a quarter of a mile wide. Our horses jumped down the bank, and wading through the water, or galloping freely over the hard sand-beds, soon reached the other side. Here, as we were pushing through the tall grass, we saw several Indians not far off; one of them waited until we came up, and stood for some moments in perfect silence before us, looking at us askance with his little snake-like eyes. Henry explained by signs what we wanted, and the Indian, gathering his buffalo-robe about his shoulders, led the way towards the village without speaking a word.

The language of the Arapahoes is so difficult, and its pronunciation so harsh and guttural, that no white man, it is said, has ever been able to master it. Even Maxwell, the trader who has been most among them, is compelled to resort to the curious sign-language common to most of the prairie tribes. With this sign-language Henry Chatillon was perfectly acquainted.

Approaching the village, we found the ground strewn with piles of waste buffalo-meat in incredible quantities. The lodges were pitched in a circle. They resembled those of the Dahcotah in everything but cleanliness. Passing between two of them, we entered the great circular area of the camp, and instantly hundreds of Indians, men, women, and children, came flocking out of their habitations to look at us; at the same time, the dogs all around the village set up a discordant baying. Our Indian guide walked towards the lodge of the chief. Here we dismounted; and loosening the trail-ropes from our horses' necks, held them fast as we sat down before the entrance, with our rifles laid across our laps. The chief came out and shook us by the hand. He was a mean-looking fellow, very tall, thin-visaged, and sinewy, like the rest of the nation, and with scarcely a vestige of clothing. We had not been seated a moment before a multitude of Indians came crowding around us from every part of the village, and we were shut in by a dense wall of savage faces. Some of our visitors crouched around us on the ground; others sat behind them; others, stooping, looked over their heads; while many more stood behind, peering over each other's shoulders, to get a view of us. I looked in vain among this throng of faces to discover one manly or generous expression; all were wolfish, sinister, and malignant, and their complexions, as well as their features, unlike those of the

Dahcotah, were exceedingly bad. The chief, who sat close to the entrance, called to a squaw within the lodge, who soon came out and placed a wooden bowl of meat before us. To our surprise, however, no pipe was offered. Having tasted of the meat as a matter of form, I began to open a bundle of presents,—tobacco, knives, vermilion, and other articles which I had brought with me. At this there was a grin on every countenance in the rapacious crowd; their eyes began to glitter, and long thin arms were eagerly stretched towards us on all sides to receive the gifts.

The Arapahoes set great value upon their shields, which they transmit carefully from father to son. I wished to get one of them; and displaying a large piece of scarlet cloth, together with some tobacco and a knife, I offered them to any one who would bring me what I wanted. After some delay a tolerable shield was produced. They were very anxious to know what we meant to do with it, and Henry told them that we were going to fight their enemies the Pawnees. This instantly produced a visible impression in our favor, which was increased by the distribution of the presents. Among these was a large paper of awls, a gift appropriate to the women; and as we were anxious to see the beauties of the Arapahoe village, Henry requested that they might be called to receive them. A warrior gave a shout, as if he were calling a pack of dogs together. The squaws, young and old, hags of eighty and girls of sixteen, came running with screams and laughter out of the lodges; and as the men gave way for them, they gathered round us and stretched out their arms, grinning with delight, their native ugliness considerably enhanced by the excitement of the moment.

Mounting our horses, which during the whole interview we had held close to us, we prepared to leave the Arapahoes. The crowd fell back on each side, and stood looking on. When we were half across the camp an idea occurred to us. The Pawnees were probably in the neighborhood of the Caches; we might tell the Arapahoes of this, and instigate them to send down a war-party and cut them off, while we ourselves could remain behind for a while and hunt the buffalo. At first thought, this plan of setting our enemies to destroy one another seemed to us a master-piece of policy; but we immediately recollected that should we meet the Arapahoe warriors on the river below, they might prove quite as dangerous as the Pawnees themselves. So rejecting our plan as soon as it presented itself, we passed out of the village on the farther side. We urged our horses rapidly through the tall grass, which rose to their necks. Several Indians were walking through it at a distance, their heads just visible above its waving surface. It bore a kind of seed, as sweet and nutritious as oats; and our hungry horses, in spite of whip and rein, could not resist the temptation of snatching at this unwonted luxury as we passed along. When about a mile from the village, I turned and looked back over the undulating ocean of grass. The sun was just set; the western sky was all in a glow, and sharply defined against it, on the extreme verge of the plain, stood the clustered lodges of the Arapahoe camp.

REMINISCENCES OF GENERAL WILLIAM LARIMER AND OF HIS SON WILLIAM H. H. LARIMER

William H. H. Larimer

Denver City, Kansas Territory
23rd November, 1858

Dear Wife:

I AM KEEPING CAMP TODAY and I thought I would commence this letter not to be closed until the last of the month. In the first place, Will and I are in clover. ... Will and I have agreed so well we have never had a cross word, and I do say with pleasure that he ever consults my wishes and does all the work for him and me both. In short, he is the finest boy I ever saw in every way. He is noted here and along the road as very promising. Truly I cannot express my feelings when I think of his feelings towards me: and he so often talks of you and all the family. One Sunday he said to me: "Only think how they are so uneasy until they hear from us." Will and I have had a hard trip, but we stand it so well we do not feel the cold. Still I may say we are out of doors and in the weather nearly all the time. I may want either John or Mr Jones to come here: still I will get along, if possible. We cannot make any rash calculations yet as something might occur to spoil our calculations.

The weather is not favorable for digging and nearly everyone is fixing for winter; still some are digging and doing well. There is a man above here a few miles that everybody says is making from $5 to $10 every day. I did not see him myself but I believe it. I have seen plenty specimens of gold, one lot about $70. The immigration appears about over for this season: very few have arrived since we came. I guess some have stopped over upon the Arkansaw. Captain Humphreys was to leave Leavenworth the Monday after we did, but he had not yet arrived here. A part of the road we came over has now, they say, about two feet of snow. We got here at the nick of time.

I want you to tell all inquirers about roads to be sure to take the Laramie Road to Fort Ramsey, and they will find a good road up the South Platte and save at least 150 miles. Over the route we came it took us at least two weeks longer than it should have done. St. Matthews, the man that was in the office with the two dogs, has never reached here: neither has Mr Wade. I think Mr Wade must have gone back from Topeka.

We made a mistake by coming so many in one wagon. Our load was too heavy; moreover, when we divided we had small portions. If Will and I had each taken a light wagon with two yoke of oxen we should have done better. Only think: Will and I never rode one mile on our Wagon, nor did any of us. We had to trudge along day after day on foot, while the Oscaloosa boys could lay all day in their wagon and we, too, had no one driver, but had to drive day about, and had to whip the oxen from morning till night. It surprises me to think we ever got through. Our team was fortyseven days on the road, only think of it. I am very anxious to hear from home. Our Laramie Express will run once a month. By the 12th of December I expect to get your letters. It will cost twenty-five cents for each letter and fifteen cents for newspapers. Let all your letters be good large ones and send me no papers except important ones: but do write me often, I have plenty of money with which to pay postage.

Will and I now cook by ourselves. We have the little stove, and I was so fortunate in drawing it, when we divided our baggage. A few little sticks will get a breakfast.

I wish you could look into our quarters, you would go up! I am writing while sitting on my trunk with a little board stuck through the logs with one end to write upon. It works nicely. Mr Sanders, James Sanders, has just called in to see me. I want you to direct your letters to me in care of Sanders & Co. Express. This will save the trouble of sending an order every time.

25th November: The weather is now mild and beautiful, very much like Pennsylvania weather. Will is out busily engaged chopping logs for our house. We expect to get them all hauled tomorrow. I am keeping camp today again. You would laugh to see Will and me eating breakfast and supper. We eat only two meals a day. Will makes first rate cakes (biscuits). We have venison nearly all the time, if not we have plenty of bacon. Will and I both feel rich. We shall have about 500 lots, each, in Denver City. I am selected to donate lots to actual settlers. We shall have at least fifty

Artist unknown, "Seven Views in Denver, Colorado, 1859," from Beyond the Mississippi *by Albert D. Richardson, 1867.*

houses up this fall and winter and no one knows how many in the spring. We expect a second Sacramento City, at least. Everybody here is delighted with the prospects, and none more so than Will and I … . We may open an office here. Everyone has it that I am going to do so. We haven't the whole matter at present in our own hands, but there is nothing to do, nor can anything be done, until they dig the gold and a regular express starts. But all this is in the future, and I will write you every chance after we get fixed up. Will is going to dig. We have our claims staked off about four miles above here. … Everybody here is confident of success. …

Sunday, 28th: I have just returned from Church. A Mr Fisher, a Methodist minister, came in our party. He preached here last Sunday also. You can imagine my feelings last Sunday when we had Mr McLane to lead the music. He was not here today: he is stopping four miles below town. Mr Moyne, a young Omaha deacon, is also here; his cabin and ours are right opposite each other. Mr Moyne is that young man with fair hair that you always saw at our church in Omaha, so you see that we are not out of the world yet. The church was better attended last Sunday than this. Everybody is busy today building and hunting. The weather is now very warm and pleasant. We have got all our logs and hope to get well housed next week. We have plenty of dry wood nearby, so you need not fear for one moment about Will and I being warm and comfortable. Besides, I think the weather here is warmer than with you, certainly warmer than in Nebraska,—the mountains protect us. …

Everything looks cheering. Will and I get along nicely, so think no more about us. We are perhaps more comfortable than you and we have plenty of people all around us. We shall have a good hotel here by spring. Stephens of Omaha is going to keep it; he is starting early in the spring. Stephens formerly kept the Douglas House and is now keeping the Saratoga Hotel. Old Spooner is here building the hotel in our City. Our town is now the County seat. I believe I wrote you I was appointed Treasurer. I am also Treasurer of Denver City, our town.

30 November: I'll have to close my letter tonight, I guess. I will send it by the hands of Ed. Wynkoop and Dr. A. B. Steinberger of Bellevue. They leave tomorrow. The express also leaves tomorrow.

Say to Mr Reed that Mr Lawrence and Dorsett are well. We will stick together. Whitsett and Jewett have gone to Montana, six miles above here: they are also very well. Mr Whitsett was down today. The news of gold diggings are better and better every day. … If things go well here I may be home by mid-summer, if not before. I have instructed Mr Wynkoop to leave John a map of Denver City when he gets them lithographed. … When you get this map notice that my lot is on the northwest corner of C and Larimer streets: Will's lot is on the northeast corner of D and Larimer streets. Larimer street at present is the best, Lawrence and McGaa next.

Yours affectionately,

Wm. Larimer, Jr.

A HIT AT THE TIMES

A. O. McGrew

Way out upon the Platte, near Pike's Peak we were told
There by a little digging, we could get a pile of gold,
So we bundled up our duds, resolved at least to try
And tempt old Madam Fortune, root hog, or die.

So we traveled across the country, and we got upon the ground,
But cold weather was ahead, the first thing we found.
We built our shanties on the ground, resolved in spring to try,
To gather up the dust and slugs, root hog, or die.

Speculation is the fashion even at this early stage,
And corner lots and big hotels appear to be the rage,
The emigration's bound to come, and to greet them we will try,
Big pig, little pig, root hog, or die.

Let shouts resound, the cup pass 'round, we all came for gold,
The politicians are all gas, the speculators sold,
The "scads" are all we want, and to get them we will try,
Big pig, little pig, root hog, or die.

Surveyors now are at their work, laying off the towns,
And some will be of low degree, and some of high renown.
They don't care a jot nor tittle who do buy
The corner lots, or any lots, root hog, or die.

The doctors are among us, you can find them where you will,
They say their trade it is to cure, I say it is to kill;
They'll dose you, and they'll physic you, until they make you sigh,
And their powders and their lotions make you root hog, or die.

The next in turn comes Lawyers, a precious set are they;
In the public dairy they drink the milk, their clients drink the whey.
A cunning set these fellows are; they'll sap you 'till you're dry,
And never leave you 'till you have to root hog, or die.

A Preacher, now is all we want, to make us all do good;
But at present, there's no lack of *spiritual* food,
The kind that I refer to, will make you laugh or cry,
And its real name is Taos, root hog, or die.

I have finished now my song, or, if you please, my ditty;
And that it was not shorter, is about the only pity.
And now, that I have had my say, don't say I've told a lie;
For the subject I've touched, will make us root hog, or die.

AN OVERLAND JOURNEY

Horace Greeley

Denver, June 15, 1859

I KNOW FEW GREATER contrasts than that between the region which stretches hundreds of miles eastward from this spot toward the Missouri, and is known as *The Plains,* and that which overlooks us on the west and, alike by its abrupt and sharp-ridged foothills seeming just at hand, and its glittering peaks of snow in the blue distance, vindicates its current designation, *The Mountains.* Let me elucidate:

The Plains are nearly destitute of human inhabitants. Aside from the buffalo range—which has been steadily narrowing ever since Daniel Boone made his home in Kentucky, and is now hardly two hundred miles wide—it affords little sustenance and less shelter to man. The antelope are seldom seen in herds—three is the highest number I observed together, while one, or at most two, is a more common spectacle. One to each mile square would be a large estimate for all that exist on the plains. Elk are scarcely seen at all, even where they have hardly ever been hunted or scared. Of deer, there are none, or next to none. For the Plains are the favorite haunt of beasts and birds of prey—of the ravenous and fearless gray wolf, of the coyote, the raven, and the hawk—the first hanging on the flanks of every great herd of buffalo, ready to waylay any foolish calf or heedless heifer that may chance to stray for water or fresher grass beyond the protection of the hard-headed and chivalrous patriarchs, behind whose vigilant ranks there is comparative safety, and counting as their property any bull, even, whom wounds or disease or decrepitude shall compel to fall behind in the perpetual march. For, while a stray buffalo, or two, or three, may linger in some lonely valley for months—for all winter, perhaps—the great herds which blacken the earth for miles in extent cannot afford to do so—they are so immensely numerous and find their safety in traveling so compactly that they must keep moving or starve. Avoiding, so far as possible, the wooded ravines of the slender watercourses, where experience has taught them to dread the lance-like arrow of the lurking Indian, they keep to the high "divides," or only feed in the valleys while they have these well covered by sentinel bulls to give warning of any foe's approach. Take away the buffalo, and the Plains will be desolate far beyond their present desolation; and I cannot but regard with sadness the inevitable and not distant fate of these noble and harmless brutes, already crowded into a breadth of country too narrow for them, and continually hunted, slaughtered, decimated, by the wolf, the Indian, the white man. They could have stood their ground against all in the absence of firearms, but "villainous salpeter" is too much for them. They are bound to perish; I trust it may be oftener by sudden shot than by slow starvation.

Wood and water—the prime necessities of the traveler as of the settler—are in adequate though not abundant supply for a hundred miles and more on this as they are throughout on the other side of the buffalo range; at length they gradually fail, and we are in a desert indeed. No spring, no brook, for a distance of thirty to sixty miles (which would be stretched to more than a hundred if the few tracks called roads were not all run so as to secure water so far as possible)—rivers which have each had fifty to a hundred miles of its course gradually parched up by force of sun and wind, and its waters lost in their own sands, so that the weary, dusty traveler vainly digs for hours in their dry beds in quest of drink for his thirsty cattle—rivers which dare not rise again till some friendly brook, having its source in some specially favored region, pours in its small but steady tribute, moistens the sands of the river bed, and encourages its waters to rise to the surface again. In one case, an emigrant assures me that he dug down to the bedrock of one of these rivers, yet found all dry sand.

Artist unknown, "Busted, by Thunder!," from Beyond the Mississippi *by Albert D. Richardson, 1867.*

I know not that I can satisfactorily account, even to myself, for the destitution of wood which the Plains everywhere present, especially the western half of them. The poverty of the soil will not suffice, for these lands, when sufficiently moistened by rain or thawing snowdrifts, produce grass, and are not so sterile as the rocky hills, the pebbly knolls, of New England, which, nevertheless, produce wood rapidly and abundantly. On the prairies of Illinois, Missouri, and eastern Kansas, the absence of wood is readily accounted for by the annual fires which, in autumn or spring, sweep over nearly every acre of dead grass, killing every tree sprout that may have started up from scattered seeds or roots running from the timber in the adjacent ravine beneath the matted grass. But here are thousands of acres too poorly grassed to be swept by the annual fires—on which the thinly scattered reed stalks and bunch grass of last year shake dryly in the fierce night winds—yet not a tree nor shrub relieves the sameness, the bareness, the desolation, of thousands after thousands of acres—not a twig, a scion, gives promise of trees that are to be. For a time, the narrow ravine or lowest intervale of the frequent streams were fairly timbered with cottonwood, and low, sprawling elm, with a very little oak, or white ash at long intervals intermixed; but these grew gradually thinner and feebler until nothing but a few small cottonwoods remained, and these skulking behind bluffs, or in sheltered hollows at intervals of twenty to forty miles. Once in ten or twenty miles, a bunch of dwarf willows, perhaps two feet high, would be found cowering in some petty basin washed out by a current of water many years ago; but these, like the cottonwoods, are happy if able to hold their own; indeed, I have seen much evidence that wood was more abundant on the Plains a hundred years ago than it now is. Dead cottonwoods, of generous proportions, lie in the channels of dry brooks on which no tree nor shrub now grows; and, at one or more stations of the express company, near the sink of the Republican, they find dead pine eight miles up a creek, where no living pine has been seen for generations. I judged that the desert is steadily enlarging its borders and at the same time intensifying its barrenness.

The fierce drought that usually prevails throughout the summer doubtless contributes to this, but I think the violent and all but constant winds exert a still more disastrous potency. High winds are of frequent, all but daily, occurrence here, within a dozen miles of the great protecting bulwark of the Rocky Mountains; while, from a point fifty miles eastward of this, they sweep over the Plains almost constantly, and at times with resistless fury. A driver stated on our way up, with every appearance of sincerity, that he had known instances of tires being blown off from wagon wheels by the tornadoes of the Plains; and, hard to swallow as that may seem, I have other and reliable assurance that when the Missourians' camp on the express road was swept by a hurricane five or six weeks ago, so that, after the wreck, but three decent wagons could be patched up out of their six, as I have already narrated, one of the wheel tires was not only blown off but nearly straightened out! There is almost always a good breeze at midday and after, on the Plains; but, should none be felt during the day, one is almost certain to spring up at sunset, and blow fiercely through the night. Thus, though hot days, or parts of days, are frequent on the Plains, I have experienced not even a moderately warm night. And thus trees are not; mainly because the winds uproot or dismember them, or so rock and wrench them while young, that their roots cannot suck up even the little nourishment that this soil of baking clay resting on porous sand would fain afford them. Thus the few shoots that cleave the surface of the earth soon wither and die, and the broad landscape remains treeless, cheerless, forbidding.

But the dearth of water and wood on the Plains is paralleled by the poverty of shrubbery and herbage. I have not seen a strawberry leaf—far from me be the presumption of looking for a berry!—since I left the Missouri three weeks ago; and the last blackberry bramble I observed grew on Chapman's Creek—at all events, the other side of the buffalo range. A raspberry cane has not blessed my sight these three weary weeks, nor aught else that might be hoped to bear an old-fashioned fruit, save the far-off blackberries aforesaid, and two or three doubtful grapevines on some creek a great way back. The prickly pear, very rare and very green, is the only semblance of fruit I discovered on the Plains; a dwarfish cactus, with its leaves close to the ground; the Spanish nettle—a sort of vegetable porcupine—a profusion of wild sage, wild wormwood, and other such plants, worthless alike to man and beast, relieved by some well-gnawed grass in the richer valleys of winter watercourses (the flora usually very scanty and always coarse and poor)—such are my recollections of the three hundred miles or so that separate the present buffalo range from the creeks that carry snow water to the Platte and the pines that herald our approach to the Rocky Mountains.

THE ROCKY MOUNTAINS

And now all changes, but slowly, gradually. The cactus, the Spanish nettle, the prickly pear continue, even into and upon the mountains; but the pines, though stunted and at first scattered, give variety, softness and beauty to the landscape, which becomes more rolling, with deeper and more frequent valleys, and water in nearly all of them; the cottonwoods along the streams no longer skulk behind bluffs or hide in casual hollows; you may build an honest campfire without fear of robbing an embryo county of its last stick of wood, and water your mules generously without drying up some long, pretentious river, and condemning those who come after you to weary, thirsty marches through night and day. The cottonwoods, as you near the wind-quelling range of protecting heights, which rise, rank above rank, to the westward (the more distant still white-robed with snow) grow large and stately— some of them sixty to seventy feet high, and at least three feet in diameter; the unwooded soil ceases to be desert and becomes prairie once more; but still this is in the main a sandy, thinly grassed region, which cannot compare with the prairies of Illinois, of Iowa, or eastern Kansas.

There seems to be as rich and deep soil in some of the creek bottoms, especially those of the South Platte, as almost anywhere; and yet I fear the husbandman is doomed to find even this belt of grassed and moderately rolling land, which stretches along the foot of the mountains to a width of perhaps twenty miles, less tractable and productive than fertile. It lies at such an elevation—from five thousand to six thousand feet above the ocean level—that, though its winters are said to be moderate, its springs cannot be early. There was a fall of a foot of snow in this region on the 26th of May, when ice formed to a quarter-inch thickness on the Plains; and when summer suddenly sets in, about the 1st of June, there are hot suns by day, and cool, strong winds by night, with a surfeit of petty thunder squalls, but little or no rain. The gentle rain of last Thursday in the mountains fell, for a short time, in sheets just at their feet—say for a breadth of five miles—and there ceased. Hardly a drop fell within five miles west, or for any distance east of this place, though the earth was soaked only ten miles further west. Hence, the enterprising few who have commenced farms and gardens near this point tell me that their crops have made no progress for a week or two, and can make none till they have rain. I trust wheat and rye will do well here whenever they shall be allowed a fair chance; barley and oats, if sowed very early on deeply plowed land, may do tolerably; but corn, though it comes up well and looks rank at present, will hardly ripen before frost, even should it escape paralysis by drought; while potatoes, peas, and most vegetables will probably require irrigation, or yield but sparingly. Yet, should the gold mines justify their present promise, farming, in the right localities at the base of these mountains, even by the help of irrigation, will yield—to those who bring to it the requisite sagacity, knowledge, and capital—richer rewards than

elsewhere on earth. Everything that can be grown here will command treble or quadruple prices for years; and he who produces anything calculated to diversify and improve the gross, mountainous diet of salt pork, hot bread, beans, and coffee, now necessarily all but universal in this region, will be justly entitled to rank with public benefactors.

And the Rocky Mountains, with their grand, aromatic forests, their grassy glades, their frequent springs, and dancing streams of the brightest, sweetest water, their pure, elastic atmosphere, and their unequalled game and fish, are destined to be a favorite resort and

Artist unknown, "Return of Pike's Peakers," from Beyond the Mississippi *by Albert D. Richardson, 1867.*

home of civilized man. I never visited a region where physical life could be more surely prolonged or fully enjoyed. Thousands who rush hither for gold will rush away again disappointed and disgusted, as thousands have already done; and yet the gold is in these mountains, and the right men will gradually unearth it. I shall be mistaken if two or three millions are not taken out this year, and some ten millions in 1860, though all the time there will be, as now, a stream of rash adventurers heading away from the diggings, declaring that there is no gold there, or next to none. So it was in California and in Australia; so it must be here, where the obstacles to be overcome are greater, and the facilities for getting home decidedly better. All men are not fitted by nature for gold-diggers; yet thousands will not realize this until they have been convinced of it by sore experience. Any good phrenologist should have been able to tell half the people who rushed hither so madly during the last two months that, if these mountains had been half made of gold, they never would get any of it except by minding their own proper business, which was quite other than mining. And still the long procession is crossing the Platte and Clear Creek, and pressing up the Hill of Difficulty in mad pursuit of gold, whereof not one-fifth will carry back to the states so much as they brought away. New leads will doubtless be discovered, new veins be opened, new diggings or districts become the rage— for it were absurd to suppose that little ravine known as Gregory's, running to Clear Creek, the sole depository of gold worth working in all this region—and in time the Rocky Mountains will swarm with a hardy, industrious, energetic white population. Not gold alone, but lead, iron, and (I think) silver or cobalt, have already been discovered here, and other valuable minerals, doubtless will be, as the mountains are more thoroughly explored—for as yet they have not been even run over. Those who are now intent on the immediate organization and admission of a new state may be too fast, yet I believe the Rocky Mountains, and their immediate vicinity— say between Fort Laramie on the north, and Taos on the south—will within three years have a white population of one hundred thousand, one half composed of men in the full vigor of their prime, separated by deserts and waste places from the present states, obliged to rely on their own resources in any emergency, and fully able to protect and govern themselves. Why not let them be a state so soon as reasonably may be.

Mining is a pursuit akin to fishing and hunting, and, like them, enriches the few at the cost of the many. This region is doubtless foreordained to many changes of fortune; today, giddy with the intoxication of success—tomorrow, in the valley of humiliation. One day, report will be made on the Missouri by a party of disappointed gold-seekers, that the "Pike's Peak humbug" has exploded, and that everybody is fleeing to the states who can possibly get away; the next report will represent these diggings as yellow with gold. Neither will be true, yet each in its turn will have a certain thin substratum of fact for its justification. Each season will see its thousands turn away disappointed, only to give place to others thousands, sanguine and eager as if none had ever failed. Yet I feel a strong conviction that each succeeding month's researches will enlarge the field of mining operations, and diminish the difficulties and impediments which now stretch across the gold-seeker's path, and that, ten years hence, we shall be just beginning fairly to appreciate and secure the treasures now buried in the Rocky Mountains.

ARTEMUS WARD: HIS TRAVELS

Artemus Ward

QUEEN OF ALL TERRITORIES

So DREARILY, WEARILY WE drag onward. We reach the summit of the Rocky Mountains at midnight on the 17th [of February, 1864]. The climate changes suddenly, and the cold is intense. We resume runners, have a breakdown and are forced to walk four miles.

I remember that one of the numerous reasons urged in favor of General Fremont's election to the Presidency in 1856 was his finding the path across the Rocky Mountains. Credit is certainly due that gallant explorer in this regard, but it occurred to me, as I wrung my frost-bitten hands on that dreadful night, that for me to deliberately go over that path in mid-winter was a sufficient reason for my election to any lunatic asylum, by an overwhelming vote. ...

🐾 🐾 🐾

We strike the North Platte on the 18th. The fare at the stations is daily improving, and we often have antelope steaks now. They tell us of eggs not far off, and we encourage (by a process not wholly unconnected with bottles) the drivers to keep their mules in motion. Antelope by the thousand can be seen racing the plains from the coach windows.

At Elk Mountain we encounter a religious driver named Edward Whitney, who never swears at the mules. This has made him distinguished all over the plains. This pious driver tried to convert the Doctor, but I am mortified to say that his efforts were not crowned with success. ...

On the 20th we reach Rocky Thomas's justly celebrated station at five in the morning and have a breakfast of hashed black-tailed deer, antelope steaks, ham, boiled bear, honey, eggs, coffee, tea and cream. That was the squarest meal on the road except at Weber. Mr. Thomas is a Baltimore "slosher," he informed me. I don't know what that is, but he is a good fellow and gave us a breakfast fit for a lord, emperor, czar, count. A better couldn't be found at Delmonico's or Parker's. He pressed me to linger with him a few days and shoot bears. It was with several pangs that I declined the generous Baltimorean's invitation.

To Virginia Dale. Weather clear and bright. Virginia Dale is a pretty spot, as it ought to be with such a pretty name, but I treated with no little scorn the advice of the hunter I met there, who told me to give up "literatoor," form a matrimonial alliance with some squaws and "settle down thar."

Bannock on the brain! That is what is the matter now. Wagon-load after wagon-load of emigrants, bound to the new Idaho gold regions, meet us every hour. Canvas-covered and drawn for the most part by fine large mules, they make a pleasant panorama, as they stretch slowly over the plains and uplands.

We strike the South Platte Sunday, the 21st, and breakfast at Latham, a station of one-horse proportions. We are now in Colorado ("Pike's Peak"), and we diverge from the main route here and visit the flourishing and beautiful city of Denver. Messrs. Langrish & Dougherty, who have so long and so admirably catered to the amusement lovers of the Far West, kindly withdrew their dramatic corps for a night and allow me to use their pretty little theatre.

We go to the Mountains from Denver, visiting the celebrated gold-mining towns of Black Hawk and Central City. I leave this queen of all the territories, quite firmly believing that its future is to be no less brilliant than its past has been. ...

A TRIP TO PIKES PEAK

C. M. Clark

AFTER LEAVING ST. VRAIN'S, a distance of two miles brought us to the junction of the Denver City road, at which place a shoe maker had erected his tent, and had displayed on a rough board, in one corner, a row of black bottles, containing, doubtless, a variety of whisky, from *proof* to *water-proof.* He was evidently on his *last pegs,* and, with his a(w)ll had located there, having been disappointed in his *findings* at the mountains, to raise the wind to get home, and for the want of boots to *sole,* he frequently *tapped* the bottles and *sold* the contents, which was decidedly the most profitable business.

We continued back, following along over the road, which no doubt the reader is sufficiently familiar with; and after thirty-five days of hard travel, over the monotonous prairie, through rain and shine, heat and cold, and many times through the entire night, for the purpose of escaping the torturous fangs of innumerable mosquitoes, and at times when the night was as dark as Erebus, and we could not see the length of our noses, when one of us would start ahead with the lantern, in order that we might keep the track, we finally reached our starting point of the Spring previous—having accomplished an over-land travel of some fifteen hundred miles in six months, behind slow bullocks, that had required about as much effort on our part as on theirs, to keep them moving—feeling rich in experience, if not in money.

A large emigration is expected next Spring, by those remaining in the mountains, and doubtless they will not be disappointed, for the country is fast being developed and settled; and as the mists of uncertainty that have hung over that country for the past two years, are fast dissolving before the warming rays of a progressive and determined spirit, disclosing that substance of things hoped for—"that more than philosopher's stone"—the public confidence is being restored, and thousands will again prepare to try their fortune and their fate.

The country is destined to be more than is "dreamt of in their philosophy," and its mines will yet open richly, and reward the persevering industry of the many who have not "fear'd their fate too much," and whose deserts are fully equal to their hopes.

Quartz mining is to be the permanent feature of the region, and it is the only mining that will hold out and pay. The gulches and bars that have been discovered and worked, have not generally paid, and they never will, unless means can be adopted to facilitate the working of them, and to save the gold, much of which is very fine, and wastes in the washing.

It is not at all probable that all who again start on the expedition, will realize a tithe of their expectations, and for reasons that have been enumerated in the previous pages, and for reasons that cannot but be apparent to every man who possesses common sense. All men are not successful in their avocations and experiments at home, and the laws that govern their finances and fortunes in the States, will not be suspended in the mountains. If they are not suited for the business, and if they have not the means to carry it forward successfully, they will necessarily fail; and if they have not the courage to face difficulties, the ability for hard labor, and the perseverance and patience that is necessary, the probability is that they will be disappointed; and if any man goes there with the hope of making a fortune in one season, he will find himself mistaken, unless he is content with a very small one.

A large number went last spring without knowing exactly what they should do on reaching the mountains; and the majority of them left without finding out, after standing around through the various mines, with the hope of "jumping into somebody's shoes," for which there is seldom a chance. Capitalists can do well there, for they can turn their money in half the time that would be possible elsewhere; but the laboring man, who has but little means, or with scarcely sufficient to furnish a comfortable outfit, and who will be entirely dependent on his wits or muscle, had better remain at home, for he cannot get rich there any sooner than at home, and he will escape much hardship, toil and privation, which is necessarily entailed on those who sojourn amid the mountains. But it is not my purpose to either encourage or discourage any person. If a man think he can do well, and wants to go—let him go—"*chacun son goux!*"

The best route is, I think, the one that I have described; but perhaps the one from Omaha is the most direct and shortest, and it will eventually take precedence over all the others, when the railroad is completed to that point. All persons intending to start for that country next spring, should be at their starting point as early as the 20th of April, and proceed out as soon as the feed will permit—the grass is generally far enough advanced at that time to afford good forage.

The outfit of companies would be too tedious to mention. Generally, a light wagon—one sufficiently strong to convey two thousand or two thousand five hundred pounds—is the best vehicle; and, with regard to team, cattle are best where you have much load to draw, and they are by far the most sure and safe, and will not occasion one-half the anxiety and trouble that horses or mules do; but then the latter will perform the journey in one-half the time that is required where bullocks are used, as they will not travel to exceed an average of fifteen miles per day.

The best method to pursue in the matter of traveling is, to get as early a start in the morning as possible—say four o'clock, and proceed until nine o'clock, and halt until two o'clock P.M.; then resume, and travel until six o'clock, or until such time as may suit convenience. By pursuing this course, you will avoid the heat of the day, your team will travel faster and better, and they, as well as yourself, will reach the end of your trip in better condition than those who follow the old methodic system of reaching certain specified camps each night, where the feed is poor, and perhaps all consumed by those who have preceded.

As regards the many other items that constitute a proper outfit, one will be governed by his own peculiarities, or according to their taste and means. Every one should be well supplied with waterproof clothing, and with a sufficient quantity of blankets and bedding, if they desire to pass the nights comfortably. The items of flour, meal, bacon, potatoes, molasses, sugar and coffee, are the essentials; dried and preserved fruits, the condiments, and a good article of whisky are the (so considered) luxuries.

Every company should make it a point to take a cow, as she will more than pay for herself and the trouble during the trip, and can be sold to good advantage after reaching the mountains.

The items of beans and Bologna sausage should be left out. The first can never be properly cooked, especially while traveling, and will ever occasion more or less sickness, when they are not properly prepared; and sausage, when eaten, creates great thirst, which cannot always be gratified, and even if it can be, the drinking of large quantities of water should be guarded against, as it weakens the system.

COLORADO: A SUMMER TRIP

Bayard Taylor

Denver, Colorado, July 15, 1866

THIS IS MY LAST NIGHT in Denver. After a month beside and among the Rocky Mountains, I am going (as the people here say) "to America." My place is taken in the stage which leaves to-morrow morning for the East, by the Platte route.

Had not the commencement of the rainy season and the condition of our animals prevented me from reaching Cañon and Colorado cities, my tour would have embraced all of the mountain regions which are easily accessible, and some that are not so. What I have seen is amply sufficient to convince me how much more there is to see. During a journey on horseback of four hundred miles, which led me through two of the three Parks, and thrice across the great range, I have obtained a tolerably extensive knowledge of the climate, scenery, and other features of a region which is destined, I think, to become for us what Switzerland is to Europe. Our artists, with true instinct, have first scented this fact, and they are the pioneers who point out to ignorant Fashion the way it should go.

Whoever comes to the Rocky Mountains with pictures of the Alps in his memory, expecting to find them repeated on a grander and wilder scale, will certainly be disappointed. He will find no upper world of unbroken snow, as in the Bernese Oberland; no glaciers, thrusting far down between the forests their ever-moving fronts of ice; no contrast of rich and splendid vegetation in the valleys; no flashing waterfalls; no slopes of bright green pasturage; no moss; and but rarely the gleam of lakes and rivers, seen from above. With no less lofty chain can the Rocky Mountains be measured, it is true; but it is merely a general comparison of height, not of resemblance in any important feature.

In the first place, the atmospheric effects are those which result from the intense dryness of the heart of a continent in the temperate zone. The Alps not only touch the Mediterranean at either extremity, but are no further from the Atlantic than from here to the Missouri River. Four or five cloudless days in succession are considered a rare good fortune by the tourist; the higher peaks are seldom without their drapery of shifting cloud. Here a clear sky is the rule. There is seldom vapor enough—except just at present, during the brief rainy season—for the artist's needs. Perspective is only obtained by immense distances. The wonderful, delicate grays of the mountain landscapes demand changes of light and shadow which are often lacking; they lie too barely in the broad, unobstructed sunshine. Yet an air more delicious to breathe can scarcely be found anywhere. It is neither too sedative nor too exciting; but has that pure, sweet, flexible quality which seems to support all one's happiest and healthiest moods. Moreover, it holds in solution an exquisite variety of odors. Whether the resin of the coniferous trees, the balm of the sage-bush, or the breath of the orchis and wild rose, it is equally grateful and life-giving. After a day in this atmosphere you have the lightest and most restorative slumber you ever knew.

On first entering the Rocky Mountains, you find the scenery rugged, cramped, and somewhat monotonous. Press forward, and they open anon—the higher the summits become the more breadth of base, the clearer outline they demand. They push away the crowd of lower ridges, leaving valleys for the streams, parks with every variety of feature, and finally gather into well-defined ranges, or spurs of ranges, giving you still broader and grander landscapes.

The San Luis Park, from the accounts I have heard, must be equally remarkable. It is on a much grander scale, and has the advantage of a milder climate, from its lesser elevation above the sea-level. The North Park is rarely visited except by an occasional prospecter or trapper. It has no settlement, as yet, and I have met with no one who has thoroughly explored it. There are a number of smaller parks on both sides of the main chain, and some of them are said to possess great natural beauties. The singular rock formations at the eastern base of the mountains furnish in themselves a rare and most original field for the tourist and the artist. The glimpse I had of those on the south bank of the Platte, on my return from the South Park, satisfy me that they surpass in magnitude and picturesque distortion the celebrated basaltic formations of Saxony.

It was part of my plan to have ascended either Pike's or Long's Peak, but I find that it is too soon in the season to make the attempt. Pike's Peak is comparatively easy of ascent; the summit, thirteen thousand two hundred feet above the level of the sea, has several times been reached by ladies. It is a very laborious, but in no sense a dangerous undertaking. On account of its isolated position, the view from the top, in favorable weather, must be one of the finest panoramas in the world. Long's Peak has never yet been ascended. Mr. Byers, two years ago, reached a point about five hundred feet below the summit, and was then compelled to return. He is quite confident, however, that it can be scaled from another side, and if the summer were six weeks further advanced, I should be willing to join him in making the attempt. On the northern side he says there is a valley or rather gulf, with walls of perpendicular rock between two and three thousand feet in height, resembling a section of the Yosemite.

A comparison of this peak with Mont Blanc—the altitude of both being just about the same—may give a clear idea of the differences between the Alps and the Rocky Mountains. When you see Mont Blanc from the western part of Lake Leman, in July or August, he appears to you as a dome of complete snow, the few rocky pinnacles which pierce his mantle being hardly discernible specks. He is a *white* vision on the horizon. Long's Peak, at the same distance, is of the faint blue or purple which a rocky mass assumes, veined and streaked with white, but showing only one snow-field of much apparent extent. His outline is very fine,—a little sharper than Mont Blanc,—the western side (as seen from Denver) having convex, and the eastern principally concave curves. He rests on a dark, broad base of forest and rock, his snows marking the courses of deep clefts and ravines. At present, the top-most summit is bare on the southern side. It is rare that one sees Mont Blanc from summit to base: I have not yet seen Long's Peak (except during a passing thundershower) otherwise.

I do not think the parks and the upper valleys of the mountains will produce anything except hardy vegetables, and perhaps barley and rye. But they abound with the richest grasses; and "Colorado cheese" may one day be as celebrated as Gruyère or Neufchatel. They offer precisely those things which the summer tourist seeks—pure air, lovely nights, the finest milk, butter, trout, and game, and a variety of mineral springs. The summer climate I know; and I am told that the winter is equally enjoyable. It sounds almost incredible to hear of persons in the latitude of New York, and eight thousand feet above the sea, rarely needing an overcoat during the whole winter season. There is a great depth of snow, and an occasional severe day, but the skies are generally cloudless, and the air temperate and bracing. The extremes of heat and cold are greater in Denver than in the mountains. As nearly as I can learn, the coldest weather yet experienced in San Luis Park, was seven degrees below zero; in the Middle Park, fifteen degrees; and in Denver, thirty degrees below.

The heavy snow-fall, while it is a godsend to the agriculture of Colorado, by swelling all the streams at the very season when water is needed for irrigation, nevertheless interferes with the mining interests. There are many rich placers in the mountains where gold-washing can only be carried on for three or four months in the year, and even the stamp and smelting mills are hindered in procuring their supplies. It will also be the principal difficulty which the Pacific Railroad will be obliged to overcome. All other obstacles are much less than I had imagined. Greater achievements have already been done in railroading than the passage of the Rocky Mountains. By the Clear Creek, the South Park, or the Arkansas Valley, the Pacific slope can be reached, with not much more labor than you find on the Baltimore and Ohio road between Piedmont and Grafton. The facilities of construction *beyond* the range, however, must determine where the range should be crossed. A thorough exploration of the region watered by the Green and Blue Rivers must first be made.

I am, therefore, quite unable to tell you where the road will cross the Rocky Mountains; it is enough that they will be crossed. My conjectures—given for what they may be worth—take this form: that the Central Pacific Railroad, now rapidly advancing up the Platte, will cross in the neighborhood of Bridger's Pass; that the Eastern Division will follow the Smoky Hill, and make directly for Denver; that a road running northward along the base of the mountains will connect the two; that this road will then be extended to Montana on one side and New Mexico on the other; and that, finally, a second central road will be pushed westward from Denver into and across the Middle Park, and so to Nevada. The business of Colorado alone, with the stimulus which a completed road would give, will keep that road fully employed. By the time the last rail is spiked down on the road connecting New York and San Francisco, we shall want, not one line across the continent, but *five*.

I hazard nothing, at least, in predicting that Colorado will soon be recognized as our Switzerland, The enervated luxury, the ignorant and imitative wealth, and the overtasked business of our cities, will come hither, in all future summers, for health, and rest, and recreation. Where Kit Carson chased Arapahoes, and Frémont's men ate mule-meat, and Jim Beckworth went through apocryphal adventures, there will be drawling dandies, maidens both fast and slow, ungrammatical mammas, and the heaviest of fathers. The better sort of people will come first, nor be scared away afterward by the rush of the unappreciating. We shall, I hope, have Alpine clubs, intelligent guides, good roads, bridges, and access to a thousand wonders yet unknown. It will be a national blessing when this region is opened to general travel. That time is not now distant. Before the close of 1868 Denver will only be four days from New York, and you can go through with one change of cars. Therefore I am doubly glad that I have come *now*, while there are still buffaloes and danger of Indians on the Plains, camp-fires to build in the mountains, rivers to swim, and landscapes to enjoy which have never yet been described.

The weather continues intensely hot by day, with cool and perfect nights. Sometimes the edge of the regular afternoon thunder-storm overlaps Denver, and lays the hot dust of the streets. These storms are superb aërial pictures. After they pass, their cloudy ruins become the material out of which the setting sun constructs unimaginable splendors. If I were to give the details of them it would seem like color run mad. Such cool rose-gray, such transparent gold, such purple velvet as are worn by the mountains and clouds, are fresh wonders to me every evening. The vault of heaven seems ampler than elsewhere; the lines of cloud cover vaster distances,— probably because a hundred miles of mountains give you a more palpable measure of their extent,—and your eye recognizes infinite shades, gradations, and transitions either unseen before or unnoticed. This amplification of the sky and sky-effects struck me when I first entered upon the Plains. It is grand, even there; but here, with such accessories, it is truly sublime.

I do not wonder at the attachment of the inhabitants of the territory for their home. These mountains and this atmosphere insensibly become a portion of their lives. I foresee that they will henceforth be among the clearest and most vivid episodes of mine.

THE ROCKY MOUNTAIN WEST IN 1867

Louis L. Simonin

TRAVEL BY TRAIN IS TOO swift when one is crossing picturesque country; then the tourist curses the speed and would willingly prefer the old stagecoach, voyaging comfortably, watching the landscape unroll little by little. But on the prairie, since the landscape is monotonous and always horizontal, train travel is more appropriate. From North Platte to Julesburg, all the natural grasses, families, species, varieties, pass in a few hours before one's eyes; also the fragrant plants of the desert, sage, artemesia, the everlasting flower, and certain dwarf cacti. Trees are scarce, and only rarely does one encounter along the streams certain poplars, one species of which, the Canadian poplar (*populus monilifera*), here bears the name of *cottonwood*, doubtless because the leaves are covered underneath with a white cottony fuzz. The cottonwood is especially dear to the plains hunter and gladly sighted, since, like the palm of the African oasis, it is the tree which announces the presence of water.

Clumps of the river birch mingle with the cottonwood along the streams, a wood valued by those crossing the prairie by wagon train for starting the campfires for the night.

The fauna of the great American desert is no more varied than the flora. Everywhere are the buffalo, or bison, enormous bulls with great heads and thick pelt. The Indian hunts the buffalo for food and for hides to tan. The hide, or "robe," serves as a coat or covering for the Redskin, and forms the principal object of commerce with the whites. The tanned hide is used to cover his tent; the flesh, drawn out into narrow strips like straps and dried in the sun, lasts indefinitely. The smoked tongue, a delicate morsel, is the only part which the whites willingly eat.

The Indians make spoons and powder horns from the horns of the buffalo; from the bones they make scratching knives, scrapers, to scrape the hides which they tan with the brains of the animal; from the tendons of the muscles they make cords and a lining for their bows, and with the gelatine from the hoofs a glue to hold the points of their arrows. The Indian thus finds everything in the buffalo, beginning with his chief diversion, hunting. So he follows it in all his migrations; and there is a saying on the prairies: Where the buffalo is, there is the Indian. The Redskin adds further that a tradition runs through all the tribes, namely, that there will be no more Indians when the day arrives that there are no more buffalo. As in so many other places, primitive man will disappear with the primitive animal. For this reason the Redskin is so hostile to civilization, which, invading the prairies, disperses the buffalo in all directions and little by little brings about his own disappearance.

Along with the buffalo as the principal animals of the great plains are the beaver, which build their clever dams along the streams, and the prairie dogs, not too unlike the marmot, the cony, and the squirrel, which live in a republic of underground villages covering immense areas. We must add the prairie wolf, or coyote, an ever hungry meat eater, and the graceful antelope, herds of which go by as swiftly as the wind. The antelope lives, like the buffalo, on the grasses of the desert; turf is nowhere lacking, and the prairie has rightly been named the terrestrial paradise of animals.

As one approaches the mountains, the fauna changes, or rather increases, into new species. There the deer, elk, hart, bear, and wildcat give the resolute hunter something to exercise his skill on.

This digression on the zoology and botany of the Great West has taken me away from Julesburg. I return. This improvised city is at the moment the last railroad station of the Pacific, a title which it will very soon yield to Cheyenne, 140 miles to the west and soon to be reached. The iron path advances swiftly here. Originally the land belonged to no one, then nature took care to level it off and give it a gentle ascent, better than the most skilled of engineers could have done. Thus the grade is gradually prepared from the Missouri to the Rocky Mountains, and up to several kilometres of railroad can be laid daily. Everybody moves west with the railroad; the very inhabitants of Julesburg will little by little abandon that city for Cheyenne.

Only recently it was the railroad which advanced where there were no cities; now the cities precede the iron path, establishing themselves in the midst of the desert and saying to the railroad, "Come to us!" The mysterious advance of the human race, since earliest times in history, has always pushed westward; but has it ever been witnessed in a livelier and more striking fashion? Indeed, there is a whole new era revealed in this great labor of the United States, at the very hour when we are discussing the piercing of the Isthmus of Panama. It is the ribbon of iron in our era which will pierce isthmuses; in two years, the iron path of the Pacific will carry those who wish to tour the world in three months. Asia will come to visit Europe, and Europe, Asia by this great commercial route, by way of what has so well been called the center of gravity of the United States.

From Paris one will visit Japan or China in thirty or forty days by the shortest route, straying very little from the great circle of the terrestrial globe. Two steamboat lines and one railroad, and the thing is done. Le Havre or Brest, New York, San Francisco, such will be the major stops of the journey. But while we await the completion of such a project, let us return to our own more modest one.

Julesburg, where we are, is defended by Fort Sedgwick. We have just visited the fort, where Colonel Heine has discovered several companions in arms, among them General Potter, commandant of the place. The General has had his young wife and children brought in. It takes a certain courage to exile oneself thus in the heart of the desert, but American women do not bargain over their devotion, and besides are great travelers.

Certain Indians are camped around the fort, Sioux, of the Oglala and Brulé bands. One sees their conical tents rising in the midst of the prairie. Red Cloud and Spotted Tail have come with their men to treat with the commissioners of the Union. Peaceful today, these bands may perhaps tomorrow take up again their terrible chant of war.

A few years ago Fort Sedgwick was surrounded by Cheyennes, Sioux, and Arapahos in league against the whites, during the time of the War of Secession. The Redskins had forgotten for the time their former intestine wars, and turned their efforts against the common enemy. Emigrants, pioneers, fleeing in fright, took refuge in the fort. The prairies had been set on fire all around. The Indians, to the number of several thousand, threatened to subdue the besieged by hunger. The attackers could be repulsed only by cannon and grapeshot.

But I must leave Julesburg; I hear the continental stage just arriving, the "overland mail."

We have one portion of our journey yet to make, my companions and I, a stretch of 190 miles across the great desert. We have with us an escort of six soldiers, perched on our vehicle, from where they survey the terrain. I shall write you from Denver if we arrive safe and sound, or if we are scalped en route by the Cheyennes and Arapahos, whose territory we cross, and have to buy a wig to adorn our occiput.

Mary Elizabeth Michael Achey, "Soldier's Camp on the Arkansas River, Colorado (1862)."

MY LIFE ON THE FRONTIER

Miguel Antonio Otero

I SHALL NEVER FORGET our first trip from Kansas City to Kit Carson. Of course we had been following the building of the railroad from the Missouri River to Wallace, Kans., but this was the first through trip we ever made from Kansas City to Kit Carson. More especially do I remember the last day before reaching Kit Carson. Very early in the morning we sighted an immense herd of buffalo. They were only a short distance south of the railroad track; indeed, many small bunches separated from the main herd were only about two hundred yards from our train, but as far as eye could reach toward the west were buffalo. They were scarcely moving—just grazing along slowly, while many were lying down, apparently unafraid of the train. All day long our train advanced toward the setting sun, stopping at many stations along the route for wood, water, meals and orders, and consequently we were always in sight of that same herd of buffalo. It is hard to imagine such a thing today, but it is an absolute fact.

Owing to the great danger of Indians, who were constantly burning the old wooden trestlework bridges, our train did not travel at night, stopping over at a regular station until after breakfast the next morning. We reached Kit Carson early in the day. The large herd of buffalo was no longer in sight, for it had turned south toward the Arkansas River.

We found our new residence quite comfortable and well-located, about two hundred yards west of the commission house of Otero, Sellar & Co. Frequently, very early in the morning, I have seen large herds of buffalo lethargically crossing the railroad track, grazing quietly not over three hundred yards from our back fence.

During the summer of 1871 my brother Page and I devoted much of our spare time to catching prairie-dogs and taming them. This we found was profitable business for we had little or no trouble in selling them to the tourists. Some account of how we caught these elusive little animals may be of interest. Enlisting the assistance of some of our friends among the freighters, we could borrow a wagon and team, as well as a few teamsters. We would fill the wagon with empty whiskey barrels, and then would drive to the well on Big Sandy Creek, where we filled the barrels with water. Along with the barrels we would provide ourselves with a number of gunny sacks from the store.

With this equipment we would proceed to the prairie-dog town, which was a few miles west of our home, between Kit Carson and Wild Horse. Then we would start catching the prairie-dogs. … We would locate a hole into which we had just seen a family of young dogs scurry. It was easy enough to distinguish the young dogs from the old ones by the way they would bark. When a young dog barked, he would leap erect and merely give one bark, whereas the old dogs would first

Charles Craig, "Utes, Winter Camp," n.d.

scurry back into their holes with their families and then expose merely the top of their heads and bark continuously until we got too close.

The next thing we would do was to drive the wagon to the hole we had selected and empty about two barrels of water into it, a quantity usually sufficient to fill an ordinary hole. In the course of a minute or so the little fellows would begin to come out, half-drowned, and then it was a simple matter to grab them by the back of the neck and store them in one of the gunny sacks. Very frequently they were alive enough to turn and bite our hands, and I do not know of any bite more painful. My hands today show where the prairie-dogs took nips more than fifty-five years ago.

We would carry our captives home and then proceed to tame them. After the taming process was well under way, we would allow the little animals to make homes in our back yard. We would begin the holes for them with our knives, digging to a depth of three feet and leaving it to the prairie dogs themselves to finish the job. They made nice pets, often becoming as affectionate as house dogs. At feeding hours we would go out into the yard and call them by name, and it was great fun to see them come, all in a bunch, to be fed. In their eagerness for food they would crawl all over us, poking their heads into our pockets; then when they had finished their meal they would crawl into our pockets, where they would sleep for some time, never attempting to bite, even when we happened to disturb them during their nap.

On one occasion when we were out catching prairie-dogs, I saw the largest herd of antelope that I remember having seen on the western plains; they were running very fast and it took fully half an hour for the herd to cross the railroad track. They were going south, and we judged that the herd was at least a half-mile wide—they must have numbered up into the millions. Today there are only 21,000 antelope in the United States!

Another sport we greatly enjoyed was catching buffalo calves. Mounting our horses, we would borrow two or three wagons with good fast teams and would have these follow us as we rode ahead. Each one in the party would have several pieces of quarter-inch rope, about three feet long, which would be tied to the horn of his saddle. Of course, before making these preparations we had already located a herd of buffalo, and when we were all ready away we would go.

If the herd happened to be on the move, we could with no difficulty ride up to it, or very close to it, before the buffalo would realize what was up, but once they perceived our presence the race would begin in dead earnest. Our horses were trained to their part in the game; we would run them against a calf and down it would go sprawling, the horse stopping dead in his tracks. Then we would jump down beside the fallen calf, which was so clumsy that it would need some time to get on its feet again, and would quickly tie its feet with one of the pieces of rope, leaving it where it fell for the wagon to pick up, while we continued the chase.

We found the sport the more zestful because we had to work rapidly. If a cow happened to recognize her calf among the victims, she might turn and make matters critical for us. We usually escaped such encounters by giving the mother a wide berth and going on after the herd, which was generally too busy to notice the loss of a single calf. If the solicitous mother lingered beside her offspring, the driver of the wagon would usually shoot her and take the meat to the freighters' camp. During one of these calf chases it was an easy matter to fill all of the wagons with calves, and, this done, we would turn homeward.

We would place the young buffalo in the corral belonging to our father's firm, where we would feed them. Usually, we had a few antelope in the corral, which the herders would bring in with them, capturing them in the tall grass which impeded their escape. We did a good business of selling both our buffalo calves and young antelope to the tourists. We took orders from them, which we promptly filled and shipped by express; usually in the course of time more orders would follow from either our customers or their friends.

Large numbers of wild horses grazed around Kit Carson, but we did not participate actively in capturing any of them. Hunters, however, would go out after them, using a bunch of tame horses, which they would induce to mingle with the wild ones. Then the hunters would start a stampede of the hybrid herd in the direction of the town. The tame horses would naturally head for their accustomed corral and some of their wild mates would follow them into it. I remember on one occasion that nearly fifty head of wild horses were caught in this way, and some were really fine animals.

TIME EXPOSURE: THE AUTOBIOGRAPHY OF WILLIAM HENRY JACKSON

William Henry Jackson

WHEN WE REACHED THE TOWN of Fairplay, we found letters from Dr. Hayden and Stevenson telling us that they would arrive with the supply train about three days later. Another small division of the Survey was already on hand, and with an unexpected holiday before us we proceeded to use it with enthusiasm, if not to anyone's permanent advantage. Fairplay was not quite as wide open as Cheyenne in 1869. But we found it would serve. Purely as a side issue—a sort of constitutional, really—I climbed Mount Lincoln, twelve miles away, and made a few pictures. Among my best early photographs are the ones of the famous Montezuma silver mine near the top.

After Hayden came in we all spent a week comparing notes, studying our common problems, and mapping our courses for the remaining weeks. My assignment was to cross the Sawatch Range to the Elk Mountain region between the Gunnison River and the Grand (so called until 1921, when it received the name of the great river to which it is a tributary, the Colorado), and then to wind up the season by photographing the Mountain of the Holy Cross.

On July 18, I started from Fairplay with my new instructions, a fresh batch of plates, and Dolly. Dolly was a white mule with cold eyes and a haughty manner. I selected her as a temporary mount in Fairplay after my horse became badly injured; but soon I found her the most docile as well as the most sturdy and surefooted of beasts. For the next five years, as long as I was with the Survey, Dolly was mine, and I rode her in preference to any horse.

Criss-cross and detour was the rule as we struck a northwesterly course toward Holy Cross—there were so many pictures that I *had* to take. Mount Massive—Mount Harvard—Mount Elbert, highest point in Colorado—La Plata—Snowmass—these and many more fell before my camera. But many did not, and I regretted the lost ones deeply. Today favorable atmospheric conditions—clear sky, bright sun, still air, clouds to punctuate the background—are always desired by the photographer. In the '70's bright weather was even more important. We had no fast emulsions to counteract the effects of overcast skies, or to "stop" wind-driven foliage, and we had no filters to define clouds and horizons against the sky. If the weather was good, I could take as fine a picture as can be made today. But on bad days much patient manipulation of the chemicals was needed to produce acceptable negatives.

The several parties were proceeding westward in the general direction of Holy Cross along more or less parallel routes. Periodical notes came to me from Dr. Hayden by messenger from beyond some distant ridge. Always these notes included, among more specific instructions, the urgent plea: "Hurry. You are losing golden opportunities."

Early in August all of us were together once more, on the high divide between East River and Rock Creek. And the catastrophe struck us. An evil mule named Gimlet slipped his pack and broke many of my exposed plates.

The Doctor himself was the first person to notice what had happened. Following directly behind my party, he found plates along the trail and galloped up to learn the cause. By that time Gimlet had scattered most of his load, and it was too late to do anything except right the pack and go back to pick up the pieces. Many plates were unbroken or but slightly nicked; many more, however, all 11 x 14's, were irreparably shattered.

I think I have never been so distressed in my life—my finest negatives lost before anyone had even seen a print. Nothing could be done to repair the damage, nothing. Dr. Hayden, who had started in to be severe, quickly realized that it was the fault of no single person; and, as always under trying circumstances, he dropped his customary nervous attitude and became the calmest man in the world. It was unfortunate, he agreed, but by no means disastrous—I could go back and retake the more important pictures. It really didn't matter at all, he assured me; there was plenty of time for all that, as well as for the other work ahead. And so I went back. What is more, Dr. Hayden was right. There *was* time enough for everything: the new negatives proved to be better than the old ones, and the delay brought me to the Mountain of the Holy Cross at the exact moment when every condition was close to perfection.

In the Middle Ages there was the legend of the Holy Grail. Sixty-seven years ago in Colorado there was the legend of a snowy cross upon a mountain.

No man we talked with had ever seen the Mountain of the Holy Cross. But everyone knew that somewhere in the far reaches of the western highlands such a wonder might exist. Hadn't a certain hunter once caught a glimpse of it—only to have it vanish as he approached? Didn't a wrinkled Indian here and there narrow his eyes and slowly nod his head when questioned? Wasn't this man's grandfather, and that man's uncle, and old so-and-so's brother the first white man ever to lay eyes on the Holy Cross—many, many, many years ago?

It was a beautiful legend, and they nursed it carefully. But anyone who wanted to see Holy Cross could climb Gray's Peak on a clear day and pick it up with field-glasses. As one comes close to the cross it always disappears behind Notch Mountain—and that is how the myth established itself.

After making our way over Tennessee Pass we followed an old Indian trail right to the base of the Holy Cross. At no time en route had we been able to distinguish the snowy cross itself, and I confess that I found myself experiencing all the thrill of the old stories. And, I think, the other fifteen members of the group present felt very much the same way.

On the morning of August 23 we separated into two parties. The larger, headed by Gardner, Hayden, Professor William Dwight Whitney of Yale University, and William H. Holmes, later the distinguished head of the National Gallery, were off to climb Holy Cross, for the purpose of completing a triangulation from the summit. Coulter and Tom Cooper, one of my packers, went with me to try for some photographs from Notch Mountain across the ravine. Tom carried the cameras, Coulter the plate boxes, and I the chemicals and dark tent. Each man's load weighed about forty pounds.

When prospecting for views it was my custom to keep well ahead of my companions, for in that way they could often be spared the meanderings that I had to make. On this day, as usual, I pushed on ahead, and thus it was that I became the first member of the Survey to sight the cross. Near the top of the ridge I emerged above timber line and the clouds, and suddenly, as I clambered over a vast mass of jagged rocks, I discovered the great shining cross dead before me, tilted against the mountainside.

It was worth all the labor of the past three months just to see it for a moment. But as I sat there waiting for Tom and Coulter to catch up, my instincts came to the fore, and I quickly devoured the hefty sandwich I had brought with me. No art was ever any better because the artist was hungry at his work.

By the time all three of us had arrived at the summit, the sky was too overcast for successful photography. While we waited for a break, we could hear faint voices across the gorge. We were that close to the other party.

Had we not been so engrossed in a single objective, our long wait on top would have been delightful. Below us as well as before us the clouds billowed majestically. Then when the mist was heavy in the valley the sun came out—not enough for picture-taking, but enough to create a great circular rainbow at our feet. I have never seen another like it.

But we were too impatient to enjoy such idle pleasures. Seething inwardly, and all to no purpose, we watched the evening approach. We *must* have pictures before going down. And we *would* have pictures. Foodless, without blankets or even coats, we determined to spend the night on the peak. Leaving our equipment at the crest, we walked down to timber line and built a fire. There we rested on the stony ground until morning. Across the way our friends had a fire of their own, and every time it flared up we hallooed and heard their own halloos in answer.

At dawn we were cold, stiff, hungry—and elated. The day, or at least the morning, promised to be magnificently clear and sunny. In order not to lose a single moment I hurried wearily back to the top and set up my cameras. But I need not have rushed. The sun was still too low, even in midsummer, to have melted any snow, and without water I could do no work.

By the time I had enough to develop and wash a few plates the long flamelike shadows on Holy Cross were rapidly sweeping down into the valley, and, using two cameras, I had made just eight exposures when they were gone. But, with the early sun, those shadows had already helped me to take the finest pictures I have ever made of Holy Cross.

Since 1873 I have been back four or five times. I have used the best cameras and the most sensitive emulsions on the market. I have snapped my shutter morning, noon, and afternoon. And I have never come close to matching those first plates.

SECTION III

SHINING MOUNTAINS

WHEN IT'S SPRINGTIME
IN THE ROCKIES

Mary Hale Woolsey

The twilight shadows deepen into night, dear;
The city lights are gleaming o'er the snow;
I sit alone beside the cheery fire, dear;
I'm dreaming dreams from out the long ago.
I fancy it is springtime in the mountains;
The flowers with their colors are aflame;
And ev'ry day I hear you softly saying:
"I'll wait until the springtime comes again."

CHORUS

When it's Springtime in the Rockies,
I am coming back to you,
Little sweetheart of the mountains,
With your bonny eyes of blue;
Once again I'll say "I love you,"
While the birds sing all the day,
When it's Springtime in the Rockies,
In the Rockies, far away.

I've kept your image guarded in my heart, dear;
I've kept my love, for you, as pure as dew;
I'm longing for the time when I shall come, dear;
Back to that dear, old Western home and you.
I fancy it is springtime in the mountains;
The maple leaves, in first sky-green appear;
I hear you softly say, my Queen of May-time:
"This spring-time you have come to meet me here."

THE SPELL OF THE ROCKIES

Enos A. Mills

EARLY ONE SUMMER, while exploring a wide alpine moorland above the timber-line, I—and some others—had an experience with one of those sudden stormbursts. The region was utterly wild, but up to it straggling tourists occasionally rode for a view of the surrounding mountain world. All alone, I was studying the ways of the wild inhabitants of the heights. I had spent the calm, sunny morning in watching a solitary bighorn that was feeding among some boulders. He was aged, and he ate as though his teeth were poor and walked as though afflicted with rheumatism. Suddenly this patriarch forgot his age and fled precipitately, with almost the speed of frightened youth. I leaped upon a boulder to watch him, but was instantly knocked headlong by a wild blast of wind. In falling I caught sight of a straw hat and a wrecked umbrella falling out of the sky. Rising amid the pelting gale of flung hail, ice-water, and snow, I pushed my way in the teeth of the storm, hoping for shelter in the lee of a rock-pile about a hundred yards distant. A lady's disheveled hat blew by me, and with the howl of the wind came, almost drowned, excited human utterances. Nearing the rock-pile, I caught a vague view of a merry-go-round of man and horse, then a glimpse of the last gyration, in which an elderly Eastern gentleman parted company with a stampeded bronco.

Five tourists had ridden up in the sunshine to enjoy the heights, and the suddenness and fierceness of the storm had thrown them into a panic and stampeded their horses. They were drenched and severely chilled, and they were frightened. I made haste to tell them that the storm would be brief. While I was still trying to reassure them, the clouds commenced to dissolve and the sun came out. Presently all were watching the majestic soaring of two eagles up in the blue, while I went off to collect five scattered saddle-ponies that were contentedly feeding far away on the moor.

Though the winter winds are of slower development, they are more prolonged and are tempestuously powerful. Occasionally these winds blow for days; and where they follow a fall of snow they blow and whirl this about so wildly that the air is befogged for several hundred feet above the earth. So violently and thickly is the powdered snow flung about that a few minutes at a time is the longest that one can see or breathe in it. These high winter winds come out of the west in a deep, broad stratum that is far above most of the surface over which they blow. Commonly a high wind strikes the western slope of the Continental Divide a little below the altitude of eleven thousand feet. This striking throws it into fierce confusion. It rolls whirling up the steeps and frequently shoots far above the highest peaks. Across the passes it sweeps, roars down the cañons on the eastern slope, and rushes out across the plains. Though the western slope below eleven thousand feet is a calm zone, the entire eastern slope is being whipped and scourged by a flood of wind. Occasionally the temperature of these winds is warm.

These swift, insistent winds, torn, intercepted, and deflected by dashing against the broken skyline, produce currents, counter-currents, sleepy eddies, violent vertical whirls, and milling maelstroms that are tilted at every angle. In places there is a gale blowing upward, and here and there the air pours heavily down in an invisible but almost crushing air-fall.

A LADY'S LIFE IN THE ROCKY MOUNTAINS

Isabella L. Bird

Estes Park, Colorado, October

🐜 🐜 🐜

... I HAVE NO HEAD AND no ankles, and never ought to dream of mountaineering; and had I known that the ascent was a real mountaineering feat I should not have felt the slightest ambition to perform it. As it is, I am only humiliated by my success, for "Jim" dragged me up, like a bale of goods, by sheer force of muscle. At the "Notch" the real business of the ascent began. Two thousand feet of solid rock towered above us, four thousand feet of broken rock shelved precipitously below; smooth granite ribs, with barely foothold, stood out here and there; melted snow refrozen several times, presented a more serious obstacle; many of the rocks were loose, and tumbled down when touched. To me it was a time of extreme terror. I was roped to "Jim," but it was of no use; my feet were paralyzed and slipped on the bare rock, and he said it was useless to try to go that way, and we retraced our steps. I wanted to return to the "Notch," knowing that my incompetence would detain the party, and one of the young men said almost plainly that a woman was a dangerous encumbrance, but the trapper replied shortly that if it were not to take a lady up he would not go up at all. He went on the explore, and reported that further progress on the correct line of ascent was blocked by ice; and then for two hours we descended, lowering ourselves by our hands from rock to rock along a boulder-strewn sweep of 4,000 feet, patched with ice and snow, and perilous from rolling stones. My fatigue, giddiness, and pain from bruised ankles, and arms half pulled out of their sockets, were so great that I should never have gone halfway had not "Jim," *nolens volens*, dragged me along with a patience and skill, and withal a determination that I should ascend the Peak, which never failed. After descending about 2,000 feet to avoid the ice, we got into a deep ravine with inaccessible sides, partly filled with ice and snow and partly with large and small fragments of rock, which were constantly giving away, rendering the footing very insecure. That part to me was two hours of painful and unwilling submission to the inevitable; of trembling, slipping, straining, of smooth ice appearing when it was least expected, and of weak entreaties to be left behind while the others went on. "Jim" always said that there was no danger, that there was only a short bad bit ahead, and that I should go up even if he carried me!

Slipping, faltering, gasping from the exhausting toil in the rarefied air, with throbbing hearts and panting lungs, we reached the top of the gorge and squeezed ourselves between two gigantic fragments of rock by a passage called the "Dog's Lift," when I climbed on the shoulders of one man and then was hauled up. This introduced us by an abrupt turn round the south-west angle of the Peak to a narrow shelf of considerable length, rugged, uneven, and so overhung by the cliff in some places that it is necessary to crouch to pass at all. Above, the Peak looks nearly vertical for 400 feet; and below, the most tremendous precipice I have ever seen descends in one unbroken fall. This is usually considered the most dangerous part of the ascent, but it does not seem so to me, for such foothold as there is is secure, and one fancies that it is possible to hold on with the hands. But there, and on the final, and, to my thinking, the worst part of the climb, one slip, and a breathing, thinking, human being would lie 3,000 feet below, a shapeless, bloody heap! "Ring" refused to traverse the Ledge, and remained at the "Lift" howling piteously.

From thence the view is more magnificent even than that from the "Notch." At the foot of the precipice below us lay a lovely lake, wood embosomed, from or near which the bright St. Vrain and other streams take their rise. I thought how their clear cold waters, growing turbid in the affluent flats, would heat under the tropic sun, and eventually form part of that great ocean river which renders our far-off islands habitable by impinging on their shores. Snowy ranges, one behind the other, extended to the distant horizon, folding in their wintry embrace the beauties of Middle Park. Pike's Peak, more than one hundred miles off, lifted that vast but shapeless summit which is the landmark of southern Colorado. There were snow patches, snow slashes, snow abysses, snow forlorn and soiled looking, snow pure and dazzling, snow glistening above the purple robe of pine worn by all the mountains; while away to the east, in limitless breadth, stretched the green-grey of the endless Plains. Giants everywhere reared their splintered crests. From thence, with a single sweep, the eye takes in a distance of 300 miles—that distance to the west, north, and south being made up of mountains ten, eleven, twelve, and thirteen thousand feet in height, dominated by Long's Peak, Gray's Peak, and Pike's Peak, all nearly the height of Mont Blanc! On the Plains we traced the rivers by their fringe of cottonwoods to the distant Platte, and between us and them lay glories of mountain, canyon, and lake, sleeping in depths of blue and purple most ravishing to the eye.

As we crept from the ledge round a horn of rock I beheld what made me perfectly sick and dizzy to look at—the terminal Peak itself—a smooth, cracked face or wall of pink granite, as nearly perpendicular as anything could well be up which it was impossible to climb, well deserving the name of the "American Matterhorn."

Scaling, not climbing, is the correct term for this last ascent. It took one hour to accomplish 500 feet, pausing for breath every minute or two. The only foothold was in narrow cracks or on minute projections on the granite. To get a toe in these cracks, or here and there on a scarcely obvious projection, while crawling on hands and knees, all the while tortured with thirst and gasping and struggling for breath, this was the climb; but at last the Peak was won. A grand, well-defined mountain top it is, a nearly level acre of boulders, with precipitous sides all round, the one we came up being the only accessible one.

It was not possible to remain long. One of the young men was seriously alarmed by bleeding from the lungs, and the intense dryness of the day and the rarefication of the air, at a height of nearly 15,000 feet, made respiration very painful. There is always water on the Peak, but it was frozen as hard as a rock, and the sucking of ice and snow increases thirst. We all suffered severely from the want of water, and the gasping for breath made our mouths and tongues so dry that articulation was difficult, and the speech of all unnatural.

From the summit were seen in unrivalled combination all the views which had rejoiced our eyes during the ascent. It was something at last to stand upon the storm-rent crown of this lonely sentinel of the Rocky Range, on one of the mightiest of the vertebrae of the backbone of the North American continent, and to see the waters start for both oceans. Uplifted above love and hate and storms of passion, calm amidst the eternal silences, fanned by zephyrs and bathed in living blue, peace rested for that one bright day on the Peak, as if it were some region

Where falls not rain, or hail, or any snow,
Or ever wind blows loudly.

Estes Park, December 7

Yesterday morning the mercury had disappeared, so it was 20° below zero at least. I lay awake from cold all night, but such is the wonderful effect of the climate, that when I got up at half-past five to waken the household for my early start, I felt quite refreshed. We breakfasted on buffalo beef, and I left at eight to ride forty-five miles before night, Dr. Hughes and a gentleman who was staying there convoying me the first fifteen miles. I did like that ride, racing with the other riders, careering through the intoxicating air in that indescribable sunshine, the powdery snow spurned from the horses' feet like dust! I was soon warm. We stopped at a trapper's ranch to feed, and the old trapper amused me by seeming to think Estes Park almost inaccessible in winter. The distance was greater than I had been told, and he said that I could not get there before eleven at night, and not at all if there was much drift. I wanted the gentlemen to go on with me as far as the Devil's Gate, but they could not because their horses were tired; and when the trapper heard that he exclaimed, indignantly, "What! that woman going into the mountains alone? She'll lose the track or be froze to death!" But when I told him I had ridden the trail in the storm of Tuesday, and had ridden over 600 miles alone in the mountains, he treated me with great respect as a fellow mountaineer, and gave me some matches, saying, "You'll have to camp out anyhow; you'd better make a fire than be froze to death." The idea of spending the night in the forest alone, by a fire, struck me as most grotesque.

We did not start again till one, and the two gentlemen rode the first two miles with me. On that track, the Little Thompson, there a full stream, has to be crossed eighteen times, and they had been hauling wood across it, breaking it, and it had broken and refrozen several times, making thick and thin places—indeed, there were crossings which even I thought bad, where the ice let us through, and it was hard for the horses to struggle upon it again; and one of the gentlemen who, though a most accomplished man, was not a horseman, was once or twice in the ludicrous position of hesitating on the bank with an anxious face, not daring to spur his horse upon the ice. After they left me I had eight more crossings, and then a ride of six miles, before I reached the old trail; but though there were several drifts up to the saddle, and no one had broken a track, Birdie showed such pluck, that instead of spending the night by a camp-fire, or not getting in till midnight, I reached Mr. Nugent's cabin, four miles from Estes Park, only an hour after dark, very cold, and with the pony so tired that she could hardly put one foot before another. Indeed, I walked the last three miles.

SPECIMEN DAYS IN AMERICA

Walt Whitman

AN HOUR ON KENOSHA SUMMIT

JOTTINGS FROM THE Rocky Mountains, mostly pencill'd during a day's trip over the South Park RR. returning from Leadville, and especially the hour we were detain'd, (much to my satisfaction,) at Kenosha summit. As afternoon advances, novelties, far-reaching splendors, accumulate under the bright sun in this pure air. But I had better commence with the day.

The confronting of Platte cañon just at dawn, after a ten miles' ride in early darkness on the rail from Denver—the seasonable stoppage at the entrance of the cañon, and good breakfast of eggs, trout, and nice griddle-cakes—then as we travel on, and get well in the gorge, all the wonders, beauty, savage power of the scene—the wild stream of water, from sources of snows, brawling continually in sight one side—the dazzling sun, and the morning lights on the rocks—such turns and grades in the track, squirming around corners, or up and down hills—far glimpses of a hundred peaks, titanic necklaces, stretching north and south—the huge rightly named Dome-rock—and as we dash along, others similar, simple, monolithic, elephantine.

AN EGOTISTICAL "FIND"

"I have found the law of my own poems," was the unspoken but more-and-more decided feeling that came to me as I pass'd, hour after hour, amid all this grim yet joyous elemental abandon—this plenitude of material, entire absence of art, untrammel'd play of primitive Nature—the chasm, the gorge, the crystal mountain stream, repeated scores, hundreds of miles—the broad handling and absolute uncrampedness—the fantastic forms, bathed in transparent browns, faint reds and grays, towering sometimes a thousand, sometimes two or three thousand feet high—at their tops now and then huge masses pois'd, and mixing with the clouds, with only their outlines, hazed in misty lilac, visible. ("In Nature's grandest shows," says an old Dutch writer, an ecclesiastic, "amid the ocean's depth, if so might be, or countless worlds rolling above at night, a man thinks of them, weighs all, not for themselves or the abstract, but with reference to his own personality, and how they may affect him or color his destinies.")

NEW SENSES—NEW JOYS

We follow the stream of amber and bronze brawling along its bed, with its frequent cascades and snow-white foam. Through the cañon we fly—mountains not only each side, but seemingly, till we get near, right in front of us—every rood a new view flashing, and each flash defying description—on the almost perpendicular sides, clinging pines, cedars, spruces, crimson sumach bushes, spots of wild grass—but dominating all, those towering rocks, rocks, rocks, bathed in delicate vari-colors, with the clear sky of autumn overhead. New senses, new joys, seem develop'd. Talk as you like, a typical Rocky Mountain cañon, or a limitless sea-like stretch of the great Kansas or Colorado plains, under favoring circumstances, tallies, perhaps expresses, certainly awakes, those grandest and subtlest element emotions in the human soul, that all the marble temples and sculptures from Phidias to Thorwaldsen—all paintings, poems, reminiscences, or even music, probably never can.

STEAM-POWER, TELEGRAPHS, &C.

I get out on a ten minutes' stoppage at Deer creek, to enjoy the unequal'd combination of hill, stone and wood. As we speed again, the yellow granite in the sunshine, with natural spires, minarets, castellated perches far aloft—then long stretches of straight-upright palisades, rhinoceros color—then gamboge and tinted chromos. Ever the best of my pleasures the cool-fresh Colorado atmosphere, yet sufficiently warm. Signs of man's restless advent and pioneerage, hard as Nature's face is—deserted dug-outs by dozens in the side-hills—the scantling hut, the telegraph-pole, the smoke of some impromptu chimney or outdoor fire—at intervals little settlements of log-houses, or parties of surveyors or telegraph builders, with their comfortable tents. Once, a canvas office where you could send a message by electricity anywhere around the world! Yes, pronounc'd signs of the man of latest dates, dauntlessly grappling with these grisliest shows of the old kosmos. At several places steam saw-mills, with their piles of logs and boards, and the pipes puffing. Occasionally Platte cañon expanding into a grassy flat of a few acres. At one such place, toward the end, where we stop, and I get out to stretch my legs, as I look skyward, or rather mountain-topward, a huge hawk or eagle (a rare sight here) is idly soaring, balancing along the ether, now sinking low and coming quite near, and then up again in stately-languid circles—then higher, higher, slanting to the north, and gradually out of sight.

AMERICA'S BACK-BONE

I jot these lines literally at Kenosha summit, where we return, afternoon, and take a long rest, 10,000 feet above sea-level. At this immense height the South Park stretches fifty miles before me. Mountainous chains and peaks in every variety of perspective, every hue of vista, fringe the view, in nearer, or middle, or far-dim distance, or fade on the horizon. We have now reach'd, penetrated the Rockies, (Hayden calls it the Front Range,) for a hundred miles or so; and though these chains spread away in every direction, specially north and south, thousands and thousands farther, I have seen specimens of the utmost of them, and know henceforth at least what they are, and what they look like. Not themselves alone, for they typify stretches and areas of half the globe—are, in fact, the vertebrae or back-bone of our hemisphere. As the anatomists say a man is only a spine, topp'd, footed, breasted and radiated, so the whole Western world is, in a sense, but an expansion of these mountains. In South America they are the Andes, in Central America and Mexico the Cordilleras, and in our States they go under different names—in California the Coast and Cascade ranges—thence more eastwardly the Sierra Nevadas—but mainly and more centrally here the Rocky Mountains proper, with many an elevation such as Lincoln's, Grey's, Harvard's, Yale's, Long's and Pike's peaks, all over 14,000 feet high. (East, the highest peaks of the Alleghanies, the Adirondacks, the Cattskills, and the White Mountains, range from 2000 to 5500 feet—only Mount Washington, in the latter, 6300 feet.)

THE PARKS

In the midst of all here, lie such beautiful contrasts as the sunken basins of the North, Middle, and South Parks, (the latter I am now on one side of, and overlooking,) each the size of a large, level, almost quadrangular, grassy, western county, wall'd in by walls of hills, and each park the source of a river. The ones I specify are the largest in Colorado, but the whole of that State, and of Wyoming, Utah, Nevada and western California, through their sierras and ravines, are copiously mark'd by similar spreads and openings, many of the small ones of paradisiac loveliness and perfection, with their offsets of mountains, streams, atmosphere and hues beyond compare.

MY ROCKY MOUNTAIN VALLEY

James Grafton Rogers

NO GENTLE SPRING

January 1

A NEW CALENDAR YEAR begins in the Rocky Mountains. The calendar, here at least, is merely an invention of astronomers. It means little or nothing out of doors. Our shortest days are already past. The real winter, if winter means cold, is still ahead. If winter means heavy snowfalls, it is even months ahead. There are early snowstorms in the high mountains in September and October and the spruce woods above ten thousand feet where the sun cannot reach are choked with snow drifts but in open spaces the ground is usually dry in the uplands until after Christmas. The big snowfalls will come in March, April or even May. The real year begins at some date other than January. January in the Rocky Mountains is only a last chapter of a long, dry, sunny autumn that begins in September and ends in February.

The four seasons, spring, summer, autumn and winter, are terms that belong to the language of Europe and of Eastern North America. These divisions would never have occurred to dwellers in the West. Some of the nomad Indian tribes that followed the buffalo on the plains used words that approximated our division of seasons but these Indians came westward in historic times, in recent centuries, from the moist woods of the East. They brought a language with them. No western Indian talks of spring, summer, autumn and winter. There is, in the Rocky Mountains, no gentle spring, no gradual awakening of life, no slow emergence of vegetation. Summer comes suddenly, some day in early June, on the heels of winter.

We know three seasons in the Rocky Mountains. One is summer, from June to September. Then plants flourish; animals are intensively active. Turquoise skies are broken by cottony thunderheads, drifting slowly east. There are downpours in the afternoons. At night the skies are cloudless and spangled with wide-eyed stars. This is real summer.

Autumn, for lack of a better word, follows and lasts until well after Christmas. In September plant growth stops. The migrant birds depart. Frost begins to arrive at night. This is a long period of pause, of suspense. The word autumn does not describe this season. We need a new word. The mountains are dry, sunny and hospitable. There is now and then a snow storm but its traces are gone in a few days, except in deep, high and shaded woods. At night frost settles over the world but by day the skies are clear, the hills are sun-baked.

Winter begins in February or March and lasts until May. Again the word winter carries many sensations quite foreign to our western world. Winter in Europe is gray, cloud-bound, moist, heavy and imprisoning. In North Europe and New England snow accumulates and hampers traffic. Farther south rain drizzles and snow flurries succeed each other. None of that here. Our winter is not gloomy or snowbound. It takes turns with sunshine and snow storms. Great snowfalls occur in March and April. Avalanches break loose in the high mountains. The thermometer may fall to ten or twenty below zero for a day or two, but the intervals are sunny and even warm. Plants are tricked into sprouting, only to be crushed in an April snow or frozen in May. The native trees like aspen and cottonwood are not deceived. They stay dormant until June. Then suddenly summer arrives without warning. The snow in the high forests melts into torrents. Thunder storms begin. Plants and animals burst into activity.

Truly we have three seasons. A short and rain-swept summer; an open autumn that lasts half the year; a winter siege of cold and snow at a time when spring is tiptoeing up in other lower eastern states. I have puzzled always for the proper descriptive words. We have a burst of life, a long pause and then a few months of intermittent snow and arctic cold.

SOLITUDE

January 20

The wilderness slips in upon us. These are the days, these chilly sunlit days in the stillnesses of winter when there is neither deep snow underfoot nor any wind above to stir the pine tops, that one broods most on the vastnesses of the mountain ranges. In every direction they roll in emptiness. There is a trickle of human commerce on the high speed highways below us, it is true. Some wisps of smoke drift up from fireplaces, thin, straight and elusive, where a few dozen families in a settlement cuddle around drafty hearths while their damp clothes dry from perspiration. The world is almost noiseless, as if even motor cars were awed a little.

There is no deep snow to battle or firewood to carry for defence against besieging storm. The chatter that the birds scatter in summer is gone. Even owls are silent for their prey of birds and ground animals are hiding or asleep for winter. No water gurgles. No gaudy carpets of flowers charm us. No insects hum. One thinks a traveller from this cabin today could take a compass in hand and tramp all through daylight in every direction except to the prairies without seeing a single red-blooded man or animal in the dusk. It is wilderness that envelopes us, silence, solitude. Bare peaks tower, defying life all about us. Armies of trees carpet the slopes. We suppress shivers.

🐾 🐾 🐾

BLUENESS

June 26

The plains are parching. Yucca and evening star begin to bloom along the roadsides.

Here, high in the mountains, flowers are luxuriant. There is no drouth. The blue columbine grows in its slim aristocratic fashion all along the edge of the woods. It seems so frail, so brittle, so vividly blue, like a piece torn out of the sky above. The two harebells are also blue, one a frail little drooping cup and the other, Parrys harebell, stouter, darker, looking firmly upward from the grass. The cranesbill or geranium is showing its magenta blossoms, usually in some shaded corner. Already the mertensia reaches high along the water courses. Its lush stems crush easily. It grows almost rankly. Thousands of its tiny trumpet-shaped blossoms droop in racemes.

The world seems tinted with blue in truth. Sky, flowers, distant mountains all are stained with it.

🐾 🐾 🐾

BLUE AS THE AEGEAN

September 19

Fall is half-way down the mountains. "Fall" I say for lack of another term. Slumber, repose, cessation—none will do. All nature suspends animation. Even the weather. Birds depart on their migration. Ground animals from bears to gophers, prepare to hibernate. Grass and flowers dry and scatter into ashes. Little streams stop flowing and big streams idle at their endless business of cutting and carrying away the mountains.

Fall is half-way here. On the plains, the noons are hot, the town lawns green, the leaves still untarnished on the trees, the crops not quite harvested. Here half a mile higher, the aspen and cottonwood groves are sprinkling down their leaves. The woods are rusty. Some of the aspen groves high on the crests are yellow but not yet golden or crimson. The ground-squirrels come out only at noon when the rocks are warm to their feet but the bluejays and Fremont squirrels who work in the woods all year are busy at dawn. The deer mice and mountain rats are active at night looking for winter quarters, gnawing at weak spots in our fortress of a house. At night it freezes hard above timberline and now for the first time also here.

The only flowers that survive are tattered. The little creeks have almost stopped flowing for their sources are above timberline and there water melts only for two or three hours just after noon. Clear Creek runs quietly below us. It is limpid, low and modest. Insects are disappearing. The sky is intense, unbroken turquoise. The world indeed is blue above—the blue of the Aegean Sea but in the wrong place for Homer. The hills have become tawny. Summer vegetation fades on the mountains, painted however with mile-wide brush-strokes of deep shutter green where the evergreen forests refuse to change their coats.

ROCKY MOUNTAIN HIGH

John Denver

He was born in the summer of his twenty-seventh year,
comin' home to a place he'd never been before.
He left yesterday behind him,
you might say he was born again,
you might say he found a key for ev'ry door.
When he first came to the mountains his life was far away,
on the road and hangin' by a song.
But the string's already broken and he doesn't really care,
it keeps changin' fast and it don't last for long.
But the Colorado Rocky Mountain high,
I've seen it rainin' fire in the sky.
The shadow from the starlight is softer than a lullaby.
Rocky Mountain high,
Rocky Mountain high.

He climbed Cathedral Mountains,
he saw silver clouds below,
he saw ev'rything as far as you can see.
And they say that he got crazy once and he tried to touch the sun,
and he lost a friend but kept his memory.
Now he walks in quiet solitude,
the forests and the streams seeking grace in ev'ry step he takes.
His sight has turned inside himself to try and understand
the serenity of a clear blue mountain lake.
And the Colorado Rocky Mountain high,
I've seen it rainin' fire in the sky.
Talk to God and listen to the casual reply.
Rocky Mountain high,
Rocky Mountain high.

Now his life is full of wonder but his heart still knows some fear
of a simple thing he cannot comprehend.
Why they try to tear the mountains down to bring in a couple more,
more people more scars upon the land.
And the Colorado Rocky Mountain high,
I've seen it rainin' fire in the sky.
I know he'd be a poorer man if he never saw an eagle fly.
Rocky Mountain high,
Rocky Mountain high.

It's a Colorado Rocky Mountain high,
I've seen it rainin' fire in the sky.
Friends around the campfire and ev'rybody's high.
Rocky Mountain high,
Rocky Mountain high.

ONE MAN'S WEST

David Lavender

LONG AGO DAVID SANG, "I will lift up mine eyes unto the hills."
   Their majesty is inescapable, yet very few alpine dwellers ever climb. Mountaineering in many of its aspects entails a devilish amount of work, and those who wring livelihood from the high country already have enough of that.

To be sure, a valley rancher after forty years in the shadow of some crag may at last want to see what his domicile looks like from above. He inveigles his neighbors into a picnic; they slog up the easiest side of the peak, point out their fence lines to each other, and slog back down. Prospectors occasionally make an ascent while looking for outcroppings, and now and then a sheepherder will assuage boredom by heaping a mound of rocks on top of some pinnacle to show he has been there.

None of these ventures is mountaineering, however. None is undertaken with the idea that spiritual values or even plain fun might lie in them. This viewpoint is reserved for certain city dwellers who physically are by no means as well fitted for it as their country cousins. Nonetheless, climbers during the past half century or so have become an integral part of the mountain scene. Oblivious to the stares of the natives, they clump in growing numbers through the streets of the decaying mining towns, sounding like horses in their hobnail boots. Thousands of them have banded together in clubs which publish bulletins, conduct outings, and lobby vigorously in the legislatures for pet conservation bills. During any week of the summer and many weeks of the winter you are apt to find in some remote, hard-to-reach vale groups of from two to sixty ragged, sunburned people enjoying a side of the mountains that the early pioneers seldom saw. Today they are as real to the high country as the miners or sheepherders, and some of my happiest times were spent in the company of these strangers who my compatriots at the Camp Bird and elsewhere sincerely believed were a little "tetched."

My brother Dwight was first infected with the virus, for the mountains had always been a passion with him. We had been born in the mining town of Telluride, Colorado, where the canyon of the San Miguel heads in a U-shaped basin half a mile deep. The boys of the village scrambled about the bases of the bright-colored cliffs as boys elsewhere climb trees and barns. It was an aimless zeal, however, and the idea of focusing it on a peak top never occurred to us until we had theoretically reached the age of better judgment. And then Dwight met some members of the Colorado Mountain Club.

When it developed that the club was planning a week-end assault on Mount Wilson, near Telluride, there was no restraining him. The great day arrived; we threw a pack on an old horse—we were living on the ranch then—and made a two-day ride across the hills to town.

I shall never forget the look on the hotelkeeper's face when we entered the lobby and it dawned on him that we were there to join the mountaineers. He was an odd little man, very frail and very neat, with the thin, high-domed face of an aesthete. His soft eyes peering blandly through thick spectacles made him look as though he should have been on the lecture platform of some university rather than behind the counter of a moribund hostelry. But behind it he had been since the glamour days of gold, when Telluride boasted twenty-six saloons and no church;

when a quarter was the smallest coin in circulation and the conductor on the little narrow-gauge railway announced the town by bawling "To Hell You Ride." In those times champagne and caviar and terrapin had been staple items on the hotel menu; engineers' wives and mineowners' mistresses had come to its parties in Parisian gowns. Sudden death, sudden fortune, sudden poverty—all this the proprietor had seen and shared. Yet he looked at Dwight and me as though he could not believe his eyes.

"Are you going with this outfit?" he said, glancing at the climbers. We hung our heads and mumbled an admission. It was a painful moment.

As I recall it, nineteen people showed up for the trip, twelve men and seven women. Now Telluride was not as populous as it had been. The last of the great mines, the Smuggler-Union, had closed down a few years before. However, the town still remained the county seat; here and there a fresh green lawn showed that some stubborn settler was hanging on. A few fat-bellied, rusty-faced politicians wandered through the red sandstone courthouse; mountain ranchers occasionally stopped by to trade, and bewhiskered placer miners still hopefully poked about the dumps. But for the most part the stores were boarded up, and broken windows gaped in the abandoned houses. The arrival of nineteen people in a body could not escape note.

The astonished city fathers did their best. They gave us a banquet. A good one, too, with the ghosts of the hotel's old chefs rising nobly to the occasion. Instead of receiving the pieces of high-grade ore that in former days had been passed out to distinguished guests, we were treated to abundant samples of the town's last going industry—brewing. There were speeches. The beauties of the landscape were rhapsodically extolled by men whose axes and dredges and dynamite had done their best to destroy that beauty. The old phrase "Switzerland of America"—every mountain sector of the West calls itself that—was trotted out and dusted off by half-a-dozen willing throats.

Warmed by their own voices and their own beer, the hosts began having a wonderful time. Then, just as the party was taking on a faint blush of former celebrations, the climbers all stood up and went to bed. They were leaving for the assault at four o'clock the next morning and they wanted to leave fresh. Incomprehensibility worse confounded! If the dismayed city fathers needed further evidence of idiocy, here it was.

Four o'clock the next morning was cheerless. Dawn had not yet come, and no stars were visible in the sodden sky. However, weather is one of the accepted hazards of climbing. We piled into cars and away we went along the narrow, breath-taking dirt road that skirts the vast upper gorges of the San Miguel. Eventually, after passing through the huddle of huts which is Ophir and skidding wildly along the greasy branch road that leads to Dunton, we reached a high, alpine vale known as the Dunton Meadows. Here we left the cars and set out afoot. It was daylight now, but Mount Wilson was not to be seen. Clouds lay on the treetops.

🐾 🐾 🐾

Our leaders ran the gamut on that Wilson climb. Trail finding was the worst. At lower elevations we encountered mazes of timber falls and impenetrable thickets of underbrush. We struggled through what seemed miles of scree and talus, steep slopes of shattered slide rock that have fallen from the cliffs and roll backward under you with every step you take. Rain drenched us, and as we climbed higher we were presented with the odd spectacle of snow going straight up instead of down.

This phenomenon was occasioned by the wind whipping through the basin below. When it met the towering ridge along whose knife-edged summit we were worming our way it was deflected upward with its burden of sleet. The effect, as we crouched there in our lonely miasma of mist, was indescribably weird. It was also cold. I had no gloves, but for some reason I had slipped an extra pair of woolen socks in my pocket. I put these on my hands. The luxury was wonderful—until I noticed, though I tried hard not to, that one of the ladies of the party was also gloveless. I surrendered my socks. Never have I enjoyed so rich a feeling of chivalry or suffered so from frigid fingers.

🐾 🐾 🐾

When we finally staggered onto the fog-shrouded summit it was 6:00 P.M. We had no desire to wolf out the night on the mountaintop, yet we knew that fatalities might well repay any attempt by nineteen tired people to descend in pitch-darkness the exposed cliffs we had climbed. Brows knit, the board of strategy went into a huddle. It was decided to select a much longer but safer route to the sheltering timber some three thousand feet below. Westward, long snow slopes dropped into a basin—Killpacker Basin, some disgusted packer had named it long ago. After reaching its bottom, rounding its southern arm, and then doubling back through the spruce forests, we could, we hoped, regain our cars without breaking our necks.

With nineteen ice axes and the ability to use them, the descent of the snow fields could have been accomplished in minutes by a glissade. This is simply skiing without skis. You slide on your feet, crouching with the hip-high, T-headed, steel-pointed ax braced behind you, serving as both rudder and brake. There is nothing more exhilarating; on a thousand-foot run you can build up tremendous speed. Like skiing, the glissade is best done with swishing zigzags and swoops and as few cartwheels as possible. Just make sure there are no crevasses in the way.

On this Wilson trip, however, we had only two or three ice axes, which the leaders used for hacking out steps on icy pitches. So we had to creep downward like snails with the freezing night crowding hard on our heels. Suddenly one of the men flopped in the snow and refused to budge another inch. Nervously we cajoled him and in desperation even shook him up a bit. In the end we had to take him by the arms and drag him down the hill. He became violently ill, retching pitifully.

It was a thing which might have happened to any of us. Mountain sickness is no respecter of apparent physical condition. In extreme form it affects the brain, and by undermining the powers of judgment has played a tragic part in some of the Himalayan fatalities of recent years. At the lower elevations of American mountains the results are not so fantastic. Here headaches, listlessness, nausea, vomiting, cold hands and cold feet are the main symptoms.

The trouble is apparently caused by insufficient oxygen in the blood stream. Aviators rising from sea level to fourteen thousand feet sometimes faint without artificial oxygen and compensation for pressure changes. A climber ascending on foot affords his body more time to adjust itself. Even so, before he rushes his peak he should spend a day or two conditioning himself in a high-altitude camp. He should also take salt. A short teaspoonful the night before an ascent and another at the start will help keep him healthy, for it seems that mountain sickness, like heat prostration, can be aggravated by loss of essential body salts through perspiration.

When we at last reached timber line on Mount Wilson we tried to bivouac, but the ground was a sea of mud, and the smoky, stuttering fire we managed to kindle was inadequate to cope with the mass miseries of nineteen exhausted souls. In despair we blundered on, clambering endlessly through deadfall and under-brush, falling into ravines, tripping on roots, wallowing knee deep in mountain bogs. Toward dawn we located the cars, returned to Telluride, and collapsed into bed. My first organized climb was over.

The next evening I came down to the hotel lobby, ravenous and creaking in every joint. The proprietor asked, with some maliciousness, I thought, "Well, did you like it?"

I considered. Fortunately God gave man a poor memory for physical discomfort. The active ingredients which made the hurt so brutal at the moment lose their keen edge in retrospect; we are able to look back on them with certain detachment and even make them subject matter of our dearest conversation pieces. Pleasure is different. Memory fondles it. It becomes a nostalgia, poignant and real and difficult to put into words. And so I remembered Mount Wilson. Not the cold and the cruel fatigue, but rather the multitude of tiny things which in their sum make up the elemental poetry of rock and ice and snow. The feel of granite under your fingers, the obedient flex of your muscles swinging you upward to the stance you must reach or fail, the taste of a cigarette when you hunker for a moment under a shelving rock. A flash of sunlight, a laugh, an incongruous patch of dwarf flowers at the base of an icy boulder.

"Yes," I said, "I liked it."

NARROW GAUGE IN THE ROCKIES

Lucius Beebe and Charles Clegg

LEGEND CLUSTERED THICKLY around the patrician person of General William Jackson Palmer, founder of the fortunes of the Rio Grande railroad and no man to shirk a fight. He was outraged when the *Rocky Mountain News* printed the intelligence that aboard his business car *Nomad* the master bedroom with its brass bed … boasted both hot and cold running water. As an aristocrat, he resented the invasion of his privacy; as an old campaigner, he resented the implication of a luxurious way of life and immediately ordered the hot water disconnected. Probably

Artist unknown, wood cut of narrow-gauge train in the Rockies, n.d.

the hot was replaced once the general had time to recover from his pique, for he wrote to the future Mrs. Palmer: "I am having a nice house car made just convenient for you and me to travel up and down when business demands and this car will have every convenience of living while in motion." In its active lifetime *Nomad* knew many notables, such as Cecil Rhodes, Otto Mears, Theodore Roosevelt. Aboard it President U. S. Grant rode the first Rio Grande train into Leadville. It was, too, a sensation in a railroad-minded generation and was exhibited at the San Louis World's Fair in 1904, the San Francisco Fair of 1915 and at Chicago's Century of Progress in 1933. Today a restoration of *Nomad* is on the private car track of the D&RGW at Durango, the property of H. B. Wood and Ted M. White, a well-to-do oil man with large holdings in the San Juan, and it is without any doubt at all the only narrow gauge car in operable commission to be privately owned in the United States.

🐾 🐾 🐾

In its final years of decline and improvisation when the pulse of the Southern flickered weakly before ceasing forever, one of the management's devisings of economy that attracted something more than purely local attention was the type of railcar built to handle both freight and passengers the length of the line and known as The Galloping Goose. The Goose varied and had several models, but generally speaking, comprised a vast box-car-like van behind and a crowded passenger cabin forward mounted on the ancient but durable chassis of Cadillacs and Pierce Arrows that had seen better days. Equipped with flanged wheels, augmented brake systems in the form of a compressor and air brakes, and in the custody of a single operator who combined the functions of engineer, brakeman and conductor, the Geese weighed only a fraction of the tonnage of a conventional steam train, required a minimum crew and represented a very real and effective economy. Attracted by the rapid and noisy passage across the landscape, they even carried a certain tourist trade anxious to experience the satisfactions of narrow gauge even at the risk of some discomfort. The Geese carried parcel freight and the mails as well as paying passengers and did business in everything but tonnage freight in ore concentrates and stock movements which still went in steam.

Occasionally, a Galloping Goose driven furiously in an effort to keep to schedule down a four per cent grade, got out of hand and imitated its prototype in everything but actual flight. When at last its mad progress left the rails, the entire contrivance disintegrated like a powder mill exploding and a reserve Goose was dispatched to pick up the mails and the maimed from the hillside they occupied. The Galloping Geese inherited most of the thrills of mountain railroading in its most primitive state of development but no fatalities were ever attributed to them.

WOLF CREEK PASS

C. W. McCall

Me and Earl was hauling chickens on the Flatbed out of Wiggins
When we spent all night on the uphill side
of 37 miles of hell called Wolf Creek Pass
Which is up on the Great Divide.

We were sitting there sucking toothpicks and drinking Nehis and
    onion soup mix
And I said "Earl, let's mail a card to mother and then send them
    chickens on down the other side."
Yeah, let's give 'em a ride.

Wolf Creek Pass way up on the Great Divide
Comin' on down the other side.

Well, Earl put down his bottle,
Mashed his foot down on the throttle,
And then a couple of boobs with a thousand cubes in the 1948 Peterbilt
screamed alive.
We woke up the chickens.
We roared up offa' that shoulder, spraying pine cones, rocks and boulders
And put 400 head of them Rhode Island Reds and a couple of burnt out
roosters on the line.
Look out below, 'cuz here we go …

Wolf Creek Pass way up on the Great Divide
Swingin' on down the other side.

Well, we commenced the truckin',
And them hens commenced a cluckin',
Then Earl took out a match and scratched his pants
And lit up the unused half of a dollar cigar.
Took a puff, said, "My, ain't this pretty up here."
I said "Earl, this hill can spill us.
"You'd better slow down or you're going to kill us.
"Just make one mistake and it's the pearly gates for them 85 crates of USDA
approved cluckers.
"You wanna hit second?"

Wolf Creek Pass way up on the Great Divide
Truckin' on down the other side.

Well, Earl grabbed on the shifter
And he stabbed her into fifth gear
And then the chromium plated folie aluminated genuine accessory shiftknob
Come right off in his hand.
I said, "You wanna screw that thing back on, Earl."
He was trying to thread it on there when the fire fell off his cigar
And dropped on down and sorta rolled around
And then lit the cuff of Earl's pants and burned a hole in his socks.
Yessir set 'em right on fire.
I looked on outta the window and I started counting phone poles
Going by at the rate of 4 to the 7th power.
Well, I put 2 and 2 together and added 12 and carried 5;
Come up with 22,000 telephone poles an hour.

I looked at Earl and his eyes were wide,
His lip was curled and his leg was fried and his hand was froze to the wheel
Like a tongue to a sled in the middle of a blizzard.
And I says, "Earl, I'm not the type to complain
"But the time has come for me to explain
"That if you don't apply some brake real soon
"They're going to have to take us up with a stick and a spoon."
Well, Earl reared back and caught his leg, stepped down as hard as he
        could on the brake;
The pedal went clear to the floor and stayed right there on the floor.
… Sorta like steppin' on a plum.
Well, from there on down it just wasn't real pretty,
It was hairpin county and slick back city.
One of them looked like a can full of worms
Another one looked like malaria germs.
Right in the middle of the whole damn show
Was a real nice tunnel now wouldn't you know.
The sign said clearance at the 12 foot line
But the chickens was stacked to 13' 9".
When we shot that tunnel at a hundred and ten
Like gas through a funnel and eggs through a hen.
We took that top row of chickens off slicker than a storm off a Louisiana swamp.
Went down and around and around and down

We run out of ground at the edge of town.
Bashed in at the side of the feed store in downtown Pagosa Springs.

Wolf Creek Pass way upon the Great Divide
Truckin' on down the other side.

Wolf Creek Pass way up on the Great Divide
Truckin' on down the other side.

THE 10TH MOUNTAIN DIVISION

David Lissy

"IF A CAMERA COULD possibly show the wonder of such a spot I'd send you some pictures but it's hard even to believe one's eyes so no photograph could ever catch it."

The year was 1943. The location was the snowy slopes above Camp Hale, Colorado, the training ground of the U.S. Army's 10th Mountain Division. The writer—Sergeant Ralph Hulbert—was describing scenery he'd climbed thousands of vertical feet to witness. On his feet were seven-foot wooden skis; on his back was a 90-pound rucksack.

Forty-five years later I'm standing on a similar slope, but my skis are lightweight Fiberglas and my 60-pound pack contains cameras and film instead of a stove and sleeping bag. My mission is not to train for mountain combat against the Nazis, but to capture the wonder and the beauty of Colorado's ski country.

Like most of the men of the 10th Mountain Division, I was born east of the Mississippi River. I too was lured west by the Rocky Mountains. And like many "phantoms of the snow" who returned after the war ended, I decided to make Colorado my home. Even now, after 12 years of photographing in these mountains, I am still left with the empty feeling of not being able to put it all on film. It's simply too big, too wonderful, too beautiful. Surely the mountains reveal part of God's glory and nature to us.

To reach the slope where I now stand I did not strap "climbers" to my skis and sweat my way up like Ralph Hulbert and the other "soldiers of the snows." A chair lift carried me to this mountaintop, giving me time to think back on the early days of skiing in Colorado.

When Camp Hale was built in 1942, the industry was fledgling: single rope tows at Loveland and Berthoud, a rope tow and T-bar at Winter Park, a sled-like lift that had to be manually hauled up the hill at Aspen. When Camp Hale's mile-and-a-10th-long T-bar was built on Cooper Hill, it was the longest in the world.

The Army chose the Camp Hale site because of its 9,300-foot elevation, steep terrain, light powder snow and long, hard winters. A glamorous recruitment campaign brought Ivy League skiers, rugged outdoorsmen and even a few ski champions to the mountain valley. During the winters of 1942 to 1944, 14,000 soldiers learned and refined ski and outdoor survival techniques on Cooper Hill and in the backcountry above Camp Hale. During the "D" Series maneuvers, described by Harris Dusenbery in this book, the entire division took to the mountains for 30 days of mock warfare, fighting minus-30-degree temperatures as well as the "enemy," fellow soldiers posing as Germans.

The same qualities that drew the Army to Colorado brought thousands of 10th Mountain Division skiers back to its slopes after the war. Tenth Mountain veterans helped launch many of the state's ski areas, including Vail, Aspen, Buttermilk, Snowmass, Breckenridge, Arapahoe Basin and Loveland. These men, more than any other group, had a profound impact on Colorado's ski industry.

Three dimensional artifacts from the 10th Mountain Division—including skis and poles, clothing, sleeping bags and food rations—are on permanent display at the Colorado Ski Museum in Vail and are periodically on display at the Colorado History Museum in Denver. Written materials ... are housed at the Denver Public Library.

Private Harris Dusenbery, who is quoted extensively in this book, was 29 when he joined the 10th Mountain Division in September 1943. He trained as a rifleman at Camp Hale for eight months, then served in Italy's Northern Apennines until the war ended in 1945. Portions of his *Ski the High Trail* memoir were written while stationed at Camp Hale. Sergeant Ralph Hulbert, whose letters to his mother are excerpted in this book, was 22 when he arrived at Camp Hale in 1943. He taught skiing, glacier climbing and mountain climbing, then went overseas to fight the Nazis in the mountains of Italy.

Every American is indebted to the men of the 10th who fought in Italy to preserve our freedoms. To those who died for that cause and to those who returned to Colorado to build our great ski industry—my special thanks.

TRUST YOUR HEART:
AN AUTOBIOGRAPHY

Judy Collins

PETER HAD BEEN MY sweetheart for three years and he and my family were very close. I was eighteen when we were married and Peter had already finished his tour of duty in the navy and was planning to go back to school in the fall to finish the two years necessary for his undergraduate degree in English literature. It was the beginning of the summer, so we agreed that we would work in the mountains for three months, then move to Boulder. In June 1958, we headed for the town of Estes Park to look for a job. We stayed in godfather Holden's cabin in Rocky Mountain National Park, a preserve of mountains and rushing streams, raw wilderness and beauty. Peter went to town the first day, and came home to our cabin very excited.

"There's a job for us running Fern Lake Lodge. It's owned by Jim Bishop, who owns the big lodge at Bear Lake. It's a nine-mile round-trip hike to get to Fern; the lodge has no electricity, and our food will be brought in by packhorse once a week; the water has to be pumped from the mountain springs, and I will chop wood for the fires, and you will—here's the catch—bake bread and pies on the wood stove!"

"Of course I will!" I already knew I was pregnant with Clark and I felt vibrant and healthy, capable of anything. Euphoric.

We first moved into Bear Lake Lodge, where Jim Bishop made us comfortable. The cook taught me to bake bread, and we waited for the snow to melt enough so we could start for Fern Lake. Jim told us how for years his mother had run Fern Lake Lodge year in and year out, accommodating two dozen guests at a time. Burros were sent in loaded with steamer trunks, and she kept three wood stoves burning all year. People would walk the nine-mile round-trip on snowshoes and go ice fishing on the lake in the winter. The lodge had been closed for a few years, but Jim wanted to open it up again because it had been so special in his mother's time and it was his favorite lodge in the national park.

Finally, when the snow was melted enough to get over the high trail, Peter and I each assembled a fifty-pound pack of clothes and food for a week and started out for our new home. It was a brilliantly sunny morning the day we began our trek. The wild mountain flowers were in bloom, the snowmelt roared down in streams and waterfalls. There were a million purple, white, and yellow columbines blooming, and I saw an orange hummingbird, a little bigger than my thumb. I have never seen one that color since, and I have been told that this species lives only in the Andes at very high altitudes. I have always thought of those red-orange wings as a special sign.

We arrived after four and a half hours and put our packs down. The lodge sat on the banks of Fern Lake, nestled beside the crystal water, its windows boarded up. We began opening doors with the big loop of keys Jim had given us, and as the slats came off, the daylight flooded the puncheon-floored main room. On the walls were enormous old photographs of people in furs with long wooden skis, snowshoes stacked against the lodge. There was a blackened stove in the huge kitchen, and behind the main lodge were eleven cabins scattered throughout the pines. Each cabin had beds and a potbellied Franklin wood-burning stove in perfect condition. A storage cabin was filled with quilts, ancient canned goods, parts for lanterns, pillows for thirty. We made up a bed in the cabin closest to the lake, and Peter went out to chop kindling. I lit the Coleman lamps in the kitchen and got the stove going. We were home.

That first night Peter and I fell asleep exhausted. Next day, he got the spring water running through the pipes; I got the bread baking. Soon mountain hikers were stopping in at the lodge for lunch.

A few days later our packhorse arrived with my old National guitar, a quart of Jack Daniel's, and food for a week. Occasionally friends would hike in to spend

Charles Partridge Adams, "Golden Hour of the Rockies," n.d.

a few days, bringing avocados, Mexican beer, and fresh tomatoes, but mostly we relied on the arrival each week of the packhorse loaded with fresh meat and vegetables, letters from home, and sometimes a newspaper. Peter fished trout out of the lake, and in the woods under the pine trees was our "Girl Scout refrigerator," a cooler made by dripping water from one of the spring pipes over a tin box covered with cheesecloth. Primitive, but it worked just fine.

In the mornings, after the fires were started, the bread baked, the chores done, the wood chopped, and the spring pipes checked, Peter and I would sit out on the porch of the lodge and play chess as we looked across the clear surface of Fern Lake, awaiting our hikers. We would hear their voices first, coming down from Emerald Lake, above us at thirteen thousand feet. I would go into the kitchen and make the final preparations for the pies and slice the bread for sandwiches.

"It's amazing to find you here in the middle of 'nowhere,' " they would often say. Peter would settle them around the wood tables, get them mugs of coffee, and then I would serve the hot apple and cherry pies and sandwiches while they oohed and ahhed.

After lunch I would bring out the guitar and sing "Spanish Is the Loving Tongue" and "Barbara Allen." People leaned their faces back in the sun, their eyes closed, sometimes singing along on the choruses. With their legs stretched out, hiking boots crossed, they often had a look of reverie that told of their innermost dreams. Fern answered a need I had not known I had—during the day we had the company of friends and strangers, but at night, as the light of the sun left the lake, there was solitude. The only sounds were the owls calling and the stream talking to itself as it ran out from the lake down the mountain. I was happy with only my husband and the moon for company. Fern Lake was a dream in the wilderness, something we knew was rare, like the hummingbird of a color not seen everywhere.

ASPEN POTPOURRI

Mary Eshbaugh Hayes

POTPOURRI

Use the wild pink roses which bloom in the Rockies in late June, the yellow roses which bloom in Aspen in early July—or a mixture of wild flowers. I always include some rosebuds whole—but as tiny as possible.

Pick the petals of flowers in the early morning, toss lightly on waxed paper in a cool, airy place to dry. Sprinkle with salt. Allow to stand 10 days stirring daily. Then put in your Potpourri jar. New petals can be added until jar is full.

RECIPE WHICH FOLLOWS IS FOR TWO QUARTS.

> *1 tablespoon Mace*
> *2 tablespoons allspice*
> *2 tablespoons cloves*
> *2 tablespoons stick cinnamon broken in bits*
> *2 tablespoons nutmeg*
> *4 tablespoons powdered Orris root*
> *1 tablespoon dried orange peel*

Mix these ingredients together, then add to dried flower petals—a layer of spices, a layer of petals, a layer of spices—on up to the top of the jar. Keep in large bottles for looks or decanter into small bottles with holes punched in lid to let out aroma. Keep in dresser draws for a breath of summer.

IN THE SHADOW OF THE ROCKIES

Gene Lindberg and Blanche M. Tice

Ev'ning shadows falling,
Wandering days are thru.
Soon you'll hear my calling,
Comin' swingin' down a mountain trail to you.

CHORUS

In the shadow of the Rockies.
Blending with the sunset hue.
We discovered love together,
Where the streams sing of dreams come true.
In the Golden West together.
To a "Nest o' Rest" we'll stray.
In the shadow of the Rockies,
At the rose-colored close of day.

Ev'ning breezes humming,
Soft, when day is thru.
Whisper, dear, I'm comin'
Thru the columbines that line the trail to you.

BEYOND THE ASPEN GROVE

Ann Zwinger

I COUNT THE SPRING year well begun when the aspen dangle their three-inch catkins, fuzzy earrings which dust the cabin deck with pollen. The buds spill them out anywhere from late March to the end of April. The catkins appear before the leaves do, open to the pollinating spring breezes. The amount of pollen is prodigious. When I cut a bouquet of spring branches, the table on which they sit is deep in pale sulphur-yellow pollen the next day.

Our log notes the appearance of the first leaves between May 14 and May 20, the third week in May consistent over the years. The leaves are a pale lucid green, circles cut out of green tissue paper and overlaid in shifting patterns. Now is the time to hang out the hammock and feel, in the chill warmth, intimations of summer. A week ago the light was too bright for reading comfortably in the grove; now the leaves make kaleidoscopic shadows on the book page.

Lying in the hammock, looking up at the leaves, I can see the gall swellings which appear almost as soon as the leaves open, opaque against the translucent leaf. Galls usually appear in the early leaves, looking like green peppercorns. Leaf miners make meandering mines in the thin galleries between the upper and lower leaf surface when the leaves are larger.

🐜 🐜 🐜

These young trees sprouted in this area when it was suitable to their needs, just as the annuals and perennials invaded the bare ground of the meadows. The preparation was done by pioneer willows and sedges which created land out of marsh, and by beaver cuttings which let in the light.

As the young trees become established, they begin to infringe upon each other's needed space. Competition shows in the slenderness of trunk and paucity of leaf. Competition begins when the demands of the plants are in excess of the site's ability to fulfill them, and is keenest among plants of the same species which have identical requirements. Those trees which survive the competition will have about fifty years of rapid growth and a life expectancy of about one hundred years, rarely much longer.

This is one of the reasons aspen is considered a "trash" tree. Not being especially long-lived, the fallen trunks open the ground to erosion. To the lumberman, aspen takes up space that might better be used for more commercially desirable stands. By the time an aspen is large enough to cut for lumber, it is usually infested with heart-rot fungi and is therefore useless. We had to cut down a twenty-year-old aspen while surveying; rot had already begun in the heartwood.

Thomas Worthington Whittredge, "In the Rockies [Bergen Park, Colorado]," 1870.

Aspen is really useful only for smaller things; young trees make fine fence posts. Susan loves to carve it, and I still have a smooth satiny spoon she made years ago from sapwood. The sapwood in the tree we cut broke like gypsum. It was slippery wet and sweet-smelling with summer, a pale, creamy lemon-yellow.

Westerners have a special feeling about aspen that encompasses none of these ideas. It is the only tall deciduous grove-forming tree of the montane area. Alder, willow, dogwood, and mountain maple are all shrubs or shrublike trees and, on our land, are never over twelve to fourteen feet high. Conifers have a majestic monotony, like someone who is always right. They are too timeless to mark the seasons. But aspen has éclat, a glorious brashness in defiance of the rules, the flapper who does the Charleston in the midst of the grand waltz. The landscape would be dull indeed without them.

🪵 🪵 🪵

In the center of the aspen grove is a small clearing, scarcely big enough to be called a meadow, which in summer is sweet and soft with white clover and edged with black-eyed Susans, lupines, and fleabanes. It is open and sunny and level, large enough to put up a badminton net or for playing volley ball. Herman mows it, bemoaning the fact that without any care it is an impeccable lawn and that his carefully manicured city frontyard often doesn't look as well.

Like the aspen grove itself, it is a people place, and because it is much lived in and played in, some of the happiest memories of Constant Friendship are tied to it.

Some years ago several families with young children planned an old-fashioned Fourth of July with us, to be shared with other friends who enjoy the out-of-doors. A bachelor brought a boiler-size watermelon. He chose to sleep on the raft in the middle of the lake and nearly congealed in the early morning dews and damps. He was just getting to sleep in the warmth of the sunshine when Herman shot off his carbide cannon announcing breakfast and a glorious Fourth.

There were watermelon-seed-spitting contests and fishing (which was largely unsuccessful due to the noise); there was a one-legged race and a treasure hunt. Susan and her house guest Jean planned a flag ceremony which the younger children carried out. They requested silence as we crossed the footbridge to the flagpole. Small hands struggled with stiff latches and stubborn grommets. Then slowly and carefully they raised the American flag to catch the morning breeze in a Colorado sky. Beneath it flew the bright blue flag of Constant Friendship with its blazon of five aspen leaves. The dignity and propriety of the boys, stilling the giggles of the girls, invested the mountain clearness with ideals and hopes. There are those moments that we remember with clarity because they epitomize a time or an awareness, that by caring for the things close to us we are able then to care for a larger world. No one had to ask for silence back across the footbridge.

The children wove in and out of the day on their own errands. It was as if the adults watched from the wrong end of a telescope trained on a section of stage landscape. Periodically figures came into view, a frieze of youngness running across the set, first from one wing of aspen, then the other of pine, diagonally upstage or down, sometimes stage front, sometimes behind a scrim of aspen leaves, sometimes swiftly, sometimes in a pavane. They belonged to the land that day, not to their parents. They were small sprites of the substance of leaf and shadow, interweaving with the patterns of flickering sunlight. The figures seemed to pause briefly, then rearrange—moments of stop-motion alternating with moments of movement.

Once a tree is grown there is no return to the seedling stage, and so the adults who watched could only remember and see arabesques of life and sunshine and unaware grace as natural as a flower or branch in the varying small figures. Even out of sight, the sound of their voices came carried on the aspen breeze. They were small exotic creatures at home in a world of wind and light. Here in these mountain meadows and groves they were all Peter Pans.

And then dinner, complete with fried chicken, corn-on-the-cob, baked beans, salad, sliced tomatoes, cucumber and watermelon pickles, homemade bread, coconut cake decorated with a red, white and blue pennant, all the good things brought and all the good things remembered from an Indiana Fourth of July. After darkness we went up to the ponderosa hill overlooking the lake. Herman set off fireworks from the lake rock, each shower reflecting in the blackness beneath, hissing upward to drop sizzling into itself. When the last rocket fell, it was hard to know whether it was fireworks or a shooting star.

SECTION IV

GROWING UP
WITH COLORADO

THE SWITZERLAND OF AMERICA

Samuel Bowles

Denver, Colorado, September, 1868.

INEXHAUSTIBLE AS IS Colorado's mineral wealth; progressive as henceforth its development; predominant and extensive as are its mountains; high even as are its valleys and plains,—in spite of all seeming impossibilities and rivalries, Agriculture is already and is destined always to be its domin-ant interest. Hence my faith in its prosperity and its influence among the central states of the Continent. For agriculture is the basis of wealth, of power, of morality; it is the conservative element of all national and political and social growth; it steadies, preserves, purifies, elevates. Full one-third of the territorial extent of Colorado,—though this third average as high as Mount Washington,—is fit, more, rich for agricultural purposes. The grains, the vegetables and the fruits of the temperate zone grow and ripen in profusion; and through the most of it, cattle and sheep can live and fatten the year around without housing or feeding. The immediate valleys or bottom lands of the Arkansas and Platte and Rio Grande and their numerous tributaries, after they debouch from the mountains, are of rich vegetable loams, and need no irrigation. The uplands or plains are of a coarse, sandy loam, rich in the phosphates washed from the minerals of the mountains, and are not much in use yet except for pastures. When cultivated, more or less irrigation is introduced, and probably will always be indispensable for sure crops of roots and vegetables; but for the small, hard grains, I have no idea it will be generally found necessary. It is a comparatively dry climate, indeed; but showers are frequent, and extend over a considerable part of the spring and summer.

At a rough estimate, the agricultural wealth of Colorado last year was a million bushels of corn, half a million of wheat, half a million of barley, oats and vegetables, 50,000 head of cattle, and 75,000 to 100,000 sheep. The increase this year is at least 50 per cent; in the northern counties at least 100. Indeed, the agriculture of the northern counties, between the Pacific Railroad at Cheyenne and Denver, which has grown to be full half that of the whole state, is the development almost entirely of the last three years. South, in the Arkansas and Rio Grande valleys, the farming and the population are older, going back to before the gold discoveries. This is the Spanish-Mexican section, and was formerly a part of New Mexico. Its agriculture is on a large but rough scale, and only the immense crops and the simple habits of the people, chiefly ignorant, degraded Mexicans, permit it to be profitable. The soil yields wonderfully, north and south. There is authentic evidence of 316 bushels of corn to the acre in the neighborhood of Denver this season; 60 to 75 bushels of wheat to the acre are very frequently reported; also 250 bushels of potatoes; and

60 to 70 of both oats and barley. These are exceptional yields, of course, and yet not of single acres, but of whole fields, and on several farms in different counties. Probably 30 bushels is the average product of wheat; of corn no more, for the hot nights that corn loves are never felt here; of oats say 50, and of barley 40, for the whole state. Exhaustion of the virgin freshness of the soil will tend to decrease these averages in the future; but against that we may safely put improved cultivation and greater care in harvesting.

The melons and vegetables are superb; quality, quantity and size are alike unsurpassed by any garden cultivators in the East. The irrigated gardens of the upper parts of Denver fairly riot in growth of fat vegetables; while the bottom lands of the neighboring valleys are at least equally productive without irrigation. Think of cabbages weighing from 50 to 60 pounds each! And potatoes from 5 to 6 pounds, onions 1 to 2 pounds, and beets 6 to 10! Yet here they grow, and as excellent as big.

🐜 🐜 🐜

Stock-raising on the Plains is simple and profitable business. The animals can roam at will, and a single man can tend hundreds. The only enemies are the Indians and the diseases that the Texas cattle bring up from the South. But the former are the great evil; the confusion, danger and loss they have created this season sum up a serious blow not only to stock-raising, but to all farming. Even if the evil is suppressed hereafter, this season's raids are a year's loss to the agricultural interests of Colorado. Many farmers have given up in despair from danger and disaster, and retired from the field; others hesitate and refuse to come, who otherwise would be here at once and in force of capital and energy, to enter upon the business.

These great interests of mining and farming shade naturally into others, and already there are the beginnings of various manufacturing developments, as there are the materials and incentives for such undertakings without stint. Some fifteen or twenty flouring-mills are in operation throughout the state. The Colorado wheat makes a rich hearty flour, bearing a creamy golden tinge; and I have eaten no where else in America better bread than is made from it. There is a baker in Georgetown, whose products are as rich and light as the best of German wheat bread. The wheat will rank with the very best that America produces, and is more like the California grain than that of "the States." Coal mines are abundant, and several are being profitably worked along the lower range of the mountains; as, indeed, they have been found and opened at intervals along the line of the Pacific Railroad over the mountains, and are already supplying its engines with a most excellent fuel,—a hard, dry, brown coal, very pure and free-burning; in Boulder valley and Golden City, iron is being manufactured from native ore; at Golden City, there is a successful manufactory of pottery ware and fire brick; also a paper-mill and a tannery, and three flouring-mills; the state already supplies its own salt; soda deposits are abundant everywhere, and will be a great source of wealth; woolen mills are projected and greatly needed, as wool-growing is the simplest of agricultural pursuits here; a valuable tin mine has been lately discovered and its value proved, up in the mountains; and next year the Railroad will be one of Colorado's possessions, and bring harmony and unity and healthy development to all her growth, social, material, and political. Also, by that time she will be a state, and so responsible for her own government, be it good or bad.

I AM NOT MOUNTAIN-BORN

Nellie Burget Miller

I did not love these mountains—not at first—
For I am prairie-born. Like prison-walls
Set stone on stone, they barred the western sun
And brought chill shadows in mid-afternoon.
All my eager youth had claimed with joy
Was but a memory stretched taut across
The rusty plains to where the urbane sun
Sank graciously to rest in crimson fire;
Where nights were hot and good for tasseling corn;
Where sleepy rivers sucked incessantly
At grass-roots on low banks, and smug black bass
Nibbled fat earthworms to make the bobbing cork
Go under; where patchwork fields of yellow wheat
Were primly stitched to pasture lands and strips
Of posied clover, tied close with big red barns.

I am not mountain-born, I was not fed
On epic tales of wild emprise; my forebears
Did not strike pay dirt in "Dead Man's Gulch"
Nor tap a silver vein on Fryer's Hill;
Such deeds are not my rightful heritage.
The storied past is theirs who helped to make it,
On their legacy, perhaps, to sons and daughters—
Heroic themes, at secondhand, are musty
At the best and make but slender singing.
But, as a master-poet once observed:

"There's something strikes a balance, no doubt."
If I had been indigenous I might
Have written more, or *less*, perhaps …
Blinded by pride of gold and gay romance,
I might have taken tragedies of dust
For granted. I saw with eyes unprejudiced
And sensed the agony of thirst-parched plains,
The heartsick longing for a tree, and rain;
The madness of a fleeing tumbleweed.

To my foster-state I have surrendered utterly.
Like twisted tree at timberline I cling
To alien soil with fierce possessive passion.
Still, I do not sing of mountains very much;
The shock of mountains to one prairie-born
Is far too violent for rhapsody—
Fit paean of sublimity is silence.

At long last I shall sleep where white-coifed peaks
Lie like a sculptured dream athwart the sky—
Ave, Colorado!
No native singer loves you more than I.

HIGH, WIDE AND LONESOME

Hal Borland

I WANTED WINTER TO be exciting. I wanted some real storms. Summer storms were fun, and they gave you a shivery feeling sometimes, when the great, towering clouds boiled like foam in a kettle and lightning flashed in all directions and the thunder made the hills bounce. But there weren't many Summer storms like that. And with the exception of the Christmas storm, when Dick brought me home from the big sheep camp, last Winter hadn't amounted to much. I wanted a real, rip-tearing blizzard.

I got it.

The Saturday when we were all set to try to get to Gary in the buggy it began to snow in mid-morning. It was just a slow, quiet snowfall with hardly any wind, but Mother said we'd better not start out in it. I thought she was being too cautious, but by the middle of the afternoon I knew she was right. The wind came up and it really began to blizzard.

★ ★ ★

While we ate supper the wind sifted snow in around every window and made such eddies in the air that the flame in the lamp flickered and smoked. We hung old quilts over the windows to break the gusts of fine snow and we stuffed a towel under the door. Mother put the hot flatirons in our beds and I tried to read for a while, sitting with my feet in the oven. But the fire died, sucked right up the chimney, and I went to bed. The wind was shaking the house so much that the dishes rattled on their shelves.

It snowed and blew all night. When I wakened the next morning there was a little drift of snow on the edge of my bed and when I stepped down I went into a drift a foot deep on the floor. There was a drift under every window in the house. We ate breakfast before I tried to get to the barn. When I opened the house door I found a solid wall of snow. The drift there was six feet deep.

We knew it was still blowing. We could hear it. But we didn't know it was still snowing until I tunneled through that drift at the door and got into the open. It took me an hour to get clear, and it was still snowing. It was eleven o'clock when I reached the barn and got the door open there.

Everything was all right at the barn. The snow had banked it and the animal heat made it almost as warm as the house. I did the milking and rationed out the extra hay I had got in the day before and started back to the house. I had to dig out every path because they'd all drifted full again. Before I got to the house the milk was full of slush, half frozen though it had been warm when I left the barn.

The wind eased off somewhat that evening, but the snow continued. The second day I had to dig out all over again. And that day I had to water the stock. They couldn't go any longer without it. Mother said she was going to help. She'd learned what the wind could do to her skirts, so she put on a pair of Father's overalls, belted them at the waist, tied them at the ankles, and put on overshoes, coat and scarf. She carried kettles of boiling water and thawed the pump while I got on Mack and broke trail from the barn to the well. When we had a trail opened through the shallower drifts, Daisy and the calves followed to the well, drank, and were very happy to get back in the barn. And that afternoon I had to find some way to get hay. The only way was to dig a path to the stacks, carve off a big slice of one stack with the hay knife, and carry it into the barn.

Before I got the hay into the barn I began to wonder if I really wanted a blizzard. My arms ached, my ears stung, I was sweating like a horse and when I stopped to catch my breath the sweat seemed to turn to icicles in my armpits. But I got the hay in, and I did the evening chores, and I shoveled my way back to the house, where the big bowl of steaming pinto beans was worth all the sweating. The Mexican wants his beans hot with chili peppers. The New Englander wants his sweet with molasses and salt pork. We had ours simmered for hours with no seasoning but salt and swimming in their own brown juice. To us they were bread and butter and meat and potatoes, as they were to many an isolated homesteader. On a cold, blizzardy night they were more than sustenance; they were warmth and comfort and a promise for tomorrow.

That was our pattern for four days, wind and snow and shoveling, and pumping and milking and carrying sheep chips. Soft snow turned to ice crystals which, wind-driven, bit cheek and knuckle and made you a sentient part of the storm. It became a kind of game to see how much cold you could take, how much wind you could face, how much snow you could shovel. And, as the storm progressed, it even added comfort to the house. Until the snow banked the house to the eaves the stove cast so small a circle of warmth that I could stand with my hip pockets practically on the stove lids and still see my breath. Then we were drifted in and I could go clear across the room before my breath was visible.

The snow probably stopped on the third day, though we couldn't tell. There were flashes of sunlight, but the air was still full of snow, undoubtedly blown from the hilltops. It seemed impossible that the snow could continue to drift, but it did. It seemed that the drifts had been built as high as they could stand and all the ridges had been swept bare. But they weren't. The wind continued to reshape the world.

But at last the wind eased away and the plains lay white and silent. And new— white, gleaming, pristine new.

🐾 🐾 🐾

After such a storm, the world of the plains is a strange and magnificent place. It is as though all the earth-shaping forces have been at work on a vastly quickened scale of time. Hills, valleys, hollows and hummocks have all been reshaped to a new pattern. The wind has had its way, at last, the wind that is forever trying to level the hills and fill the valleys. It has been able to work its will with an obediently plastic, though transient, material.

Our wind had been somewhat thwarted, by a fence post, a hay stack, even by a tall weed stem. It had swirled and eddied, and we could see all the swirls and eddies frozen in the snow. Change was everywhere, but there was one constant, the soft curve. You saw it in the eddy around a fence post, the swirl around a hay stack, the shape of a hill, the flow of a valley, and in a thousand variations of the amazing curl of a snowdrift.

The wind had all but obliterated the house, the barn, the fences, the hay stacks. They were still there, but they had been merged into the drifted landscape, their own shapes lost and distorted. There was virtually no trace of human tenancy except the smoke from our chimney. Paths were drifted over. Fences were buried under the drifts. Hay stacks were only larger drifts, as were both the house and the barn. And we, the human survivors, had been driven back, in a way, into a cave; the house was little more than a cavern in a hillside of snow. There we had survived as a kind of human outpost in a world suddenly engulfed in a new ice age. An ice age, though, that would retreat and vanish in a matter of weeks rather than centuries and eons.

The initial vacancy of that world was beyond belief. It was a vast white void, without a wing in the sky or a moving paw upon the snow. In time, of course, in another day or two, the prairie quail huddled in bunch grass caves beneath the drifts would work their way out. Field mice, tunneling under the snow from one seed storehouse to another, would come to the surface and explore. Jack rabbits would break through the drifts that sheltered them beside the soap weed clumps. Prairie dogs would open their snow-sealed burrows and yelp at the white and hungry world. And coyotes would come from their dens and make lean shadows on the starlit snow and send their hungry yelps echoing among the white hills. But now they were as snowbound as we were.

ROUND BY ROUND:
AN AUTOBIOGRAPHY

Jack Dempsey

I REMEMBER MANASSA

WHEN I WAS SEVEN years old, in the small town of Manassa in southern Colorado, I had a run-in with a boy named Fred Daniels, about my own size, who went to school with me. Just what started us fighting I can't remember; in fact, it is from my father that the description of the set-to comes—but at any rate we tangled in one of the wide, dusty, road-like streets of the country town.

We went to it hammer and tongs, as small boys will, with ferocious swinging blows that missed a mile. The noise attracted men from the country store, and a half-circle gathered, amused, to watch us, as they might watch a dogfight. Apparently, in that pioneer atmosphere of the Rockies, nobody thought of interfering. Fred's father was there, and so was mine, laughing and slapping their thighs, watching us scrap it out.

The going kept getting rougher and rougher. The two of us tried everything we could think of, wrestling and butting and kicking and everything else. Presently Fred's father yelled encouragingly, "Bite him, Fred!"

Everybody laughed, and Fred turned his head to find out what his father had said. It left him wide open, and they tell me I instantly took advantage of it and bopped him on the chin as hard as I could. Over he went! The fight was finished.

Years later, as you will see, that early fight had its influence on many of my

A. Howard Brodie, "Jack Dempsey," 1958.

battles in the ring. It affected my entire career. ...

The whole San Luis Valley, in which Manassa lies, was, and still is, exactly suited to a fight like that. ... When I was born there and christened William Harrison Dempsey, in June 1895, there were only thirty or forty houses. Picture a flat, high-lying, western valley about a hundred miles long and nearly seventy miles across, entirely surrounded by rugged mountains, many of them over 14,000 feet high. Warm in summer, freezing in winter, with lots of snow. Just to the west lies the backbone of the whole country, the great Continental Divide. It is still wild, open country, with cattle and sheep ranches, flat meadows and sagebrush between widely separated towns. ...

The first white settlers of the valley ... were Mexicans, who came up the Rio Grande from the southwest. Most of the towns still have Spanish names—San Acacio, Del Norte, La Garita, Estrella, La Jara. They contrast sharply with the later names given other towns by farmers who moved into the valley, following the gold rush, from eastern states—Russell, Center, Henry, Bountiful, McGinty. Together the widely differing strains have populated the valley side by side. ...

🐜 🐜 🐜

Manassa was strong on religion. When I was a small boy a great Mormon church was built there and painted white. ... Every evening we had family prayers. A blessing was always asked at the beginning of each meal. Regularly the Teachers of the Mormon church, corresponding to preachers in other religions, visited our house to see how things were going. They would exhort my father to do right, as they saw the right ... but in spite of all the religion, Manassa was like every other pioneer town, tough and ready for anything.

My parents were poor. Although there was plenty to eat, we were otherwise a poverty-stricken household. My father was of a roving, happy-go-lucky disposition. He didn't like to stick to the same job, the same farm. He wanted endless variety. When he had money, he spent it generously, but he rarely had any. He loved to have a good time. He used to play the fiddle, without notes, but with nimble fingers, running the same rollicking melody over and over and over—"Turkey in the Straw," "Arkansas Traveller," "The Wild Goose." Occasionally he'd make up a little tune of his own. Sometimes he played for dances.

Any inconsistency between his religion and his manner of living never bothered him. "The Morman religion," he would explain, "is a good thing. It shows you what you ought to do. That's the main thing, always to know what you ought to do. Of course, you don't always do it. Nobody does. That's human nature. But at least you always ought to know what's right. I reckon that's what religion is for." ...

My mother was very different. She was much more ambitious than my father. She was scrupulously clean. She was always scrubbing floors, always washing dishes or washing windows or cooking or putting up fruits or vegetables for winter. ... Mother had great dreams for all of us. We were all to be well educated and successful, rich and powerful ladies and gentlemen. And above all, "good citizens," whatever that meant. We were to make the country better. My mother wasn't as religious as my father, but she was more sincere.

🐾 🐾 🐾

We were always surrounded with horses, cows, pigs and chickens. Also innumerable dogs. I learned to ride a horse almost as soon as I learned to walk. One summer my father took me over to Cumbres Pass with him, when he had a contract for getting out ties for the railroad. I can remember helping my older brothers snake out logs with a mule.

Mostly, during those days at Manassa, my mother was too crowded with work, and my father too busy with his own schemes and expeditions to have much time for us. We had to be shaped by our day-to-day adventures and experiences, the fights with Mexican boys and trying to throw ropes on horses, rather than by much guidance from our parents. ... We never had any "store" toys. We had to make our own playthings. Chips of wood became boats, sticks became spears, bits of rope became lariats. We were able to make fairly respectable bows and arrows, and we had a lot of fun with these things.

Looking back at it now, it seems as if I almost always had a good time. The only bad thing was the feeling of being so very poor.

SECOND HOEING

Hope Williams Sykes

OUT OF THE CHURCH, dodging and shrinking, trying to avoid the rain of barley, corn, and wheat which showered round them from numerous pockets and small sacks, the bridal party ran to the parsonage to get coats and have witnesses sign the marriage license.

Hannah tried to shake the grain from her clothes. Small red spots showed on her throat where the grain had pelted. She tried to dislodge the last of the seeds as she rode with the bridal party to the photographer's.

They waited awkwardly for the photographer to get ready. She looked at Henry Goelzer, small, skinny, and loose jointed. Not much like his huge fat mother, more like his bullet-headed father. He had the same drooping shoulders, the same watery blue eyes. Henry looked simple, ashamed. No wonder he wouldn't meet her glance.

"Well, that's over." Jake Heist took Hannah's arm and led the way to the car. "Now for the wedding eats. I'm starved." He grinned at them all.

Down through the wide streets of Valley City they went, across the river to the narrow streets and little houses of Shag Town, to the dingy home of the Goelzers.

A group of young men held a thick rope stretched across the gateway.

"You gotta pay to get in," they shouted in unison.

"Open that gate, or I get out and throw you away," one of the bride's boys called loudly from the car.

"One dollar you pay before you get in to eat. You know the bride gotta have some money. She don't feed you for nothin'. One dollar."

"We don't! Twenty-five cents is all we pay," Jake replied loudly.

The four bride's boys each threw a quarter to the gate keepers, and the rope was lowered.

As the car came into the yard, three old men standing under a tree started playing, "Jesus, now lead on 'til the peace is won." The bass horn, clarinet and cornet sent a high lilting melody across the yard, the bass horn boomed.

Older women came running out of the house to kiss Olinda and shake Henry's hand.

The bridal party made their way through the crowded Goelzer kitchen. The odor of cooking was thick in the warm air. The old women cooks bustled about in woolen dresses covered by great aprons.

"In the front room," shouted one, motioning.

Stepping sideways, turning and twisting, they made their way.

Hannah stepped over the board seats and slid along until she was beside

Jenne Magafan, "Country Dance," c. 1941.

Olinda at the long bride's table. It was covered with snowy linen and set with thick white dishes.

A cook brought a glass pitcher. "For the bride's flowers," she said, and waited while Olinda soberly placed her pink carnations and sweetpeas within. She placed it in the center of the table directly in front of Olinda, moving the huge bride's cake to one side.

Bowls of butterball soup, with the tin dippers resting in their depths, were brought in by the cooks, and each guest at the bride's table ladled out the delicious yellow butterballs and finely cut noodles into his own individual soup bowl. The great platters of brown and sizzling turkey, goose, and chicken were brought in. The browned potatoes followed with rich dressing, pickles, and homemade bread.

Henry poured a small wine glass of whisky and passed it. The glass was returned, filled again and passed to the next one at the table, and so on until every one had drunk. Soberly, Hannah emptied the glass; stolidly, she set to eating her butterball soup.

Fingers curved around her ankle, then moved on. Hannah felt Olinda move slightly, and sensed that she moved one of her feet backward so that the unseen prowler could not touch it. At the same time, Hannah knew that Olinda put her other foot forward so that her slipper could be taken off, but in such a manner as would give the impression that she didn't want any one to steal her slipper.

One of the cooks came in with her right arm bandaged in a huge white cloth.

"I burn mineself mit the bride's soup," she shouted loudly, holding up her arm for all to see.

"Money, I got have so I pay a doctor. Two, three, might five dollar it take. I take up a collection so I pay him," she shouted.

Hannah watched while the fat cook squeezed around people, reaching her long-handled tin dipper across the table so that the nickels, dimes, and quarters could be tossed in. She slapped some of the men boisterously upon the back, telling them loudly to put in plenty of moneys.

Every one knew the cook's arm wasn't hurt.

As the men sampled the liquor, talk and laughter flowed louder.

Old lady Heist shouted for silence. She elbowed her way to the tables holding a huge white pillow in a fancy embroidered case. In the center of the pillow was a small paper basket surrounded by great paper roses. Across one corner stood two dolls, dressed as bride and groom.

"Money to buy the bride's bedclothes! The bride and her man got have some covers so they don't freeze when they sleep mit each other." Quarters dropped into the elaborate basket.

Hannah woodenly watched the whole procedure.

Daniel Kniemer held aloft Olinda's white bridal slipper. A great pink bow of crêpe paper and a pink carnation were tied around the instep.

"You're some bride's boys," Kniemer said in mock severity. "Why don't you take care mit the bride more better? There she sit mit cold feets. You want her to catch cold so Henry lose her right away?" He laughed loudly.

"Well, boys, I got the bride's slipper, here. You wasn't smart enough to keep it for her, so now you got to buy it back for her. You know a bride's got to have her slipper or she don't can dance mit you. If you want to dance mit the bride, she's gotta have shoes. You have to pay so you get it back.

"What am I bid for it?"

"Fifty cent," came a call from an adjoining table.

"Just fifty cents for this beautiful bride's slipper? Ach, too cheap. Who'll make it one dollar?"

"Two dollar," came a deep rumbling voice from the other room.

"You make it two dollars?" The auctioneer nodded to the bride's boys. Jake soberly nodded his head answering for all of them. This was serious business for the bride's boys had to chip in and buy the slipper at the highest price bid.

Three dollars, four, five, six, seven. Then it jumped to ten dollars. It sold at twelve dollars. It was too high. It meant that each of the four bride's boys would have to pay three dollars apiece. Resentment boiled up inside of Hannah, but none of the turmoil showed in her face. Then the older women brought out the wedding presents, placing them on the cleared table.

Henry and Olinda stood up, and according to the custom, Henry unwrapped each present, saying aloud to Olinda the name of the giver. Olinda took the present from his hand, held it aloft, and thanked the giver. She passed it around for each to see and feel, to decide whether it was worth much or little.

Expensive gifts: bedspreads, linens, curtains. Cheaper gifts of dishes, cooking utensils, towels and small useful articles from the fifteen cent store. A motto from the minister, "The Lord Is My Shepherd." More suitable, Hannah thought, would have been, "Forgive Us Our Sins." Foolish gifts: a bright pink baby hood in a purple box. Olinda held it up, a faint smile touching her blushing face. The crowd roared, and jokes and suggestive stories began.

Jake pressed Hannah's hand, giving her a slight shove. "Come on, let's get out," he whispered.

Daniel Kniemer blocked her way.

"Have a drink, Hannah," he urged, holding up a pitcher. Hannah shook her head and moved around him.

Old lady Kniemer, unable to get out, slid down and crawled under a table. Hannah helped her to her feet.

Hannah stood on the porch. The cool air blew upon her hot, powder-streaked face. The party was breaking up and some of the young people pushed past her.

"Come on, let's ride around a while before we go on to Schreissmillers'," someone shouted.

In the brightly decorated cars, laughing loudly, with horns honking, they tore down the dirt streets. It was four o'clock in the afternoon when they stopped near the Schreissmiller barn.

"Hurry, you don't wanta miss the dance," Jake shouted, pulling Hannah up the rickety ladder to the barn loft.

Benches were ranged along the walls. In one corner cake, sandwiches, and glasses were piled upon boards laid on trestles. This was for the midnight lunch. On one corner of the table was the wedding cake, waiting to be cut into the smallest pieces possible. Each piece would be auctioned off at midnight. Each piece would probably bring from ten to twenty-five cents.

In a far corner, near the window, were the two violinists, and Fred Hergenboch with his big harpboard, laid on a table in front of him.

Hannah looked at Fred's strong dark face and at his big husky body clad in his best suit. Fred was good looking. No wonder Frieda was proud of him. It was too bad Frieda couldn't be here, her baby had come just a week ago, a puny boy. Fred had had to come. He had the finest harpboard in all the country and played for all the weddings. His harpboard had a six-inch sounding board and was handmade of solid oak, with many wires strung across its broad surface. In the sunlight streaming through the window the brass bound corners gleamed and the many tightly strung wires glistened like silver.

Daniel Kniemer stepped up and held his hand high for silence.

"Everybody's what dance with the bride will have to pin a dollar bill on her dress, or they have to give one silver dollar. The womens can dance for fifty cents." He turned to Fred. "Go on with the dance," he ordered.

Fred struck the wires with two curled, soft-wood sticks. Instantly the room was filled with sound, as though a dozen violins were wailing in slow mournful tones.

Olinda and Henry stood stiff and straight before the harpboard, faces serious, looking down as Fred played the slow music. This was the bride's music. Fred's strong hands flew faster, the music quickened, and the two Ochmidt boys raised their violins and joined in the fast and joyous tune.

Henry danced this first dance with Olinda. The older men and women crowded around the open doorways and against the walls. Hannah saw her mother crying. Great tears were splashing down her cheeks and she was wiping them away with her broad hands. Tabia was comforting her, and Lizzie and Mary stood near. Lizzie straight as a rod, Mary dumbly patting Ana's shoulder.

This was the groom's dance, the only time during all the wedding dancing that he had to dance. He had it easy, Hannah thought, and Olinda will be sick. For the bride was compelled to dance every dance that was played.

Olinda had sinned but she would pay, Hannah thought grimly. She watched Olinda dance by with her long white veil tied to her arm by a pink satin ribbon. Rice and grain showered around Olinda and Henry. It fell on Olinda's hair, rattled as it hit the worn boards of the bare floor.

Mrs. Hergenboch, Fred's mother, who was Olinda's godmother, wriggled her way through the packed crowd and, raising her arm high, shouted, "Hockzeit!" (Wedding Time) and dashed a large dish to the floor, where it broke into bits. Olinda and Henry kept on dancing, and the scrunch of the broken dish under the soles of their shoes sent shivers racing up Hannah's back. Some of the older women and men stooped down and picked up the largest of the broken pieces. The smaller pieces were left to be ground into the floor.

Henry danced with Olinda for three rounds before the music stopped.

Jake nudged Hannah's arm. "You dance with Olinda next, Hannah. I'll pay for it."

Hannah started to shake her head, but she saw Ana nod and smile at her, so she consented. Jake pinned the dollar bill to Olinda's dress, Fred struck up the music, slow and mournful, and Olinda and Hannah stood side by side, facing the harpboard. When the music quickened Olinda and Hannah went into the dance. Every one watched.

Hannah felt that she dared not look at Olinda. She held the pudgy body lightly, but even so it seemed to her that all who danced with the bride must know. Round and round she danced, three whole rounds. It was the custom to allow members of the wedding party three rounds with the bride; all others paid their dollar for but two rounds. When each of the wedding party had danced with the bride, guests were allowed the privilege of dancing with her.

The old women smiled happily as they watched each man pin a dollar bill upon the bride's dress. Their jiggling feet kept time to the music. Some of the old women danced with each other, their faces wreathed in smiles.

Whenever the musicians stopped to rest the old men, as well as the younger, stamped their feet on the wide boards of the loft until it sounded like the thunder of stampeding cattle.

LITTLE BRITCHES

Ralph Moody

WHEN WE LIVED IN East Rochester, Mother used to let Grace and me take the money to pay the grocery bill every Saturday. Mr. Blaisdell always gave us a little bag of candy when we came in to pay, but since we had moved out to the ranch we never got any. I liked all kinds of chocolate, but I liked the bitter kind Mother baked cakes with best. The last Christmas before we came west, she had made fudge with some of it. It was the best candy I ever tasted. I got thinking about fudge, and one night I asked her when she was going to make some more. She said maybe she'd make some when Christmas came, but sugar cost too much to be using it up in candy we didn't need.

The more I thought about fudge, the more I thought about the bar of Baker's chocolate we got with our last groceries, and the more I wanted some of it. Baked beans, pea soup, and fried sidemeat had tasted all right before, but thinking about chocolate, they didn't even make me feel hungry.

The next afternoon when I was helping Father on the winnower, I was thinking of what he had said about going to meet your troubles and how much less they would be. I don't know if I'd even stopped thinking about that when I began daydreaming about chocolate again. It was right then I got the idea: If I should whack a chunk off the end of that bar of chocolate, Mother would be sure to miss it. Then, before she had any idea who had done it, I could confess and probably wouldn't even get a spanking for it, any more than I did for going up to Two Dog's.

I waited till she was out feeding the chickens, then told Father I was thirsty and thought I'd go in for a drink of water. All the time I was going into the house and getting the bar of chocolate down out of the cupboard, my head kept wanting to think about tearing boards off my house, but I wouldn't let it, because I told myself that was only when you did things you shouldn't and then lied about it. I wasn't going to lie at all about the chocolate.

I heard Mother coming just when I had the knife ready to whack off the end of the bar, so I had to slip it into the front of my blouse and pick up the water dipper quick. Before I went back to help Father I went to the barn and hid the bar of chocolate back of the currycomb box.

All the rest of the afternoon, I didn't like to look at Father. I tried to get him to let me go over to see Willie Aldivote, but he wouldn't. Every time he spoke it made me jump, and my hands got shaking so I couldn't hold the pieces still enough for him to solder. He asked me what was the matter, and I told him it was nothing except that my hands were getting cold. I knew he didn't believe me, and every time he looked my way my heart started pounding, because he could always tell what was going on inside my head. It seemed it would never come time to go for the cows. I didn't want the chocolate any more; I just wanted a chance to put it back without being caught.

On the way out for the cows, my heart stopped pounding so hard, and I could think better. I hadn't really stolen the whole bar of chocolate, because I had only meant to take a little piece, and that's as much as I would have taken if Mother hadn't come in just when she did. If I put back the whole bar, I wouldn't have done anything wrong at all. I'd nearly decided I would do it, but just thinking so much about chocolate made my tongue almost taste the smooth bitterness of it. It didn't seem as if it would be very wrong if I only took a small piece. Then I got thinking that if I took a sharp knife and cut about half an inch off the end—with a good clean slice—Mother might never notice it.

I was nearly out to where the cows were picketed when I remembered what Father had said when I got my trap: some of the money in his pouch was mine because I had earned it. Why wouldn't it be all right to figure that the bar of chocolate had been bought with my own money, and in that way I wouldn't be stealing it at all. That seemed to fix everything, and I got planning how I would go out to the barn every night after school and whittle off a little piece of chocolate.

I could have felt all right about the whole business if it hadn't been for Mother's reading. Sometimes, on Sunday afternoons, she used to read just to Father, but any of us could stay in the house and listen if we wanted to. He often had her read Shakespeare's plays, and the one he liked best was about Hamlet. I liked it, too, and used to listen every time she read it.

I had just pulled the picket pins and was heading the cows home when the bad king's prayer came into my head, and I couldn't get it out. I tried to think about how Hi dived off his horse and came up on his feet, and about Two Dog, and King, and everything else, but my head kept saying, "Oh, my offense is rank," until I thought I'd go crazy.

We were nearly to the railroad track when I decided to leave the whole matter

Frank Mechau, "Wild Horse Race," n.d.

to the Lord, and twisted out a dried soapweed stalk with seed pods on it. When you slung one of them up in the air it would wobble and twist all around so that you never knew which way it would come down. I told myself that if it came down with the pods to the west I'd take the whole bar of chocolate back. If it came down pointed to the south, I'd take half an inch off the end, but if it came down pointed to the east, it had been bought with my own money and it wouldn't be stealing to keep it.

I swung the pod stalk around my head a few times and flung it as high as I could, then I shut my eyes tight till I heard it land. When I opened them the pod end of the stalk was pointed almost toward the west, but not quite. It was a little bit toward the south.

There was a bright moon when I went to bed that night, and it was sharp and frosty. I couldn't go to sleep and kept trying to remember how much the pod end of that stalk had really been pointing toward the south. At last I heard Father put King outside for the night, and a little later when I peeked under my curtain I could see that he had blown out the lamp.

I pulled my overalls up over my nightgown and took my shoes in my hand. After I was out in the yard I slipped them on and took the axe from the chopping block. It was good and sharp, and I was sure I could peel off a smooth, thin slice of chocolate with it.

It was dark as tar inside the barn, but I felt along the wall for the currycomb box, and lifted the chocolate box out from behind it. King had followed me, and I nearly fell over him when I was groping for the door, but it was so light outside that you could almost have read a book. I shook the bar out of the box, unwrapped it, and laid it on the lower rail of the corral fence. Just as I was starting to cut it with the axe, Father said, "Son!"

I couldn't think of a thing to say, but I grabbed up the bar of chocolate and shoved it inside the bib of my overalls before I turned around. He picked me up by the shoulder straps—just as he'd have picked up a kitten that had wet on the floor—and took me over to the wood pile. I didn't know anybody could spank as hard as he spanked me with that little piece of board. It felt as if my bottom were going to catch fire at every lick.

Then he stood me down and asked me if I thought I'd deserved it. He said it wasn't so much that I took the chocolate, as it was the way I took it, and because I tried to hide it when he spoke to me. But it was the next thing he said that hurt me worse than the spanking.

He said, "Son, I realize a lot better than you think I do that you have been helping to earn the living for the family. We might say the chocolate was yours in the first place. If you had asked Mother or me for it, you could have had it without a question, but I won't have you being sneaky about things. Now if you'd rather keep your own money separate from the family's, so you can buy the things you want, I think it might be a good idea."

I never knew till then how much I wanted my money to go in with Father's. Ever since we bought the cows, I had been able to feel I had a part in all the new things we were buying to make ourselves real ranchers, and it looked as though it were all slipping away from me. I had felt I was beginning to be a man, but I guess I was still just a baby, because I hid my face against Father's stomach and begged him to let me put my money in with his.

Father hadn't been coughing nearly so much that fall as he used to, but he coughed and it seemed as if he choked a little before he answered me. He said he didn't want a sneaky partner, but if I could be open and aboveboard he didn't know a man he'd rather be in business with.

I couldn't help crying some more when he told me that; not because my bottom was still burning, but just because I loved him. I told him I'd never be sneaky again, and I'd always ask him before I did things. We walked to the house together. At the bunkhouse door he shook hands with me, and said, "Good night, partner." When I went to sleep, my hand was still hurting—good—from where he squeezed it when we shook hands.

FOUNDER'S PRAISE

Joanne Greenberg

IT GOT SO THAT THE old man would sit in his chair by the front window and conduct the storm. When it scoured up from the south, he would dare it to drown them. When the storm lay its gritty black winds about them, he would shake his fists at it. Sometimes the wind would change in mid-storm, layering the colors—gray and black and red, and their own pale earth flung back at them, after a ride to Texas or Oklahoma. It was a game the winds were playing, setting down red dunes with black edges in one storm and carrying them off in the next, and whipping three years of dry seeds through air suddenly gone solid.

Now the ground was so dry that it wouldn't even clump if it was wetted. Inside the houses, the dust that had forced its way through every crack blew the air dark. They wore it, ate it, breathed it, spat it out black from dry throats every morning. "Like livin' in a coal mine," Charlie cursed. "Dark as a mine, even in the daytime."

When the winds were at their worst, there was nothing to do but stay inside. They wore dampened rags over their faces to keep the dust from their lungs. Between the dry storms, they worked until they were exhausted. The old man had to dig the house out, Edgar the northeast side of the barn. The wind drove dry bushes and the roots of old trees against their fences and piled the rubbish of distant farms against their outbuildings. The well went foul and silted up. There was no water, and they had to haul emergency supplies from town. More and more families picked up and left. There came to be a place in the services on Sunday when one or two or three men would get up and announce that they were leaving. "Anyone who feels I got a debt to 'em, come on over and take what's fair. There's tools and things—the wife's got a tea set and a cherry-wood chest." And he might laugh a little, embarrassed, at the joke he had not meant, a laugh that had no humor in it.

The Bissets did not see them go. Their place was east of town and no one went east.

The road beside the farm was a minor one, used once and now forsaken for the larger one, a mile or so to the north, that led directly through the town. On this road, people said, the cars and carts and horses and wagons moved in a slow stream. Stopping in town, people would look around through shocked, road-dulled eyes. "We thought it would be better here—they told us it was better here—" and they would go on.

It moved Edgar to see his father's rage. The old man had more energy in his wiry body than Edgar did—enough to curse the dunes that danced and changed, east, southeast, south-southeast, back and forth, changing color, as the wind changed direction. He noticed that after every blow the old man would shoulder his shovel and go to the same banked place that buried the front porch, the same downed fence. Edgar wondered how long the old man's spirit would last. He wondered how long he and Charlie would be kept from insanity, how much less they could eat and not starve to death, how many weeks it was to ruin. He did not speak. He seldom spoke five words at all between sunup and dark.

At the end of March the winds stopped abruptly and on the third of April it rained. It was a black rain, full of the north-winding dust that had been held in the clouds, and it left black grit wherever it fell. After the rain, Edgar drove their remaining four cows to browse on whatever new grass might have come up. The cows looked skeletal, and they barely had the strength to move. Erosion had made a cleft through what had once been Mutcher's farm, and at the bottom of this cleft there was a protected place and the barest haze of new grass. Edgar left them there and went scouting in the arroyos and dry creek beds for whatever else there might be. By noon he had worked all the way around to the east of the farm without finding anything on which the cows could feed. At lunch, Ralph told Edgar to go on scouting to the south for new grass. He would bring the cows back before dark. It was a scanty meal, barely enough to keep Edgar from cramping as he walked in and out of the eroded places in the vast, flat land. Edgar kept looking up at the sun, which seemed suddenly cold. He walked quickly to keep warm. Here and there he found a web of grass, hair-thin and almost too delicate to see on the south-facing sides of the arroyos. Too little. Too fragile. He noted the places and started for home.

As he walked, he thought of the cows, once good stock. The dust had filtered into their fodder as it had into everything else, and their teeth had been ground down, almost by half. They were so thin—

He was crossing the broom field near home when he saw the old man coming toward him, running, his arms out as though to stop himself from falling. Edgar began to run. As they neared each other, Edgar heard his father yelling his name and he ran faster, until they met between barn and house and Charlie Dace came running up from where he was working.

"Edgar!" the old man gasped. "The cows!"

"What?"

"The cows has been took!"

"What, stolen?"

"Took, took!" The old man coughed, gasping for breath, while Edgar in an agony of frustration almost jumped from one foot to the other.

"The cows has been took!" the old man finally gasped.

"Not stole, took, took against nature!" And before he recovered, half staggering, he led them to the old Mutcher place and the draw.

Looking down the draw, they saw all four cows, wandering aimlessly, having eaten all the grass there was. "You—don't—see—!" The old man gasped. "But I seen. Growin'. Growin' grass. The cows—is growin' grass!"

Edgar caught Charlie's eye. They might have laughed, except that Ralph's voice had hysteria in it, and his face showed terror sharp as the marks of a slap.

"What do you think?" Charlie murmured under his breath. Edgar shook his head. Slowly, they walked toward the bony cows.

"They seem okay," Charlie whispered. "Still got their winter hair, and they are awful skinny, but they seem okay."

Looking back, they could see Ralph standing above them, motionless now. "You reckon he's lost his mind?" Charlie whispered. Edgar said nothing. They went closer.

At first it seemed like winter hair, a thicker coat against the winds, and then they saw that what the old man said was true. The cows were green. Patches of new-sprouted prairie grass were growing from the backs and down the flanks of Juliet, Surprise, and Independence. Movie Star, whose place was near the far wall of the barn, had the left side of her body evenly covered with prairie grass, young clover, and wild wheat. Neither of the men wanted to touch the cows—there was a whiff of the old man's horror in them—but Edgar made himself remember that he had been on battlefields, and seen grass growing between the fingers of a severed hand. After a moment, he pushed himself forward and grabbed at Movie Star, raking at the green on her flank. She lowed and pulled away from him. Charlie, beside him, was cursing in a self-absorbed monotone as he pulled at the green weeds caught among the rotting hair of Independence's back.

"You can't get under it!" Charlie cried. "The dust has been drove up right into the skin and it's all matted in there with roots. These cows must be carryin' twenty, thirty pounds of dirt on 'em."

"You ever hear of this before?" Edgar asked him.

"One time, a long time ago, I heard a fellow tell about a tornado come through one year and done like that, drove dirt into cows' hides so hard it couldn't be got out."

"What happened to the cows?" Edgar asked.

Charlie stood, embarrassed, fussing with Movie Star and then Independence. "Man didn't say," he muttered.

Edgar sighed. Charlie had kept to himself so long that he had lost the talent for telling a convincing lie.

The next week another sandstorm crested and broke on the fields. Ropes of dust were held upright like cobras swaying from a basket. And the old man shouted curses at the storm in his dried-out plains voice. It lasted for four days. The air in the house was gray. The drying, abrading dust found each hair-thin fault and secret way inward to the heart of the house and the men there. They coughed and spat gray. They burned their kerosene lamps all day and still had to grope for doorways.

When the night-pots were full, the old man went to dump them out the back door away from the wind, but it saw him and turned and blew his piss, turned black with its moment in the air, back in his face. At the sight of him crusted, black, and stinking, Charlie and Edgar had a fit of hysterical laughter, but they couldn't laugh long because they began to choke—the air had gone solid again.

When it was over, they went out to the barn and slaughtered the cows. The hides were useless, the green patches gone to mold, rotten under their knives. Although the meat was not good, they boiled, smoked, pickled, and oven-dried it. They used every jar that could hold a seal, and processed them in the sour black water that the well pumped. They were stupid with exhaustion and threw the saved parts out with the rotten; there was no time to boil and settle the water they needed. So much was wasted and useless that the old man cried in rage.

BUTCHER'S CROSSING

John Williams

By THE TIME HE GOT back to the camp, the sun had gone behind the western range of mountains; there was a chill in the air that went through his clothing and touched his sweaty skin. Charley Hoge trotted out from the camp to meet him.

"How many?" Charley Hoge called.

"Miller counted a hundred and thirty-five," Andrews said.

" 'I God," Charley Hoge said. "A big one."

Near the camp, Andrews halted his horse and untied the rope from the saddle horn.

"Nice little calf you got," Charley Hoge said. "Make good eating. You going to dress her down, or you want me to?"

"I'll dress her," Andrews said. But he made no movement. He stood looking at the calf, whose open transparent eyes were filmed over blankly with a layer of dust.

After a moment, Charley Hoge said: "I'll help you fix up a scaffold."

The two men went to the area where earlier Charley Hoge had been working on the corral for the livestock. The corral, roughly hexagonal in shape, had been completed; but there were still a few long aspen poles lying about. Charley Hoge pointed out three of equal length and they dragged them back to where the buffalo calf lay. They pounded the ends of the poles into the ground, and arranged them in the form of a tripod. Andrews mounted his horse, and lashed the poles together at the top. Charley Hoge threw the rope, which was still attached to the calf's head, over the top of the tripod, and Andrews tied the loose end to his saddle horn. He backed his horse up until the calf was suspended, its hooves barely brushing the short grass. Charley Hoge held the rope until Andrews returned to the tripod and secured the rope firmly to the top, so that the buffalo would not drop.

The buffalo hung; they surveyed it for a moment without speaking. Charley Hoge went back to his campfire; Andrews stood before the hung calf. In the distance, across the valley, he saw a movement; it was Schneider and Miller returning. Their horses went in a swift walk across the valley bed. Andrews took a deep breath, and put his knife carefully to the exposed belly of the calf.

He worked more slowly this time. After he had made the cuts in the belly, around the throat, and around the ankles, he carefully peeled the hide back so that it hung loosely down the sides of the animal. Then, reaching high above the hump, he ripped the hide from the back. It came off smoothly, with only a few small chunks of the flesh adhering to it. With his knife he scraped the largest of these chunks off, and spread the skin on the grass, flesh side downward, as he had seen Schneider do. While he stood back, looking down at his hide, Miller and Schneider rode up beside him and dismounted.

Miller, his face streaked with the black residue of powder smoke and smears of brownish-red blood, looked at him dully for a moment, and then looked at the hide spread on the ground. He turned and shambled unsteadily toward the campsite.

"Looks like a clean job," Schneider said, walking around the hide. "You won't have no trouble. Course, it's easier when your carcass is hanging."

"How did you and Miller do?" Andrews asked.

"We didn't get halfway through. We'll be working most of the night."

"I wish I could help," Andrews said.

Schneider walked over to the skinned calf and slapped the naked rump of it. "Nice fat little calf. She'll make good eating."

Andrews went to the calf and knelt; he fumbled among the knives in his case. He raised his head to Schneider, but he did not look at him.

"What do I do?" he asked.

"What?"

"What do I do first? I've never dressed an animal before."

"My God," Schneider said quietly. "I keep forgetting. Well, first you better de-gut her. Then I'll tell you how to cut her up."

Charley Hoge and Miller came around the tall chimney rock and leaned against it, watching. Andrews hesitated for a moment, then stood up. He pushed the point of his knife against the breastbone of the calf, and poked until he found the softness of the stomach. He clenched his teeth, and pushed the knife in the flesh, and drew the knife downward. The heavy, coiled blue-and-white guts, thicker than his forearm, spilled out from the clean edge of the cut. Andrews closed his eyes, and pulled the knife downward as quickly as he could. As he straightened up, he felt something warm on his shirtfront; a gush of dark, half-clotted blood had dropped from the opened cavity. It spilled upon his shirt and dripped down upon the front of his trousers. He jumped backward. His quick movement sent the calf rocking slowly on the rope, and made the thick entrails slowly emerge from the widening cut. With a heavy, liquid, sliding thud they spilled upon the ground; like something alive, the edge of the mass slid toward Andrews and covered the tops of his shoes.

Schneider laughed loudly, slapping his leg. "Cut her loose!" he shouted. "Cut her loose before she crawls all over you!"

Andrews swallowed the heavy saliva that spurted in his mouth. With his left hand he followed the thick slimy main gut up through the body cavity; he watched his forearm disappear into the wet warmth of the body. When his left hand came upon the end of the gut, he reached his other hand with the knife up beside it, and sliced blindly, awkwardly at the tough tube. The rotten smell of the buffalo's half-digested food billowed out; he held his breath, and hacked more desperately with his knife. The tube parted, and the entrails spilled down, gathering in the lower part of the body. With both arms, he scooped the guts out of the cavity until he could find the other attachment; he cut it away and tore the insides from the calf with desperate scooping motions, until they spread in a heavy mass on the ground around his feet. He stepped back, pale, breathing heavily through his opened mouth; his arms and hands, held out from his body, dripping with blood, were trembling.

Miller, still leaning against the chimney rock, called to Schneider: "Let's have some of that liver, Fred."

Schneider nodded, and took a few steps to the swinging carcass. With one hand he steadied it, and with the other reached into the open cavity. He jerked his arm; his hand came out carrying a large piece of brownish purple meat. With a few quick strokes of his knife, he sliced it in two, and tossed the larger of the pieces across to Miller. He caught the liver in the scoop of his two hands, and clutched it to his chest so that it would not slide out of his grasp. Then he lifted it to his mouth, and took a large bite from it; the dark blood oozed from the meat, ran down the sides of his chin, and dropped to the ground. Schneider grinned and took a bite from his piece. Still grinning, chewing slowly, his lips dark red from the meat, he extended the meat toward Andrews.

"Want a chew?" he asked, and laughed.

Andrews felt the bitterness rise in his throat; his stomach contracted in a sudden spasm, and the muscles of his throat pulled together, choking him. He turned and ran a few paces from the men, leaned against a tree, doubled over, and retched. After a few moments, he turned to them.

"You finish it up," he called to them. "I've had enough."

Without waiting for a reply, he turned again and walked toward the spring that trickled down some seventy-five yards beyond their camp. At the spring he removed his shirt; the blood from the buffalo was beginning to stiffen on his undershirt. As quickly as he could, he removed the rest of his clothing and stood in the late afternoon shadow, shivering in the cool air. From his chest to below his navel was the brownish red stain of buffalo blood; and in removing his clothing, his arms and hands had brushed against other parts of his body so that he was blotched with stains hued from a pale vermilion to a deep brownish crimson. He thrust his hands into the icy pool formed by the spring. The cold water clotted the blood, and for a moment he feared that he could not remove it from his skin. Then it floated away in solid tendrils; and he splashed water on his arms, his chest, and his stomach, gasping at the cold, straining his lungs to gather air against the repeated shocks of it.

A TENDERFOOT IN COLORADO

Richard Baxter Townshend

ON A BLAZING HOT NOON in early summer I was riding around over the range looking for a stray horse. The endless rolling surface of the prairie seemed absolutely bare of cattle, so far, at least, as one could depend upon what the eye told one. For it was one of the days when the "smoke" was strong, "smoke" being the name we used to give to the mirage. Out in Colorado all the baffling uncertainty of vision that makes for mystery, all illusion, all glamour, belong to the dazzling hours of midday and not to the gloaming.

In the early morning, and towards evening, there is no "smoke" and no mystery, for out there on the great plains, five thousand feet above sea level in the very driest part of the American continent, the air is of an incredible transparency. Forty miles from my ranch the huge red granite dome of Pike's Peak heaved up its beetling crags against the western sky, and at sunrise every crack and crevice of the rocks showed as sharp and clear-cut as though they were only half a mile off. Northwards the stem of one solitary pine, ten miles away, made a thin black line against the sky, and I once knew a single horseman detected by the keen sight of a frontiers-man standing in front of my ranch over on Holcombe bluffs across a distance of fully two leagues.

But as the summer sun mounted high and poured his scorching rays on the bare ground there came a change. The lowest layer of air absorbed the heat from the heated soil and presently began to rise up in wavering currents such as one may observe to quiver perpetually over the mouth of a furnace.

Through this flickering veil of mirage all things were seen distorted, shifting, uncertain. A solitary soapweed a hundred yards away might suddenly stand up and develop legs and become a horse; again the horse's back would swell and arch itself into a great hump, and lo! there stood a buffalo instead; presto! the buffalo would sink, elongate himself, and be transformed into a thicket of reeds, shaking in the wind, alongside a pool of clear delicious water. And then in a moment the scene would change back again, the illusion pass, and the common soapweed was a weed once more.

However, I had no time to waste over fancies, but pushed on in search of my stray horse, on whom, if chance willed, and the "smoke" were not too confusing, I might happen at any minute. ...

&   &   &

I turned back to the rolling prairie, ... and as I went I noticed half a dozen dun and brindle Texas cows, who had already slaked their thirst, travelling steadily away from the water in the same direction as myself. A few young heifers and steers accompanied them, though the mass of the cattle, as I well knew, would stay by the water till the heat of the day was over; but this party of long-horned, long-legged Texas ladies clearly had business elsewhere. They struck into one of the innumerable cattle trails leading from the high pastures to the water and pressed up it, travelling one close behind the other at a steady walk that occasionally became a trot. I rode parallel to them, curious to see the goal they were making for so eagerly.

Up we went into the high rolling sand-hills, and there, in the middle of them, in a little cup-like hollow, I saw a regular Texas nursery. Eight little dun-coloured Texas calves lay there, squatted close to the sandy ground with which their coats matched so well, their heads lying out flat, with the chins pressed down on the sand, just as little antelope fawns would have crouched. In this pose they were all but invisible. Beside them lay two elderly Texas cows, whose office had been to guard the crèche.

The mothers, who had travelled till now in perfect silence, began to low loudly and lovingly when they caught sight of their offspring, and in a moment each young hopeful had jumped up and rushed to his own dam, where his wriggling tail and nuzzling head, the busy lips frothing with milk, soon showed he was getting the dinner he had waited for so patiently. Meantime the two guardian cows had risen to their feet, and lost no time in starting off in their turn to make their trip to the water, leaving their own two calves safe in the care of the rest of the band.

The system of mutual protection was perfect. Brer' Wolf might prowl around and watch with hungry eyes till his lips watered—there was no chance for him to get veal for his dinner while the sharp horns of those fierce Texas mothers guarded their children. Broadly speaking, one might say the Texas cow, the cow of the wilderness, had evolved an institution that has enabled her and her offspring to survive the dangers of savage life.

This institution has been long superseded by the civilized life of the farm for the well-bred short-horn cow; but take her away from her sheltered surroundings and turn her loose on the range, and she is as helpless as most duchesses would be if left on a desert island. The pedigree daughter of fifty prize-winners must inevitably succumb to the dangers of her new life unless she has initiative enough to revert to the social system of her own primitive ancestors who fought with the wolf and bear in the woodlands of early Britain.

Artist unknown, "Cutting Out," from New Colorado and The Santa Fe Trail *by A.A. Hayes, Jr., A.M., 1880.*

THE GAMBLER

Baxter Black

When the corn's all gone to tassel in the Colorado fall
And the April future's crowdin' ninety cents,
An electric kinda feelin' gets to floatin' in the air
That makes you take your leave of common sense.

Them Texas calves look better than they ever have before.
You can buy'em now for eight cents on the dime.
And lay'em in the feedyard at under eighty-five.
They're ripe for pickin', boy, and now's the time.

So you call the order buyer and put him on the road.
You want to get'em before the market peaks.
You tell the cattle foreman to get the crew in gear
And you fill 'er up, eight thousand in two weeks!

They arrive in good condition for a thousand mile trip.
The weather's holdin' pretty much the same
And you finally get'em processed and started up on feed
Then, by gosh, it settles into rain.

The pens that looked so pretty with the straw all scattered 'round
Become a quagmire; puddles, ponds and bogs.
The mud behind the feed bunk is gettin' ankle deep
Them calves look less like cattle, more like hogs.

It hangs all gray and cloudy as the days drip slowly by
'Neath overcast November, sorry skies.
The cowboys' workin' overtime to pull the sick ones out
But they keep dyin', dyin' just like flies.

There ain't no magic potion, nothin' seems to work
The vet'inary's done pulled out his hair.
The crew is gettin' owly and fightin' with theyselves
And lookin' back it just don't seem quite fair.

'Cause you had them cattle bought right, it really shoulda worked.
You didn't plan on losin' ten percent.
Plus the fact May futures down the limit once again
Plus all the time and money that you spent.

But then you say, "Aw, what the hell, tomorrow it might change.
There ain't no point in settin' here agrievin'
If corn goes down to one O five and calves hit two fifteen
Then I may stand a chance of breakin' even!"

"The springtime winds'll dry me out, by summer I'll be healed
And ready for another free-fer-all.
'Cause I don't need Las Vegas, just a set of Texas calves
And Colorado weather in the fall."

THE CATTLEMEN

Mari Sandoz

SOME DEDICATED MEN

THOROUGHLY DISGUSTED AT last, Charlie Goodnight gave up ranching in Texas. Too many Indians and no use begging for help from that Reconstruction gathering of scalawags and carpetbaggers down at Austin. ... But the mining regions of the Rockies seemed to have some money left. ... Steers worth at the most $8 or $10 in Texas brought $60 up there.

🐾 🐾 🐾

It would take real time, money, and sand to swing down an unknown trail through waterless country to get around the Comanches, or most of them. Yet Charlie Goodnight, an old cowman at thirty, insisted he was heading for Colorado and going around the south to do it. He gathered up little herds of loose, unmarked cattle here and there ..., claiming they belonged to him but with no brand to prove it.

Old Charlie, as some called him now, was convinced by his wartime experience with the Rangers, and since, that any crossing of the Indian country of northwest Texas was to be avoided.

🐾 🐾 🐾

Goodnight also knew something of the country he would have to cross on the southern swing and the turn westward to the Pecos and up its briny, forbidding canyon and beyond. The reputation of the stretch to the Pecos was bad ever since the first cattle came to Texas with Coronado. The other two ranchers who were to go with Charlie Goodnight to Colorado got scared out just chewing it over. In the end the old rancher Oliver Loving, who had tried to talk Goodnight against it, too, asked to go along.

🐾 🐾 🐾

Goodnight had planned his drive in the hope that there was some nice money loose for beef in Colorado and certainly there would be grass to hold any stock not readily salable. Now another and, by his planned route a more immediate, hope came up—the hope of selling beef to fill Indian contracts in New Mexico on the way. There was even a chance of cornering a little of the often-exorbitant prices that some Indian contractors seemed to get.

   ❧ ❧ ❧

So, in 1866, trailing a mixed herd of 2,000 steers, cows, and calves, with eighteen hands, mostly armed, they set out, the fifty-four-year-old tough and range-hardened Loving in charge of the herd.

PULLING FOR NEW GRASS

Perhaps it was true that in Colorado a cattleman could still make a living.

He let his impatient horse out, pointing his hat at arm's length before him, signaling the direction. So Goodnight scouted the trail for water, for range and bed ground, doubling back to give his signals. Loving, behind him, knew how to get the most from the men and the herd. All but the two point riders, the best men of the outfit, shifted positions daily to relieve those on the dusty side and those riding drag—always keeping the herd strung out well and yet close enough to let them feel each other, hold them in an unbroken file to crawl like a thin, dark, thousand-segmented joint snake over the rolling prairie. It was a pretty route through the mirage region, the Phantom Hill country. By then the herd was a fine traveling unit, the leader taking his place every morning, keeping it day after day. As in most beef herds, the steers had traveling companions and when separated they raised their heads to get wind of each other, bawling until they got together. Each strong young cow gathered her own following within the herd. As in most good-sized drives, there were a few muleys, born hornless, and within a few days these bedded down together, a little apart. As usual, too, there was a loner or two who went prowling up one side of the herd and down the other, apparently searching for the never lost. Sometimes there was an outcast, hooked at everywhere, with even the muleys making the horning motion. All these, unless steadied down early, ended up with the drags, with the poor, the old, and the very young.

   ❧ ❧ ❧

Loving had the herd traveling very well in the heat and dust by the time they reached the head of the Middle Concho, where they rested and fed before starting over the dry, horse-killing jump of around eighty miles to the Pecos, with twelve, fifteen miles considered a good drive in the burning sun. Then, after days without water, and the smell of it from the river to drive the cattle wild, they would have to pass the poison lakes marked by whitened bones long before the first Spaniard rode through that way. They had been warned against the poison lakes, the alkali strong enough to kill everything that drank the water, and just beyond was the Pecos, with most of the bank very steep, the crossing a swift, swimming current.

Goodnight and Loving watered the herd, steers, cows, and calves, with all they would drink and filled the canteens and the water barrels of the grub wagon to overflowing. Then in the afternoon they pointed the herd to follow the sloping sun out upon the pale baked earth.

They trailed late that first evening, made dry camp, and pushed on early. While the Longhorn on the range often went without water for three days, driving dried out stock as it did men. The second night the herd was too thirsty to bed down, many trying to break back as they walked and milled all night so it took most of the men to hold them. Goodnight realized that this wouldn't do—the cattle had walked enough on the bed ground to take them most of the way to the Pecos. He got the herd started very early, knowing that the cattle would have to be pushed today, the faltering whipped up by the sleepy, worn-out cowboys under the sun that shimmered in great rippling mirage lakes ahead. The canteens dried up, the water barrels began to rattle in the wagon, and the dust rose in bitter white clouds that grayed them all. It cracked the lips under the protecting kerchiefs tied loosely enough to be drawn up over the nose, almost to the hat-brim, the dust-rimmed eyes bloodshot and burning; it stung and burned in the sweated saddle galls.

🐜 🐜 🐜

Charlie Goodnight was suddenly less angry with Texas, less impatient for a look at Colorado ranch possibilities. He hurried back on the 700-mile trail to gather up another herd for the Indians before winter. He rode ahead, followed by a pack mule carrying the $12,000 in gold

🐜 🐜 🐜

Up near Fort Sumner Oliver Loving put a little meat on the cows and calves the Indian agent had turned back, and then trailed them slowly to the Raton Mountains, the Arkansas River, and beyond, blazing the trail most of the way. Near Denver he sold the whole lot to John W. Iliff for his range in northeast Colorado, in the heart of a new cattle region.

Down in Texas, Goodnight collected his second herd of the summer, 1,200 head, all steers, able to travel fast and strong.

🐜 🐜 🐜

By now it was too late for the Indian contracts, and when the herd finally reached Sumner Goodnight headed it on toward Colorado. From the Raton Pass region he looked down over the mountain slopes to the great fall-yellowed grasslands of the upper Arkansas River so like the cloud-shadowed swells of a golden sea. He pointed the herd along the north-flowing creeks and up near the head of one of these, the Apishapa, Goodnight stopped. The canyon was around twenty miles long, not very deep, but with walls steep enough so it was practically inaccessible except at the two ends, which could be kept closed very handily by casual line riding. The creek, between banks lined by box elders, shyly sank out of sight during the day and ran again when the sun settled behind the canyon walls. The cowboys joked about it, glad they could laugh after the very grueling drive.

Here Goodnight established his ranch in what seemed to him a most beautiful cow country and perhaps his would be the first extensive cattle venture in southern Colorado. At least he had the world to himself again, with, so far as any of them knew, little danger from raiding Indians, probably more danger from outlaws. So they turned the cattle loose and set to cutting pines for a log cabin.

SECTION V

MINING TOWNS

CASEY'S TABLE D'HOTE

Eugene Field

Oh, them days on Red Hoss Mountain, when the skies was fair 'nd blue;
When the money flowed like likker, 'nd the folks was brave 'nd true!
When the nights wuz crisp 'nd balmy, 'nd the camp wuz all astir,
With the joints all throwed wide open 'nd no sheriff to demur!
Oh, them times on Red Hoss Mountain in the Rockies fur away—
There's no sich place nor times like them as I kin find to-day!
What though the camp hez busted? I seem to see it still
A-lyin', like it love it, on that big 'nd warty hill;
And I feel a sort of yearnin' 'nd a chokin' in my throat
When I think of Red Hoss Mountain 'nd of Casey's tabble dote!

Well, yes; it's true I struck it rich, but that don't cut a show
When one is old 'nd feeble 'nd it's nigh his time to go;
The money that he's got in bonds or carries to invest
Don't figger with a codger who has lived a life out West;
Us old chaps like to set around, away from folks 'nd noise,
'Nd think about the sights we seen and things we done when boys;
The which is why I love to set 'nd think of them old days
When all us Western fellers got the Colorado craze,—
And that is why I love to set around all day 'nd gloat
On thoughts of Red Hoss Mountain 'nd of Casey's tabble dote.

This Casey wuz an Irishman—you'd know it by his name
And by the facial features appertainin' to the same,
He'd lived in many places 'nd had done a thousand things,
From the noble art of actin' to the work of dealin' kings,
But, somehow, hadn't caught on; so, driftin' with the rest,
He drifted for a fortune to the undeveloped West,
And he come to Red Hoss Mountain when the little camp wuz new,
When the money flowed like likker, 'nd the folks wuz brave 'n true;
And, havin' been a stewart on a Mississippi boat,
He opened up a caffy 'nd he run a tabble dote.

The bar wuz long 'nd rangey, with a mirrer on the shelf,
'Nd a pistol, so that Casey, when required, could help himself;
Down underneath there wuz a row of bottle beer 'nd wine,

'Nd a keg of Burbun whiskey of the run of '59;
Upon the walls wuz pictures of hosses 'nd of girls,—
Not much on dress, perhaps, but strong on records 'nd on curls!
The which had been identified with Casey in the past,—
The hosses and the girls, I mean,—and both wuz mighty fast!
But all these fine attractions wuz of precious little note
By the side of what wuz offered at Casey's tabble dote.

There wuz half-a-dozen tables altogether in the place,
And the tax you had to pay upon vitals wuz a case;
The boardin'-houses in the camp protested 'twuz a shame
To patronize a robber, which this Casey wuz the same!
They said a case was robbery to tax for ary meal;
But Casey tended strictly to his biz, 'nd let 'em squeal;
And presently the boardin'-houses all began to bust,
While Casey kept on sawin' wood 'nd layin' in the dust;
And oncet a trav'lin' editor from Denver City wrote
A piece back to his paper, puffin' Casey's tabble dote.

A tabble dote is different from orderin' aller cart:
In one case you git all there is, in t'other, only part!
And Casey's tabble dote began in French—as all begin,—
And Casey's ended with the same, which is to say, with "vin";
But in between wuz every kind of reptile, bird, 'nd beast,
The same like you can git in high-toned restauraws down east;
'Nd windin' up wuz cake or pie, with coffee demy tass,
Or, sometimes, floatin' Ireland in a soothin' kind of sass
That left a sort of pleasant ticklin' in a feller's throat,
'Nd made him hanker after more of Casey's tabble dote.

The very recollection of them puddin's 'nd them pies
Brings a yearnin' to my buzzum 'nd the water to my eyes;
'Nd seems like cookin' nowadays aint what it used to be
In camp in Red Hoss Mountain in that year of '63;
But, maybe, it is better, 'nd, maybe, I'm to blame—
I'd like to be a livin' in the mountains jest the same—
I'd like to live that life again when skies wuz fair 'nd blue,
When things wuz run wide open 'nd men wuz brave 'nd true;
When brawny arms the flinty ribs of Red Hoss Mountain smote
For wherewithal to pay the price of Casey's tabble dote.

And you, O cherished brother, a-sleepin' way out west;
With Red Hoss Mountain huggin' you close to its lovin' breast,—
Oh, do you dream in your last sleep of how we use to do,
Of how we worked our little claims together, me 'nd you?
Why, when I saw you last a smile wuz restin' on your face,
Like you wuz glad to sleep forever in that lonely place;
And so you wuz, 'nd I'd be, too, if I wuz sleepin' so.
But, bein' how a brother's love aint for the world to know,
Whenever I've this heartache 'nd this chokin' in my throat,
I lay it all to thinkin' of Casey's tabble dotc.

BEYOND THE MISSISSIPPI

Albert D. Richardson

ON THE MORNING AFTER reaching Denver we started for the Gregory Diggings, forty miles to the northwest. Along the bank of the Platte which bounds the town on the north, immigrant wagons extended for a quarter of a mile, waiting to be ferried across for two dollars and fifty cents each. The boat was propelled by the current, and its daily receipts were from two to three hundred dollars.

Immediately beyond, stretched a succession of low sandy hills, entirely destitute of trees, and with thin ashen grass, dreary enough to eyes familiar with the rich green prairies of Kansas and Missouri. But we passed several ranches where idle cattle and horses, whose owners were in the diggings, were kept and guarded by the month at from one to two dollars per head. By day they grazed on the desert and really fattened upon its unpromising diet. At night they were *corraled*—driven into enclosures—to prevent them from stampeding and protect them against the cattle-thieves, which infest all our frontier regions until exterminated or frightened away by the sudden, decisive administration of lynch law.

From Denver to the foot of the range seemed only a stone's throw, but we found it fifteen miles. The only well-defined spur is Table Mountain; which rises five or six hundred feet from the valley, with symmetric stone walls. It looked down upon two little tents, then the only dwellings for miles; but in the intervening years it has seen a thriving and promising manufacturing town spring up under the broad mountain-shadow.

At its base we found Clear creek, greatly swollen so we left the coach, saddled our mules and rode them through the stream amid a crowd of emigrants who sent up three hearty cheers for Horace Greeley. The road was swarming with travelers. In the distance they were clambering right up a hill as abrupt as the roof of a cottage.

It seemed incredible that any animal less agile than a mountain goat could reach the summit; yet this road only five weeks old, was beaten like a turnpike; and far above us toiled men, mules and cattle pigmies upon Alps. Wagons carrying less than half a ton were drawn up by twenty oxen, while those descending dragged huge trees in full branch and leaf behind them, as brakes.

We all dismounted to ascend except Mr. Greeley, still so lame that his overtaxed mule was compelled to carry him. The astonished brute yielded to destiny and climbed vigorously, experiencing painfully the climax of Ossa upon Pelion.

In an hour and a half we reached the summit. Far below, on the top of Table Mountain gleamed a little lake. At the foot of the long hill were the pigmies again; and beyond, the valley of the Platte with its dark timber and shining water. Before us mountain lay piled upon mountain; some grassy, others gaunt and bare. From most rose the pine, spruce and hemlock in perfect cones, interspersed with quivering aspens; while brilliant flowers clothed the desolate rocks with beauty.

Our road led us past the new-made grave of a young immigrant, one of many victims to the careless use of fire-arms. Up and down the steep mountain sides, across swift-running, ice-cold streams, over jagged rocks and through deep canyons overshadowed by sullen walls, we wound our toilsome way. An eager crowd kept pace with us; some walking, others with ox-wagons, pack-horses or mules, and all pressing toward the mines.

At night we turned our patient animals out to graze, and encamped under a sloping roof of fir and pine boughs. Our cook elect kindled a blazing fire, by which we sat listening to the conflicting reports of the sanguine or disheartened gold seekers; those going forward led by buoyant hope, and those coming back bringing dearly-bought experience.

Wrapt in our blankets upon the hard ground, we gazed through fir boughs at the far-off stars, until the deep soothing music of the pine, the Eolian harp of the forest, mingled with our dreams.

The next morning we started early, and descending a steep hill reached at last the Gregory Diggings. The valley presented a confused and constantly-shifting picture, made up of men, tents, wagons, oxen and mules. The first miner we

Artist unknown, "Gregory Gold Diggings, Colorado, May, 1855," from Beyond the Mississippi *by Albert D. Richardson, 1867.*

encountered was digging a hole like a grave beside a little rivulet, but reported to us that he had not yet 'struck the color.'

Along the rocky gulch for five miles were scattered log cabins, tents and camps covered with boards sawn by hand or with pine boughs. At the grocery tents, meat was selling at fifty cents per pound; and beside the stream women were washing clothes at three dollars per dozen.

After breakfasting in the open air, we went from camp to camp talking with miners, and studying their operations. They found no gold in the stream-beds; but were washing out the 'rotten' quartz which they gathered from narrow crevices in the granite on hill-sides. Gregory, Green Russell and the other old Georgia miners, very expert in detecting lodes, found abundant employment in 'prospecting' for new-comers at one hundred dollars per day. In our presence one miner washed two dollars and fifty cents from a pan-full of dirt, and told us that another pan had just yielded him seventeen dollars and eighty-seven cents.

Some twenty sluices were in operation. In gulch or placer-mining the dirt is shoveled into a long wooden sluice or trough, through which a stream of water pours, washing away the earth and leaving the heavy gold dust at the bottom. These sluices were of lumber, which was cut with hand-saws and commanded three hundred dollars per thousand. There was much speculation in claims; some had sold as high as six thousand dollars, cash.

Most of the miners were exultant and hopeful; but a few, utterly discouraged, were about to return to the States. There were five thousand people in the Gregory Diggings, and hundreds more were pouring in daily.

Mr. Greeley, Henry Villard of the Cincinnati *Commercial* and myself, spent two days in examining the gulches and conversing with the workmen engaged in running sluices. Most of the companies reported to us that they were operating successfully. Then we joined in a detailed report, naming the members of each company and their former places of residence in 'the States,' (that any who desired might learn their reputation for truthfulness,) and adding their statements as to the number of men they were employing and the average yield of their sluices per day. We endeavored to give the shadows as well as the lights of the picture, recounting the hardships and perils of the long journey, and the bitter disappointment experienced by the unsuccessful many; and earnestly warning the public against another general and ill-advised rush to the mines. Little time is required to learn the great truth, that digging gold is about the hardest way on earth to obtain it; that in this as in other pursuits great success is very rare. The report was widely copied throughout the country as the first specific, disinterested and trustworthy account of the newly-discovered placers.

THE SNOW-SHOE ITINERANT: AN AUTOBIOGRAPHY OF THE REV. JOHN L. DYER

John Lewis Dyer

As ALL THE MINING WAS gulch or placer diggings, a great part of the people left in the fall to winter—some for Denver, others for Cañon City or Colorado City, some crossing the Missouri River with ox-teams. Only a few would come back in the spring; for men did not come to Pike's Peak—as it was called—to stay, but to make a raise, and then go back.

In the summer of 1861 a troop of theatrical performers came across to Summit County, and played in all the camps—Sunday morning at one place, and in the evening at another. I thought the devil was traveling the circuit as well as myself. I have thought less of theaters ever since. There is little about them but evil. We had some miners who would go to the dance or theaters.

But the best work done was a revival at Gold Run, in the midst of winter. The snow was about six feet deep. We concluded to hold a protracted meeting at the above place, where we had four members, and only about twenty-five people, all told. From the first, the meetings were interesting. Irrespective of denominations, all began to work in earnest. Seventeen was the average attendance, and about that number were warmed up, reclaimed, or converted. We called it a good revival on a small scale. A more enjoyable time I have seldom had. Among those present were Dr. John McKaskill and wife, and J. T. Lynch, the former of whom were in Kansas the last I heard, and the latter in Utah.

In March, 1863, I received my appointment from Kansas Conference. My work up to this time had been as a supply. Through the presiding elder, L. B. Dennis, I was readmitted. It was a surprise, for I had not made up my mind to stay in the mountains. This decided me to stand the storms and leave the events with God, and do the best I could to build up the Church in this wilderness country. I was put down for South Park, and on the third day of April left Lincoln City and stopped at Mr. Silverthorn's, in Breckenridge, until about two o'clock in the morning, when I took my carpet-sack, well filled, got on my snowshoes, and went up Blue River. The snow was five feet deep. It might be asked, "Why start at two o'clock?" Because the snow would not bear a man in daytime, even with snow-shoes. From about two o'clock until nine or ten in the morning was the only time a man could go; and a horse could not go at all. When about three miles up the Blue River, back of McCloud's, the wolves set up a tremendous howling quite near. I was not armed, but passed quietly along, and was not disturbed. It was not likely, I thought, that the good Lord would let anything disturb a man going in the night to his appointment, although wolves and bears, with some Rocky Mountain lions, were numerous.

I reached Montgomery about nine o'clock in the morning. The snow drifted above the tops of the doors. All along the streets steps had been made in the snow, and served as stairs to get into the stores and houses. There were some two or three hundred people in town, among them seven members. I must mention Brother and Sister Gurton, and Brother and Sister Fowler. I stayed eight days, and held service each evening; on Sunday twice. Two or three professed to be reclaimed, and we all were revived. My circuit embraced the above, with Buckskin Joe, Mosquito, Fair Play, and Tarryall. Buckskin Joe was so called from the nickname given to a prospector wearing a suit of that material.

Tarryall was discovered in 1860. Some very rich claims were opened, and soon all were taken. The news spread, and prospectors by the thousands came, but with no chance to get a foot of ground; so they all tarried, and hence the name Tarryall. From there the prospectors went every way, and some struck pay dirt in the Platte, and called it Fair Play, as they claimed to be more liberal.

This was a two-weeks' circuit. Brother Wm. Howbert was preacher in charge a part of 1860 and 1861, and Brother Loyd in 1862, a part of the year.

Mosquito got its name from this circumstance: The miners met to organize. Several names were suggested, but they disagreed, and a motion was made to adjourn and meet again, the place for the name to be left blank. When they came together on appointment, the secretary opened the book, and a large mosquito was mashed right in the blank, showed it, and all agreed to call the district Mosquito.

In addition to the above places, I went to California Gulch, as that place was not supplied.

Two Mexicans, called Espanosa, who had become enraged against the government of Colorado, came from near Fort Garland, armed to kill as many Americans as they could find. They struck Arkansas River at Hard Scrabble, met Judge Bruce, and shot and murdered him. Thence they went north to Park County, and murdered Mr. Addleman, and from there to near the Kenosha House, where they found two men camped and murdered them. Next, about half-way between Fair Play and Alma, they shot down and killed a Mr. Carter in the road. Just after they had rifled his pockets and taken his pistol and most of his clothes, Mr. Metcalf came along with a wagon and oxen, loaded with lumber. As he sat on the load, they shot at him from a tree about seventy yards off, and gave him a close call—the ball striking right opposite his heart. But the ball struck a pamphlet in his side pocket, and glanced so that it did not hurt him. He of course halloed, and the oxen took fright and ran. They shot again at him, but missed him; and as there was a house in a half mile, he got clear of them. He was the first one that got away from them to describe them. He said they were negroes or men blackened. I suppose he had never seen a Mexican. One of them had a broad-rimmed white hat; and after he was captured, and his hat brought in, Metcalf recognized it as having been worn by the man who shot at him. From the above place they went east to the Red Hill crossing of the Denver road, where any one could be seen coming from either way. There they waited until two men came along on their way from Denver to California Gulch. They shot one dead, and it was supposed wounded the other in the arm. He retreated down the hill to the foot or level, where they caught him and knocked a hole in his skull. This was the last murder they committed. This was late in the evening. The next morning the word came to Fair Play that just over Red Hill there were two men that had been murdered, lying by the roadside.

At this time were were a few soldiers at Fair Play. A number were sent to bring in the dead bodies, and try, if possible, to capture the murderers. Just as the soldiers passed the second dead body, they saw a man coming on the road, whom they at first thought to be a traveler. But seeing them about the same time, and having heard of the numerous murders on the road, he thought they would surely kill him; and dropping his coat in the road, put out south. The soldiers seeing him run, thought he was the man they wanted, and so followed after him at full speed. He, being a man in the prime of life and active, especially on this occasion, made a good race. The word came to Fair Play that they were after the murderer, and another company started on horses to try to head him off. But Mr. John Foster—for that was his name—evaded them all. At one time his pursuers were very close on him, as he passed over a sharp ridge, but he got over before they got quite to the top, and that gave him a chance to turn his course and throw them off his track. After running fifteen or twenty miles, he reached Fair Play in his socks, without coat or hat. As the people saw him in his plight, they halloed: "There comes the murderer!" But I recognized him, as he kept a "Methodist hotel" in California Gulch, and kept in between them and him until he got to the first house. The door being open he went in, and it was some time before he could relate his feat, as he was very short of breath and badly scared, and did not know till then but it was the murderers that had been running him so close. After a while his pursuers came, feeling mortified that he got away from them; but when the facts were known, they felt relieved, for although they had been outrun, they had been saved from killing an innocent man.

I shall not forget that week or ten days of intense excitement. Everybody was alarmed. The five murdered men were buried at Fair Play. The sickening sight of the dead, and the thought, Who would be the next? set the few inhabitants into almost a panic. During the time, word came that a man was harbored at a ranch some fifteen miles east, and a company went over about night and demanded him. The family would not let them in. They guarded the house. There was a shot fired from within which killed a mule. When daylight appeared they gave the inmates just a few minutes to surrender the man, under the alternative of having the house burned. They went in and took the man, and made the ranchman give property to the full value of the mule, and ordered him to leave. They took the prisoner near to Fair Play, and without trial or jury, hanged him, although he denied being guilty of any crime for which he deserved death. But poor Baxter had fallen into the hands of hard men in an evil hour. This was a mob, and nothing better ever comes of such work.

But to return to the pursuit of the Mexicans. The people started a company on their trail from Red Hill. As they had two ponies, they were easily trailed south, and finally were overtaken at breakfast in the chaparral. The pursuers waited for them to go out of the brush to get their ponies. At last only one of them went out, and John said to Joe: "Can you shoot him?" He said, "Yes;" and with his deadly rifle, brought him to the ground. The Mexican tried to shoot, but was not able to do it. One of the avengers, whose brother had been shot by them, craved the privilege to finish the wounded man by shooting him in the head. The other Mexican ran, and got upon a pinnacle of rocks that hung almost over where they were. While Mr. Lamb, who shot first, was stooping over the dead Mexican, to see whether he had shot him as he intended, the other Mexican shot at him from the rocks, the ball passing through his hat-rim, ranging down through his clothes, but fortunately doing no harm. He then made his escape back to near Fort Garland, but was afraid to be seen. He got one of his nephews, and they took up their residence in the mountains for some time. They would come into the settlements on the sly for provisions. A woman found out where they kept themselves, and told it. Mr. Thomas Tobin took a company of five or six men, and went in search of them. As there was a bounty for their heads, both were shot—the old man falling dead in his tracks; the young one, although mortally wounded, running some distance before he expired. That ended the Espanosa trouble. What I have given was most of it done on my route of travel, so I had a good opportunity to know the facts. It was a hard blow on Park County. One mother yet lives to mourn the loss of her son; and sorrowful traces remain in the memory of all the inhabitants. It was a most daring and deplorable outrage.

A VICTORIAN GENTLEWOMAN IN THE FAR WEST

Mary Hallock Foote

THERE WAS A YOUNG Englishman who spent his evenings rather often in the cabin, whom Arthur called Pricey. His name was Hugh Price. He had no "wife," no pal, no special fireside unless it was ours. The other boys teased him about being always in our sitting room, always silent and buried in a book; they called it a "free reading room for Pricey"; and he defended himself candidly, to everyone's delight, with the badgered apology: "A man can't sit in his bedroom, you know!" He was a public-school boy, an Oxford man, a student in Germany, a traveler—an impecunious younger son; if he had any remittances, they were small ones. He was a doleful duffer when it came to handling things in a laboratory or stepping about among coffeepots and frying pans at a campfire, but he had read enormously, and when alone with one or two who could catch what he was trying to say in his shy, hampered fashion, he was awfully good company.

Every evening in the cabin he took the same chair in the corner by the bookshelves (unfortunately it was a rocking chair) and read and rocked until all the others were gone. The rocking annoyed Arthur who was sensitive to little personal habits; he did not hesitate to correct this habit in Pricey in a somewhat crude manner. One evening when Pricey was deep in a book and the chair in full career, A. stepped behind it and slipped a book under each rocker. It surprised Pricey and caused a general laugh, but he took it with touching good nature; he was not thin-skinned in such ways. We had many long quiet talks when the merrier part of the company had left. His mind was the most abstruse and cultivated and the least available of any of the younger men's in Leadville.

Yet he had his happy moments—never indoors! Once when we were riding in the valley—the valley of the little wild Arkansas near its source, with that towering and stainless sky resting on the mountain peaks, he looked up like a worshipper and said in his fine Oxford accent:

'O tenderly the haughty day
Fills his blue urn with fire—

Who in Leadville could have done that but Pricey, or would have thought of doing it! But alas! he was one who stayed in Leadville too long. It was the winter after, when we were in New York, A. received a letter from him and laid it down with a queer look, "Either Price was drunk when he wrote that letter or he has gone out of his mind." It was the last he feared, and drink had nothing to do with it. When Emmons returned from Washington in the spring and Van Zandt from his wild trip to New Mexico (of which more later), those two took care of poor Pricey and sent him back to his relatives in England at their own expense. He had been taken up on the streets wandering about insane and lodged in the common jail for mere safety, lacking every comfort or even decency. No one knew him and he could give no account of himself—so quickly the little fireside groups dispersed in that senseless, rootless place. "The altitude of heartbreak," it was sometimes called.

    🐿 🐿 🐿

The mountains of the Great Divide are not, as everyone knows, born treeless, though we always think of them as far above timberline with the eternal snow on their heads. They wade up through ancient forests and plunge into cañons tangled up with watercourses and pause in little gemlike valleys and march attended by loud winds across high plateaus, but all such incidents of the lower world they leave behind them when they begin to strip for the skies: like the Holy Ones of old, they go up alone and barren of all circumstance, to meet their transfiguration.

We spent the early part of the day steadily climbing; our horses had no load to speak of, yet before noon one of them was hanging back and beginning to show signs of that rapid lung fever which if a horse has taken cold in those altitudes has but one end. A. thought he might hold out till we reached English George's, but from that on, the drive was spoiled by seeing the gasping creature kept up to his work. On the last and steepest grade, before you got to English George's, a sharp turn with a precipice on one side narrowed the road suddenly. The view was cut off ahead, and here we met the stage coming down, all six horses at full speed—they had the precipice on their right, we had the bank and we had to go up the side of it if only on two wheels, for there was no room to pass. I felt that moment I would just as soon die myself as see my husband force that dying horse up the bank, but it had to be done. He stood out on the buggy step, throwing his weight on the upper wheels, and laid on the lash; we did not turn over and we did get by, with a few inches to spare. The two men driving exchanged a queer smile—they understood each other; and I am glad I have forgotten what I said to my husband in that moment when he saved our lives, and I hope he has too! The horse died after we got to English George's and there we hired another, or the remains of one, and he died the day after we reached Leadville. A. paid for both—and how much more the trip cost him (both trips) I never knew, but that is the price of Romance: to have allowed his wife to come in by stage in company with drunkenness and vice, or anything else that might happen, would have been realism.

We knew that we were nearly "in" when corrals and drinking places and repair shops began to multiply, and rude, jocose signs appeared on doors closed to the besieging mob of strangers: "No chickens, no eggs, no keep folks—dam!" was one that A. pointed out to me. ... "Shall we drive out or walk?—there is a trail?" he asked. ... "Let's walk, of course!"

AT A NEW MINING CAMP

Richard Harding Davis

I MET SEVERAL OF these prominent citizens while in Creede, and found them affable. Billy Woods fights, or used to fight, at two hundred and ten pounds, and rejoices in the fact that a New York paper once devoted five columns to his personality. His reputation saves him the expense of paying men to keep order. Bob Ford, who shot Jesse James, was another prominent citizen of my acquaintance. He does not look like a desperado, but has a loutish apologetic air, which is explained by the fact that he shot Jesse James in the back, when the latter was engaged in the innocent work of hanging a picture on the wall. Ford never quite recovered from the fright he received when he found out who it was that he had killed. "Bat" Masterden was of an entirely different class. He dealt for Watrous, and has killed twenty-eight men, once three together. One night when he was off duty I saw a drunken man slap his face, and the silence was so great that we could hear the electric light sputter in the next room; but Masterden only laughed, and told the man to come back and do it again when he was sober. "Troublesome Tom" Cady acted as a capper for "Soapy" Smith, and played the shell game during the day. He was very grateful to me for teaching him a much superior method in which the game is played in the effcte East. His master, "Soapy" Smith, was a very bad man indeed, and hired at least twelve men to lead the prospector with a little money, or the tenderfoot who had just arrived, up to the numerous tables in his gambling-saloon, where they were robbed in various ways so openly that they deserved to lose all that was taken from them.

There were also some very good shots at Creede, and some very bad ones. Of these latter was Mr. James Powers, who emptied his revolver and Rab Brothers' store at the same time without doing any damage. He explained that he was crowded and wanted more room. The most delicate shooting was done by the Louisiana Kid—I don't know what his other name was—who was robbed in Soapy Smith's saloon, and was put out when he expostulated. He waited patiently until one of Smith's men named Farnham, appeared, and then, being more intent in showing his skill than on killing Farnham, shot the thumb off his right hand as it rested on the trigger. Farnham shifted his pistol to his left hand, with which he shot equally well, but before he could fire the Kid shot the thumb off that hand too.

This is, of course, Creede at night. It is not at all a dangerous place, and the lawlessness is scattered and mild. There was only one street, and as no one cared to sit on the edge of a bunk in a cold room at night, the gambling-houses were crowded in consequence every evening. It was simply because there was nowhere else to go. The majority of the citizens used them as clubs, and walked from one to the other talking claims and corner lots, and dived down into their pockets for specimens of ore which they passed around for examination. Others went there to keep warm, and still others to sleep in the corner until they were put out. The play was never high. There was so much of it, though, that it looked very bad and wicked and rough, but it was quite harmless. There were no sudden oaths, nor parting of the crowd, and pistol-shots or gleaming knives—or, at least, but seldom. The women who frequented these places at night, in spite of their sombreros and flannel shirts and belts, were a most unpicturesque and unattractive element. They were neither dashing and bold, nor remorseful and repentant.

They gambled foolishly, and laughed when they won, and told the dealer he cheated when they lost. The men occasionally gave glimpses of the life which Bret Harte made dramatic and picturesque—the women, never. The most uncharacter-istic thing of the place, and one which was Bret Hartish in every detail, was the service held in Watrous and Bannigan's gambling-saloon. The hall is a very long one with a saloon facing the street, and keno tables, and a dozen other games in the gambling-room beyond. When the doors between the two rooms are held back they make a very large hall. A clergyman asked Watrous if he could have the use of the gambling-hall on Sunday night. The house was making about three hundred dollars an hour, and Watrous calculated that half an hour would be as much as he could afford towards the collection. He mounted a chair and said, "Boys, this gentleman wants to make a few remarks to you of a religious nature. All the games at that end of the hall will stop, and you want to keep still."

The clergyman stood on the platform of the keno outfit, and the greater part of the men took the seats around it, toying with the marking cards scattered over the table in front of them, while the men in the saloon crowded the doorway from the swinging-doors to the bar, and looked on with curious and amused faces. At the back of the room the roulette wheel clicked and the ball rolled. The men in this part of the room who were playing lowered their voices, but above the voice of the preacher one could hear the clinking of the silver and the chips, and the voice of the boy at the wheel calling, "seventeen and black, and twenty-eight and black again and—keep the ball rolling, gentlemen—and four and red." There are two electric lights in the middle of the hall and a stove; the men were crowded closely around this stove, and the lamps shone through the smoke on their tanned upturned faces and on the white excited face of the preacher above them. There was the most excellent order, and the collection was very large. I asked Watrous how much he lost by the interruption.

"Nothing," he said, quickly, anxious to avoid the appearance of good; "I got it all back at the bar."

CREEDE

Cy Warman

Here's a land where all are equal—
    Of high or lowly birth—
A land where men make millions,
    Dug from the dreary earth.
Here the meek and mild-eyed burros
    On mineral mountains feed.
It's day all day, in the daytime,
    And there is no night in Creede.

The cliffs are solid silver,
    With wondrous wealth untold;
And the beds of running rivers
    Are lined with glittering gold.
While the world is filled with sorrow
    And hearts must break and bleed—
It's day all day, in the daytime,
    And there's no night in Creede.

Artist unknown, "A Mining-Camp Court-House," from The West from a Car-Window *by Richard Harding Davis, 1892.*

THE LIFE OF AN ORDINARY WOMAN

Anne Ellis

NELLIE SMELTZER WAS THE town dressmaker and milliner. As a girl, she had money and some of the good things it brings; such as education and breeding. She always boasted of going to a private school. When quite young she married a mining man in Georgetown and had followed him from one mining camp to the other. Finally they came to Bonanza; here she planted herself and said, 'No more moves.'

She has often told me of how she shocked the 'natives' when she first came to town with her lovely and daring clothes. I think a low-necked, black tarletan dress was the knock-out. I know she must have been beautiful in those days, as she always had very good features, and such an air; talked with her eyebrows and shoulders. The first thing I remember of her was the enticing colored pictures in her windows. She could twist a scarf around a hat and give it *that* look. These pictures in the window attracted me, and I paid her my first visit, finding a fairyland, mirrors, flowers, hats, Japanese parasols, furniture, and pictures. For many years, her house was a stopping-place for me, always warm and pleasant. She was a good dressmaker and considered very expensive. Once, when we were flush, she made Mama a dress and charged ten dollars for it; this seemed awful, but in spite of shirrings, ruffles, pinkings, and puffings, a big howl went up over it and it was shown to all of the neighbors.

In those days you never held a dress up so that your friends could see the outside, oh, no! It was the wrong side which was turned outward and examined to the smallest detail. How it was lined, and interlined; how bound; how the seams were finished; the smallness and evenness of the stitches; how the steels were put in—there was the test of the dressmaker's art: they should be put up and down every dart and seam, with fancy stitches in bright colored silk thread; from fourteen to seventeen were required for the usual basque.

In this dress of Mama's, which looked very stylish, the lining in the overskirt was pieced and patched. This ruined it, and many times I have seen it held at arm's length, and have heard, 'Now, I just wish you would cast your eye over that; the nerve of a woman to charge me ten dollars for making a gacy thing like that; it takes the cake, that's all I've got to say.' Nevertheless, we children bragged a good deal over the dress that cost ten dollars to make.

Mrs. Smeltzer got her spring millinery just before the Fourth of July, but this was soon enough, as it was never warm before this, and the Fourth was the event of the year; and if one had a new hat it would not be worn before this day, anyway. I had many new hats of her, some paid for (in small 'dribs,' depending on how the washing came in or how much milk was sold) and some given me. Always, when

I visited her, she would give me good advice, none of which I remember. Only once was I asked to eat with her. The linen napkins and the egg cups of silver filigree impressed me very much. She would tell of Paris fashions, the lack of appreciation in Bonanza, of her girlhood, of balls she attended (I only knew dances); of a dead brother she had loved dearly, and of how she tried to talk to him through the spirits; of her stepmother beating her out of her money; of (when I was older) my love affairs, or rather the lack of them. She would say: 'Now, Annie, aren't you mashed on any one? Do you know why you haven't as many beaus as the other girls? Your breasts are too small; you should eat more butter and eggs.'

For many years she would go on the mountainside, cut huge pine trees, and drag or carry them home and put them in holes in front of her house, where they would last for months; strangers wondered why she had such fine shade trees. She always got her own wood off the mountain, hauled it home, sawed and split it. If you think this is an easy job, you should try it once.

The years pass, each day she looks for the return of her husband. But he never comes. She has no intimate friends, neither women nor men, and never seems to feel the want of them. No relative ever came to see her.

She is never talked about, although many men have tried their luck with her, and have left sadder but wiser men. One was told to come late at night; he went, tapped gently on the door; it was opened a crack, he stepped eagerly forward and had his eyes filled with red pepper. Another was also told to 'come ahead.' When he tapped, a sweet voice whispered, 'Come,' but a bucket of cold water had been left hanging above the door which tipped, drenched him, and cooled his ardor. There was another one whom she enjoyed visiting with, as he was clever, a good talker, and more one of her own kind. By now she was washing, as the sewing had played out, and when this man would come for his washing, he would slip out the back way if he saw any one coming. I expect he wanted the other men to think he had a clear thing. She never said one word, but at the back door was a steep step; this she loosened and slipped so that the next time her friend sidled through her bedroom, so that he could go out the back way (our houses always had the rooms in a row), he fell, heels over head. She lost his washing!

She was one of the proudest persons I have ever known; she would never allow any one to help her or give her anything. When she would be out hunting her cow, dressed in gunnysacks, maybe one foot in an old rubber boot and the other wrapped in an ore sack, if you could coax her in, wanting to give her something to eat, you had to make an affair of it, and drink tea along with her. One Christmas people knew she was hungry. They filled a sack with groceries, and put it on her doorstep. When she found it, she took it by the bottom, and dumped it first to the right, then to the left, threw the sack over the fence, went into the house and slammed the door. She held on to one blue velveteen dress, which she wore on election days, when she dressed for the occasion; for years she wore gunnysacks, and sometimes these were very scant, but whatever she wore, she wore it with an air. She even walked with a tripping sort of strut, and each day of her life powdered, white as snow, with flour; in later years she was very dirty, but always powdered thick over the dirt.

Once, when a woman whom she disliked very much left town, Mrs. Smeltzer slipped over and hung crêpe on the door. Once, while pulling a bale of hay up the snowy, icy street, a young miner, coming off shift, stopped and offered to help her. She peered up at him, and said, 'Young man, I don't want to get you talked about!'

She carried her money in her mouth and the store kept a glass of water to drop it in!

She was honest to a degree; I have known her to walk to Saguache to pay her taxes, seventeen miles over a high mountain pass. Once she borrowed our cart, piled it high with millinery, put herself in the shafts, and hauled it to Villa Grove, fifteen miles away.

A year or two ago, she was brought to the county seat on an insanity charge, and after the jailer's wife had washed her hair, it was lovely. Then they got one of those cheap straw garden hats, and she insisted on a piece of cheesecloth to trim it, and finished with a creation. She and I laughed over the charge; one of the complaints was, that she kissed her cow! The cow had come to be her only means of livelihood, and she said to me, 'She's the only creature who loves me; why not kiss her?' It was at this time she gave me this advice: 'Annie, don't ask people their business. If they want you to know they will tell you, and if they don't they will lie.'

During all these years there was never one word of complaint at an unkind fate. She died, as she lived; proud and alone, asking no odds of any one. At the last she was with the only things on earth that loved her, the cow and chickens; these chickens roosted on the foot and under the bed, and were blinded by the light when brought out. But, even to the end, there was a sign creaking above the door, 'Fashionable dressmaking'; and ladies, yellow and fly-specked, dressed in beautiful colors, with tiny waists, big sleeves, and long trains, looked and smiled at you from the fashion sheets in the bay window.

TOMBOY BRIDE

Harriet Fish Backus

SHORTLY AFTER THAT CHRISTMAS day I had a new adventure. Johnny Midwinter, the foreman, suggested that he and George take me into the mine. George thought I would enjoy it.

Johnny met us at the entrance. Outfitted in a miner's long rubber coat and sou'wester I entered the tunnel where Johnny fastened a miner's candlestick in the loop on my hat and with a dramatic gesture of his pudgy hand, lighted the candle.

Possibly, because I had made the effort to send help to the roustabout which prevented an accident, Johnny decided my interest in the mine warranted a wider understanding of its ramifications. After we walked some distance along the main tunnel he turned to me with a smile and said, "We'll start up this ladder in what we call 'a vertical raise.' Just climb slowly behind me and George will follow you. When we get up to the stope, take the candle out of your hat and carry it straight up and as far from your face as you can."

What did he mean by a *stope*, and would I recognize it when I reached it?

Step by step, clinging to the rungs, we climbed straight up the three by four opening in the rock. As water dripped from above and hit my hat and face, the candle sputtered. I stepped carefully for fear of tripping on my skirt. With the strange feeling of carrying a candle on my head I stared steadily at the ladder. The flickering light shone dimly on the walls caging us in, three sides of solid rock and the fourth made of timbers for the ore chute alongside. Each rung was a little harder for me to reach and cling to. By the time fifty rungs were beneath us I began to waver, then I hesitated, but remembering that George was close below and might be thrown off balance, I plunged on. After one hundred feet of this fearsome climb we reached the top of the ladder where the rock closed in over our heads.

Even today, many years later, the memory of that moment hits hard at the pit of my stomach!

Broken ore almost completely filled the cross shaft, leaving only a crooked passage to crawl through, two feet wide, three feet high.

Artist unknown, "Down the Shaft" from Beyond the Mississippi *by Albert D. Richardson, 1867.*

Faintness and vertigo swept through me. But not for anything would I let George or Johnny know how desperately fear gripped me. I could hardly breathe. There must have been oxygen but I couldn't pull any of it into my lungs. To cover the sick feeling of panic I made the excuse, which was real enough, that I needed to catch my breath after the exhausting climb. Unable, in that flat space, to sit up I lay flat on my stomach, resting, doubting that I could go on.

Through the pounding of my heart I could hear myself saying, "Hattie, you *must* go on. You are the wife of a miner. Keep going and get it over!" But my head was swimming and my stomach churning. I lay there until terror subsided somewhat, then told Johnny I was ready.

Holding the candle safely before me I inched along, face down, clawing at the rocks with my one free hand, dragging my legs forward, my long skirts hampering every move. Only occasionally could I catch the gleam of Johnny's candle ahead. Unable to look back I could hear George calling a word of encouragement as he followed.

But what if the rock overhead should cave in? The thought was torture. I struggled to wipe it from my mind. In the darkness, broken only by a flicker of the nearby candle, I twisted, turned, writhed like a snake, stopped many times to rest and capture a mite of courage.

It was one hundred and fifty feet of pure hell! Yet I lived through it. We had crossed the awful stope and there remained the descent, straight down another hundred foot ladder in a well, scarcely four feet square, cut in solid rock. It seemed easy. I had room to breathe. With each rung lower there was more space above my head. The tunnel at last! I hurried toward the streak of daylight at its mouth, and the great outdoors. Heaven!

FATHER STRUCK IT RICH

Evalyn Walsh McLean

... A FEW DAYS later Annie told me Father wanted me in the bedroom.

"Daughter, close the door."

I did and then rested my chin on the cold, shining footboard of the big brass bed.

"You must keep a secret I am going to tell you. Promise?"

"Yes, Papa."

"Remember the trip we made up near the Gertrude? I found some gold in those samples I made that day. It ran about two dollars a ton. Now I have had reports on samples I took this last trip."

He hesitated; after all, I was only ten. If Mother had been there I am sure he would have told her instead. Feeling as badly as he did, he had to tell someone, someone he could trust. He motioned to me to come around to the side of his bed and showed me a piece of grayish quartz; it was not very impressive. He wet it with his tongue and held it near my eyes. Like thread-ends in its texture were glistening circles and specks of black.

"That's gold."

I was ready to whoop with joy, but he sharply interrupted: "Whoa! Remember this is a secret. If you should tell a single person before I say you can, you might ruin our whole future." I have forgotten most of his words, of course, but I remember their import: the report he had received on his samples was better than his wildest dreams.

In the intervening years I have thought often about that action of my father. Why did he tell me, a ten-year-old child? He dared not tell a soul outside the family until he had completed all his pending deals for the claims and prospects and mines in that long deserted region. He had no partners; it was all his own. Yet he was a sick man who knew his clutch on life was none too firm. If he died his secret would die with him, and we who were so deeply loved by him, for whom he had scaled mountains and dug and worried—we should be left in want. He had to tell. Mother was in Denver, Vin was a little too young, but I was ten and I knew where the gold was. So he told me and the secret was kept as securely as if we had been a family of mountaineer Corsicans. Almost the whole of his message was imparted with a single spoken sentence. He did not have to write anything that a prying eye might see. Even if he died he knew that some day I would grow up and sensibly interpret what he meant when he whispered,—

"Daughter, I've struck it rich."

CRIPPLE CREEK DAYS

Mabel Barbee Lee

THE STORY IN THE *Times* next morning was tantalizingly brief. Every word was burned in my heart:

> Pearl De Vere, madam at the Old Homestead, died early today from an overdose of morphine. According to a denizen in the house, a gay party was in full swing when Pearl excused herself, saying that she felt indisposed. She refused to let anyone go with her to her room. She was in high spirits all evening, a woman said, and never seemed happier or more carefree. No one could offer any reason why the madam should want to end her life. The body was discovered by the wealthy patron of the lavish affair. It was lying across the bed fully clothed in the ball dress that came only last week from a salon in Paris. The name of the patron could not be learned. It was understood that he left suddenly on business in Denver. Funeral arrangements will be announced later pending word from the deceased's relatives in the East.

Doris Lee, "Eagle's Rest, Cripple Creek," c. 1938.

Kitty's lips tightened as she pushed the paper aside. "Another one of those poor unfortunates has taken poison," she said grimly. "It's just as well. Places like the Old Homestead, together with its inmates, should be wiped from the face of the earth!"

It was the saddest Christmas of my life. I had no interest in the gifts that banked our tree, no desire to help Kitty string cranberries and popcorn. The thought of Pearl De Vere cold in death, forsaken and alone in Fairley Bros. and Lampman's back room pulled at my heartstrings. It was all I could do to keep from crying. My mother had no inkling of my grief and if I wept she would grow suspicious and pry out my secret. So I escaped to my retreat at the Lone Pine Shaft on Mineral Hill, to sit on the dump and mourn over the tragedy of my idol.

Then a daring obsession began to grip me. It was nothing less than a visit to the funeral parlor to gaze once more on Pearl De Vere's lovely face. I had never seen a corpse; the very word made me shiver with horror. I would cross the street any time rather than pass near a house with black crepe on the door. But my urge to see her was stronger than my fear; and besides, the saying came to me that if you touched a dead person his ghost would never return to haunt you. Even so, several days passed before I could muster sufficient courage to take such a bold step. The arrival of Pearl's sister from the East brought things to a head; now there wasn't a moment to lose.

At first glance, the entry of the mortuary was so inviting that it might have been a parlor in anybody's house. An enormous fern hung down from an iron stand in the sunny window. Green Brussels carpet covered the floor and comfortable chairs were scattered around. I waited at the desk a moment for the undertaker to appear but the place seemed empty. A large glass case on a table caught my eye. It contained mementos of people who had met violent death in Cripple Creek and been laid out at the mortuary. Each bore a typewritten label. There was the lunch bucket of a miner who had been struck by lightning, sidecombs of Two-go Ruby who had swallowed strychnine, the pistol of a gambler who shot himself through the mouth, a piece of fuse that another used to blow off his head with dynamite. It was the lock of Pearl De Vere's red hair that made me shudder and try to escape through a back door. But instead, I found myself facing the morgue.

Four shadowy coffins stood along the wall of the dimly lit room and I recalled with a shiver the mine explosion up on Gold Hill. I was tempted to run out before anyone discovered me, but all at once low, insistent voices near a far window caught my ear. A thin, sharp-nosed woman and a man in a dirty oilcloth apron were standing alongside a lavender casket. They apparently didn't notice me as I tiptoed closer.

"She's dead," the man was saying; "her sins won't rub off on you now."

"The stain on our family will never rub off," the woman said bitterly. "It is as red as the dye on her hair! You should have told me what she was, the kind of life she had been leading, before I made the long, futile trip to this loathsome place." And yanking on her gloves, added, "I'll take no further responsibility. I'm washing my hands of the disgraceful business!"

"But she is penniless!" the man urged. "Do you want your sister buried in the potter's field?"

"This harlot is no sister of mine!" the woman shot back, as she started to leave. I was trembling so that I dropped my new purse. "What're you doing here?" she screamed, seemingly aware of me for the first time. "A fine place this is for a child!" And she flung out, slamming the door so hard the calendar on the wall fell to the floor.

"There's a lot a' mean-hearted folks in the world," the man said, shrugging, "but for my money she takes the cake!"

"Is Pearl De Vere's hair really dyed red?" I asked, struggling with disillusionment.

"Sure," he bantered, "that's nothing. All the girls on the row do it. Sometimes black, sometimes blond, and now and then it's red, like De Vere's. I done my damnedest to bleach it before any of her hoity-toity relations got here, but it was no use—came out a dirty pink—the ungodliest sight I ever seen on a cadaver!"

I leaned over the coffin for a better view. She looked so natural that she might have opened her eyes and smiled up at me slantwise through her long lashes. If there had been any stain of wickedness in her face Death had erased it. She seemed much younger than my mother; the hurt, wistful expression about the mouth was like that of a girl. "Do you care if I touch her?" I asked, reaching over to brush a pinkish wisp of hair from her forehead.

"Go ahead," the man replied, "but make it snappy. I got work to do—can't hang 'round here all day. Say," he eyed me sharply, "ain't I seen you somewheres—whose kid are you, anyhow?"

I turned and ran out of the room, afraid that he was one of my father's friends.

The whole town was in an uproar when word spread that Pearl De Vere's sister had disowned her. The editor of the *Times* wrote, "Cripple Creek can bury its own dead!" The Reverend Jim Franklin preached a sermon called, "Let Him Who Is without Sin Cast the First Stone!" And Johnny Nolon, the owner of the camp's biggest gambling rooms, started a movement to auction off the Parisian ball gown, "and give the little girl the finest funeral that money can buy!" But before the exquisite shell-pink creation could be handed over to the highest bidder, Fairley Bros. and Lampman announced receipt of a mysterious, unsigned letter. It was postmarked Denver and enclosed a thousand dollars in crisp new bills to pay all burial costs. The only request was that Pearl De Vere be laid out in the elegant dress in which she had danced on Christmas Eve.

A throng turned out the day of the funeral, mostly children and miners. I watched from the top of a barrel in front of Roberts' Grocery. Somebody claimed he saw ladies from up on the hill sitting in the shadows of upstairs office windows. The Elks Band headed by Joe Moore led the procession, playing the "Death March." Then came the heavily draped hearse with the lavender casket almost hidden by a blanket of red and white roses. Just behind, a man walked solemnly beside the empty rig with the shiny red wheels, driving the span of restive black horses. A large cross of shell-pink carnations lay on the seat.

My throat ached; I swallowed hard to choke back the tears. Now four mounted police were coming down the avenue, pushing back the crowd to make way for all the lodge members in brilliant regalia trying to keep in step. The sight of their red fezzes, feathered helmets and gold braided scabbards sent thrills of ecstasy through me. Bringing up the rear were buggies filled with thickly veiled women who, a man said, were Pearl's friends from the row.

I ran along the alley to the edge of town where Bennett Avenue narrowed into the road to Pisgah graveyard. Except for a few squatters' cabins, that part of camp was barren and windswept. I climbed on a rock from where I could get a clear view of the cemetery. It was late afternoon and the sun had begun to slant toward Pisgah Mountain. I watched a man chopping wood in front of a tar-papered shack. Not far away a boy was trying to hitch an obstinate burro to a cart while a dog yelped and snapped at the animal. A chicken hawk soared and dipped above an acrid, smoldering dump ground. My feet were getting chilly and I hugged myself to keep warm.

The last of the procession had passed by and the marchers were gathering around the freshly dug grave. I wondered uneasily if the services would be long. Soon the train would be coming in from Beacon Hill and Kitty would call me up and down the neighborhood to help her with supper. The thought had scarcely crossed my mind when I saw some of the mourners scattering and climbing back into the rigs. But a few of the lodge members had moved in closer to the grave and one of them seemed to be reading from a book. All at once, through a break in the ranks, I caught a glimpse of the flower-laden casket being lowered into the ground; and then came the sad sweet notes of Joe Moore's cornet playing "Good-bye, Little Girl, Good-bye." That was too much for me to bear; my heart was broken and I buried my face in my coat and sobbed.

When I looked up again, the long line of carriages and men had begun to file through the cemetery gate and down the slope back to camp. But the order had been reversed. The women, coming first, had thrown the veils off their faces and were laughing merrily as the trotting horses kicked up dust. Lodge members hurried willy-nilly, flapping their arms up and down, crossing them from side to side to get warm. The driver of the buggy with the shiny red wheels had jumped on the seat and the frisky steeds galloped wildly while he held the reins with one hand and pulled for a bottle from under the seat with the other. Even the hearse had picked up speed and the wheels rattled clumsily over the stones. The musicians came last and as they approached me, dapper Joe Moore looked over and winked. Then he trilled the whistle, the snare drums rolled and the whole band burst into "There'll Be a Hot Time in the Old Town Tonight!"

I waited until they were out of sight and the tune had faded in the distance. I felt suddenly weary, older and more grown up. ...

ABROAD AT HOME

Julian Street

HOWEVER, WE DID get to Cripple Creek, and for all its mountain setting, and all the three hundred millions of gold that it has yielded in the last twenty years or so, it is one of the most depressing places in the world. Its buildings run from shabbiness to downright ruin; its streets are ill paved, and its outlying districts are a horror of smokestacks, ore-dumps, shaft-houses, reduction-plants, gallows-frames and squalid shanties, situated in the mud. It seemed to me that Cripple Creek must be the most awful looking little city in the world, but I was informed that, as mining camps go, it is unusually presentable, and later I learned for myself that that is true.

Cripple Creek is not only above the timber-line; it is above the cat-line. I mean this literally. Domestic cats cannot live there. And many human beings are affected by the altitude. I was. I had a headache; my breath was short, and upon the least exertion my heart did flip-flops. Therefore I did not circulate about the town excepting within a radius of a few blocks of the station. That, however, was enough.

After walking up the main street a little way, I turned off into a side street lined with flimsy buildings, half of them tumbledown and abandoned. Turning into another street I came upon a long row of tiny one story houses, crowded close together in a block. Some of them were empty, but others showed signs of being occupied. And instead of a number, the door of each one bore a name, "Clara," "Louise," "Lina," and so on, down the block. For a time there was not a soul in sight as I walked slowly down that line of box-stall houses. Then, far ahead, I saw a woman come out of a doorway. She wore a loose pink wrapper and carried a pitcher in her hand. I watched her cross the street and go into a dingy building. Then the street was empty again. I walked on slowly. As I passed one doorway it opened suddenly and a man came out—a shabby man with a drooping mustache. He did not look at me as he passed. The window-shade of the crib from which he had come went up as I moved by. I looked at the window, and as I did so, the curtains parted and the face of a negress was pressed against the pane, grinning at me with a knowing, sickening grin.

I passed on. From another window a white woman with very black hair and eyes,

Artist unknown, "When Cripple Creek District Towns Were Wide Open," from Yellow Gold of Cripple Creek *by Harry J. Newton, 1928.*

and cheeks of a light orchid-shade, showed her gold teeth in a mirthless automatic smile, and added the allurement of an ice-cold wink.

The door of the crib at the corner stood open, and just before I reached it a woman stepped out and surveyed me as I approached. She wore a white linen skirt and a middy blouse, attire grotesquely juvenile for one of her years. Her hair, of which she had but a moderate amount, was light brown and stringy, and she wore gold-rimmed spectacles. She did not look depraved but, upon the contrary resembled a highly respectable, if homely, German cook I once employed. As I passed her window I saw hanging there a glass sign, across which, in gold letters, was the title, "Madam Leo."

"Madam Leo," she said to me, nodding and pointing at her chest. "That's me. Leo, the lion, eh?" She laughed foolishly.

I paused and made some casual inquiry concerning her prosperity.

"Things is dull now in Cripple Creek," she said. "There ain't much business any more. I wish they'd start a white man's club or a dance hall across the street. Then Cripple Creek would be booming."

I think I remarked, in reply, that things did look rather dull. In the meantime I glanced in at her little room. There was a chair or two, a cheap oak dresser, and an iron bed. The room looked neat.

"Ain't I got a nice clean place?" suggested Madam Leo. Then as I assented, she pointed to a calendar which hung upon the wall. At the top of it was a colored print from some French painting, showing a Cupid kissing a filmily draped Psyche.

"That's me," said Madam Leo. "That's me when I was a young girl!" Again she loosed her laugh.

I started to move on.

"Where are you from?" she asked.

"I came up from Colorado Springs," I said.

"Well," she returned, "when you go back send some nice boys up here. Tell them to see Madam Leo. Tell them a middle-aged woman with spectacles. I'm known here. I been here four years. Oh, things ain't so bad. I manage to make two or three dollars a day."

As I passed to leeward of her on the narrow walk I got the smell of a strong, brutal perfume.

"Have you got to be going?" she asked.

"Yes," I answered. "I must go to the train."

"Well, then—so long," she said.

"So long."

"Don't forget Madam Leo," she admonished, giving utterance, again, to her strident, feeble-minded laugh.

"I won't," I promised.

And I never, never shall.

THE WILLOW-BENDER

Helen Rich

ON THE DREDGE THE winchman coaxed the fouled bucket-lines until at last the bucket ladder and its weight of iron scoops drew clear of the green water. It stretched awkwardly, like a man with a stiff leg, part on deck, part over the pond. The grunting shore crews dug new postholes, setting the deadmen, the posts, in them and fastening the shorelines to hold the boat steady as she turned. By the end of the week, floundering, wallowing, McClain's bellows echoing over the camp, she was turned, headed toward Divide Street, her points set, her spud anchored, the buckets let down into the water again.

By the end of the week men had already cleared the ground as far as the Moffat house. The company owned land to the town limits, and that was where the Moffat house stood, just on the edge. Jett Moffat watched grimly while she packed. Her old mouth quivered sometimes as she saw the lodgepoles rend from their stumps and fall, saw the quaking aspens die, took the final bouquet of sagebrush into her wide nostrils.

One day while she watched, she took down a frayed denim jacket that belonged to her husband, Breck, and put it on over her tremendous calico. She laced her gnarled feet into a pair of Breck's workshoes and clumped out across the flat, her white hair standing about her head like a ragged cloud.

"Here comes old lady Moffat," one of the workmen said, "looking like she was going to sink a pick into somebody."

She had remembered an *albino mertensia* that grew on this land. It was her tender possession, although it did not grow on her ground. She had found the rare bells years before and never told a living soul where they were, not even Breck, for fear they would be dug up and taken away. She had even concealed the plant, arranging brush so skillfully that it was open to sun and rain yet no one would think to look where it grew.

She strode fiercely up to Lam Hunter, the gang foreman. "If you've gone and tromped my white bluebells, I don't know what I'll do," she said in her mighty voice.

"What white bluebells, Jett?" Lam asked. "Whereabouts would they be?"

"You've already tore away my marks," Jett moaned, "but they'd be about here somewheres if you ain't destroyed them to death." She began searching for the plant. "Oh, the little dear things!" she cried, then shouted at Lam standing close. "You stand back with your great feet! You stand clear back!" She began a slow circling then, her deep eyes probing for the dusty-green plant that would, by now, be bowing with delicate carillon.

She found it while the gang waited anxious and silent, not daring to grub out a clump of sage or put an ax to a tree. Her hands came together in a great clap of thanksgiving. "You fetch me a shovel, one of you!" she called. She dug it up herself, deep down and widely circled, and when she had delivered it from its birthplace she took off her jacket and laid the plant on it, the gravelly dirt sifting only a little.

She let the men see it before she gathered the jacket around it. "Why, they's hunderds of them bells around this country," one of them said.

She looked at him with majesty. "Blue," she said. "Show me white." She bore it away then in her great arms, bare to the river wind. When she got back home she planted it in an eight-pound lard bucket to take with her on her migration.

MOUNTAIN WOMAN

Belle Turnbull

God love these mountain women anyway,
Said Mr Probus. Not to say they're fair
Or sleek with oils, for woodsmoke in the hair
And sagebrush on the fingers every day
Are toughening perfumes, and the sunstreams flay
Too dainty flesh. But what remains is rare,
Like mountain honey to the mountain bear.
He finds his relish in a rough bouquet.

Days when their wash is drying, off they'll go
And fish the beaver ponds. Hell or high water
They'll wade the slues in sunburnt calico
Playing a trout like some old sea-king's daughter.
Hell and high water women … Steady now,
Not all of them, he said. One, anyhow.

EAST TINCUP

Pete Smythe

DEEP IN THE MOUNTAINS of beautiful Colorado is a place where progress is about as popular as a Cuban bomber over New York City. Here progress is actually looked down on by some people. Like being poor in the city is. You see when the fellows who run things in the cities and capitals of the world make speeches, they tend to lump progress in one great big successful ball. Everything is big, wonderful, and good for everybody.

Well, it just ain't so. There's a bad side to that progress ledger too. And the books are sort of out of balance. Not so much moneywise, but livin'wise. Extremes in progress are like extremes in drinkin' Moat Watkin's Rhubarb Red. If you don't come up with a headache next day, you're dad-burned lucky or you were pourin' your drinks in the fern.

So I suppose that's why we like it here in East Tincup. **"The Slowest Growin' Town in the Nation—And We Aim to Keep it That Way."** We operate Smythe's General Store, next door to the Postoffice. Free parkin' for your buckboard and free hay for your horses. I've been Mayor for over 15 years and probably will be from now on. It's not because I'm a good mayor, but I've got a platform they can't beat. It's real simple. **NO TAXES AND NO PARKIN' METERS.**

We broadcast directly from the store by stimulated remote control over the Bobwire Network. And most of the neighbors are cooperating to keep their gates up so we can stay on the air. Instead of the Rotary and the Optimists and the Kiwanis and the Lions and all those service clubs, we have the Tincup Anti-Development League. The purpose of this organization is to keep any person or syndicate from constructing any big buildings or freeways or factories in our City. **"KEEP TINCUP SMALL"** is our slogan.

Most everyone has lived in a small town during some exciting period of their lives. They might not have thought it exciting at the time, but you are always hearin' people tell stories at standarounds about the good old days in Ruptured Falls or some other town. I don't think it's because they are tryin' to impress people. It's just that if they come from a small town to the city and make good, it helps them to hang onto their humility. Makes them appear a self-made man. But if you figure it out cost-plus you find there may be a loss somewhere along the line.

Anyway, small towns are good because everything is simplified. The work, the gettin' there, goin' fishin' and huntin', goin' to church, savin' money, buildin' friendships and enjoyin' life. And after all that last one should be one of our main goals. And to enjoy it you just have to have a sense of humor. A man without a sense of humor is like a wagon without springs. For instance, ol' Rube Lucas was in the store the other day and he kept pacin' up and down, up and down. I asked him why and he said he was worried about his wife. I said, "What's she got?" and ol' Rube says, "The car."

Now that is a real simple incident but it got a chuckle out of me. And things like that happen all the time in small towns. Maybe it's because people have more time for things to happen to them, and maybe it's just that people notice these things when they happen. I suppose it is a matter of attitude, of havin' the spark turned up a little higher on the funny bone.

Check your spark on the following happenin's that we've witnessed, or heard about, occurin' around East Tincup. But we warn you, if you want to move to East Tincup to live, we just won't have room until somebody moves out.

—Mayor Pete

SILVER CAKE AND GOLD CAKE

The La Jara Cook Book

SILVER CAKE

Scant half cup of butter, cup of sugar, half cup sweet milk, one and one-half cups flour, one-half cup corn starch, whites of four eggs, half tea spoonful soda, one teaspoonful cream tartar.

GOLD CAKE

Yolks of four eggs, one cup sugar, beat eggs and sugar together, half cup sweet milk (not a bit of cream), scant half cup butter, one and one-half cups flour, half teaspoonful soda, one teaspoonful cream tartar. Bake in layers and use the silver and gold alternately. Use any filling you like.

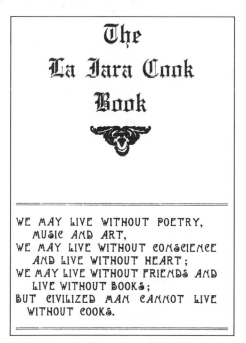

The La Jara Cook Book

WE MAY LIVE WITHOUT POETRY,
    MUSIC AND ART,
WE MAY LIVE WITHOUT CONSCIENCE
    AND LIVE WITHOUT HEART;
WE MAY LIVE WITHOUT FRIENDS AND
    LIVE WITHOUT BOOKS;
BUT CIVILIZED MAN CANNOT LIVE
    WITHOUT COOKS.

The La Jara Cook Book, *published by the Sewing Circle of La Jara, n.d.*

STAMPEDE TO TIMBERLINE

Muriel Sibell Wolle

WHEN THE SIGHTSEEING bus climbed the long, steep mile from Black Hawk to Central City in the midst of the Colorado Rockies, I sat up a little straighter and could hardly believe my eyes. Wooden sidewalks! Gingerbread frets under eaves; houses tier on tier and mine dumps, with rusty shaft houses everywhere.

"What you see here," said the man in the next seat to me, "is what's left of the old West. You won't see it much longer for it is disappearing fast."

Craning my neck and looking from side to side I watched the old houses slip by together with the gaping mine tunnels, and the monument commemorating the discovery of Colorado's gold on this spot. Still the car climbed toward more mines. Ahead, to the left, was an empty fire house with its bell, standing beside a gulch down which gray tailings poured, proof that the mines in the distance were working. On the right were streets, one above another built on terraces cut from the hillside and on one stood the native stone high school from which, I was told, were graduated the first trained teachers of the state.

Crowning the hill was another school building, this one surmounted with a cross. "That," said my neighbor, "was St. Aloysius' Academy, and just below it, on Eureka Street, is one of the most famous hostelries in the west—the Teller House. And beyond it is the Opera House, and beyond it Gilpin County Courthouse, and farther up the streets, the Brewery, and at the top of the hill the cemeteries." My head reeled.

Buildings everywhere, many of them deserted and definitely built many years ago. Few people were in sight when we stopped for soda-pop and a quick walk along the main street, and our footsteps echoed as we climbed the wooden steps to the Masonic Lodge, one of the sights of the city. This was Central City, once the biggest place in Jefferson Territory, and in the sixties surpassing even Denver in size. And here *I* was, fresh from the east and surrounded by a culture which flowered in the seventies and eighties and slowly faded in the nineties.

We stayed all too short a time in Central City and were hurried on toward Idaho Springs and our objective, St. Mary's Glacier, where there would be skiing—a great attraction to easterners on the Fourth of July! We climbed the long, curving hill that led out of Central to Russell Gulch and Idaho Springs, and before we reached the top of the grade I glanced back for a last look at Central City, cupped in a hollow of the mountains and emanating such a strong flavor of the past. The rest of the day I do not remember. The skiing and the snowballing are hazy recollections, for my whole attention was centered on Central City and my mind was made up then and there to know more of its history and to return to its picturesque streets and sketch its tumbling buildings and gaping mines.

A year passed before I could carry out my decision, a year spent in New York. But now New York had lost its fascination: more and more I longed for the mountains and the West. And I well remember the day that I walked into the president's office at the Art School where I was teaching and tendered my resignation.

"What's this?" said that gentleman, "Are you going to be married?"

"No," I replied with a wicked gleam in my eye, for I knew how he loved the city, "I'm tired of New York and I want to go west to live."

So, a few months later, having sought positions from Montana to Arizona, I was fortunate enough to find an opening in the Art Department at the University of Colorado and I knew that my Central City dream was beginning to materialize.

During the summer of 1926, while teaching at the University, I asked questions about Colorado's past, its mining booms and its ghost towns, but my real interest in the history began when I returned to Central City to start my pictorial record of the place. As soon as school closed at the end of August, ignorant of the lack of regular transportation in the west to many mountain points at any time, I made preparations to spend the vacation in Central City, forty miles from Boulder, and when I was ready to start, there was no way to go. The sightseeing companies had left until the following season; the daily stage up the canyon went only halfway— and twenty miles is a long hike at seven thousand feet elevation. In desperation I called the local taxi company and presented my problem to them. They seemed a little stunned at the request but did some quick calculating and announced that the trip would cost $15.00. Knowing that the canyon stage to Nederland, twenty miles away, cost considerably less I decided to take it and hunt the rest of my transportation there.

Armed with sketching materials, I set out on Labor Day on what seemed an innocent excursion. I reached Nederland by noon. Surely someone would be willing to drive me to Central City for a modest sum, and I began inquiring at the garages and hotels; but seemingly no one was interested in a trip to Central. Finally one man agreed to drive me over. "And how much will the trip cost?" I asked. "Fifteen dollars," was his prompt answer. At this point the hotel proprietor came to my aid by assuring me that if I spent the night in his hotel I might be able to get a ride over the next day with the Boulder bread man who served the mountain towns once a week and who sometimes took passengers. Such an arrangement seemed worth trying, and much more economical; so I settled down to stay in Nederland, a small mining town, which by the twenties had become a summer resort. All afternoon I tramped the streets, sketching the false-fronted stores, the log cabins, and the big tungsten mill on the creek. To the west was the Continental Divide and up the winding road to the south lay Central City, twenty miles away. From time to time during the afternoon great roars and cheers came from the Baseball Park where a game was in progress, and upon inquiry I learned that the

Nederland team was playing the Black Hawk Club. That was the last straw, for I knew that Black Hawk was one mile from Central City and here in front of me were nine men who in a few hours would be going to within one mile of my destination while I sat in Nederland waiting for the bread man. But I was from the east, and one doesn't just offer oneself to a ball team and beg transportation. Yet, the more I mulled it over in my mind the more foolish it seemed to spend the night in Nederland with Central so accessible. I entered a restaurant for an early supper, perhaps because, parked in front of it, was a car with a Black Hawk license! At one table sat a ballplayer with his wife and family, and as I ate I gathered courage. Just as they were leaving I told them my plight and said that since I saw they were from Black Hawk maybe they would know someway that I might get to Central. This thin disguise worked, and while I ran for my suitcase they filled the tank of the touring car with gasoline and in less than five minutes I was on my way to the Teller House.

It was a ride I shall never forget. The road in those days was steeper than the new highway and was not surfaced. The car pulled slowly but steadily up the long grades while the driver told me of seeing some autos which couldn't make them and had to back up the worst hills. All the while I sat in the backseat between two small boys, with a gaily flowered coverlet tucked under our chins to shut out the cold wind of a September evening.

I watched the sunset colors fade, as we drove between stands of lodgepole pines and passed occasional ranch houses. Just before dark we dropped down into Black Hawk with its mills and smelters and its homes perched crazily on the mountainsides. With true western hospitality my "benefactors" drove up to Central and deposited me in front of the Teller House, refusing to take any remuneration for the trip. I thanked them profusely and was so confused at my temerity in thumbing a ride that even their names have escaped me, and to this day I regret that I do not know to whom I am indebted for starting me on my ghost town hobby.

                                                                 🐿 🐿 🐿

For four days I explored Central City, returning to the hotel only for meals and to sleep. There was so much to see and sketch that the days were all too short. At noon time if I were halfway down the gulch I had only to put my painting paraphernalia in a deserted cabin and climb up the hill to the hotel for lunch knowing that they would be safe during my absence. Children and passers-by stared curiously as I worked and made comments about the pictures. One lady admired a watercolor of Eureka Street showing several residences including her own. When her husband returned from work she brought him to see the picture and he, seeing her interest offered to buy it for her. "No," said she emphatically, "I don't want it unless she will paint it again and make our house look bigger."

One morning I was sitting in an alley making a watercolor of some buildings and a crazy flight of wooden stairs to the next street level when a girl of about ten stopped to look over my shoulder, and as we talked she found that I was an art teacher. Later she returned with several little friends and standing just within earshot said of my work, "It's pretty good for her being just a teacher and not an artist."

Each day was a new experience, and my enthusiasm to capture the town on paper was greater than my resistance to the cold September winds which swept down the empty streets and up my arms. As a greenhorn I had not realized how much warm clothing I should have brought for these mountain altitudes. I had planned to spend two weeks in the town but at the end of five days I had caught cold in one shoulder and could neither sketch nor move about with any comfort. The Teller House was cold, and dank too in those days, and hot water could be gotten only at intervals, brought in a pitcher by a solicitous but elderly bellhop. Plainly it was time for me to return to Boulder. But how was I to get there? Inquiry after inquiry convinced me that no one ever went to Boulder, and again I was marooned forty miles from my destination. Then someone remembered the Boulder bread man who was due the following day. Maybe he would take me. I mentally resolved that he jolly well would, and an hour before he was due I was sitting in front of the store where he made his deliveries, my suitcase beside me. He was not glad to see me and when I told him of my plight he did not say that he would take me; so desperately, I insisted, "But I won't take up very much room," and began to move my luggage toward the automobile. I remember no more except that in a few minutes I was riding beside him with my feet braced against the dashboard as we bounded down the canyon toward Boulder. The truck was short on springs and air-cushions but speedy, and by the time I was unloaded in front of the apartment house in Boulder I felt as if I'd had a thorough osteopathic treatment. Out came the suitcase from the bread wagon, and slowly but gratefully I limped into the house, my first adventure with Central City over.

Muriel Sibell Wolle, "Teller House, Central City," n.d.

SECTION VI

THE TABORS

Promotional brochure for the Tabor Grand Opera House, 1881.

HORACE TABOR

Duane A. Smith

Oro City, December 27, 1876. Is a very shrewd businessman and not liable to lose money, has a good chance to make money as he has no competition. Estimated worth say $15,000.

THIS R. G. DUN REPORT FAIRLY and accurately described the pre-Leadville and bonanza Horace Tabor. An 1859er who had spent nearly two decades following the will-o-the-wisp Colorado mining frontier, Tabor was then living and working in out-of-the-way Oro City, near where Leadville would be one day.

Soon thereafter came the Little Pittsburg silver strike, and Tabor's fortune took flight. Very quickly, Colorado—and the rest of the nation—was hearing about

Horace Tabor. "Denver's lucky star was on high when Governor Tabor decided to spend his fortune here," praised the *Denver Tribune* (September 7, 1881). The *Leadville Daily Herald* (July 8, 1882) also understood his contribution: "Colorado has produced fortunes for many men, but no man who has met with success has so freely made investments in this state, as has Governor Tabor."

The events that followed that amazing silver discovery on Fryer Hill, May 1878 unfolded like a classic Greek tragedy. Tabor weathered them all, and his name has resounded through the suc-

Artist unknown, "Horace Tabor," n.d.

ceeding decades. No other Coloradan of his generation is so well remembered, nor does anyone else so typify the tempo of this legendary mining era. While the others—Henry Teller, David Moffat, Jerome Chaffee, Edward Wolcott—have faded in memory, Tabor is still alive, thanks in no small measure to that epoch-capturing opera, *The Ballad of Baby Doe*.

He is perhaps remembered for all the wrong reasons—the love triangle, the divorce, the decline and collapse—rather than for the faith, the optimism, and the investments that built Colorado. Even more regrettable is the fabrication that became fact; as far as can be ascertained, he never told Baby Doe to "hang onto the Matchless." Her later life—and death—these are catalyst enough for the legend, without adding a 1938-concocted story that seems unlikely ever to die.

CABIN LIFE IN COLORADO

Mrs. H. A. W. Tabor

I WAS THE FIRST WOMAN in California Gulch. There was only one party ahead of us, one of seven men, and we were to join with them, but I was sick in Denver and they all went off a few days ahead of us. We were all this time trying to get track of them. We knew they had gone somewhere into the mountains prospecting about 150 miles southwest of Denver. They were prospecting along as they went, tried several gulches before they found California Gulch. When we got to Cache Creek we stopped one month. My husband whip-sawed some lumber to make sluice boxes and put them in. We found plenty of gold but there was so much black sand and we did not know how to separate it. We had no quicksilver, so we had to abandon it. I would work all day long picking out with a little magnet and when night came I would not have a pennyweight, it was so fine. Afterwards those mines turned out to be very rich, if we had stayed right there we would have had enough. It is owned by capitalists now, 20 miles below California Gulch. The town of Granite is there now. We abandoned Granite. We were the first there and camped there just one month. Three gentlemen, Nathaniel Maxey, S. P. Kellogg, Mr. Tabor and myself and baby, now a young man.

Someone came down California Gulch and reported they had found gold, they were looking us up and wanted to get in supplies. He came to our camp and told us to move up, telling us to go up until we came to the first large bald mountain on the road, then turn up that gulch around the bald mountain; it would take us all day to go with the ox-team, we would probably see the smoke of their camp fire. We went up there and found Slater and Abe Lee. Those were the first men that panned out in California Gulch. They got a dollar to the pan and that encouraged them right off. We killed our cattle that we drove in and divided the beef among them. We lived on that a few days until the man got back with some Mexicans coming in with flour. They turned to and built me a cabin of green logs, had it finished in two days. We lived there all summer. Mrs. C. L. Hall was the second lady to cross the South Park, now living at 412 Broadway, Denver. Dr. Bond came from Iowa. Had a very interesting wife, he was a gambler. He is blind now and she has to support him.

In the winter time when everything was frozen up, there was no mining and the men who had a little means would go out to the cities and spend all their money and go back in the spring.

Really the women did more in the early days than the men. There was so much for them to do, the sick to take care of. I have had so many unfortunate men shot by accident, brought to my cabin to take care of. There were so many men who could not cook and did not like men's cooking and would insist upon boarding where there was a woman and they would board there all they could.

We arrived in California Gulch May 8th, 1860, and in 1861 we had acquired what we considered quite a little fortune, about $7,000 in money. We came over into Park County, started a store and stayed there six years. We rode over Mosquito Range. My husband was Postmaster. It was called Buckskin Joe when we lived there. A man who wore buckskin clothes whose name was Joe discovered the first mine there. There was a little mining excitement, about 200 people were there so we went over with the rush and started a store there until the mines all played out. Then we went back and opened a place in California Gulch, still continued the mercantile business. My husband kept the Post Office and Express Office and I kept a boarding house in California Gulch. We were in better fix to keep those places as most everyone who came in just had a pack on his back. We had a little house and things in shape to keep them.

A man named Wm. Van Brooklyn, who did not like mining as it was too hard work, said he had a pair of mules and he would start an express, would ride the mules alternately. He brought our letters in and we paid him 75 cents each for them and paid accordingly for any little express matter he could bring on a mule. He was a heavy man and could not bring much. I kept the express books, started the letters out and took the money. He said if I would board him while he was running the express he could give me his claim, but I would not board him for it, so he sold it to a man named Ferguson and Stevens and that summer there was $80,000 taken out of that claim by those two men. I weighed all the gold that was taken out of the upper end of the gulch that summer. There was many a miner who did not know one thing about weighing gold. I never saw a country settled up with such greenhorns as Colorado. They were mostly from farms and some clerks. They were all young men from 18 to 30. I was there a good many years before we saw a man with grey hair. They thought they were going to have a second California, they gathered all the knowledge they could from books. Some Georgia miners reported there was gold here and they came out to search for it. Thousands turned back. We met them every day and they advised us to go back; but we started with six months provisions and thought if we did not find anything here we would go on to California.

When we came here everybody said nothing would ever grow on this sandy desert, and no one could ever build a railroad in those mountains.

Mr. Tabor supplied the first 300,000 ties to the A. T. & S. F. Railroad. It took five months to get those ties down the mountain. He was under contract to get them down to the road at such a time and was under bonds and he was a man who would not allow his bondsmen to pay. He expected to get them down when the water was high in the spring, but we did not have any snow that spring and could not float them, so he had to hire teams to get them out of that canyon. I stayed at home all that five months and kept the store going. We had a good deal of money to take care of, we had the only safe in the country and had to keep everybody's treasures in that safe, and I was a little afraid for the five months he was gone from home.

A man named Green took the contract to get out the ties for the A. T. & S. F. The ties were got up where California Gulch is. They were owing Mr. Tabor a good deal of money for supplies and he found out the man was not going to make a success of it and became alarmed, so he took the contract off Green's hands to get his money out of it, and that is where he missed it.

After he got through with the tie business we found that we had worked two years and had not made a dollar. Had done all the hard work for nothing. He worked hard with the rest of the men. He was terribly pushed to get food enough for them. They would eat an ox at one meal, and more too. All that time I had the store for him to get money to run those ties through.

He wanted our boy to go into the store, but I wanted him to go to school. I told him I would go into the store and do all the boy could do. I went into the store and he found I was a better hand at keeping the books than he was. I made all the returns for the Post Office for seven years, and General Adams said that during these seven years he only sent back one paper for correction. ...

I have been taken along as a body-guard a great many times when Mr. Tabor was going to Denver with treasure, because he thought he would not be so liable to be attacked. I have carried gold on my person many a time. He would buy all the gold that he could and would carry it down ourselves rather than trust the express, because our express was often robbed. I have gone across the Mosquito Range with him on horseback. Then we had no road at all. I had the gold in buckskins, then put in gunnybags, then laid on the horse and then my saddle put on over the blanket, and bring it that way. Then there would be nothing visible but the saddle. If anyone came along they would rather search him than me. There were some miles that we could not ride our horses on account of the wind, it blew so fiercely. We had to have our clothes tied on firmly. In some places it was so steep we had to hang on to our horses' tails, it was all the horses could do to get up.

Artist unknown, "Mining Camp in Colorado," from The West from a Car-Window *by Richard Harding Davis, 1892.*

SILVER QUEEN:
THE FABULOUS STORY OF
BABY DOE TABOR

Caroline Bancroft

HER STORY HAD BEEN A drama of contrasts, from rags to riches and from riches back to rags again, the whole play enacted against the backdrop of Colorado's magnificent and munificent mountains. But what those ruthless snow capped peaks give, they also take away and almost as if they are gods, they single out certain characters in history to destroy by first making mad. Mrs. Tabor went to her death with a delusion about the Matchless Mine.

She had lived during the last years of her life largely through the charity of the citizens of Leadville and the bank that held the mortgage on the Matchless. The mine had produced no ore in years and was not really equipped to work although she could not find it in her soul to admit this harsh fact of reality. She dressed in mining clothes and off and on during the last twenty years made a pretense of getting out ore with a series of men she inveigled to work on shares. But she either quarreled with these partners when she became suspicious of their honesty or the men became disillusioned about the supposed fortune hidden in the Matchless and drifted off.

I only met her once, in the summer of 1927, when I called on her with my father, a mining engineer, who was making a swing around the state to report on the mining situation. Mrs. Tabor, who had known my father for many years, showed us over the premises. She was polite to me but largely ignored me since she was concentrating on my father with the hope he might get her new backing.

The tiny cabin she lived in had been a former tool and machine shop of the Matchless and the actual shafthouse was perhaps a hundred feet or so away. When we entered the shafthouse, it already had an aura of ghosts. Dirt and rust were accumulating from disuse and covered the hoist, cables and machinery that were still there. It was my father's opinion, voiced to me as we drove off past the Robert E. Lee mine, that quite a lot of machinery had been stolen from the shafthouse without her being aware of it. Or perhaps "the old lady," as he spoke of her, had sold it to get enough to eat and had forgotten the transaction in the forgetfulness of what mountaineers call "cabin fever," a strangeness that overtakes elderly people who live alone.

I was not so interested in the mining aspects of her situation as my father (who was always avid on the scent of ore—gold, silver, copper, tungsten, and at the end, rare minerals such as vanadium, molybdenum, uranium, titanium and tantalum).

What interested me about Mrs. Tabor were her looks and her personality. I studied her quietly while she and my father talked about the glorious riches that would be uncovered if she "could just drift a little further north on the sixth level" or "sink a winze through to that stope on the fourth."

She was a little woman, very withered, and unattractively dressed in men's corduroy trousers, mining boots and a soiled, torn blouse. She had a blue bandana tied around her head and when we first drove up back of the Matchless, as close as the car could make it and started to walk to her cabin, she met us halfway, a very belligerent expression on her face. My father and she had not met in several years and it was not until after he gave his name that her manner changed.

She smiled then and said, "Why, of course, pray do forgive me. And what a beautiful daughter you have! It is my lasting sorrow that the Lord's work has taken my own daughter ..."

I could not have been more startled. The smile, the manner, the voice and the flowery speech were anomalous in that strange figure. Her smile was positively, although very briefly, gay and flashing; the teeth, even and white and the voice, clear and bell-like while the manner I can only describe as queenly despite her diminutive size.

C. Waldo Love, "Baby Doe Tabor," 1935.

I only remember two other things about that afternoon. After we had spent some time in the shaft house and walking about outside, while she and my father talked about the direction of veins and probable apexes, the price of silver and other matters not very interesting to my youthful ears, Father suggested that in the car he had a jug of homemade wine his housekeeper had made. It was during Prohibition and wine of any sort was a rarity so that when he invited her to have a drink for old times' sake, she seemed pleased and asked us up the ledge to her cabin.

While Father went back to the car for the wine, she and I strolled on ahead. I complimented her on the spectacular view of Mt. Massive and Mt. Elbert, Colorado's highest peaks, off to the west beyond the town of Leadville.

She did not say anything but she turned her eyes full upon me, the only time I think that she looked directly at me. Again I was startled. They were very far apart and a gorgeous blue, their unusual color preserved through all the violence and drama and bitterness of her then nearly seventy years.

Her cabin, really no more than a shack, was crowded with very primitive furniture and stacked high in newspapers and mementoes. It was quite neat although, to my mind, it could have stood a good dusting and the window panes had evidently not been washed since the winter snows. We drank our wine from an assortment of cups, one of them tin. She apologized for their not being very clean and said something about hauling her drinking water from some distance and using boiled mine water for other purposes.

I did not listen—to my shame, now. While they went on talking, I entertained myself with my own thoughts. I knew almost no Colorado history in those days; I had been out of the state for nine years at school, college and working in the East, my interests completely disassociated. To me, she was just one more of the queer mining characters my father knew, and he knew dozens. But I lived to regret my youthful ignorance and indifference.

LET'S REMEMBER THE REAL CAROLINE BANCROFT

Sandra Dallas

In WESTERN HISTORY SHE WAS—both literally and figuratively—a giant. Just as she loomed over most women and a goodly number of men in stature, so did Caroline Bancroft, who died recently at 85, tower above other writers of history from this region.

Caroline did a great deal for Western history. She made it palatable. I suspect more people learned Colorado history from her two dozen Bancroft booklets than anything the rest of us wrote. She actually supported herself with her writing, which is more than most Western writers can say.

And she was unfailingly generous, especially to aspiring writers. While many other historians choose to hoard their collections of photographs and make money from them, Caroline long ago turned over her valuable pictures of the Tabors and others to the Western History Department of the Denver Public Library. Anyone who cares about history is indebted to her for saving the stories and recollections of the old-timers she interviewed.

But before we whitewash Caroline Bancroft and bury her with pallid eulogies, we ought to remember her as she was. It wasn't her writing (which wasn't very good) or even her history (which could be thinly researched) that made her a monumental figure. It was Caroline herself.

She was a vibrant, opinionated woman who when stirred showed the wrath of an angry god. She relished her enemies as much as her friends. She loved a good time and up to the end had a capacity for liquor that awed even Tom Noel, author of a book on the saloons of Denver. And Caroline had a presence that turned the rest of us into wimps.

I had known her slightly in my childhood as an eccentric family friend who wore orange braids on top of her head entwined with paper flowers. But my first real encounter with her came 20 years ago, when she wrote a withering review of my first book. How, I wondered, could this nice old lady be so brutal? She vilified anybody who made errors—including James Michener after he wrote *Centennial*.

An even worse sin was failing to agree with her. She often wrote in a review that if the author had only read her own writing on the subject, he or she wouldn't have made such a foolish mistake. But when the author did as she suggested, she might charge plagiarism.

Many of us wrote with a sense of Caroline looking over our shoulders, and that was another of her contributions to Western history. More than one author went back to the library to double-check a fact for fear Caroline would catch an error. When I was writing up one of the towns included in my recent *Colorado Ghost Towns and Mining Camps*, I discovered that my date for the town's founding was different from Caroline's. I went back to my source, the autobiography of the town founder, and found I was right. Did I dare stand up to Caroline? Are you crazy? I fudged it.

Caroline's scrutiny and caustic tongue made her many enemies. She relished her feuds. The most famous was with photo historian Fred Mazzulla, who had once been her great "pal," as she dubbed her friends.

As I recall, he said she had swiped a photograph from him; Caroline claimed he had made a pass at her and blamed herself for being indiscreet enough to tell. Whatever it was, neither missed an opportunity to stick it to the other. When the late Olga Curtis wrote an *Empire* magazine article about the two and mentioned that as a young woman Caroline had raced camels in Egypt, Fred wrote a sly letter asking who had won, Caroline or the camels.

While most historians sit on the sidelines and observe life, Caroline lived it. Born into a prominent Denver family—she could get a bit dotty on the subject of the Bancrofts—Caroline shocked her set by going to work for the *Denver Post*. "It was the same as going down to Market Street and working in a house," she liked to say.

She was part of cafe society, a chum (another Bancroft word) of Evalyn Walsh McLean and Lucius Beebe, and she was even on friendly terms with old Mrs. Crawford Hill, leader of the Sacred 36.

Caroline ("It rhymes with sin, gin or jasmine, take your pick," she would say) also was a friend of Dorothy Parker, and once she and Mary Coyle Chase threw a party for Parker in Denver and invited Denver's underworld. A friend got copies of the invitation and sent them to Denver's upper crust as well, and Caroline had to station someone at the door to turn away the elite.

She never mellowed. That was the reason we all thought she would go on forever. And perhaps she will, since she believed in reincarnation.

But in one lifetime she had an enormous impact. She won't be remembered as much for her history or her writing as for herself. Like Baby Doe Tabor and Maggie (Molly) Brown, whose lives she chronicled, she was a character. With Caroline Bancroft gone, there aren't many of them left.

THE BALLAD OF BABY DOE

Douglas Moore and John Latouche

HOW THE BALLAD OF BABY DOE WAS WRITTEN

WHEN I FIRST READ THE newspaper accounts of the death of Baby Doe in 1935, I began to think of writing an opera about her. Here was a woman once famous for her beauty, who had been married to the richest man in Colorado, whose wedding had been attended by the President of the United States, and who had been found frozen to death in a miserable shack beside an abandoned silver mine.

Investigating the story with a friend, I discovered other fascinating characters: Horace Tabor, who literally stumbled upon millions and lost them in his fanatical devotion to silver; Augusta, his first wife, who had sustained him through the years of poverty, only to be mortified by his divorcing her when the young and beautiful Baby Doe appeared.

Although our planned libretto did not materialize at the time, I found myself always returning to the theme and wondering how it could be realized in an opera. Imagine my delight when, in 1953, Donald Oenslager, who had been urging the Central City Opera Association to put on an original American opera, invited me, on behalf of the Association, to write an opera about Baby Doe.

Meanwhile John Latouche had been suggesting that we write an opera together, and when he got to work on the story, all the problems of the libretto were miraculously solved.

NEW YORK CITY OPERA COMPANY
(Julius Rudel, General Director)

THE BALLAD OF BABY DOE

AN OPERA BY
DOUGLAS MOORE & JOHN LATOUCHE

The opera house, a union grand
of capital and labor;
g will the stately structure stand,
a monument to Tabor."

Eugene Field
(Upon the opening of
he Tabor Grand Opera House.)

"So fleet the works of man:
Back to the earth again
Ancient and holy things
Fade like a dream . . ."

Charles Kingsley
(Inscription on the curtain
of the Tabor Grand.)

CAST OF CHARACTERS
(In order of their appearance)

An Old Silver Miner	Grant Williams
A Saloon Bartender	Chester Ludgin
Horace Tabor, Mayor of Leadville	Walter Cassel
Sam, Bushy, Barney, Jacob; Cronies and Associates of Tabor	
Jack DeLon, Keith Kaldenberg, George DelMonte and Arthur Newman	
Augusta, Wife of Horace Tabor	Frances Bible
Mrs. Elizabeth (Baby) Doe, a Miner's Wife	Beverly Sills
Kate and Mag, Dance Hall Entertainers	Greta Wolff and Helen Baisley
Samantha, a Maid	Lynda Jordan
A Clerk at the Clarendon Hotel	Keith Kaldenberg
Albert, a Bellboy	Robert Atherton
Sarah, Mary, Emily, Effie; Old Friends of Augusta	
Mary Lesawyer, Jennie Andrea, Lou Rodgers and Dorothy White	
Mama McCourt, Baby Doe's Mother	Beatrice Krebs
Four Washington Dandies	
Edson Hoel, Dan Marek, Peter Silker and John Dennison	
McCourt Family	
Greta Wolff, Helen Baisley, Donald Arthur and William Saxon	
Father Chapelle, Priest at the Wedding	Grant Williams
A Footman at the Willard Hotel	Arthur Newman
Chester A. Arthur, President of the United States	Jack DeLon
Elizabeth, Child of Horace and Baby Doe Tabor	Lynn Taussig
The (Later) Mayor of Leadville	William Saxon
William Jennings Bryan, Democratic Presidential Candidate	Joshua Hecht
Stage Doorman at the Tabor Grand Theatre	Grant Williams
A Denver Politician	Chester Ludgin
Silver Dollar, Younger Child of Horace and Baby Doe Tabor (grown-up)	Helen Baisley

Dance Hall Girls, Guests at the Clarendon, Baby Doe's Family and Foreign
Diplomats at the wedding reception, Miners and Miners' Wives.

NEW YORK CITY OPERA CHORUS: Jennie Andrea, Donald Arthur,
Robert Atherton, Anthony Balestrieri, George DelMonte, John Dennison,
Frank Ehrhardt, William Golden, Edson Hoel, Lynda Jordan, Mary Le-
sawyer, Dan Marek, Rita Metzger, Margaret Rae, Lou Rodgers, William
Saxon, Peter Sliker, Lynn Starling, Marshall Stone, Dorothy White, Greta
Wolff, Mara Yavne.

Original cast list for the New York production of "The Ballad of Baby Doe," 1958.

The first performance of the opera was given July 7, 1956, in Central City, where Baby Doe had actually lived at one time. Donald Oenslager did the sets, Hanya Holm directed, Emerson Buckley conducted performances which featured Walter Cassel as Tabor, Martha Lipton as Augusta, and Dolores Wilson as Baby Doe. The alternating cast included Clifford Harvuot, Frances Bible, and Leyna Gabriele. When the opera was produced in New York at the City Center in 1958, Beverly Sills appeared for the first time as Baby Doe.

After the performances in Central City, Latouche and I discussed some revisions, principally the addition of the gambling scene in Act Two. This and a new aria for Baby proved to be the last things he was ever to write. He died at the age of thirty-nine in August, 1956. I am glad that from the warmth of the reception that Coloradans gave him, he knew he had been equal to the challenge of this great American story.

(John Latouche and) Douglas Moore

THE STORY

The chief characters in *The Ballad of Baby Doe* are drawn from actual figures in American history. Baby Doe, Horace and Augusta Tabor, and their fellow-citizens in Leadville and Denver, are re-created from pages of Colorado's fabulous era, at the turn of the century. William Jennings Bryan and President Chester A. Arthur, who touch on the story at certain points, reflect the larger American scene, as the struggle concerning free gold and silver coinage nearly split the nation asunder.

The dramatic treatment of Tabor's life, and the two women who dominated it, closely follows the pattern of fact. Any shifts in the time element and character emphasis have been made in order to shape the robust chronicle of these lives into the framework of the musical theatre.

The story begins in 1880 at the peak of Tabor's success. After twenty years of poverty, he and his wife, now in their fifties, have attained wealth and power. The classic triangle is formed when Mrs. Elizabeth Doe, known to the miners of Central City as Baby, leaves her husband, Harvey Doe, and comes down to Leadville to better her fortunes.

What begins as flirtation ends as a deep and abiding love for the man thirty years her senior. But the price of this love is ruin for Tabor. Baby Doe remained true to his memory, however. In 1935, she froze to death at the Matchless Mine, ending the long vigil she had kept there since Tabor's demise in 1899.

ACT ONE

Time: 1880. A summer evening.

Scene: The exterior of the Tabor Opera House in Leadville, Colorado. It is not a very big building, but it strains toward grandeur in a timid rural way. To one side can be seen part of the façade of a saloon. On the other side the entrance to a hotel is indicated. As the curtain rises, there are wild shouts and screams mingled with laughter. A few pistol shots crack out, and figures can be seen struggling in the section of the saloon window visible on stage. An Indian in slipshod regalia, a woman and child, and a cowboy run along the street to watch the fun. The bouncer of the saloon throws a miner out the door. The miner is an aging man. He waves a pistol in one hand, and holds a pot of silver ore in the other.

SCENE ONE

🐜 🐜 🐜

(The doors of the Opera House open, and Augusta and the other women stand aghast at the scene.)

AUGUSTA

Horace, what is this? Have you taken leave of your senses? Just one evening, can't you act with a bit of dignity? Can't you manage to cooperate in our efforts to provide some change of tone in this money-grubbing town—some touch of beauty and refinement? The ladies and I worked hard to secure artists of the highest caliber for this concert, and you men walk out in the sight of all, making us look silly there, sitting in the box alone. All the more ridiculous when we find you here, cavorting with these harridans, dancing with these Jezebels—an insult to your wives!

TABOR

Now, Augusta, wait a bit. We just stepped out for a cigar while the string quartet is on. Lecture us, but why on earth snub the girls and call them names? Like I say, they work for me, and you owe them some respect. Dollars from that old saloon, same as dollars from the mines, helped to build this handsome Opry House— helped to put this shindig on. Yep, these painted Jezebels, doin' high kicks for the boys, helped to put this concert on much as your committee did.

AUGUSTA

Really, Horace, you're too much! Remember who you are.

LADIES

Intermission's over now. Let's go in.

MEN

Yes, my dear, you're right—you're always right.

(They start to go back into the Opera House. Tabor lingers behind. Baby Doe enters,

followed by a Welsh servant, a cook from the mining camp. She is a beautiful woman in her early twenties, neatly but not too expensively dressed. She goes up to Tabor.)

BABY DOE

I beg your pardon,
Can you direct me
To the Clarendon Hotel?
I've just arrived from Central City
So I don't know my way about.
Cousin Jack there
Knows so little English,
I have to find the way by myself.

TABOR

Yonder is the Clarendon
And welcome to our city.
My name is Horace Tabor;
If I can be of any help
I hope you'll let me know.

BABY DOE

You're very kind.

AUGUSTA

(From the doorway of the Opera House)
Horace, we're waiting!

TABOR

I hope we'll meet again.
(He bows and goes into the Opera House with Augusta.)

BABY DOE

I'm sure we'll meet again, Horace Tabor.
Indeed we'll meet again.
(She enters the Clarendon.)

CURTAIN

SCENE TWO

Time: Later that evening.
Scene: The exterior of the Clarendon Hotel. Stage right is an out-size window through which a lamp glows. The shades are drawn. Two large windows upstairs are also functional, as are the lower door and window. Augusta, Tabor and their cronies enter on their way from the concert. The women wear shawls and carry fans. The men carry capes.

LADIES

What a lovely evening

All the charms of music
Wedded to poetry
Like as if the muses
Had've all descended
Crowning us with blessings
What a lovely evening
We're so glad you liked it
MEN
Lovely, lovely evening
Charming, charming music
Borne aloft by Pegasus
Clad in classic draperies
Bringing classic laurels
Their immortal benison
Thanks to all you ladies
Thank you, thank you, ladies
AUGUSTA
Thank you, one and all.
TABOR
Till we meet tomorrow.
(The friends exit.)
AUGUSTA
It's nice they enjoyed it.
But now the whole thing's over
I have to admit
I'm a wee bit tuckered out.
CHORUS
(Fading)
Lovely, lovely evening
We must do it again.
AUGUSTA
(Yawning)
La, la, la, la.
I like Adelina Patti.
She sings divinely
And quite a lady too.
Are you coming up?
TABOR
Soon.
AUGUSTA
Don't be too long.

(She goes in. Tabor sits in a chair to the left of the center door and puffs his cigar thoughtfully. Two girls come in, returning from the saloon. They are in animated conversation and do not notice Tabor.)

KATE

Her with a servant boy and all, what airs!

MAG

Did you see her making up to Tabor?

KATE

Asking for the Clarendon!

MAG

Baby Doe! Ain't that silly?

KATE

That's what the miners call her. She's so *sweet!*

MAG

Sweet! That little stuck-up thing, Baby Doe? Ain't she got a husband somewhere?

KATE

Harvey Doe, up in Central City.

MAG

Guess he can't afford that kind of baby.

KATE

Tabor'd better watch out.
She'll make trouble.

BOTH

She's no better than us, Baby Doe, Baby Doe, Baby Doe!

(As the girls go out, Baby Doe raises the window shade and seats herself at the piano. Tabor watches in rapt attention.)

TABOR

So that's her name. Baby Doe!

(Baby Doe begins to play the piano.)

BABY DOE

Ah!

Willow, where we met together
Willow, when our love was new
Willow, if he once should be returning
Pray tell him I am weeping too.
So far from each other
While the days pass
In their emptiness away.
Oh my love, must it be forever
Never once again
To meet as on that day?

And never rediscover
The way of telling
The way of knowing
All our hearts would say.
Gone are the ways of pleasure
Gone are the friends I had [loved] of yore
Only the recollection fatal
Of the word that was spoken:
Nevermore.
Oh, willow, where we met together
Willow, when our love was new
Willow, if he once should be returning
Pray tell him I am weeping too.
Ah!
(Tabor, in the darkness, applauds, and Baby comes to the window.)
Oh, Mr. Tabor, you startled me!
I had no idea anyone was listening.
Tabor
(Deeply moved)
Baby Doe!
Baby Doe!
Baby Doe!
That's the prettiest name
I ever had the luck to hear.
Baby Doe
You know my name?
How is that possible?
Tabor
Baby Doe, the miners' sweetheart.
I'm just a miner too.
Baby Doe
But you are Horace Tabor,
Fabulous Horace Tabor
And no one ever mentioned
You're still a young man.
Amazing Horace Tabor
With hair like a raven's wing,
Eyes afire with dreaming
Like a boy of seventeen.
Tabor
Warm as the autumn light

Soft as a pool at night
The sound of your singing,
Baby Doe.
And while I was listening
I was recalling [all the things]
Things that once I had wanted so much
And forgotten as years slipped away
A girl I knew back home in Vermont
The sea in New Hampshire
The first sight of the mountains
They say I've been lucky
There's nothing my money won't buy
It couldn't be I was unhappy
Or was missing the good things of life.
But only tonight came again in your singing
That feeling of wonder, of longing and pain.
Deep in your lovely eyes
All of enchantment lies
And tenderly beckons, Baby Doe
Dearest Baby Doe.
(*They gaze at each other tenderly. Tabor takes her hand and kisses it. A light goes
on in one of the upstairs windows and Augusta is seen looking out.*)
AUGUSTA
Horace, are you still down there?
I thought I heard you calling
Horace, are you down there?
TABOR
Yes, Augusta.
Yes, my dear.
I am here.
AUGUSTA
Aren't you coming up?
It's getting on to midnight.
TABOR
Just as you say, my dear.
Anything you say.
(*Baby Doe and Tabor silently bid farewell. He goes in the door of the hotel.*)

OUR PRESIDENT ROOSEVELT'S COLORADO HUNT

Silver Dollar Tabor

Roll up in a Navajo blanket
And stretch 'neath the sweet pine trees,
With the moan of the panting Wild cat
Borne upon the breeze;
Watch for the Elk and Beaver,
Keep your old Winchester by,
Be up with your rifle when you hear
The Martin's teeming cry.
Away, away, to the glorious wilds,
Where life is free and the world your own,
Upon the slopes 'mid the shelt'ring pines,
And down in the valleys I'll roam,
Wrapped in a Navajo blanket,
I'll make the West my home.

Way up on the crested summits,
I'll brave the frantic storm,
And track the tardy Grissly Bear,
While still my heart is warm;
Down the snowcapped mountains,
'Mid the wafting sheen,
I'll carry my burdens homeward
Into the valleys of green.
Dream, ah! dream, of the life within the hills,
And peaceful slumber by the rippling rills
Upon the slopes 'mid the windswept pines
That stand like Sentinels round,
Wrapped in a Navajo blanket,
I'll keep watch with my hound.

Passed by the biting winds,
Still in the beaming sun,
Under the cloudless Heavens
Until the day is done;
Out of the starlit sky
The moon shines over head,
Bright in her queenly glory
Until the night has sped.
Live, oh! live, 'neath the azure
        Heaven,
Until the golden morn is giv'n,
Out to the land of freedom,
Sweet with the scented breeze,
Wrapped in a Navajo blanket,
I'll pal with the old pine trees.

STAR OF BLOOD

Silver Dollar Tabor

ON DECEMBER 3, 1896, he was tried before Judge Butler. He had no lawyer, for he needed none. He simply pleaded guilty and begged for a speedy sentence of death. Judge Butler was not satisfied with Downen appearing for himself and appointed Attorney Robert E. Foot to conduct his case.

His life story was repeated to the jury just as he had confessed it, repeated at its best and at its worst, his grewsome deeds frowning out of the shadow of the past, his little betrayals of sentiment touching the jury, and his voluntary confession of all winning their respect in a singular manner.

"I'm dead tired of life; I've had a hard one and I want to die," he frankly admitted in his natural blunt way.

Downen sank back in the witness chair, that same old sullenness clouding his drawn features. Then a quiescence of resignation and the sullen gloom had drifted into a tearful hope that he would be condemned to death.

Sixty-three seconds elapsed while the jury was deliberating, and at the end of that short time they returned.

The head of the host of dignified men stood before the silent judge and slowly read the verdict.

A pall had settled over the room, the judge and spectators were apprehensive of the pending toll of death, only one face greeted the sentence cheerfully and that was the face of the multi-murderer himself.

"Guilty of murder in the first degree!"

An agonized shriek rent the air. It was like an impassioned cry from the other world. The vibrating echo died away and the hushed spectators in the crowded court room breathed again.

A woman, as wildly sinuous as an animal, with tragical black eyes flashing from her pale face and her loosened dark hair falling about her bare throat, staggered forward.

She was bareheaded and scantily clad for the dead of winter, and a wild hopelessness deposed all other expressions from her face.

"Artie," Downen's hoarse shout expressed intense feeling.

The startled black eyes of Artie Dallas tenderly rebuked him for voluntarily confessing to the crimes that would take him to the gallows or the penitentiary. As she blindly stumbled toward him through the curious crowd, he suddenly awakened to the wrong he had done her by confessing, and he weakened when he realized the magnitude of her love.

With that old relevant bravado and dauntless reliance, he turned to the judge and jury and disavowed the statements he had made. He disclaimed every mysterious crime that he had deliberately related and proclaimed himself innocent.

But they had been verified, and it was too late.

"You voluntarily confessed to all these crimes that have convicted you, you pleaded guilty and asked for a speedy sentence of death, and you were satisfied until you saw Artie Dallas," the energetic prosecuting attorney put in.

"I knew you could not trace the murderer of Ashworth; I knew I could claim that crime, for I am dead tired of durance, and in order to get death at your hands I accused myself, but I did not kill him. I spent that night with a woman. Neither did I kill the sport in San Jose; he committed suicide, and Ashworth was killed by a jealous lover of his wife's."

The trembling woman of the slums sank in the murderer's arms like a maimed wild bird.

"Artie," he purred.

Her limp body lay heavily against him and no answer came from her white lips. Artie had swooned.

They laid her frail body upon a couch by an open window. Her motionless face lay back upon its pillow of tangled dark hair like the face of a dead slave of the Orient who had been tortured to death. Had chains been around her slender wrists, had her feet been bare and bleeding, had her body been burnt in sacrifice, that tragical visage could not have betrayed more violent anguish.

Downen broke away from his guards and shouldered his way to her. He gathered her up and clung to her with all the furious strength that despair commands.

He believed that she was dead, and did not express his feelings, whether he rejoiced for her sake or grieved for his, but he passionately caressed the marble-like face.

"Artie, Artie, Artie," he purred, in a voice so low but penetrating that it seemed capable of waking the dead.

The woman's wild eyes slowly opened and she joyously kissed him, for the fleeting moment forgetting that they were doomed to part, forgetting that the judge and jury and spectators were witnessing their valediction. Her temples were feverish and her eyes burned, for she had passed the stage of tears. All through the long trial she had rebelliously witnessed the secrets of his life, that had been so sacredly guarded by her in the shrine of her devotion, being vivisected for the inspection of the jury. There, way back in the court room, she had sobbed like a mourner at a funeral with a shawl drawn down over her bent head. Now that he was convicted of murder in the first degree, she had a vague prescience that she had not long to live on in her lawless way.

They clung together as if the parting meant death. Their hearts were united in a fusion of love which was so completely tempered that nothing earthly could mollify it, but the insoluble hand of the law abruptly interrupted their love scene and they were forcibly torn apart.

SECTION VII

PIKES PEAK

Charles Patridge Adams, "Pikes Peaks," n.d.

AMERICA, THE BEAUTIFUL

Katharine Lee Bates

I

O beautiful for spacious skies,
    For amber waves of grain,
For purple mountain majesties
    Above the fruited plain!
    America! America!
    God shed His grace on thee,
And crown thy good with brotherhood,
    From sea to shining sea!

II

O beautiful for pilgrim feet,
    Whose stern, impassioned stress
A thoroughfare for freedom beat
    Across the wilderness!
    America! America!
    God mend thine every flaw,
Confirm thy soul in self-control,
    Thy liberty in law!

III

O beautiful for heroes proved
    In liberating strife,
Who more than self their country loved;
    And mercy more than life!
    America! America!
    May God thy gold refine,
Till all success be nobleness,
    And every gain divine!

IV

O beautiful for patriot dream
    That sees beyond the years
Thine alabaster cities gleam
    Undimmed by human tears!
    America! America!
    God shed His grace on thee,
And crown thy good with brotherhood
    From sea to shining sea!

Lyman Byxbe, "Autumn," n.d.

AN ACCOUNT OF EXPEDITIONS TO THE SOURCES OF THE MISSISSIPPI

Zebulon Montgomery Pike

Nov. 25TH. MARCHED EARLY, with an expectation ascending the mountain, but was only able to encamp at its base, after passing over many small hills covered with cedars and pitch-pines. Our encampment was on a [Turkey] creek, where we found no water for several miles from the mountain; but near its base, found springs sufficient. Took a meridional observation, and the altitude of the mountain. Killed two buffalo. Distance 22 miles.

Nov. 26th. Expecting to return to our camp the same evening, we left all our blankets and provisions at the foot of the [Cheyenne] mountain. Killed a deer of a new species [*Cariacus macrotis*], and hung his skin on a tree with some meat. We commenced ascending; found it very difficult, being obliged to climb up rocks, sometimes almost perpendicular; and after marching all day we encamped in a cave, without blankets, victuals, or water. We had a fine clear sky, while it was snowing at the bottom. On the side of the mountain we found only yellow and pitch-pine. Some distance up we found buffalo; higher still the new species of deer, and pheasants [dusky grouse, *Dendragapus obscurus*].

Nov. 27th. Arose hungry, dry and extremely sore, from the inequality of the rocks on which we had lain all night, but were amply compensated for toil by the sublimity of the prospect below. The unbounded prairie was overhung with clouds, which appeared like the ocean in a storm, wave piled on wave and foaming, while the sky was perfectly clear where we were. Commenced our march up the mountain, and in about one hour arrived at the summit of this chain. Here we found the snow middle-deep; no sign of beast or bird inhabiting this region. The thermometer, which stood at 9° above zero at the foot of the mountain, here fell to 4° below zero. The summit of the Grand Peak, which was entirely bare of vegetation and covered with snow, now appeared at the distance of 15 or 16 miles from us. It was as high again as what we had ascended, and it would have taken a whole day's march to arrive at its base, when I believe no human being could have ascended to its pinical. This, with the condition of my soldiers, who had only light overalls on, no stockings, and were in every way ill provided to endure the inclemency of the region; the bad prospect of killing anything to subsist on, with the further detention of two or three days which it must occasion, determined us to return. The clouds from below had now ascended the mountain and entirely enveloped the summit, on which rest eternal snows. We descended by a long, deep ravine, with much less difficulty than contemplated. Found all our baggage safe, but the provisions all destroyed. It began to snow, and we sought shelter under the side of a projecting rock, where we all four made a meal on one partridge and a piece of deer's ribs the ravens had left us, being the first we had eaten in that 48 hours.

Nov. 28th. Marched at nine o'clock. Kept straight on down the [Turkey] creek to avoid the hills. At half past one o'clock shot two buffalo, when we made the first full meal we had made in three days. Encamped in a valley under a shelving rock. The land here very rich, and covered with old Tetau [Comanche] camps.

Nov. 29th. Marched after a short repast, and arrived at our camp before night; found all well.

Sunday, Nov. 30th. Marched at eleven o'clock; it snowed very fast, but my impatience to be moving would not permit my lying still at that camp. The doctor, Baroney, and myself went to view a Tetau encampment, which appeared to be about two years old; and from their having cut down so large a quantity of trees to support their horses, we concluded there must have been at least 1,000 souls. Passed several more in the course of the day; also one Spanish camp. This day came to the first cedar and pine. Killed two deer. Distance 15 miles.

ACCOUNT OF AN EXPEDITION FROM PITTSBURGH TO THE ROCKY MOUNTAINS

Edwin James

AT AN EARLY HOUR ON the morning of the 13th [July 1820], Lieutenant Swift, accompanied by the guide, was despatched from camp, to measure a base near the Peak, and to make there a part of the observations requisite for calculating its elevation. Dr. James being furnished with four men, two to be left at the foot of the mountain to take care of the horses, and two to accompany him in the proposed ascent to the summit of the Peak, set off at the same time.

This detachment left the camp before sunrise, and taking the most direct route across the plains, arrived at eleven o'clock, at the base of the mountain. Here Lieutenant Swift found a place suited to his purpose, where also was a convenient spot for those who were to ascend the mountain, to leave their horses in a narrow valley, dividing transversely several sandstone ridges, and extending westward to the base of the Peak.

After establishing their horse camp, the detachment moved up the valley on foot, arriving about noon at the Boiling spring, where they dined on a saddle of venison, and some bison ribs, they had brought ready cooked from camp.

The Boiling spring is a large and beautiful fountain of water, cool and transparent, and highly aerated with carbonic acid. It rises on the brink of a small

Titian Ramsay Peale, "Rocky Mountains ... from a Sketch by S ... ," n.d.

stream, which here descends from the mountain, at the point where the bed of this stream divides the ridge of sandstone, which rests against the base of the first granitic range.

The water of the spring deposits a copious concretion of carbonate of lime, which has accumulated on every side, until it has formed a large basin overhanging the stream. This basin is of a snowy whiteness, and large enough to contain three or four hundred gallons, and is constantly overflowing. The spring rises from the bottom of the basin, with a rumbling noise, discharging about equal volumes of air and of water, probably about fifty gallons per minute, the whole being kept in constant agitation. The water is beautifully transparent, and has the sparkling appearance, the grateful taste, and the exhilarating effect of the most strongly aerated artificial mineral waters.

Distant a few rods from this, is another spring of the same kind, which discharges no water, its basin remaining constantly full, and air only escaping from it. We collected some of the air from both of these springs, in a box we had carried for the reception of plants, but could not perceive it to have the least smell, or the power of extinguishing flame, which was tested by plunging into it lighted splinters of dry cedar.

The temperature of the water of the larger spring at noon was 63° the thermometer at the same time in the shade, stood at 68°; immersed in the small spring, at 67°. This difference in temperature, is owing to the difference of situation, the higher temperature of the small spring, depending entirely on its constant exposure to the rays of the sun, and to its retaining the same portion of water, while that in the large spring is constantly replaced by a new supply.

After we had dined, and hung up some provisions in a large red cedar tree, near the spring, intending it for a supply on our return, we took leave of Lieutenant Swift and began to ascend the mountain. We carried with us, each a small blanket, ten or twelve pounds of bison meat, three gills of parched-corn meal, and a small kettle.

The sandstone extends westward from the springs, about three hundred yards, rising rapidly upon the base of the mountain. It is of a deep red colour, usually compact and fine, but sometimes embracing angular fragments of petrosilx and other silicious stones, with a few organic impressions. The granite which succeeds it, is coarse, and of a deep red colour. Some loose fragments of gneiss, were seen lying about the surface, but none in place. The granite at the base of the mountain, contains a large proportion of feldspar of the rose-coloured variety, in imperfect cubic crystals, and disintegrating rapidly under the operation of frost and other causes, crumbling into small masses of half an ounce weight or less.

In ascending, we found the surface in many places, covered with this loose and crumbled granite, rolling from under our feet, and rendering the ascent extremely difficult. We began to credit the assertions of the guide, who had conducted us to the foot of the Peak; and left us with the assurance, that the whole of the mountain to its summit, was covered with loose sand and gravel, so that though many attempts had been made by the Indians and by hunters to ascend it, none had ever proved successful. We passed several of these tracks, not without some apprehension for our lives, as there was danger when the foot-hold was once lost of sliding down, and being thrown over precipices.

After clambering with extreme fatigue over about two miles, in which several of these dangerous places occurred, we halted at sunset in a small cluster of fir trees. We could not, however, find a piece of even ground large enough to lie down upon, and were under the necessity of securing ourselves from rolling into the brook, near which we encamped, by means of a pole placed against two trees. In this situation we passed an uneasy night, and, though the mercury fell only to 54°, felt some inconvenience from cold.

On the morning of the 14th, as soon as daylight appeared, having suspended in a tree, whatever articles of clothing could be dispensed with, our blankets and provisions, except about three pounds of bison flesh, we continued the ascent, hoping to be able to reach the summit of the Peak, and return to the same camp in the evening. After passing about half a mile of rugged and difficult travelling, like that of the preceding day, we crossed a deep chasm, opening towards the bed of the small stream we had hitherto ascended, and following the summit of the ridge between these, found the way less difficult and dangerous.

Having passed a level tract of several acres, covered with the aspen poplar, a few birches and pines, we arrived at a small stream running towards the south, nearly parallel to the base of the conic part of the mountain, which forms the summit of the Peak. From this spot, we could distinctly see almost the whole of the Peak, its lower half thinly clad with pines, junipers, and other evergreen trees; the upper a naked conic pile of yellowish rocks, surmounted here and there with broad patches of snow; but the summit appeared so distant, and the ascent so steep, that we despaired of accomplishing the ascent, and returning on the same day.

In marshy places about this part of the mountain, we saw an undescribed white flowered species of caltha, some Spediculariae, the shrubby cinquefoil, (Potentilla *fruticosa, Ph.*) and many alpine plants.

The day was agreeably bright and calm. As we ascended rapidly, a manifest change of temperature was perceptive, and before we reached the outskirts of the timber, a little wind was felt from the northeast. On this part of the mountain, the yellow flowered stone-crop, (Sedum *stenopetalum, Ph.*) is almost the only herbaceous plant which occurs. The boundary of the region of forests, is a defined line encircling the peak in a part which, when seen from the plain, appeared near the summit, but when we arrived at it, a greater part of the whole elevation of the mountain, seemed still before us. Above the timber the ascent is steeper, but less difficult than below, the surface being so highly inclined, that the large masses when loosened roll down, meeting no obstruction, until they arrive at the commencement of the timber. The red cedar, and the flexile pine, are the trees which appear at the greatest elevation. These are small, having thick and extremely rigid trunks, and near the commencement of the woodless part of the mountain, they have neither limbs nor bark on the side exposed to the descending masses of rocks. These trees have not probably grown in a situation so exposed, as to be unable to produce or retain bark or limbs on one side; the timber must formerly have extended to a greater elevation on the sides of this peak, than at present, so that those trees, which are now on the outskirts of the forest, were formerly protected by their more exposed neighbours.

A few trees were seen above the commencement of snow, but these are very small and entirely procumbent, being sheltered in the crevices and fissures of the rock. There are also the roots of trees to be seen at some distance, above the part where any are now standing.

A little above the point where the timber disappears entirely, commences a region of astonishing beauty, and of great interest on account of its productions; the intervals of soil are sometimes extensive, and are covered with a carpet of low but brilliantly flowering alpine plants. Most of these have either matted procumbent stems, or such as including the flower, rarely rise more than an inch in height. In many of them, the flower is the most conspicuous and the largest part of the plant, and in all, the colouring is astonishingly brilliant.

A deep blue is the prevailing colour among these flowers, and the Pentstemon *erianthera,* the mountain Columbine, (Aquilegia *coeruea*) and other plants common to less elevated districts, were here much more intensely coloured, than in ordinary situations.

It cannot be doubted, that the peculiar brilliancy of colouring, observed in alpine plants, inhabiting near the utmost limits of phaenogamous vegetation, depends in a great measure on the intensity of the light transmitted from the bright and unobscured atmosphere of those regions, and increased by reflection from the immense impending masses of snow. May the deep coerulean tint of the sky, be supposed to have an influence in producing the corresponding colour, so prevalent in the flowers of these plants?

At about two o'clock we found ourselves so much exhausted, as to render a halt necessary. Mr. Wilson who had accompanied us as a volunteer, had been left behind some time since, and could not now be seen in any direction. As we felt some anxiety on his account, we halted and endeavoured to apprize him of our situation; but repeated calls, and the discharging of the rifleman's piece produced no answer. We therefore determined to wait some time to rest, and to eat the provisions we had brought, hoping in the meantime he would overtake us.

Here, as we were sitting at our dinner, we observed several small animals, nearly of the size of the common gray squirrel, but shorter and more clumsily formed. They were of a dark gray colour, inclining to brown, with a short thick head, and erect rounded ears. In habits and appearance, they resemble the prairie dog, and are believed to be a species of the same genus. The mouth of their burrow is usually placed under the projection of a rock, and near these we afterwards saw several of the little animals, watching our approach and uttering a shrill note, somewhat like that of the ground squirrel. Several attempts were made to procure a specimen of this animal, but always without success, as we had no guns but such as carried a heavy ball.

After sitting about half an hour, we found ourselves somewhat refreshed, but much benumbed with cold. We now found it would be impossible to reach the summit of the mountain, and return to our camp of the preceding night, during that part of the day which remained; but as we could not persuade ourselves to turn back, after having so nearly accomplished the ascent, we resolved to take our chance of spending the night, on whatever part of the mountain, it might overtake us. Wilson had not yet been seen, but as no time could be lost, we resolved to go as soon as possible to the top of the Peak, and look for him on our return. We met, as we proceeded, such numbers of unknown and interesting plants, as to occasion much delay in collecting, and were under the disagreeable necessity of passing by numbers which we saw in situations difficult of access. As we approached the summit, these became less frequent, and at length ceased entirely. Few cryptogamous plants are seen about any part of the mountain, and neither these nor any others occur frequently on the top of the Peak. There is an area of ten or fifteen acres, forming the summit, which is nearly level, and on this part scarce a lichen is to be seen. It is covered to a great depth with large splintery fragments of a rock, entirely similar to that found at the base of the Peak, except, perhaps, a little more compact in its structure.

By removing a few of these fragments, they were found to rest upon a bed of ice, which is of great thickness, and may, perhaps, be as permanent and as old as the rocks, with which it occurs.

It was about 4 o'clock P.M., when we arrived on the summit. In our way we had attempted to cross a large field of snow, which occupied a deep ravine, extending down half a mile from the top, on the south-eastern side of the Peak. This was found impassable, being covered with a thin ice, not sufficiently strong to bear the weight of a man. We had not been long on the summit, when we were rejoined by the man, who had separated from us near the outskirts of the timber. He had turned aside and lain down to rest, and afterwards pursued the ascent by a different route.

From the summit of the Peak, the view towards the north, west, and southwest, is diversified with innumerable mountains, all white with snow; and on some of the more distant, it appears to extend down to their bases. Immediately under our feet on the west, lay the narrow valley of the Arkansa, which we could trace running towards the northwest, probably more than sixty miles.

On the north side of the Peak, was an immense mass of snow and ice. The ravine, in which it lay, terminated in a woodless and apparently fertile valley, lying west of the first great ridge, and extending far towards the north. This valley must undoubtedly contain a considerable branch of the Platte. In a part of it, distant probably thirty miles, the smoke of a fire was distinctly seen, and was supposed to indicate the encampment of a party of Indians.

To the east lay the great plain, rising as it receded, until, in the distant horizon, it appeared to mingle with the sky. A little want of transparency in the atmosphere, added to the great elevation from which we saw the plain, prevented our distinguishing the small inequalities of the surface. The Arkansa with several of its tributaries, and some of the branches of the Platte, could be distinctly traced as on a map, by the line of timber along their courses.

On the south the mountain is continued, having another summit (probably that ascended by Captain Pike,) at the distance of eight or ten miles. This, however, falls much below the High Peak in point of elevation, being wooded quite to its top. Between the two lies a small lake, about a mile long and half a mile wide, discharging eastward into the Boiling-spring creek. A few miles farther towards the south, the range containing these two peaks terminates abruptly.

The weather was calm and clear, while we remained on the Peak, but we were surprised to observe the air in every direction filled with such clouds of grasshoppers, as partially to obscure the day. They had been seen in vast numbers about all the higher parts of the mountain, and many had fallen upon the snow and perished. It is perhaps difficult to assign the cause, which induces these insects to ascend to those highly elevated regions of the atmosphere. Possibly they may have undertaken migrations to some remote district, but there appears not the least uniformity in the direction of their movements. They extended upwards from the summit of the mountain, to the utmost limit of vision, and as the sun shone brightly, they could be seen by the glittering of their wings, at a very considerable distance.

About all the woodless parts of the mountain, and particularly on the summit, numerous tracks were seen resembling those of the common deer, but they most probably have been those of the big-horn. The skulls and horns of these animals we had repeatedly seen near the licks and saline springs at the foot of the mountain, but they are known to resort principally about the most elevated and inaccessible places.

The party remained on the summit only about half an hour. In this time the mercury fell to 42°, the thermometer hanging against the side of a rock; which in all the early part of the day, had been exposed to the direct rays of the sun. At the encampment of the main body in the plains, a corresponding thermometer stood, in the middle of the day, at 96°, and did not fall below 80°, until a late hour in the evening.

Great uniformity was observed in the character of the rock about all the upper part of the mountain. It is a compact, indestructible aggregate of quartz and feldspar, with a little hornblend in very small particles. Its fracture is fine granular or even, and the mass exhibits a tendency to divide when broken into long, somewhat splintery fragments. It is of a yellowish-brown colour, which does not perceptibly change by long exposure to the air. It is undoubtedly owing to the close texture and the impenetrable firmness of this rock, that so few lichens are found upon it. For the same reason it is little subject to disintegration by the action of frost. It is not improbable that the splintery fragments which occur in such quantities on all the higher parts of the Peak, may owe their present form to the agency of lightning; no other cause seems adequate to the production of so great an effect.

Near the summit, some large detached crystals of feldspar, of a pea-green colour, were collected; also large fragments of transparent, white and smoky quartz, and an aggregate of opake white quartz, with crystals of hornblend.

About five in the afternoon we began to descend, and a little before sunset arrived at the commencement of the timber, but before we reached the small stream at the bottom of the first descent, we perceived we had missed our way. It was now become so dark, as to render an attempt to proceed extremely hazardous, and as the only alternative, we kindled a fire, and laid ourselves down on the first spot of level ground we could find. We had neither provisions nor blankets; and our clothing was by no means suitable for passing the night in so bleak and inhospitable a situation. We could not, however, proceed without imminent danger from precipices, and by the aid of a good fire, and no ordinary degree of fatigue, we found ourselves able to sleep during a greater part of the night.

A BLOOMER GIRL ON PIKES PEAK, 1858

Julia Archibald Holmes

AUG. 5—WE LEFT SNOWDELL early this morning for the summit, taking with us nothing but our writing materials and Emerson. We deviated somewhat from our course in order to pass the rim of Amphitheater Canyon. Here on the edge of the perpendicular walls, were poised stones and boulders of all sizes ready to be rolled, with a slight effort, into the yawning abyss. Starting these stones had been a favorite amusement with those who ascended before us, and it savored somewhat of the terrible. When a stone was started it seemed first to leap into the air, and passing from sight nothing would be heard of it for several seconds. Then would come a crashing, thundering sound from the hidden depths below, which seemed to continue until lost in the distant lower region. From these hollow distant sounds some of the men had supposed the existence of an inaccessable cave below. As we proved yesterday, however, nothing but a tremendous circular chasm exists. After enjoying this sport a short time we proceeded directly up towards the summit. Arriving within a few hundred yards of the top the surface changed into a huge pile of loose angular stones, so steep we found much difficulty in clambering up them. Passing to the right of a drift of snow some three or four hundred yards long, which sun and wind had turned into coarse ice, we stood upon a platform of near one hundred acres of feldspathic granite rock and boulders. Occasionally a little cranny among the rocks might be found in which had collected some coarse soil from the disintegration of the granite, where in one or two instances we found a green tuft about the size of a teacup from which sprung dozens of tiny blue flowers most bewitchingly beautiful. The little ultra-marine colored leaves of the flower seemed covered with an infinitude of minute sparkling crystals—they seemed children of the sky and snow. It was cold and rather cloudy, with squalls of snow, conseq(u)ently our view was not so extensive as we had anticipated. A portion only of the whitened back-bone ridge of the Rocky Mountains which forms the boundary line of so many territories could be seen, fifty miles to the west. We were now nearly fourteen thousand feet above the sea level. But we could not spend long in contemplating the grandeur of the scene for it was exceedingly cold, and leaving our names on a large rock, we commenced letters to some of our friends, using a broad flat rock for a writing desk. When we were ready to return I read aloud the lines from Emerson.

Artist unknown,
"Climbing Pikes
Peak," from
Beyond the
Mississippi *by*
Albert D.
Richardson,
1867.

"A ruddy drop of manly blood,
The surging sea outweighs;
The world uncertain comes
and goes,
The looser rooted stays."

🐜 🐜 🐜

Aug. 2d, 1858

Dear Mother: I write this to you sitting in our little house among the
rocks, about one hour's walk from the summit of Pike's Peak. It is a
curious little nook which we have selected as our temporary home,
formed by two very large overhanging rocks, and enclosed by a
number of smaller ones, while close beside it is a large snowbank
which we can reach with ease. Our couch is composed of a large
quantity of spruce boughs, (cut with that little knife which you have

used so much). These we arrange on the rock, upon which we spread
our quilts—reserving others for covering—and by the help of a good
fire which we keep burning all night, we can manage to keep the cold
off very well.

Two days of very hard climbing has brought me here—if you
could only know how hard, you would be surprised that I have been
able to accomplish it. My strength and capacity for enduring fatigue
have been very much increased by constant exercise in the open air
since leaving home, or I never could have succeeded in climbing the
rugged sides of this mountain. There were some steep climbing the
first day, and I would sometimes find it almost impossible to proceed.
I was often obliged to use my hands—catching, now at some
propitious twig which happened to be within reach, and now trusting
to some projecting stone. But fortunately for me, this did not last more
than a mile or so.

We have brought about a week's provisions, purposing to
remain here and write some letters, &c. This is the most romantic of
places. Think of the huge rocks projecting out in all imaginable
shapes, with the beautiful evergreens, the pines, the firs, and spruces,
interspersed among them; and then the clear, cold mountain stream,
which appears as though it started right out from under some great
rock—and on it goes, rushing tumbling and hissing down behind
some huge rock, and now rising again to view, it rushes on, away
down, down, until at length it turns a corner and is lost to our sight.
Then think of the fragrant little flowers—so many different kinds, and
some of them growing within reach of our snowbank:—I will send
you some of the different kinds.—There is one little blue flower here
which, for some reason, I cannot tell exactly what, whether it is the
form, color, or fragrance, but it has had the effect to carry me back
in imagination to the days of my childhood, in my far down Eastern
home.

But I shall not write any more now, for I mean to finish this
on the top of the mountain.

After reaching the topmost part of the Peak, Mrs. Holmes continued her letter
as follows:

Pike's Peak, Aug. 5, 1858

I have accomplished the task which I marked out for myself, and now
I feel amply repaid for all my toil and fatigue. Nearly every one tried
to discourage me from attempting it, but I believed that I should

succeed; and now, here I am, and I feel that I would not have missed this glorious sight for anything at all. In all probability I am the first woman who has ever stood upon the summit of this mountain and gazed upon this wondrous scene, which my eyes now behold. How I sigh for the poet's power of description, so that I might give you some faint idea of the grandeur and beauty of this scene. Extending as far as the eye can reach, lie the great level plains, stretched out in all their verdure and beauty, while the winding of the great Arkansas is visible for many miles. We can also see distinctly where many of the smaller tributaries unite with it.—Then the rugged rocks all around, and the almost endless secession of mountains and rocks below, the broad blue sky over our heads, and seemingly so very near; all, and everything, on which the eye can rest, fills the mind with infinitude, and sends the soul to God.

"Pike's Peak Gallop," sheet music, n.d.

SOUTH BY WEST

The Rev. Charles Kingsley

"Colorado Springs, Colorado, Nov. 1871.

"DEAR * * *, —HERE I AM 'LOCATED' at last, and the best thing I can do is to describe our arrival here, and my first impressions, which, to say the least, are novel.

"We pulled up at a log cabin by the side of the track, and from the door-way came a voice, saying, 'Dinner's on table.' Out we all got, and I thought—Surely we can't be going to dine in this place: but M. took me round to the back door and into the parlour, where he told me to wait while he saw to the luggage. In a few minutes he returned, and took me into the dining-room, where I found, to my amazement, two large tables on one side, and four small on the other, with clean linen, smart waiters, and a first-rate dinner; far better than any we had had on the Kansas Pacific. I was in a state of complete bewilderment: but hunger soon got the better of surprise, and we were doing ample justice to oyster-soup and roast antelope when in came General and Mrs. P. It was pleasant to find well-known faces among so many new ones.

"You may imagine Colorado Springs, as I did, to be a sequestered valley, with bubbling fountains, green grass, and shady trees: but not a bit of it. Picture to yourself a level elevated plateau of greenish-brown, without a single tree or plant larger than a Spanish bayonet (Yucca) two feet high, sloping down about a quarter of a mile to the railroad track and Monument Creek (the Soda Springs being six miles off), and you have a pretty good idea of the town-site as it appears in November 1871.

"The streets and blocks are only marked out by a furrow turned with the plough, and indicated faintly by a wooden house, finished, or in process of building, here and there, scattered over half a mile of prairie. About twelve houses and shanties are inhabited, most of them being unfinished, or run up for temporary occupation; and there are several tents dotted about also.

"On the corner of Tejon and Huerfano Streets stands the office of the Denver and Rio Grande Railway, a small wooden building of three rooms, in which all the colony work is done till the new office is finished. It is used, besides, as post-office, doctor's shop, and general lounge for the whole town. My house stands next to it; a wooden shanty, 16 feet by 12, with a door in front, and a small window on each side—they are glass, though they do not open. It is lined with brown paper, so it is perfectly wind-proof, and really quite comfortable, though it was ordered on Thursday and finished on Saturday. M. has now put his tent up over the front of the shanty, with a rough board floor, and it serves for our sitting-room by day and his bedroom at night; so we can warm both tent and room with a stove in the former:

but on Monday we forgot to bring the stove down from Denver, and I had to do without it as well as I could. In one corner of the shanty we put my little camp-bed; my trunks in the others. Our furniture had not arrived from Denver; so M. found an old wooden stool, which had been used for mixing paints upon, tacked a bit of coloured calico over it, deposited upon it a tin basin, and there was an impromptu washhand-stand. A few feet of half-inch board were soon converted into corner shelves, and, with warm yellow and red California blankets on my bed, and a buffalo-robe on the floor, my room looked quite habitable. In the tent we have put the stove, a couple of wooden kitchen chairs from the office, and a deal table; M.'s bed makes a comfortable sofa by day; and over the door into the shanty hang two bright curtains Dr. B. has brought me from Denver, as a contribution to our housekeeping. In the corner by the stove stands a pail of water; and over it hangs an invaluable tin dipper, which serves for saucepan, glass, jug, cup, and every use imaginable.

"Monday night, after paying one or two visits, we went to the office and had a game of whist with Mr. N. and Dr. G., who has been burnt out of Chicago and come down here to settle. Then I locked myself into my strange new abode, with M.'s revolver as protection against imaginary foes; and by dint of buffalo-robes and blankets, and heaps of flannel, managed to keep tolerably warm, though my breath

William Henry Jackson, untitled, n.d., photograph with color lithography

condensed on the sheets, and when I got up the bucket had a quarter of an inch of ice on it.

"This is how our day goes, now that we have got everything 'fixed' properly:— Get up at 7 A.M. in the cold frosty air. M. comes in and lights the stove; heats some water; and by eight we are ready for a walk of nearly half a mile down to the restaurant (the log cabin), with a fine appetite for breakfast. The food is good and plentiful. Beefsteak or venison; biscuit—as they call hot rolls out here; hot buckwheat cakes eaten with butter and molasses or honey; and the whole washed down with bad tea or excellent rich milk. Then if there is time we take a stroll and look for seeds and stones. There are all sorts of stones and crystals to be found here; and I hear of amethysts up the Monument. On Monday Dr. G. brought me a lump of rock-crystal as large as a man's fist, which he picked up close to our tent; and it serves me for a paper weight.

"At nine work begins, and I attend to my household duties, sweeping the room, etc., and then am ready to help M. in writing out agreements for lots and memberships. At 12:30 the train comes in, and we go down to dinner. At 5:30 it is almost dark; supper is at six, and then we shut up our tent and spend a cosy evening."

PIKES PEAK IS UNSER MOUNTAIN

Bobby Unser

THIS BOOK IS THE ONLY one that will probably ever exist—at least in more than our time—that will be anywhere near correct and will cover the real history of the Pike's Peak Auto Hill Climb. Without this there will be nothing so we would like it to be right, and give a clearer picture of the race.

My favorite experience up there can't be limited to just one. I probably have several. That first year, 1955, will always be memorable because of the intense anxiety of that one. Obviously there's nothing like the first time you race at Pike's Peak. You're an aspiring young man. You have no idea what you are capable of doing. There's really no concept of what it's like in a young man's mind when he finally goes to race up Pike's Peak. I wasn't capable of winning the race, nor did I have a car good enough to win the race—and I didn't realize I was capable of winning the race anyway.

My first win, which was my second year, 1956, was extremely memorable in my life because Pike's Peak, being the second oldest race in the United States, has a lot of importance to a race driver; especially in those days, because drivers competed in Indianapolis, then came to Pike's Peak—or the Championship trail, then came to Pike's Peak. The real live biggest American heroes for the most part came to Pike's Peak, as you will see in this book.

Another time of importance to me was 1968, my last trip in an Open Wheel, and it was a big year. My 1968 record was, in part, my brother, Louis's record, because Louis built the very special engine. He put in more than just being paid for doing a job. I mean, he babysat it for a long time. He came to the Hill Climb that year, and he took over the engine duties. He didn't just build it and send it to me; Louis worked on the engine for me on a daily basis all during practice and the race, and remember, Louis already had Multiple Sclerosis. But every day, the engine was freshened up. The heads came off and the valves got freshened up. Everything got looked at in that engine daily and as it came closer to the race, Louis started adding the nitro methane to it. Every day, Louis would ask me how much power I needed and he would mix up the alcohol and nitro and change the injection so it would carburate the same all the time. He was a genuine master at it. It was like a real good musician tuning a violin. With that car, we set a record that lasted many, many years. It is the NO. 92 car that has won the Hill Climb 7 times, and is presently on display in the Pike's Peak Hill Climb Educational Museum in Manitou Springs.

Then, in 1986, when I went back to Pike's Peak with Audi, a multi-million dollar operation, that was a big deal for me personally. I don't know that people will ever understand that, but it certainly was. Being gone for 12 years, most (not all) of the locals had written Bobby Unser off. He wouldn't be good enough to win again—times had changed and the road had changed a lot. What they didn't realize was that even though times had changed, I had changed also. I was smarter than I used to be. I hadn't stood still for the 12 years I had been away. My racing, my engineering and my knowledge about racing had progressed a long ways. So when I went back that year that was really the icing on the cake. That year I had everything to lose and nothing to gain, except my very important ego. I was racing because I wanted to go back. I told my wife, Marsha, "I can win. I not only can, but I will. The car is the best and if the Audi people will just come with an open mind (which they did) and just trust in me, Bobby Unser is going to work just like he used to." It was probably one of the most important ego things in all my life.

As for the future of the race, in my opinion, Pike's Peak should always have a future. Hopefully the city fathers of Colorado Springs will always make sure it has a plan. It's a big thing to American history. It's known throughout the world and especially in Europe—more so than the Indianapolis 500 race—so it's important that they keep that going. The City of Colorado Springs and Manitou Springs derive a tremendous amount of notoriety from that race. They get a lot of publicity so it's important to keep the race thriving and I hope they will. The city must realize they can't have just people who love the Pike's Peak race to keep it alive. It has to be a commercial business venture—it's very good for the State of Colorado.

SECTION VIII

GOOD TIMES

SUNSHINE

The Mesa Workers' Cook Book

SUNSHINE.—One pound of strawberries; one pound of sugar. Boil moderately fifteen minutes. Put on shallow dishes; set in sun until juice jellies.—Mrs. Louise McFate.

A FISH DINNER

Joseph Addison Thatcher

WE WERE TELLING STORIES which seemed to interest the cowboy, but he never made a remark—some were pretty highly overdrawn, too. Finally, I said, "Boys, I don't think I ever told you my experience fishing in the North Platte. Well, the fishing was rather poor that summer up there. One morning I took my steel rod, a buttered

Adolph Arthur Dehn, "Fishing, Colorado," 1945 or 1946.

sandwich in my basket, and set off, expecting to be out all day. About noon I had a half-dozen nice trout in my basket, and a severe rainstorm, with terrible thunder and lightning, came up.

"I left the creek and started across a clear place of ground for a clump of trees to get out of the rain. I was running with my rod held up in my right hand, when a streak of lightning struck the steel rod, darting me senseless to the ground. I came to in a short time, found I was not hurt, and looking around I saw that my creel upon the ground was a bed of live coals, and there were my trout lying upon the coals beautifully broiled. My sandwich was ready toasted, and, to show you the eccentricity of electricity, the bones had been taken out of the fish and made into toothpicks and laid beside the fish. A more dainty lunch I never had. What do you think of that?"

The cowboy couldn't stand this last story and turned on his side, laid his hand on his pistol, and said, "I will bet a dollar that's a lie." I turned to him and said, "My friend, I don't want to win your money by betting on a sure thing—but if old Bill Shakespeare was alive, I could prove it by him. Did you know him?" The cowboy said, "No; where did he range his cattle?" There was a silence in the tent; then turning, he said good evening, and went out into the night.

NEWPORT IN THE ROCKIES

Marshall Sprague

THERE IS NO QUICK WAY to bring General Palmer to the start of this story in '69. He was born in 1836 on a farm in Delaware near Delaware Bay, but he was raised by his parents, Matilda Jackson and John Palmer, in Quaker Philadelphia where he got a grade school education, and a touch of high school. At seventeen he was quietly precocious and only a desultory Quaker. He had a large, handsome head, curly brown hair, and a slight wiry frame perhaps five feet eight inches tall. He loved cricket, pretty girls, and arguing about Abolition, anti-Catholics, and freedom of the press. He was even then a sort of self-man Philadelphia aristocrat—a bit stiff and reserved on the outside but diffident, good-humored, and kind within. He was enormously persistent to achieve his own ends which had to do with a dream of building around him a neat, trim, happy, sensible world.

He turned railroader, and at nineteen he went abroad for his coal-mining uncle to see how coal burned in English and French locomotives. He sailed home eight months later full of bright ideas and a conviction that "Paris is the most wonderful city in the world." In 1857, still under twenty-one, he became private secretary to another Quaker, J. Edgar Thomson, president of the Pennsylvania Railroad. Two years later he was out west with Andrew Carnegie to decide for President Thomson where the Pennsylvania should go next from Pittsburgh—to St. Louis or Chicago.

Soon Fort Sumter fell, postponing the question, and it took Will Palmer about six weeks to decide that he had to defend the Union even if he were a pacifist Quaker. But not as a railroader. No office war for him. He read up on pack trains, mules, and litters, got a captain's commission, and recruited a carefully-picked troop of proper young Philadelphians, the nucleus of his beloved Fifteenth Pennsylvania Volunteer Cavalry. Palmer wasn't a snob, exactly, in his recruiting. He just felt that people with superior brains and energy ought to hang together and run things.

🐜 🐜 🐜

The year 1866 was release time for young Americans, a time for exploding of creative energies held in check by the war. General Palmer, aged thirty, had been trained well in railroading by J. Edgar Thomson of the Pennsylvania. He knew where to explode—west of Kansas City where new railroads could turn worthless mountains and plains into high-priced real estate. He knew that capitalists were everywhere with tons of cash to invest—dollars in Philadelphia and New York, pounds in London, guilders in Amsterdam. In 1855, he had seen for himself the land hunger of Englishmen, obsessed by fears of running out of pasture on which to feed their cattle and sheep in England.

And so Palmer began his slow demarch on his future Colorado Springs by getting the job to build the Kansas Pacific Railroad west from Kansas City. This political sop of a line was projected originally to join the Omaha-based, California-bound Union Pacific in western Nebraska, but its directors soon forgot its branch role and decided to go to California, too, through New Mexico. In June of '67, these directors in St. Louis ordered General Palmer to make a survey of southern routes through the western wilderness to San Francisco from the rail head at Salina, Kansas.

News of the proposed Kansas Pacific survey got around even to an international conclave of doctors in St. Louis who were attending a lecture series on homeopathic medicine. This homeopathy was all the rage and had to do with giving to patients pills containing minute toxins to counteract the germs which bothered them. Among those at the conclave was a small, bubbling youngster of twenty-six from London named Dr. William Abraham Bell, who had barely finished his medical training. Bell had journeyed to St. Louis at his father's request. Dr. William Bell, Senior, was one of England's most famous physicians, a man whose bedside charm brought him the trade of everybody who was anybody. He wanted fresh data on homeopathy just to be sure that he wasn't putting the wrong toxins into the stomachs of England's social and business elite.

Young Dr. Bell was pure Irish by birth, but he drank his tea at five o'clock precisely like an Englishman. Medicine, oddly, did not interest him. What he loved was horses and adventure, and when the Kansas Pacific news reached him in St. Louis, he dropped homeopathy—and medicine in general, for that matter—forever. He applied at K. P. headquarters to go on the survey and took the only job open, photographer, after three days of learning how to be one. He met General Palmer in August of '67 in the Raton Mountains part of the Maxwell Grant, 140 miles south of Pikes Peak. The ensuing survey gave the K. P. party nine months of excitement, danger, and hardship. It involved Indian battles, threats of starvation, lost trails, desert heat, and sub-zero snow storms on the passes as the men moved 5,000 miles through the Southwest to San Francisco and back to Kansas by way of Salt Lake City, Cheyenne, and Denver.

Before the trek ended in March of '68, the cavalry hero, Will Palmer, and the effervescent tea-drinker, Willie Bell, had become close friends. They had become also two of the sturdiest males in the Southwest with vast knowledge of what the Rocky Mountains were all about. Back in St. Louis, Palmer urged that the Kansas Pacific should run to California over Raton Pass and on through northern New Mexico. But Congress refused to make any more huge gifts of land to help railroad promoters, and nothing came of the General's suggestions. Young Dr. Bell went back to England to report belatedly to his father on homeopathic pills and to write a remarkable book, *New Tracks in North America.* Palmer wound up unhappily building the Kansas Pacific into Denver. There, in August, 1870, it met the Denver Pacific which ran north to join the transcontinental Union Pacific at Cheyenne, Wyoming Territory.

Failure of his K. P. hopes put the General to planning a railroad of his own. It would be, naturally, a neat, trim, orderly affair staffed by Fifteenth Pennsylvania officers and other true blue friends like Willie Bell. It would be a "North and South" road, from Denver south and over the Sangre de Cristos to the Rio Grande River in the San Luis Valley and on down to Texas and Mexico, to be fed enroute by all future east-west railroads that crossed its right-of-way. It would be a complete novelty, having a three-foot narrow-gauge track which would permit it to make sharp curves and to climb steeply in the Rocky Mountains. It would be much cheaper to build than a line with tracks four feet eight-and-a-half inches apart.

But there was a great difficulty. The government's free-land-for-railroads policy was no more. Eastern and European investors would have no interest in Palmer's proposed line unless it owned a great deal of land the value of which could be expected to increase hugely when the railroad ran through it. The government's preemption price now for Rocky Mountain wilderness was $1.25 per acre—far too high for promoting a railroad. Palmer's problem, then, was to find cheaper land.

One day it occurred to him where to find it—in that Raton Pass region which he and Dr. Bell had examined during the Kansas-Pacific survey. It consisted of two Mexican estates known as the Sangre de Cristo and Maxwell (originally Beaubien-Miranda) Grants. Governor Manuel Armijo had doled them out in the 1840s before the Mexican War, and Dr. Bell's father was physician to many of the British plungers who had money in them—men like William Blackmore, a brother of R. D. Blackmore whose novel *Lorna Doone* was about to become a classic. William Blackmore had put two of his alcoholic brothers on the Sangre de Cristo Grant to straighten them out, and Willie Bell believed that many rich Englishmen would pay well for ranches where they could send their black sheep.

        🐜 🐜 🐜

On the basis of these complicated facts, Palmer made a few simple deductions. It was plain to him that the two grants had cost their European owners only a few cents an acre. He had in England two influential friends—the Drs. Bell, Junior and Senior. Suppose the Bells called on the owners and suggested to them that General Palmer was about to build a railroad which just might run through the grants—if the owners took up his railroad bonds? Surely the Europeans would see their opportunity. Palmer's proposed railroad would quadruple overnight the value of those remote 2,752,942.47 acres along the Colorado–New Mexico border below the Spanish Peaks. Even small mortgages on the grants would raise enough capital to build the railroad at least from Denver to the Rio Grande!

At this critical point, in the spring of '69, a cataclysm occurred. Palmer had boarded the Pennsylvania at St. Louis on his way East to look up a friend of William Blackmore's, and he began describing his Colorado and Mexico railroad scheme in the palace car to a fellow passenger who introduced himself as William Proctor Mellen, a New York lawyer. Mellen revealed that he had studied law in Cincinnati as the protégé of Salmon P. Chase, who became Lincoln's Secretary of the Treasury. Both Chase and Mellen, Palmer discovered, knew William Blackmore and other British financiers who were interested in the West. Mellen suggested that he himself might be useful to Palmer in his western ventures.

The two men were joined in the car by Mellen's nineteen-year-old daughter, a small demurely-elegant, snub-nosed creature with a low musical voice. Her name was Queen. Palmer looked at her once and was lost—the typical total love-fall of a thirty-two-year-old bachelor who gazes upon a soft thing of nineteen and realizes with the suddenness of a thunderclap how empty his life has been without her. Before the train reached Cincinnati, the normally-composed General was just another frantic suitor.

Some weeks later Queen told him that she was his. Whether she loved him deeply is a moot point, but there is no doubt about her filial devotion. Queen had been raised mostly by her father, with some help from her stepmother who was also her aunt. She knew that Mellen had made unfortunate investments after the Civil War, that he was discouraged about his career in New York, that he was past his prime at fifty-three years of age, and that his health was poor. She did not mind, therefore, when Palmer combined his love-making with the acceptance of William P. Mellen as his close business associate in the Rockies.

The wedding, Queen and Will Palmer decided, would take place at the Mellen home in Flushing, Long Island, after Palmer finished building the Kansas Pacific into Denver. By June of '69, he was back at the K. P. railhead—Sheridan, Kansas— writing sonnets by the yard and seeing Queen all over the prairie. His world was upside down. Queen had upset it and he asked himself incessantly how he could bring a refined girl who was used to places like Flushing, Newport, and Saratoga to the bawdy-house environment of a place like Sheridan, or even to raw Denver.

And so—by way of two Mexican land grants and a love affair—we reach the circumstances which resulted in Colorado Springs. Before Queen came into Palmer's life, he had visualized the usual rough railroad towns which he would found along his "North and South" line at intervals to be determined by prospects for agriculture and mining. But Queen split him into two people—the tough empire builder determined to conquer the wilderness, and the Arthurian cavalier shielding his gentle lady from the facts of life. The problem was intricate. Queen, he knew, held deep prejudices against the West, derived from the frontier trials of her maternal grandparents and from the fact that her uncle, Malcolm Clarke, had been killed by Indians in Montana.

To soothe Queen, Palmer had promised to consider settling down in New York City as the eastern officer of the Kansas Pacific, even though he knew that was impossible. He had seen too much of the mountains. The tonic climate and elastic air of the Rockies, their majesty and friendliness and simplicity, the heady freedom and infinite horizons, had spoiled him forever for the cramped and soggy East.

Somehow he would have to make Queen love the mountains, too. This imperative preoccupied him in July of 1869 as he scouted for a section of his "North and South" line, circling from Sheridan, Kansas, up the Arkansas and by moonlight up Fountain Creek where the plains met the Front Range and the Spanish Peaks showed darkly to the south. On the early morning of July 27th, the General, wrapped in blankets on top of his Concord coach, passed Pikes Peak for the first time. He bathed at dawn in the sandy, ice-cold Fountain, breakfasted in moldering Colorado City, and toured that cathedral park of violent reds and deep greens which Pikes Peak pioneers had been calling the Garden of the Gods since 1859.

He loved everything—the soda springs at the foot of Ute Pass, the gray-green mesas and grassy valleys of Fountain and Monument Creeks, the deep, cool canyons smelling of spruce and pine. And Pikes Peak over all. This noble presidence, he knew, had always been the greatest of Rocky Mountain landmarks through immemorial ages of changeless mankind. It was a kingdom in itself of huge jutting spurs and majestic ridges and forested knobs, of vast secret parks and lakes. Soaring a mile above its 400-square-mile mass was the brown 14,000-foot summit, snow-streaked, friendly, placid.

On that day, Palmer believed that he had the answer to his problem. Here was the one spot in the whole wild West fit for Queen Mellen of Flushing, Long Island. And, after all, he planned to have some sort of town every ten miles along his railroad. Why not build a very special one at Pikes Peak—an attractive place for well-to-do people, on the order of Newport or Saratoga? Next day in Denver he wrote Queen about it, but furtively as to what he really had in mind. "I am sure there will be a famous resort here soon," he predicted. And, a little further on: "I somehow fancied that an exploration of the Monument or the Fountain might disclose ... perhaps some charming spot which might be made a future home."

THE WILDEST OF THE WEST

Forbes Parkhill

FROM CAPITOL HILL TO Holladay Street all Denver was atwitter with the news. Oscar Wilde was coming! The apostle of aestheticism was booked to bring culture to the uncouth Queen City of the Mountains and Plains in two easy lectures at the gorgeous new Tabor Grand Opera House on June 13 and 15, 1882.

🐾 🐾 🐾

Among those who pondered the problem of aestheticism were Madame Minnie Clifford and her boarders. Her establishment occupied the site of the original stagecoach stables of the Leavenworth City & Pikes Peak Express Co. Minnie had bought it December 23, 1880, and had converted it into a maison de joie. ...

Minnie Clifford and Emma Nelson and the rest of the girls had no use for effeminate lily-lovers. They much preferred Western he-men, who might better be symbolized by the tough, gaudy, rugged sunflower, whose acrid emanations lacked something of the fragrance of the lily.

On the afternoon of April 5 Minnie and a group described by the newspapers as "a number of her subjects" set out to promenade the length of Larimer Street, then Denver's principal business thoroughfare. Minnie's bonnet was adorned with an enormous sunflower the size of a dinner plate. Emma sported a "very intense lily."

Police Officer Thomas O'Connor was pacing his beat in front of the Windsor Hotel. Prancing up to him with mincing steps Emma Nelson, cribbing an expression attributed to Oscar, observed in a shrill feminine falsetto:

"Oh, Officer O'Connor, in that new helmet you look too, too divine! Yes, indeed—too, too!"

The sunflower-sporting Minnie bellowed, "I know what makes the wildcat wild. But who makes Oscar?" ...

   🐜 🐜 🐜

The lecturer was booked for a return engagement in Denver Saturday night, April 15. O. H. Rothacker, president of the Denver *Tribune*, had planned to take him for a tour of the city in Rothacker's "six-horse drag," or tallyho. After the lecture he was to be guest of honor at a dinner of leading citizens at the Denver Club.

At the suggestion of Charles E. Locke, Wilde's advance man and press agent, Rothacker had assigned his most brilliant reporter to cover the story of the Irishman's arrival. The reporter was none other than Gene Field, who recently had joined the *Tribune* all-star staff.

Wilde's train was late. The welcoming committee adjourned to a Larimer Street saloon. Between drinks press agent Locke remarked that it was a shame to deprive the waiting throngs of a spectacle. Field agreed to impersonate Wilde, and the nearby hairdresser who supplied the Holladay Street trade provided him with a wig resembling Oscar's flowing locks.

Wearing a wide-brim hat and an overcoat and sporting a lace handkerchief in his sleeve, Field was driven triumphantly through the streets of Denver by the press agent. For the benefit of the crowd the pseudo-aesthete languidly fluttered his fingers in his best lackadaisical la-de-da manner at the gaping throngs. There was no applause. One disgusted newsboy shouted, "Shoot Oscar!"

A huge crowd awaited the arrival of the celebrity at the *Tribune* office. On the steps stood dignified F. J. V. Skiff, the *Tribune* business manager, later to become director of the World Columbian Exposition and the St. Louis World's Fair.

Suddenly the crowd was paralyzed with horror when Skiff, instead of shaking hands, angrily threw a broom at the city's distinguished guest. The broom knocked off the wig, exposing the hoax. Skiff had, of course, recognized the masquerading *Tribune* reporter.

IMPRESSIONS OF AMERICA

Oscar Wilde

FROM SALT LAKE CITY ONE travels over the great plains of Colorado and up the Rocky Mountains, on the top of which is Leadville, the richest city in the world. It has also got the reputation of being the roughest, and every man carries a revolver. I was told that if I went there they would be sure to shoot me or my travelling manager. I wrote and told them that nothing that they could do to my travelling manager would intimidate me. They are miners—men working in metals, so I lectured to them on the Ethics of Art. I read them passages from the autobiography of Benvenuto Cellini and they seemed much delighted. I was reproved by my hearers for not having brought him with me. I explained that he had been dead for some little time which elicited the enquiry "Who shot him"? They afterwards took me to a dancing saloon where I saw the only rational method of art criticism I have ever come across. Over the piano was printed a notice:—

PLEASE DO NOT SHOOT THE PIANIST. HE IS DOING HIS BEST.

Wilde's lecture tour through America in 1882 was thus caricatured by Max Beerbohm. He was then known chiefly for his precious posturings and his aesthetic cult of the sunflower and the lily. All he liked in the United States was Walt Whitman and the Rocky Mountains.

The mortality among pianists in that place is marvellous. Then they asked me to supper, and having accepted, I had to descend a mine in a rickety bucket in which it was impossible to be graceful. Having got into the heart of the mountain I had supper, the first course being whisky, the second whisky and the third whisky.

I went to the Theatre to lecture and I was informed that just before I went there two men had been seized for committing a murder, and in that theatre they had been brought on to the stage at eight o'clock in the evening, and then and there tried and executed before a crowded audience. But I found these miners very charming and not at all rough.

Among the more elderly inhabitants of the South I found a melancholy tendency to date every event of importance by the late war. "How beautiful the moon is to-night," I once remarked to a gentleman who was standing next to me. "Yes," was his reply, "but you should have seen it before the war."

So infinitesimal did I find the knowledge of Art, west of the Rocky Mountains, that an art patron—one who in his day had been a miner—actually sued the railroad company for damages because the plaster cast of Venus of Milo, which he had imported from Paris, had been delivered minus the arms. And, what is more surprising still, he gained his case and the damages.

THE LADY OF THE GARDENS

Caroline Lawrence Dier

Shakespeare Visits Elitch's Gardens
by Ben Johnson (June, 1911)

Here we have Juliet's garden,
With Verona's moon tipping "with silver,
All the fruit tree tops."

Again, at noon-tide hour,
Transported now to Arden Forest,
Fair Rosalind is seen
Tripping to meet "the young Orlando
Beneath the shade of melancholy boughs."

Or is it Brutus' orchard
With Cassius and the rest
Resolving on the death of Caesar?

But stay, these stunted trees
Resemble much that northern wood
Where Denmark's King was killed—
"Sleeping within mine orchard
My custom always in the afternoon,
Upon my secure hour thy Uncle stole—
        Alas poor ghost!"

        Orlando's father did bequeath
To sons, who quarreled, an orchard fair,
And there, beneath the listening trees,
Good, faithful Adam proved
My gift of "thrifty hire"
To his old master's son, the sterling "service
Of the antique world."

What changeful dream is this?
Now it is Windsor Wood! old Hearn
Shakes his chain; There is "fat Falstaff!"
I can almost hear the honest laughter
Of "The Merry Wives."

I rub my eyes and look again,
For "there be elves and fairies!"
No, they are CHILDREN, Denver's own,
Secure and happy, playing 'neath the trees,
And yonder, to complete their joy, SHE comes,
Their guardian Queen—
        "The Lady of the Gardens."

J. Harrison Mills' portrait of Mary Elitch, n.d.

THE ROCKY MOUNTAIN COOK BOOK

Caroline Trask Norton

KNOWING THE DIFFICULTY OF most people in this high altitude to find their cooking always satisfactory, the author has endeavored to give them in this book the benefit obtained from teaching and housekeeping in Denver, making high altitude cooking a special study. The greatest difference between sea level cooking and here is in the cakes. Most of the sea level receipts can be used here by adding another egg to them, that gives a delicious, moist, rich cake.

Water boils at sea level at 212°. In Denver, where the air is much lighter, it boils at 202°; therefore, it does not reach as great a heat here, so vegetables or anything boiled requires a little longer cooking.

The luscious Boston baked beans can be cooked equally as good here if soaked twelve hours before parboiling. The author has endeavored to make her receipts practical, wholesome, and easily followed by the most inexperienced cooks. She has not attempted giving much information on chemistry and food values, leaving that for the cooking schools that are becoming such a necessity all over the country. No girl's education is complete without such a course. Girls should not take upon themselves the most important position in life without a thorough knowledge of its requirements. Such a knowledge will enable them to feed their families intelligently, inexpensively, and to give them the variety that the system requires.

Food for invalids should be selected and cooked with the greatest care. At the end of the book are given a few receipts that can be used for invalids. Scientific cooking should fill an important part in the training of a nurse.

The desire of the author will be obtained if the book proves helpful to all who use it and inspires them with the wish for more knowledge in the art of cooking.

HATTIE:
THE LIFE OF HATTIE McDANIEL

Carlton Jackson

BEFORE GOING TO WICHITA, AND during their stay there, Henry and Susan started what ultimately became a large family of thirteen children. Over half of them died either at birth or shortly thereafter. The youngest, born on June 10, 1895, was a bouncing baby girl, whom they named Hattie.

But life for the young Hattie did not settle down until her father's wandering urge carried the family to turn-of-the century Colorado, first in Fort Collins and then in Denver.

In Fort Collins Henry worked as a teamster. The family lived in the 300 block of Cherry Street. Two blocks away on North Meldrum lived Hattie's dearest friend, Ruth Collamer, a white girl. Ruth and Hattie were inseparable, as they walked with each other every morning, hand in hand, to the Franklin School, where they were classmates.

At school, Hattie and Ruth played jacks on the flagstone sidewalks, and a game called, "Pom pom pullaway." Hattie taught Ruth how to bounce a rubber ball while repeating in rhythm, "one, two, buckle your shoe." Each afternoon after school Ruth's father drove his cattle to pasture, always passing by the McDaniel's residence on the way. Hattie frequently came out of her house and walked with the herd for a way, she and Ruth picking flowers (violets and "johnny jump ups" in the Spring), and, hand in hand, "hippety-hopping" through the fields.

The picture of Hattie that Ruth always held was "of a sweet little colored girl about eight years old in a dainty ruffled bonnet, and a round face with one of the biggest smiles a girl could acquire. She had beautiful white teeth, which she showed very distinctly every time she smiled, and that was very often when we were together."

In 1901, Hattie was again uprooted when the family moved to another boomtown, Denver, a short distance away Henry saw working and living conditions as better for himself and family in Denver than in Fort Collins. Henry quickly got a job as a laborer on numerous construction projects, and his oldest son, Otis, became a porter in a barber shop, earning his share of the family upkeep by sweeping, and keeping the place clean. Over the next several years the McDaniels lived in at least ten different places in Denver from the time they arrived in 1901 to Henry's death in 1922. Gradually, as they grew up, his family scattered throughout the city, his sons (including Otis, James, and Samuel) going into barber shop and hotel portering, and construction work, and his daughters (including Ruby, Adele, Orlena, Etta, and Hattie), generally became clerks. Hattie, for example, worked for some time as a clerk for the Charles Lind Bakery on Lincoln Street. "Clerking" meant not only keeping books, but the place clean as well. Hattie probably got the job because of her friendly nature and her ability to "cipher." It was not, however, commonplace for blacks to become clerks in business establishments. All of the McDaniels had some talent in music and entertainment, and the children at least, who had not been directly involved with slavery, had outgoing personalities that caused them to seek employment beyond the usual maid and wash jobs. In addition, Denver was such a boom town with so many business establishments to be run that "color" was frequently put aside when managers looked for employees. Also in the western parts of the country around the turn of the century, Populist Party politics created a system in which blacks had at least a semblance of "place." Perhaps that political factor was one reason why Henry McDaniel, though frequently moving around in the city of Denver itself, stayed permanently after 1901 in the state of Colorado.

Even with all the changed ways of life Henry and Susan had left behind, the McDaniels—especially the men—could usually get only menial jobs in Denver. Their situation in the Colorado capital, however, was probably better than if they had stayed in the South. "White supremacy" took root in southern states and state legislatures put into effect a large number of "Jim Crow" segregation laws. On the other hand, much of the West at this time was so economically active, with enough work and adequate housing to go around, that there were generally too many activities for people's racial biases to become obsessive, as they had done in the South.

Nevertheless, there was some bigotry, even in Denver. In the Fall of 1916, a debate raged over a proposed ordinance to prohibit blacks from living on the same residential blocks as whites. The Denver Property Owners' Protective Association, was made up almost entirely of white real estate agents, and it supported the efforts to segregate Denver's housing. (Ironically during the late 1940s, Hattie battled exactly the same kind of housing discrimination in Los Angeles.)

Besides the housing problem, another cause for racial strife in Denver, as indeed around the country at the time, was the screening, in 1915, of D. W. Griffith's epic film, *The Birth of a Nation*. Based upon Thomas Dixon's *The Clansman*, the film glorified the Ku Klux Klan at the expense of black people, and for the first time depicted black villains on the screen. The newly formed (1909) National Association for the Advancement of Colored People fought against showing this film anywhere. The Denver chapter of the NAACP was formed in 1915, in no small part because of *The Birth of a Nation*. Thus, while Denver in the early twentieth century was quite liberal compared to other parts of the country, it did have its own racial problems.

These difficulties, though, remained unapparent to Henry and Susan's youngest child, Hattie. She was one of a few black students at Denver's Twenty-Fourth Street Elementary School, and her teachers and classmates loved her.

Her favorite teacher, Louise Poirson, often permitted Hattie to do what she liked best: to stand before the class reciting poetry or singing popular songs. Mrs. Poirson wrote to Hattie later on in Hattie's career: "The reason I remember you so well is due to the fact that as a child you were so full of rhythm. You had an outstanding dramatic ability, an ability to project to your listeners your strong personality and your ever present sense of humor. I recall with pleasure the keen enjoyment of the pupils and myself whenever you sang or dramatized a story." Hattie began singing at the Central Baptist Church in Denver almost as soon as she arrived, sang spirituals at school, and recited passages from the Bible for the pleasure of her classmates. Hattie herself said that she sang so much as a child that it sometimes got on the household nerves. "My mother would say, 'Hattie I'll pay you to hush,' and she'd give me a dime. But in just a few minutes I'd be singing and shouting again."

From an early age, Hattie was a "take charge" person, a characteristic which remained her entire life. In grammar school she organized, improvised, and directed the activities of the other children, a foreshadowing of future successes and "firsts." Being first almost became a way of life for Hattie. Later, she would be known as the first black woman to sing on radio, the first black person to win an Oscar, even the first black to be buried in a previously all white cemetery.

Her best friend at Twenty-Fourth Street School was Willa May, and after graduation Hattie and Willa went together to East Denver High School. The most "daring" thing the two friends did in high school was to have their initials tattooed in blue in the bend of their arms. Hattie could stare down at a big "HM" imbedded into her arm, while Willa gazed at "WM."

Still the center of Hattie's life at East Denver was singing and dancing, and her theatrical abilities. She was always much in demand for school plays and musical performances, and excelled at a number of dances that were popular in that era. The most notable of these were the cakewalk, the juba, the fleetfoot softshoe buck, and the wing dance, and they were among hundreds that blacks brought from Africa, or created once they were in the United States. ...

In a way, the development of black music and dancing talents was one way of compensation for their conditions of servitude. Thus, when Hattie went through the rigors of "Convict Joe" that night at East Denver High, she exemplified many generations of black talent. Her natural abilities, coupled with Henry's and Susan's encouragement, turned Hattie, at an early age, into an important performer.

In fact, as early as 1908, when she was only thirteen, Hattie was billed as part of a minstrel show, J. M. Johnson's Mighty Modern Minstrels performed at East Turner Hall (later known as German Hall). The show featured "Happy Dick Thomas and the Merry Howards," and "just a few" of the "big, mighty company," included Etta, Hattie, Otis, and Samuel McDaniels (misspelled as even press agents would do for years to come). The show was as much a competition as a performance, because its program announced that the "challenging cakewalk, fleetfoot softshoe buck, and the wing," were "open to all comers," as they had been in plantation tradition.

A few months later, in March 1909, a minstrel group, the Red Devils, came to East Turner Hall, under the management of the Colored American Amusement Company, with Miss Hattie McDaniel, "Denver's favorite soubrette," at the bottom of the bill. Already, Hattie was acquiring a reputation of acting the coquettish maid.

In 1910, Henry decided that he had had enough of hard labor and so he formed his own minstrel show, with his sons, Otis and Sam as regulars. For some time the two brothers had played with the All-Star Minstrels at both East Turner and the

Empress. Otis and Sam were clog dancers; Sam played Pappy Rufe, and Otis played Aunt Miranda of the Lime Kiln Club, leaving "the house in a constant uproar of laughter and applause," according to one reviewer. The Henry McDaniel Minstrel Show was popular entertainment for people all over Colorado. With Henry at the top of the bill with his banjo and guitar the show toured Pueblo, Colorado Springs, Boulder, Fort Collins, and other cities. Although fifteen-year-old Hattie begged to travel and perform, her mother, Susan, forbade it, protecting her from the rigors of show business life, one-night stands, tiresome travel, and stays in segregated, inferior parts of towns they visited.

Generally, black performers preferred to travel by train rather than by car to engagements, because they were not as likely to be stopped by unfriendly policemen. Sometimes, however, a remote destination required several black groups to travel together by automobile, exposing them to dangers along the way. Susan also considered that since everyone in the show was black, hotel rooms were hard to come by, compelling a dependence on a black "bed and breakfast" circuit that flourished along the black entertainment routes.

For her part, Hattie seemed to be doing just fine as a student at East High. Nonetheless Hattie quit high school at the end of her sophomore year. While she waited for her "real" career to begin, Hattie continued to perform at local theaters such as the Empress, and at carnivals. Then, in 1910 she gave her famous rendition of "Convict Joe," and after that experience nothing could stop her from full time entertainment. She enlisted the help of her brother, Otis, in convincing Susan that the time had come. Reluctantly, Susan bowed to the inevitable, even though it meant giving up her cherished dream of seeing Hattie earn a high school diploma.

The next three years were among Hattie's busiest and happiest. She toured from Colorado to the West Coast, sometimes with a minstrel group called the Spikes Brothers Comedy Stars. Primarily, though, she traveled with her father and brothers, and frequently wrote the programs that her father's minstrel group performed. Also, she began to show a lively talent for writing songs, a talent that was fully developed during the 1920s.

But in 1916, tragedy struck. Her older brother, Otis, who had always been the star of "that talented McDaniel family," died of an undisclosed cause, at the unfulfilled age of thirty-five. His funeral was conducted at the Campbell Chapel of the African Methodist Episcopal Church, and he was buried in Riverside Cemetery. For awhile it appeared that Henry's minstrel group would fall apart without Otis' guidance, and gaps increased between engagements. During these periods, Hattie worked in Denver cooking, clerking, and taking in washing. By the late 1910s, Henry had become inactive as the years and busy life began to catch up with him, forcing Hattie, Etta, and Sam, to turn to other outlets through which to display their talents.

At last around 1920 Hattie first came into contact with one of Denver's most noted black musicians, Professor George Morrison, and his "Melody Hounds," who gave her the "big break" that carried her to a greater exposure than she was accustomed to. She traveled with the Morrison Orchestra to Portland, Salt Lake City, El Paso, and even a short stint in Juarez, Mexico. Newspapers lauded Hattie's entertainment abilities. The *Portland Telegram* said that "the biggest show stopper of them all was Morrison's Orchestra and its Hattie McDaniel, billed as the female Bert Williams," (an internationally known black vaudeville performer). Hattie McDaniel was "taken in riotous fashion," said the *Telegram*. The *Oregon Daily Journal* said that Morrison's work on the Pantages Circuit was "not exactly a jazz offering of the syncopated, slam-bang order," but a "refined and accomplished act which not only hits the musical high spots, but interjects a humorous surprise in Hattie McDaniel ... who did a hop, skip, and jump act on the stage while keeping up her vocal stunts. ... " Another paper, the *Oregonian*, complimented Morrison's band for its "melodious playings" of its theme song, "By the Waters of Minnetonka," which took on "new and charming values." The paper described Hattie as a "large Negro woman who sings jazz songs." The *Evening News* of San Jose, California, called Morrison's band "as excellent a vaudeville show as anyone would care to see," and Hattie a special feature whose dances blended "to the peppiest music ever heard in this man's town."

In 1922 Hattie suffered two more losses. In his seventies, Henry had developed hearing and sight problems, which sharply curtailed his activities with the minstrel show. On December 5, 1922, he died, at the age of 82. He was buried in a special Grand Army of the Republic section of Denver's Riverside Cemetery. His death deeply affected Hattie: though she had always leaned most heavily on Susan for aid and understanding, she had adored Henry, and learned much of her musical craft from him.

THE FLICK AND I

Ralph J. Batschelet

IN THE THIRTIES, FREE DISHES (one piece per admission), was a popular method of alluring patrons. The race was on for all forms of attendance gimmicks.

A jolly fellow named "Fat" Sanders conceived the idea of giving groceries away by the bushel basket. The giveaway was advertised as " 'Fat Sanders' old-fashioned Country Store Night." He gave away everything from a squealing pig to a sack of potatoes. With his gift of gab the event became a carnival-type adventure.

After a while, we decided to reverse the horseplay of the giveaway and play it straight with dignity and aplomb.

So the *Deluxe* Country Store was born. It was an instant success! I admit that over the next eleven years we injected all the fun we could muster, while giving away tons of groceries and luxury gifts.

"Next Saturday night, ladies and gentlemen, at 8:00 P.M. at the BlueBird we will *butcher a beef on this stage before your very eyes!*"

With that announcement, our "Deluxe Country Store" was on its way. We called it "Deluxe" because we all worked in tuxedos, and in Depression days, that indeed was class! We bought good tuxes for ten dollars. Feeling luxurious in our sartorial splendor, we worked diligently to befit our elegance. Our "Store" was initiated to increase attendance of the regular movie fare and was popular for over six hundred weeks!

Baskets of groceries were heaped high with solid-value items, many of which were new on the market. It's true that Nate Naiman's Market would supply us with a bag of potatoes and a head of cabbage to "line" the bottom of the basket. Adding in a box of cornflakes, we had a head start on the filling process. Eleven regular merchants for eleven years supplied us, week after week, in return for screen advertising.

When we first began the giveaway, a bottling company owned by James A. "Bert" Gooding, Sr., had acquired a franchise for a new drink called "Pepsi-Cola." Bert offered us the product to put in our baskets. The bottle was big and the weight was good, so a deal was made. I'd lean over the footlights, bottle of Pepsi in hand, and exclaim, "Folks, you are gonna like this one." Jim Gooding, Jr., is now chairman of the board of the Denver Regional Pepsi Cola Bottling Company, and his son, Richard, is president and general manager of operations.

Such were the roots and friendships of the BlueBird Country Store. The Boscoe brothers smile as they recall the years when they had a one-store bakery beneath the West Colfax viaduct. Sam and Rudy Boscoe would meet me every week as I backed in my Chevy to load our allotment of "Star" fresh-baked bread. I devotedly informed our audiences every Saturday night, "Honest, folks, if you haven't tried Star bread, you don't know what you are missing. Frankly, I wouldn't buy any other bread!"

When we believed in a product, we would really pass the word along, and the merchants knew it. People must have believed us, because the Pepsi Cola Bottling Company, Star Bread, American Beauty Macaroni products, Bowman Biscuit Company (Keebler), and many others have become huge corporations since our Country Store plugged their products!

Butchering a side of beef was the outstanding event. Lloyd King was president of King's Soopers then, and we made a deal for the beef. He furnished a meat block, knives, wrapping paper, and their head meat cutter, who to our surprise attired himself in "tails."

"A good butcher doesn't soil his clothing, so why not?" he declared. "That's the way the meat institute personnel demonstrate."

The cuts were most generous to say the least. We even rigged up a spotlight for him as he explained the various cuts of beef to the audience. Lucky numbers were drawn out of the wheel, and the winners received a premium package of beef. Even the soup bones were something to behold. We repeated the beef night several times, always a hit.

COLORADO OWNS A CHUNK OF GLENN MILLER

Frances Melrose

GLENN MILLER, WHO DIED IN A 1944 plane crash in the English Channel, was once the highest-paid band leader in the world.

In 1944, it was estimated that one of every three nickels dropped into the nation's jukeboxes played a Glenn Miller record. In a *Downbeat* magazine poll, Miller collected more votes for swing and sweet music combined than any other orchestra leader. Benny Goodman got more for swing.

Miller always has had a special place in the hearts of Coloradans, not so much for his band's renditions of "Old Black Magic," "Tuxedo Junction," "Chattanooga Choo Choo" and the Miller theme song, "Moonlight Serenade," as for the fact that he went to high school in Fort Morgan, then attended the University of Colorado at Boulder. In fact, he worked his way through CU playing a trombone in the college band.

The university was so proud of him that a campus ballroom built in 1953 was named the Glenn Miller Ballroom. Many of these details are in the movie, *The Glenn Miller Story*, which first appeared in 1953. (Miller was born in 1904 in Clarinda, Iowa.)

Miller, who became famous both for his trombone playing and for his distinctive arrangements, earned his first instrument by doing odd jobs when he was 14. He played in bands in Fort Morgan and after graduation joined the Boyd Senter Band, which traveled in western states.

By 1923, however, he had decided college was important, and he enrolled at CU.

In Boulder he joined the Holly Moyer Orchestra, a dance band that played 3 nights a week at Citizens' Hall, where college students hung out. He was serious about a career as a musician, and declined to play football for fear of having his teeth knocked out, disastrous for a trombonist.

He was tall and thin and was not a warm personality. Before long he had earned the nickname "Gloomy Gus" because of his serious air and strict personal discipline. He also was so shy that, when he organized his own band, it was difficult for him to get up in front to lead it, but he loved the music so much that he made himself stand there.

He stayed at Boulder for a year, then left school because he wanted to get started on his musical career. For several years he worked for different bands, both on the West Coast and in New York, as trombonist and arranger.

In 1928, he married his college sweetheart, Helen Burger, in New York.

About that time Ray Noble asked Miller to help him put together an orchestra and do the arranging for it. Most of the nation knew this orchestra on Ray Noble's "Coca-Cola Hour."

Still itching to be on his own, Miller organized a combination of "strings and swing" that recorded for Columbia Records in 1935. Miller's big band was formed in 1937, but a year later he disbanded it and started over. By 1939, the band was a national hit, playing in the famed Meadowbrook Roadhouse and the Glen Island Casino. His band's recording of "Tuxedo Junction" in 1939 was the first million-disc seller in nearly 10 years.

Then came radio's "Chesterfield Show," which starred the Miller Band.

In 1942, Miller turned the band over to Harry James and enlisted in the Army Air Force. He was appointed conductor of the Army Air Force Band and given the rank of major.

The Air Force band was playing in Paris in December 1944. Miller was flying ahead of his group to another engagement in France when his plane disappeared over the English Channel. No trace was ever found.

The movie stars James Stewart as Miller and June Allyson as his wife. Henry Morgan had the role of Miller's buddy, "Chummy" MacGregor.

Much of the filming was done on location in the Denver area in 1953. About 3,000 airmen from Lowry Air Force Base performed as extras in a scene showing a USO performance in England in December 1944. Although it was an extremely hot July in Denver, and the temperature inside the hangar was around 100 degrees, the airmen wore heavy wool winter uniforms.

Another day's shooting took place on the CU campus in Boulder. In later years, Miller had remembered his college days by playing songs of the university on his radio program and by making an occasional appearance at the college with his famous orchestra.

About 5,000 Denverites were extras for scenes filmed at Elitch Gardens Trocadero Ballroom, which was torn down in 1975. Stewart's wife, the former Gloria McLean, was in the crowd.

Miller's 82-year-old mother, Mattie Lou Miller, who lived in Greeley, came to watch the ballroom scenes being filmed and met Stewart.

"He's a fine actor," she commented, "but he doesn't look a thing like my boy."

Civic Center was the locale of another scene, showing Miller stopping to make a phone call from a booth in 1926. Antique-car collector Arthur Rippey provided the vehicles for the scene.

September 22, 1985

CZ: THE STORY OF
THE CALIFORNIA ZEPHYR

Karl R. Zimmermann

THE PROTEAN CZ: IT CERTAINLY was a train that meant different things to different people. For the Interstate Commerce Commission it was a puzzlement and perhaps their hardest "train-off" decision ever. The railroads felt it a thorn in their collective sides, although for rail enthusiasts it was the great hope, the proof-positive of the popularity of the well-run passenger train. Newsmen and editorialists found in it a cause ill-starred, the best kind. Thousands of Americans whose sense of transportation esthetics had not been dulled by the jet age saw it as a straw to clutch. To children it was heaven, to the unions, gravy.

And to me? To me it was the final and ultimate train, the point where schedulers and designers, surveyors and engineers, dietitians and personnel men should have said "Stop! We've got it." To be sure, other railroads had rolling stock to equal that of the *California Zephyr*. The Union Pacific's dome diners were just about the finest place to sup on earth, let alone on rails. The Santa Fe's Pleasure Domes, the Milwaukee's Super Domes and Skytops were plush and distinctive. The deep-windowed step-down observations of the *20th Century Limited* were classic, and who could forget the *Broadway Limited*'s Pullman observations *Tower View* and *Mountain View*?

But the CZ's Vista-Dome lounge observation was no ugly stepsister to any of these, nor were the rest of the CZ's cars, especially when you consider what there was to be seen from the windows. No other train had the Colorado Rockies and California's Feather River Canyon. And five domes from which to view this splendor was hard to beat. So were the food and the service.

Still, for anything to be truly grand, the whole must be greater than the sum of its parts. So it was with the CZ, which built a reputation and established an aura few other trains could touch. In part this was no doubt inherited through the rich Zephyr lineage of its Burlington Route predecessors. Certainly the CZ continued their honorable tradition in all important ways save the emphasis on speed.

And the *California Zephyr* was a pretty train, don't forget that. Pretty, it can't be denied, in a conventional, familiar way, not much different from the other Zephyrs, but pretty from any angle. From high atop the south rim of Gore Canyon: the train was a silver snake, sinuously inching its glittering way along the opposite face of the chasm as if in slow motion. From trackside at Williams Loop: the Sierras' early-morning sun sidelit the Western Pacific's feather-emblemed F's and spiraling consist, making all seem crisp and fresh and invigoratingly new. From the dome of the *Silver Sky*: the entire train stretched gracefully ahead, then corkscrewed into

Thrills Galore!

When You Travel "The Scenic Way" Across America

Burlington
Rio Grande
Western Pacific

Promotional brochure for the California Zephyr, n.d.

another cut as Glenwood Canyon towered by. From the station platform at Salt Lake City: the consist stood quietly hissing in the cool dark, windows of Pullmans glowing a welcome.

🐾 🐾 🐾

We sometimes judge people by the way they die; why not trains? Many great runs have languished in their last years, losing their fine equipment and prestige, until little remained but a name. Though its name too lingered on, the CZ was largely spared this degradation. Instead it went out looking much as it had in its youth. The lounge-observation was not amputated to simplify switching. Service in the diner remained up to snuff until the end; the carnations in the vases never turned to plastic. Admittedly lateness was the rule in the last years, but no one seemed to mind much, unless it was so extreme that darkness fell on the more spectacular scenery. After all, the CZ was a "cruise train."

Or was it? "Cruise" implies going nowhere fast, and the *California Zephyr* went lots of places, although relatively slowly. It never stopped being transportation, and this sense of movement and purpose was central to the pleasures experienced aboard the train. Both ocean liner and streamliner lose their majesty when they idle; grandeur accompanies function and direction and urgency on the high seas and high iron alike. The CZ took you somewhere, but it did so in the most civilized possible manner, and that takes time.

🐾 🐾 🐾

The *California Zephyr* died on March 22, 1970, when the Western Pacific was allowed to discontinue its portion of the run. Any consists that have operated since under the illustrious CZ name are imposters, and must be regarded as such. And when the CZ died, the death knell was rung for the transcontinental passenger train operated in the grand manner, Amtrak notwithstanding. For if the *California Zephyr* was not worth saving at all costs, what running on lost-distance rails really is?

A twenty-one-year history is not a long one. But the CZ's career, brief as it was, had everything to delight the chronicler: glamour, warmth, drama, and controversy. Millions rode the train and loved it. Thousands spoke up in protest as it was allowed to roll to its death. It had made a lot of friends, and that in itself tells a story.

THE COLOR ORANGE

Russell Martin

YOU REALLY COULDN'T HELP but be impressed by the meteorological portent, by the way the weather presaged the start of the season. On Friday the city was hot and strangely still, the sky blue above the smog. Then on Saturday came a great drum roll of thunder and a spare and promising rain—the dark skies lowering the morning light, the chill wind abetting the nervous anticipation of the two hundred or so fans who milled, umbrellas open and jackets buttoned tight, at the edge of the turf at Mile High Stadium in Denver, waiting for a minor ritual to begin—the taking of the team photograph, annually executed the day before the Broncos' home opener, before new jerseys lost their luster, before injuries and expediencies inevitably began to change the faces in the photograph.

At last, large men in Popsicle-orange jerseys with white numerals wider than pie tins began to amble out of the locker room and onto the field. Helmetless, wincing against the weather and hunching their huge padded shoulders, they milled near the four rows of risers where they would pose, shouting "Sheee-*it*, it's cold," kidding each other about their ugliness, slapping each other's butts, and bouncing on the balls of their feet.

The fans, held at a distance by a harried team PR man, pulled cameras with long lenses from the cover of their coats, aimed them at the men in orange and chattered excitedly, the cold—at least for a few moments—no longer a concern. They watched and waited while Dan Reeves, the Broncos' forty-two-year-old head coach, took on the frustrating task that thousands of grammar school teachers know too well—trying to get his players to line up properly (in their jerseys' numerical order), to bunch up a bit, to move over this way just a little, to drop the rabbit-ears fingers they held behind each other's heads, to stop making silly faces. When Reeves made it clear that everyone could go back inside as soon as the photos were finished, his players quickly simmered down. They stiffened up and looked straight ahead, Reeves and his assistants standing attentively behind them now in matching sport shirts, nearly five dozen all told—players and coaches and trainers—hollering "Cheese" in the same instant, then "Cheese" three more times to be sure, before they bolted for the locker room, the fans breaking toward them then as if intent on some open-field tackling. But the contact was light, nothing more than the pressing of pads of paper into the players' chests, the fans—suddenly intimidated by the sea of orange and, *my God*, by the size of these men, and surely by their local celebrity— blurting only "Would you … ?" or "Please?" as they held pens up to the players' eyes.

    🐜 🐜 🐜

I wiped the rainwater off an aluminum bench and sat down, the only spectator among 75,000 empty seats. I had never been in this place before, this colossal horseshoe painted in section-coded colors—yellows, blues, oranges, and reds— some sort of outsized theater in the round, all seats focusing on a distant stage that was simply a rectangular strip of grass, a place that, even in its emptiness, offered a vision of drama, a heady sense of coming attractions. Mile High Stadium, cobbled and riveted through four series of renovations since it first served as a baseball park in 1948, had been sold out for every regular-season home game of the Denver Broncos since the beginning of the 1971 season—fifteen years, 117 games, 120 if you count the three play-off games played here in 1977, 1978, and 1984. Tomorrow it would be sold out again as 75,000 blue-capped and orange-shirted football fans, no, *Broncos* fans, streamed into this stadium to pledge their allegiance, to scream their hearts out, to die with every Denver turnover, to know true exaltation if their guys were ahead at the end of the game.

The Broncos were my team, too, if the truth were told. After ninety-four years of American professional football, they were still the only team anchored between the Sierras and Kansas City—the only game in the Great American West save the teams scattered along the Pacific Coast, which somehow didn't count. Growing up in a rat-ass town located where the Rockies descended to the Navajo desert, I had become a Broncos fan in the years during which they were indisputably the worst team trying to play the game. They wore silly vertically striped socks, their helmet logo was a dumb cartoon depiction of a bucking horse, and, back then, a .500 season would have been something worthy of wild celebration. But the Broncos were likable. Actually, they were lovable, lovable in the way that a dog who just can't manage a trick is lovable. They reminded us of ourselves, I suppose—our unabashed optimism somehow always countered by a bare reality. Throughout the mountain West, the Broncos were the boys we worried about on tattered stools in small cafes, the team we lambasted on job-site lunch breaks, the team we coached brilliantly over beers and whiskeys, then gamely cheered through the subsequent losing effort. Perhaps we cared about them so much simply because they so often broke our hearts.

After eleven losing seasons (44 wins, 105 losses, 5 ties), the 1971 Broncos were nonetheless, and for no discernible reason, able to sell out every home game. To no discernible effect: The team barely mustered a 4-9-1 record that year.

In 1972, things began to get a bit better. In their first year under former Stanford University head coach John Ralston—a Dale Carnegie advocate and a shrewd judge of football talent—the Broncos went 5-9. Then in 1973, while the rest of the nation focused on a minor skirmish called Watergate, football fans in the Rockies reveled in—can you imagine it?—a winning season, 7-5-2. It had taken fourteen years to achieve, but we are a patient people, those of us who live in the American outback. Broncomania, the term for the condition that had afflicted long-suffering fans, came into common usage, and there was indeed a growing, nearly epidemic mania about this laughing stock football team that had finally found a way to win. Four years and three more winning seasons later, the meek inherited the earth and the 12-2 Broncos, coached by a fireplug named Red Miller, went to the Super Bowl. But because life has little meaning, the 1977 season ended in defeat. In Super Bowl XII, the Wild West Bowl, the Dallas Cowboys corralled the Denver Broncos, and 40,000 visiting Denver fans milled through New Orleans's French Quarter in dazed and dangerous post-game depression. Back in the Rocky Mountains, *everybody*— except those who were in comas and had good excuses not to have watched the game—turned off the television, sighed a great collective sigh, and averred in a voice sad and deflated, "Well, what'd we expect? Shoot, we're talking *Broncos*, after all."

Yet despite that game's bitter lesson, it was a kind of watershed. Never again could the Broncos simply be lovable losers. The very fans who had become devoted to them because of their strange socks, because of their succession of aging and unathletic quarterbacks, because of their penchant for snatching defeat from the pendulous jaws of victory, now demanded something better, more than mediocrity, something akin to excellence.

The national sports media, on the other hand, and football fans elsewhere in the country really didn't give much credence to the Broncos' ascendancy that year. They didn't suppose it would last long. One hinterland team or another always seemed to be able to pull off a Cinderella season. But for the Broncos' owners, coaches, players, and for their much-abused fans, .500 seasons would never again be adequate achievements. The vertically striped socks had long ago been burned in a pre-game ceremony. Now it was time to incinerate an image—one of a team, and a town, that simply didn't amount to much.

During the decade that followed the Super Bowl season, the Broncos were a good football team. Twice they won the American Football Conference's Western Division. They recorded at least ten victories per season in all but the strike-shortened 1982 season. Under current head coach Dan Reeves, the team had won forty-five games, losing just twenty-eight. Only two other teams posted better records during that decade. Yet at the start of the 1986 season, a remnant of the Broncos' first incarnation remained, some long-standing and latent suspicion of ineptitude: The Broncos had played in four post-season play-off games since that trip to the Superdome. They weren't super, or even adequate to the task, in a single one of them.

As the 1986 season was set to open, everyone's annual anxieties were compounded by a strange new reason to worry. In addition to all the usual concerns about the adequacy of the offensive line, and the utter absence of a running game, there was this to worry about: Five national magazines that are prone to make such prognostications had recently made the Broncos their pick to be representing the

American Football Conference in Super Bowl XXI in Pasadena—a few months and a dozen and a half football games down the road. For crying out loud! Not only was the upcoming schedule a virtual mine field, not only was the running offense its usual suspect self, now there were these crazy expectations to contend with.

Sitting in the autumnal gloom on a hard seat in that silent stadium, I was eager for some football finally to be played, whatever the four-month succession of games might bring—a season unparalleled or a season like so many others. I had come to the city from the hard-scrabble sticks to observe firsthand what theretofore I had only gleaned from Sunday afternoon television and the sports pages of Denver's dailies. I wanted to get some measure of what fed this football mania, to try to understand why this team could captivate so many dissimilar people. The Broncos were the great democratizer in Denver, the one safe but shared and passionate conversation between the rich and the poor and the sea of people in the economic middle ground, between people who were white and brown and black.

Still, football was only a *game*—a diversion, an entertainment, as simple and artificial and ultimately unimportant as a Saturday schoolyard match played between neighborhood boys. And this was what intrigued me. How was it that a series of games, of contests between mercenary athletes, which had no real or concrete connection to the lives of the rest of us, could assume such vital importance? Why did the weekly fate of Denver's football team—or of other teams in other cities—garner the kind of attention that might otherwise have been given only to a summit between the superpowers? What was it, for heaven's sake, that football offered us?

PRIVILEGED INFORMATION

Stephen White

IN THE SUMMERTIME, THE Downtown Boulder Mall was an ecumenical version of Main Street in Disneyland. From the west end, where a lone Laundromat is the last evidence of the real world, there mingled a solid mass of browsing couples, wandering tourists, teenagers on the make, adults on the make, and members of sundry societal fringes.

Taken at its full length, it was a sociological microcosm of counterculture America since the beat generation. Aging Kerouac-inspired men somehow found sustenance sipping coffee at the Trident or the Bohemia. From their outdoor seats they were inured to the punks, stoners, and heavy metalists who sprawled across tiny lawns or surrounded planter boxes and benches. Teenagers spilled from

William Sanderson, untitled, n.d.

subterranean video dens, sub shops, pizza by-the-slice parlors, or an absurdly broad selection of ice-cream and frozen yogurt vendors. The most outrageous of the teens always seemed to stand sentinel at the ends of blocks, their bizarreness creating reasonable bookends for what lay in between.

New-age devotees carried take-out salads of unlikely vegetables to the small lawns in the eleven hundred block, or lined up for falafel or designer cookies farther down the street. Time-capsule hippies and hypomanic street people shared centurion duty on the lawn in front of the thirties deco courthouse. Constituents of the indigenous culture were present in small congregations, too. Adrienne called the natives "Bouldoids" but could never quite describe their mores, instead insisting that, like obscene materials, "I just know 'em when I see 'em."

The affluent were conspicuous mostly by their purposefulness, the fact that they had destinations distinguishing them from the majority merely in search of a place to be. The dollars the middle and upper classes dropped in galleries, boutiques, and restaurants kept the four-block playground in the black.

In a town where ice-cream trucks are illegal for making too much noise, where airplanes pulling banners violate the city sign code, and where municipal employees are prohibited from smoking even when alone in city vehicles, the mall was a bit of an oasis of noninterference. As long as you didn't want to skateboard, ride a bike, panhandle, or run your dog, it was Boulder's most tolerant four blocks.

Lauren and I held hands and wandered through the throngs beneath the Victorian storefronts and anachronistic architectural oddities that contained the press of people A good magician drew a crowd in front of Potter's, and an energetic piano player, who had pushed an aging baby grand on wheels to the brick walk in front of the New York Deli, played ragtime mostly to himself. He had more enthusiasm than talent.

We landed awhile beneath an umbrella on the roof of the West End Tavern and watched the western light fade over Mexican beer. Our aimlessness ended at Juanita's, where we flirted over Mexican food and too loud roadhouse music.

SECTION IX

HARD TIMES

EMILY

Emily French

February, Wednesday 26, 1890

I UP BUT SO SICK I could not eat. John Clibon came to see if I could go to wash at his father in-laws for them all. I promised if I should be able. I took the rug in the big basket, went over to Mrs F. I had a chill, in about 1 hour I had to lie down. Joe Isenberg came while I was there, he stayed that night. I slept on the lounge. I coughed so hard she fixed me some ginger tea, done all she could. I took red pepper tea, worked on her rug, cut the scallops all ready to sew.

February, Thursday 27, 1890

Got up, build both of Mrs Fricks fires. The children came out, Florence helped me start the breakfast—coffee & meat & pancakes. Old Isenberg is lazy, not up till it was on the table. He dont amount to nothing, sets & talks German. I sat on my under teeth, heard them break as I sat down to grind her coffee. Oh dear if only I could get through & go away from all this awful life. God in his mercy do help me, I am so sick, not able to wash for Agnes & I had said I would. I took a lot of pepper tea, washed the dishes, sat by the fire and worked on the rug. I must get it done if I can today sure, Mrs. F. tries to be kind. She got a good dinner—eggs, coffee & meat, crackers &c. Hellgate came, staid all night. Mrs. Baltzell came to see why I did not go to wash for Agnes, I to sick. I went over to see Agnes in the cold, told her I would try to wash tomorrow if she & John would help me.

February, Friday 28, 1890

I up but oh so sick, coughed an hour. Mrs Frick trying to get breakfast, I done all I was able to help. Isenberg still there. I could not eat anything so I put on my things to go. Mrs Frick said I ought not do such work. I washed at Joseph Oaks, the big days work. Agnes & John helped me good, I could not have done it if they had not. 2 ticks, a quilt, the stained clothes, all that a death can cause. I washed all day, so tired & cold. Laura & Jim went over to Mrs Reeds, not a good place for them. I put on Mrs Oaks cloak, came home. So cold & tired, Annis had a fireplace all nice for me. I sat down a little while, but I had to go to bed. Old Ric I fed good, she so thin. Mr Oaks brought feed, now she will get all she can eat.

March, Saturday 1, 1890

A still day, awful sick all day. Oh dear what shall I do, Old Ric she will have to go hungry, I am not able to feed her.

March, Sunday 2, 1890

I lay still for fear of having a coughing spell. I am so sick & sore, Annis sleeping so sound, she is a carless *nobody*. Oh why am I left with only her for a companion. I called her, then had a hard coughing spell. She made a fire in the grate or fireplace, it smokes so in the stove. She got her own breakfast. The wind not blowing for a wonder. I called old Ric & gave her a feed of oats. She looks so much better, the sore on her back nearly healed, has one now on her neck. I crawled to bed, oh dear I am so sick, wont somebody come, I fear not. My feet are cold. Oh why cannot I have some care when I always have done all in my power for others, must I suffer here alone & make no *sign*. God send me relief.

March, Monday 3, 1890

I felt verry bad when I awoke. Annis crawled out, made a fire, got a little to eat. I lay still, had a hard coughing spell. What will I do, no rest, I am so sore, my kidneys are so weak, I must go see the Dr. Higgins, maybe he will do something to relieve me. I had a fire in the fireplace, it smokes so in the kitchen. I tried to sew, cannot do anything. I am perfectly miserable, what shall I do. Does a kind providence send this terrible affliction for my good, or am I to do something that now I cannot seem to see or understand. My good old faithful horse Ric she must have some hay.

🐾 🐾 🐾

November, Saturday 15, 1890

Thy kingdom come—Amen

Yes, the talk at the table shows they are going to move. She is so cross I shall go unless she treats me different sure. I cannot stand such talk as she gets off about my knowing so much. All I try to do is to please her. I am to go with her to the Cinderella Mattinee to care for Maurice. I know she will abuse me, this will be the last time sure. We were just in time for the car, I run to hurry her. I carried the big boy, was worried and tired as we went up the stairs in the 15 st Theatre. I dropped off his cap, it is so verry big for him. Such talk, she abused me as much as she dare. I am going now, on the way home I see it was to be hotter than ever. I told Mr Mauck he might pay & I would go, such a scene, she charged me $1.35 for the bonnet we had made. I must stay awhile, I used reason.

November, Sunday 16, 1890

Thy will be done

I got sick, she had said finally I could go to church but I am sick. I took all the Epson salts there was, no use, I am near blind with the headache. I done the work all day, took care of the boys, they went out to ride. I lay down on the hall mat upstairs, got to sleep. I have done up the supper work, am now ready to go to rest. She is kind now as she can be, I should not mind it if she would be so all the time. She fried the corn and they eat there supper. I lay down on the sofa where I sleep. They after supper pulled all the tacks out of the carpets upstairs & down. My head feels some better.

November, Monday 17, 1890

On earth as it is in heaven

I up at 5, he called, they expect a days work. I am no more to them than an old horse. They are going to move today in a house, 2922 Downing Ave. where there is a good barn too, they can keep their horses now, he pays $20.00 per month for its keep. She is not so cross this morning but she expects me to git all the same. I got breakfast over, then washed out the didies, she packing upstairs, I down stairs, hard at it. The big wagon came at 11, $3.00 for piano and all. He had 3 loads in his Plumbing wagon, every scrap is to go, she was sure to give that order. I gathered kindling wood, all then went over to the place and worked till 11 hard, 3 of the carpets down and a good many things straightened. I had to sleep yet on the sofa in the parlor, such a hard bed, she seems not to care. The body lice, such a long siege as I have had.

November, Tuesday 18, 1890

Give us this day our daily bread

Yet we must work, I dont feel as if I could do scarce a thing I had to, life so hard. On the base burner, it is so verry heavy, has to be cleaned, tis covered with hen drop and rust, has been in the barn all summer, such a nice stove ruined. I do wish I could have such nice things, but the Mrs Mauck is jawing away and in a big ugly fit. Must I go through more of her abuse, yes, she wont try to get the bedstead set up in the back room, I would get a good nights rest, that she dont wish.

November, Wednesday 19, 1890

Again I am serving up a nice hot breakfast to a pair of such ingrates. He is the best of the two, that is not saying much. Cleaned the kitchen. She is cross, went to take him to a job, she goes & takes him and brings him home, I have the cross boys to take care of and work. We put down the last carpet and set up the bedstead. I must take that crosspatch of a Maurice in my bed, oh dear wont I be glad when this is over.

November, Thursday 20, 1890

And forgive us our debts as we forgive our debtors

I up and breakfast at 6, he cross, says two old women and nothing done, she put him up a nice lunch. I hurried to get the water over & things ready for a washing.

We will have a big one sure. She says I must do it all winter for her, she left the bulk till Monday. Tired to night.

November, Friday 21, 1890

Cleaning the baseburner and the scouring the black kitchen floor, three meals a day she will have. She twits me of getting $20.00 per month but says of late more about my earning it. Yes, I guess I do, I am so tired when night comes. Such a big time to night, Olive came to see me, Mrs Anfinger has gone to abusing her, refused her the use of the water closet, such a mean trick. She wanted to see if I was willing for her to leave, yes, she need not take a bit of her abuse—wheeling the old broken baby buggy, getting turnips, hurrying them on, making pie and buiscuits &c—she comes in, commences to abuse me, tells Maurice to strike me, he threatens to do.

MOLLIE

Mollie Dorsey Sanford

May [1865]—Camp Weld

ON THE MORNING OF THE 19th about 3 o'clock the night watchman at the corral came pounding on our door with the startling cry, "Get up. There is a flood in Cherry Creek, and hundreds of people are drowning." We could not believe but that he was fooling, until we heard the distant roar and the shouts of men like the coming of a mighty tempest. By hurriedly dressed and started away. I could not leave my sleeping boy. He came back and said I must see it. I would never probably see so awful a sight again. We bundled up Bertie and, coming over to the creek, found hundreds of people staring and shivering, some half dressed, *and* all in a state bordering on frenzy. Great inky waves rolled up 10 or 15 feet high carrying on their crests pieces and parts of houses, cattle, and for all we know human beings too. In the low places the soldiers on horseback were rescuing families, risking death to save women and children, fighting with a foe not easily vanquished. It was the chill hour of morning, hardly daylight, but huge bonfires were lighted all along the banks where drenched and half-drowned people were warmed and dried. In the confusion families were divided, and plaintive cries were heard above the roar, "O, where is my husband," or, "Where are my children," or "family."

Very little if any loss of life occurred, but homes were swept out of existence. Buildings had been erected on the sandy channel of the creek that were carried away. I came back to our shanty, got a bite of breakfast, and again we went to the scene of desolation, trying to be of some assistance. By was off on duty with the soldiers, a few only who are at Camp Weld. About 9 o'clock I heard a commotion.

A man came galloping along, shouting, "All that live on the river bottoms, look out. The Platte is booming," and looking toward my shanty, I could see the water spreading like a mighty lake, and knew that all *we* had in the world was in danger, so giving "Bertie" to a trusty friend, I rushed on to my little home, only to find the banks of the big ditch this side had burst, and water was rushing downhill to meet the coming tide from the Platte. I could go no further but could see that the boys from the corral were loading my things into the wagon. They had to swim the horses before they got through, and here *we* were in a bad plight ourselves. We were kindly taken in by a friend whose home was high and dry, and remained several days. The vacant rooms at the barracks were thrown open to the homeless, and here we are again in our quarters where little "Bert" was born. Where we used to walk over to the east side on dry sand or elevated foot bridge, or wagon bridge, now runs a mighty torrent, spanned by a rope extension bridge. A ferry has been built across the Platte, and scenes of disorder and destruction are everywhere. People are groping in the slime and mud of the receding waters for their things, as most of the houses were left standing in the inundated district.

I have not had any of my queer impressions for a long time, until the other night, after I had gone to bed, I seemed to feel there was going to be a fire! I could not sleep, and could not impress By at all. He snored away while I laid in fear and trembling. I actually got up and put my valuables and a little money we had under my pillow, fixing my clothes ready to jump into, even placing my shoes and stockings on a chair in easy reach, then crept back to bed, feeling foolish enough, and had just gotten into a sleep, when the cry of "Fire! Fire!" startled us, and all was hurry and confusion, I exclaiming, "I knew it all the time!" The large commissary building where a large amount of government stores are kept, burned to the ground, doing no further damage, so all we had to do was to go back and settle our scattered household goods again. It seems there is one excitement after another, until I wonder I'm not white-headed. We are hearing of Indian depredations and scouting parties are out now from the barracks. Co. "H" is now and has been for some months stationed at Fremonts Orchard to guard the settlers. Bro. Sam is a member of that company. We stopped overnight with them as we came from Neb. City. There had been a light engagement, and I am all the time looking for news of another, as the Indians are no longer peaceable.

We have had a few weeks of comparative quiet with only occasional rumors of Indian troubles. We had always felt secure here in Denver, but were aroused from that feeling by one night of horror. On the evening of the 19th By, with almost *all* of the men from the barracks, had gone up to Denver to a political meeting. I sat in our room with the surgeon's wife, reading aloud some thrilling story from the *N.Y. Ledger*. Our babies were sweetly sleeping and all was quiet and serene. It was about 11 o'clock that a horseman, one of our soldiers, came tearing up the road, dismounting before our door. He knocked furiously. I opened it, expecting something had happened, but what was my horror to hear him gasp out, as his knees knocked together, and his eyes almost starting from their sockets, "Run, wimmen! Run for your lives, the Injuns are coming three thousand strong! Run for the brick building at Denver! Governor's orders! But don't get skeered." (I was already about paralyzed.) "Mrs. Sanford, you tell the folks down the row while I go around," and away he went to the outside quarters. Mrs. Towles immediately went into hysterics, while I started to give the alarm, but when the woman came to the first door I went to, I could not utter a word. My tongue had cleaved to the roof of my mouth. By this time I could hear the shrieks of women and children as the flying messenger went his rounds. By an effort of will power, I overcame my terror, and was soon back to my room, where my friend was wringing her hands in agony. We could hear bells ringing and the distant sound of confusion. In a very few moments the barracks were empty, the people on the road to Denver. I knew that By would come to me, and if I started he could not find me. Beside, I could not leave my friend with her two babies nor could I run with mine, so we concluded to stay where we were for a while, thinking it as safe there as on the road to town alone. Very soon By came. He did not seem so excited, as he hardly believed it, but he said we had better go, as there was not a living soul left at the barracks, as probably if there was an attack they would come here first to seize ammunition and arms. We picked up a few little things for the children, and putting the babies in their buggy, started, walking quietly along, and by this time I had gotten over my fright and did not credit the rumor much. It was so dark we could hardly see an object. We had nearly reached the town when we heard a quick volley of shots, then shouts, and then a mighty rush of horsemen toward us. I dropped on my knees, expecting my time had come at last, when just ahead of us passed a band of loose mules that had stampeded. We came on then to the brick buildings, only to find them crowded to suffocation. Fearing a collapse of the building, we went with a friend into her cottage nearby. By was put on patrol duty, his beat being directly in front of the house. Time went by, and no Indians came.

Scouts had been sent out in every direction, alarming settlers as they went, and by daylight the streets were filled with families who had fled from their homes. The returning scouts had found no traces of the Indians, and finally this and the returning daylight gave us the feeling of security, and the "scare" was over, and in due course of time people returned to their homes. It all came from some old people living out a few miles, imagining some Mexican cattle drivers to be Indians, and in their fright running two miles to the stage station, where the alarm was sent to the Governor. It only developed the fact that had there been an attack such confusion and panic ensued that the Indians could have wiped out the town.

LIFE OF GEORGE BENT

George E. Hyde

AT DAWN ON THE MORNING OF November 29 I was still in bed when I heard shouts and the noise of people running about the camp. I jumped up and ran out of my lodge. From down the creek a large body of troops was advancing at a rapid trot, some to the east of the camps, and others on the opposite side of the creek, to the west. More soldiers could be seen making for the Indian pony herds to the south of the camps; in the camps themselves all was confusion and noise—men, women, and children rushing out of the lodges partly dressed; women and children screaming at sight of the troops; men running back into the lodges for their arms, other men, already armed, or with lassos and bridles in their hands, running for the herds to attempt to get some of the ponies before the troops could reach the animals and drive them off. I looked toward the chief's lodge and saw that Black Kettle had a large American flag tied to the end of a long lodgepole and was standing in front of his lodge, holding the pole, with the flag fluttering in the grey light of the winter dawn. I heard him call to the people not to be afraid, that the soldiers would not hurt them; then the troops opened fire from two sides of the camps.

The Indians all began running, but they did not seem to know what to do or where to turn. The women and children were screaming and wailing, the men running to the lodges for their arms and shouting advice and directions to one another. I ran to my lodge and got my weapons, then rushed out and joined a passing group of middle-aged Cheyenne men. They ran toward the west, away from the creek, making for the sand hills. There we made a stand, but troops came up on the west side of the creek and opened a hot fire on us; so after a short time we broke and ran back toward the creek, jumping into the dry bed of the stream, above the camps. Hardly had we reached this shelter under the high bank of the creek when a company of cavalry rode up on the opposite bank and opened fire on us. We ran up the creek with the cavalry following us, one company on each bank, keeping right after us and firing all the time. Many of the people had preceded us up the creek, and the dry bed of the stream was now a terrible sight: men, women, and children lying thickly scattered on the sand, some dead and the rest too badly wounded to move. We ran about two miles up the creek, I think, and then came to a place where the banks were very high and steep. Here a large body of Indians had stopped under the shelter of the banks, and the older men and the women had dug holes or pits under the banks, in which the people were now hiding. Just as our party reached this point I was struck in the hip by a bullet and knocked down; but I managed to tumble into one of the holes and lay there among the warriors, women, and children. Here the troops kept us besieged until darkness came on.

Artist unknown, "Surprise Attack on a Hostile Indian Camp," n.d., from I Stand By Sand Creek *by William R. Dunn, Lt. Colonel, 1985.*

They had us surrounded and were firing in on us from both banks and from the bed of the creek above and below us; but we were pretty well sheltered in our holes and although the fire was very heavy few of us were hit.

When the soldiers first appeared, Black Kettle and White Antelope, who had both been to Washington in 1863 and were firm friends of the whites, would not believe that an attack was about to be made on the camps. These two chiefs stood in front of their lodges and called to their people not to be afraid and not to run away; but while they were still trying to quiet the frightened women and children, the soldiers opened fire on the camps. Black Kettle still stood in front of his lodge, holding the lodgepole with the big American flag tied to its top. White Antelope, when he saw the soldiers shooting into the lodges, made up his mind not to live any longer. He had been telling the Cheyennes for months that the whites were good people and that peace was going to be made; he had induced many people to come to this camp, telling them that the camp was under the protection of Fort Lyon and that no harm could come to them; and now he saw the soldiers shooting the people, and he did not wish to live any longer. He stood in front of his lodge with his arms folded across his breast, singing the death-song:

"Nothing lives long,
"Only the earth and the mountains."

while everyone was fleeing from the camp. At length the soldiers shot him and he fell dead in front of his lodge. Black Kettle stood in his camp until nearly everyone had gone, then took his wife and started up the creek after the rest of the people. Soldiers kept firing at them, and after a while Black Kettle's wife fell. He turned and looked at her, but she seemed to be dead; so he left her and ran on up the creek until he came to the place where the people were hiding in the pits. After the soldiers had withdrawn about dark, the chief went back down the creek to find the body of his wife, but he found her still alive, although wounded in many places. He took her on his back and carried her up the creek to where the rest of us were waiting. Her story was that after she had fallen and her husband had left her, soldiers rode up and shot her several times as she lay helpless on the sand. At the peace council in 1865 her story was told to the peace commissioners and they counted her wounds, nine in all, I believe.

Most of us who were hiding in the pits had been wounded before we could reach this shelter; and there we lay all that bitter cold day from early in the morning until almost dark, with the soldiers all around us, keeping up a heavy fire most of the time. If they had been real soldiers they would have come in and finished it; but they were nothing but a mob, and anxious as they were to kill they did not dare to come in close. They finally withdrew, about 5 o'clock, and went back to spend the night in the Indian camp. As they retired down the creek they killed all the wounded they could find and scalped and mutilated the dead bodies which lay strewn all along the two miles of dry creek bed. Even this butchers' work did not satisfy them, and when they reached the Indian camp they shot Jack Smith and wished to shoot my younger brother Charlie. These two young men (they were half Cheyenne and half white) had remained in the camp when the Indians fled and had later surrendered to some soldiers they knew. Old John Smith was trading in our camp and remained with his son when the Indians fled. When the whites came back to camp after dark, an officer came and told old John that some of the Denver roughs (one-hundred-day-volunteers) were talking of shooting his son Jack. Smith induced some officers of the Fort Lyon garrison who were his friends to go to Colonel Chivington and ask him to save Jack, but Chivington in the morning had given orders to take no prisoners, so when these officers came in and asked him to prevent the shooting of young Smith, he told them roughly that he had given his orders and had nothing further to say. Old John was sitting in his lodge, waiting for the return of the officers, when shots rang out close by. Then men came into the lodge and told him that his son was dead. The Denver men then wished to shoot my brother also, but Charlie had fallen into the hands of some New Mexican scouts belonging to the Fort Lyon garrison; men who knew all of us Bent boys and who had known our father for years; so when the Denver crowd wished to take Charlie out and shoot him as they had just shot young Jack Smith, the New Mexican men ordered them off and threatened to shoot any of them who attempted to touch Charlie.

After the troops withdrew to the Indian camp, we lay in our pits for some time, suspecting that the whites might come back; but they did not return, and at last we crawled out of the holes, stiff and sore, with the blood frozen on our wounded and half-naked bodies. Slowly and painfully we retreated up the creek, men, women, and children dragging themselves along, the women and children wailing and crying, but not too loudly, for they feared the return of the whites. After a long time we met Indians with horses. These men had gone out before dawn to see that the herds had not strayed, and reaching the herds just before the troops came up, they succeeded in getting away with some of the animals before the soldiers surrounded the rest of the herds. On seeing the soldiers coming, these Indians had thrown themselves upon the first ponies they could catch and had then rounded up as many more as they could and driven them up the creek. They went away up the creek and waited until the firing stopped after dark, then came cautiously back to see what they could learn, and this was how they happened to find us. They helped the wounded upon the ponies. One of my cousins was with them and gave me a pony to ride, but my hip was so stiff and sore that I could not mount and had to be lifted on the animal's back. After meeting these young men with the horses, our party went on up the creek a few miles farther, moving very slowly, and then, as the wounded and the women and children could go no farther, we all bivouacked on the open plain for the night.

That was the worst night I ever went through. There we were on that bleak, frozen plain, without any shelter whatever and not a stick of wood to build a fire with. Most of us were wounded and half naked; even those who had had time to dress when the attack came, had lost their buffalo robes and blankets during the fight. The men and women who were not wounded worked all through the night, trying to keep the children and the wounded from freezing to death. They gathered grass by the handful, feeding little fires around which the wounded and the children lay; they stripped off their own blankets and clothes to keep us warm, and some of the wounded who could not be provided with other covering were buried under piles of grass which their friends gathered, a handful at a time, and heaped up over them. That night will never be forgotten as long as any of us who went through it are alive. It was bitter cold, the wind had a full sweep over the ground on which we lay, and in spite of everything that was done, no one could keep warm. All through the night the Indians kept hallooing to attract the attention of those who had escaped from the village to the open plain and were wandering about in the dark, lost and freezing. Many who had lost wives, husbands, children, or friends, went back down the creek and crept over the battleground among the naked and mutilated bodies of the dead. Few were found alive, for the soldiers had done their work thoroughly; but now and then during that endless night some man or woman would stagger in among us, carrying some wounded person on their back.

At last we could stand the cold no longer, and although it was still pitch-dark and long before dawn, we left that place and started east, toward the headwaters of the Smoky Hill, where we knew Indians were encamped. It was fifty miles to the nearest of these camps, and we could go but slowly, most of the people, and even many of the wounded, being still on foot. Then we had to dread the pursuit which would probably begin as soon as the coming of day made it possible for the troops to follow our trail, and we knew that if the troops overtook us on the open plain, barely a handful of us could hope to escape. But luckily for us a few of the men who had escaped on their horses at the beginning of the attack had made straight for the nearest camps on the Smoky Hill, and riding all day they had reached these camps about dark with the news that our camp had been surprised by a thousand white men. Large numbers of men had at once set out from these camps on the Smoky Hill, bringing led ponies with them loaded with blankets, buffalo robes, and food; and soon after day broke these people began to join us in little groups and parties. Before long we were all mounted, clothed, and fed, and then we moved at a better pace and with revived hope; but it was late in the day when we reached the first camp on the Smoky. As we rode into that camp there was a terrible scene. Everyone was crying, even the warriors and the women and children screaming and wailing. Nearly everyone present had lost some relations or friends, and many of them in their grief were gashing themselves with their knives until the blood flowed in streams.

The Sand Creek Massacre was the worst blow ever struck at any tribe in the whole plains region, and this blow fell upon friendly Indians. The hostiles were camped on the Smoky Hill and Republican, far away from the troops, and our camp would never have been where it was if the chiefs and people had not been assured that peace would probably be made soon and that in the meantime they need fear no attack. From a third to a half of these friendly Indians were butchered in the attack, and of those who escaped very few were without wounds. The women and children were by far the heaviest sufferers. ...

COLORADO WITHOUT MOUNTAINS

Harold Hamil

WHEN MEMBERS OF OUR CLASS of 1924 at Sterling High School got together for our 50th anniversary reunion, we could claim at least one distinction. Ours was the only class ever graduated at Sterling with hooded members of the Ku Klux Klan joining in the services.

There were many, of course, who looked upon the Klan as an intruder rather than a participant, but the drama and tension of the occasion could not be denied. This was one aspect of our commencement weekend that everyone seemed to recall in detail after more than 50 years.

Those who have dug into the history of the Klan say that 1924 was the year of its largest national membership. The surge of enthusiasm for the organization was apparent around Sterling, and some of the talk in school corridors had suggested that fathers of some members of the class of 1924 were active in the local unit.

There was a baccalaureate service at the First Presbyterian Church the Sunday evening before the actual graduation program at the high school. We seniors, some 80 of us, sat in our caps and gowns in the front pews.

At a point about midway in the service there was a commotion at the rear door and concerned looks on the faces of members of the choir who looked out on all that went on.

The presiding pastor, somewhat awkwardly and uneasily, tried to carry on as though nothing was happening. Glancing over our shoulders, we ultimately caught the outlines of peaked hoods in the rear doorway.

I could never believe that the appearance of these Klansmen, about eight in number, was a complete surprise to everyone, but it was obvious that nobody had tipped off the ushers. They had taken a firm position against any interruption of the program, and therefore the commotion. Finally, though, somebody passed the word along, and the intruders marched in single file to the front of the church and lined up before the pulpit.

The minister asked if any member of the group had something to say, and one came forward and handed him an envelope. There was a mumbled exchange, and if the minister had been taken by surprise, what he heard seemed to answer all his questions. The visitors marched silently to the exit; the minister put the service back on track, and all of us relaxed.

While the Klan engaged in all kinds of double-talk as to its ideals and purposes, there was a general presumption that its prime concern was to press the interests of white Protestants over those of Negroes, Catholics and Jews. (I was to learn many years later that some of the Protestant German-Russians in Logan County felt the Klan was antagonistic toward them.) There were no Negroes in our class and, to the best of my recollections, no Jews. But there were a half-dozen or more Catholics, and I could detect an obvious uneasiness on the part of a Catholic girl in my pew. If the truth were known, though, the uneasiness was shared by most everyone. This was our first view of the Klan in action. One could not help pondering the ability of such performers to strike terror into the hearts of persons who knew they were on the "enemies" list.

There was much talk around school the next day about our unexpected guests. The minister, as I recall, made known that the envelope he received contained a cash gift and a note of appreciation of his services to the community. Classmates were calling off the names of persons who might have been behind the hoods. One was of a very large man and one was of a fellow with a missing finger.

Most members of the faculty indicated disgust with what had happened. But one teacher, T. L. Girault, was openly scornful. He denounced the Klan and all it stood for. At the moment he seemed to make more of the incident than it deserved. Some of us, I am sure, were inclined to think it would have been a pretty dull evening if the Klan hadn't appeared.

About six weeks later, a black touring car drove into the hayfield where Father, two hired men and I were working. Four men, all in white shirts, got out and went into serious conversation with Father. They stayed for about an hour. On the way to the house that evening nothing was said about the visitors. But when Father started off to care for the hogs—a chore he reserved for himself—he asked me to join him. This was unprecedented, almost, because I was supposed to milk cows.

As we dipped half-bushel buckets of corn from the granary and spread it on the concrete feeding floor, Father explained that his afternoon visitors had come from Sterling to suggest he be a candidate for the Republican nomination for sheriff. They had known, perhaps, of his plans to leave the ranch and of his hankering to get back into county politics after one term as county commissioner. They had brought assurance of powerful support for his candidacy. But he would have to agree to join the Klan. And the question he finally put to me, in tones that carried a surprising hint my decision might be binding, was whether he should accept the offer and the conditions.

I surprised myself with the promptness of my reply. I told him I was opposed to the Klan and what it stood for in words that I had not repeated since hearing them from T. L. Girault and other teachers following our baccalaureate service. All of a sudden, I realized that I was subscribing fully to opinions I had heard but hadn't taken the time to consolidate into my own thinking.

Whether Father was merely asking me to confirm a decision he already had made is a secret he took to his grave. He didn't run for sheriff.

I went off to college in the fall and was not around to witness other activities of the Klan in Logan County, but I did observe a big Klan rally at Hastings, Neb., that fall. Delegates came from a large section of Nebraska and staged a parade that stretched for at least a mile. There were hooded men on horseback and floats depicting little red schoolhouses and other symbols of solid American tradition.

Those who have traced the history of the Klan say that what we witnessed in 1924 was the high water mark of the organization. It remained, but never enjoyed the widespread popularity that it enjoyed for a brief period in the mid-1920's.

T. L. Girault, who taught for many years in the Denver schools before retiring, came to Sterling for our 1974 reunion, and I couldn't help telling him about how his forthrightness helped me make up my mind on what seemed to be a pretty important issue back there in 1924.

SUMMER ETCHINGS IN COLORADO

Eliza Greatorex

IN THE GAY PARTY ASSEMBLED for an excursion to Pueblo and the coal mines, I had the good fortune to be included. The feelings of our entire company are expressed in a letter of warm and sincere thanks to General Palmer, and the officers of the Central Colorado Improvement Company, for their many kindnesses and courtesies.

On that trip I first comprehended the luxury of travelling by a "special" train; resting in an easy chair, listening to stories of long-ago in these regions, when railroads were unthought of—rushing at a speed of forty miles an hour, but stopping at will wherever scenery or incident invited our stay. This was the very poetry of motion, or, at least, the refinement of steam traveling. As we approached Pueblo, a great change was apparent in the character of the scenery. Pike's Peak was grander, the Spanish Peaks and Cheyenne Range more lofty and varied in outline, the Arkansas more rapid and winding, with the added beauty of tall, graceful cottonwood-trees rising to a great height on its banks.

Pueblo, now a bright and growing business town, is new and fresh in almost all its streets and buildings. A few of the low *adobe* houses, which were once the only dwellings of the town, still remain at the entrance; but the new city has taken its station on a high, breezy bluff, one of the loveliest possible sites. From Pueblo

Eliza Greatorex, "View from South Pueblo," from Summer Etchings of Colorado *by Eliza Greatorex, 1873.*

to the coal mines is the wildest bit of country I have yet seen. The climate in winter is very fine, and there is a large hotel projected close to a spring of iron and soda, where invalids may pass the whole season in comfort of sky and sunshine, both of which we nearly forget as we enter the mines. By the twinkling lamps carried in the miners' hats we see and wonder at all the dark processes of mining. A friend wrote for me some of the salient points in the

Eliza Greatorex, "Old Pueblo," from Summer Etchings of Colorado *by Eliza Greatorex, 1873.*

history of these mines and of the miners; and, only that my space is too small, I would gladly transcribe his letter. The men whose lives are spent in these sad underground shades can have but gloomy and cheerless lives. He says: "The work is very hard. Often the 'cuts' are made by the miner while lying on his side, the pick used by working it over the shoulder, the hole drilled, filled with powder, and blasted, the daring workman still in this uncomfortable position. Some compensation they do manage to find in the spending of their hardly-earned wages." Beef, mutton, vegetables, and pudding, cloth, muslin, silk, and shoes are their ideas of "comfort, of life!" As we emerged from the black pit into the day, made dazzling by contrast, a huge miner, who had been our guide and general informant, calls out to "Dave," to know if the new beer had come. Now, "Dave" has been pointed out to us as *the* character of the place—I should say, Dave and his mule, as the two are but parts of one character, whole and indivisible. The *Dave* part is a hunchback, the mule a marvel of strong thews and long ears. Dave's voice is as the herald and proclaimer of all mining movements, heard long before even the ray of his lamp or the tip of the mule's ear reach the mouth of the mine. They bring out the coal and, blessed compensation, bring in the beer. "Who will you have to bring in this beer?" calls General Palmer down the shaft. A great shout from mingled voices answers, "Dave!" and Dave responds lustily, and the mule rattles his bell gayly, as both disappear with the refreshing can. We turn away from these living tombs with a little glow of comfort in our minds, as we know that there is still even that compensation left to the hard lives passed in the Pueblo Coal Mines.

COLORADO: ITS GOLD AND SILVER MINES

Frank Fossett

So BENEFICIAL HAVE BEEN found the climatic influences of Colorado that her fame as a sanitarium is becoming world-wide, and the influx of health-seekers is annually becoming greater. The dryness and lightness of the air and its invigorating character, together with the almost constant prevalence of sunshine, impart new energy to the well, and a fresh lease of life for those whose constitutions are impaired. Here on this elevated plateau, far removed from the chilling winds and damp atmosphere of either ocean, all the conditions of life to the new comer are fresh and inspiring.

This region possesses influences that arrest the tendency to pulmonary diseases. Consumptives who do not put off their coming too long have been cured effectively, while others have had their days prolonged by months or years. Many eastern people have taken up a permanent abode in Colorado, because their health would not permit of their living elsewhere. Others have found the results of a sojourn so salutary that they return to stay. A variety of diseases, chronic or otherwise, find a speedy or partial cure in the pure air or in the health-giving mineral waters.

Investigation and long experience by the highest medical authority have summed the advantages of this climate somewhat as follows: To a person in the enjoyment of fair health, the sensations attending a first entrance into this elevated region are always pleasant. The dryness of the atmosphere, together with the electricity therein contained, combined with, perhaps, other peculiarities of climate, excites the nervous system to a peculiar degree of tension. The physical functions, which may have for some time been accomplished in a sluggish, inefficient manner, at once assume a vigor of action to which the system is a stranger. The appetite is keen, the digestion is vigorous, and the sleep sound. The result of these innovations is that all lurking ailments are swept away at once, and whatever there is in each individual to enjoy is called into the fullest action. He revels in what might be called intoxication of good health. An unclouded mind partakes of the elasticity of a healthy body, and a newly-aroused desire for activity is manifested, as well as an increased capacity to accomplish. This, in the beginning, is experienced to a greater or less degree by all who visit this section, and the pleasure attendant upon such a beginning will forever render the Rocky mountains a resort of unequaled attraction for the tourist.

But besides merely pleasure-seeking travelers who come westward every year, there are thousands of invalids, suffering from a wide range of chronic diseases, who come on a pilgrimage in search of health. In many cases the relief obtained is surprisingly rapid. The asthmatic forgets in the quiet of undisturbed slumber his nightly suffocation; the victim of chronic bronchitis discovers a new lease of life, and after the lapse of a very brief period he finds it hard to realize that he has been so recently afflicted with a cough so distressing, so violent, or so dangerous. The sufferer from malaria, in that most obnoxious form called fever and ague, is glad to have found a land where fever and ague never come.

While the climate is thus referred to in such seemingly flattering terms, the idea is not intended to be conveyed that there is no bad weather in Colorado. There are almost all kinds of climate, according to elevation and locality, from a warm temperate to that of the borders of the frigid zone, the latter being largely experienced on the lofty peaks of the main range of mountains. Under such circumstances, weather, good, bad, and indifferent must be expected. Still the belt of country skirting the eastern base of the mountains as well as a few other sections, enjoys an amount of sunshine and of delightful weather with a freedom from storms such as is but rarely encountered elsewhere, and in no section between Colorado and the seaboard. The temperature of a large portion of the foothills country, including such places as Central, Black Hawk, Idaho Springs, and Georgetown, is remarkably even for the entire year, there being less cold weather in winter and warm weather in summer than in any locality of less elevation. ...

* * *

"Infinite" is the term used by an old Coloradan to describe in brief the climate of this region. Infinite it certainly is in its variety, purity, and sunshine. But the variety comes from difference in altitude, rather than in latitude. The Italian or Virginian warmth of the plains, and the frigidity of "timber line," or of the mountain tops, are experienced on the parallel and within fifty miles one of another. It is but a short remove from a northern to a southern temperature, and from either to the eternal snows of the Sierras. Owing to the dry, bracing qualities of the atmosphere, heat or cold are not felt as severely or readily as where there is greater moisture and humidity.

The quantity of the snow-fall is not great, except on the great mountain ranges and higher elevations. It never entirely disappears from altitudes of from 12,000 to 14,400 feet. Elsewhere the sun's rays are too powerful to admit of snow laying on the ground a great while unless in case of unusually cold weather, and sleighing is of rare occurrence in many mountain towns.

KING COAL

Upton Sinclair

THERE WAS ANOTHER WAY, Old Mike explained, in which the miner was at the mercy of others; this was the matter of stealing cars. Each miner had brass checks with his number on them, and when he sent up a loaded car, he hung one of these checks on a hook inside. In the course of the long journey to the tipple, some one would change the check, and the car was gone. In some mines, the number was put on the car with chalk; and how easy it was for some one to rub it out and change it! It appeared to Hal that it would have been a simple matter to put a number padlock on the car, instead of a check; but such an equipment would have cost the company one or two hundred dollars, he was told, and so the stealing went on year after year.

"You think it's the bosses steal these cars?" asked Hal.

"Sometimes bosses, sometimes bosses' friend—sometimes company himself steal them from miners." In North Valley it was the company, the old Slovak insisted. It was no use sending up more than six cars in one day, he declared; you could never get credit for more than six. Nor was it worth while loading more than a ton on a car; they did not really weigh the cars, the boss just ran them quickly over the scales, and had orders not to go above a certain average. Mike told of an Italian who had loaded a car for a test, so high that he could barely pass it under the roof of the entry, and went up on the tipple and saw it weighed himself, and it was sixty-five hundred pounds. They gave him thirty-five hundred, and when he started to fight, they arrested him. Mike had not seen him arrested, but when he had come out of the mine, the man was gone, and nobody ever saw him again. After that they put a door onto the weigh-room, so that no one could see the scales.

The more Hal listened to the men and reflected upon these things, the more he came to see that the miner was a contractor who had no opportunity to determine the size of the contract before he took it on, nor afterwards to determine how much work he had done. More than that, he was obliged to use supplies, over the price and measurements of which he had no control. He used powder, and would find himself docked at the end of the month for a certain quantity, and if the quantity was wrong, he would have no redress. He was charged a certain sum for "black-smithing"—the keeping of his tools in order; and he would find a dollar or two deducted from his account each month, even though he had not been near the blacksmith shop.

Let any business-man in the world consider the proposition, thought Hal, and say if he would take a contract upon such terms! Would a man undertake to build a dam, for example, with no chance to measure the ground in advance, nor any way of determining how many cubic yards of concrete he had to put in? Would a grocer

sell to a customer who proposed to come into the store and do his own
and meantime locking the grocer outside? Merely to put such questions
the preposterousness of the thing; yet in this district were fifteen tho
working on precisely such terms.

Under the state law, the miner had a right to demand a check-we..ɡ....ɪɑⁿ to
protect his interest at the scales, paying this check-weighman's wages out of his own
earnings. Whenever there was any public criticism about conditions in the coal-
mines, this law would be triumphantly cited by the operators; and one had to have
actual experience in order to realise what a bitter mockery this was to the miner.

In the dining-room Hal sat next to a fair-haired Swedish giant named
Johannson, who loaded timbers ten hours a day. This fellow was one who indulged
in the luxury of speaking his mind, because he had youth and huge muscles, and
no family to tie him down. He was what is called a "blanket-stiff," wandering from
mine to harvest-field and from harvest-field to lumber-camp. Some one broached
the subject of check-weighmen to him, and the whole table heard his scornful laugh.
Let any man ask for a check-weighman!

"You mean they would fire him?" asked Hal.

"Maybe!" was the answer. "Maybe they make him fire himself."

"How do you mean?"

"They make his life one damn misery till he go."

So it was with check-weighman—as with scrip, and with company stores, and
with all the provisions of the law to protect the miner against accidents. You might
demand your legal rights, but if you did, it was a matter of the boss's temper. He
might make your life one damn misery till you went of your own accord. Or you
might get a string of curses and an order, "Down the canyon!"—and likely as not
the toe of a boot in your trouser-seat, or the muzzle of a revolver under your nose.

HISTORY OF THE
MINERS' STRIKE IN COLORADO

Emil Różański

VICTORY FOR THE MINERS CONCLUDED a bitter struggle of more than forty months
with the Colorado coal barons headed by the Colorado Fuel and Iron Company,
which is known as the greatest enemy of all labor unions and which opposes them
in every possible way. This company controls the whole state of Colorado: its
governors—both Republican and Democrat, county sheriffs, mayors, municipal and
state police and militia, and every official wearing a shiny star. All of them are on
the side of the Colorado Fuel and Iron and John D. Rockefeller. ...

Nadine Drummond, untitled, c. 1947.

Everything encompassed by the human eye belongs to "John D."—the land, coal, and other mineral [deposits], the buildings around the mines, houses, schools, churches, and even the post offices and public thoroughfares. ...

        ♣ ♣ ♣

This industrial potentate declared war on all union workers. He drove the Western Federation of Miners out of Colorado. In 1903 the coal barons smashed this union, arrested its leaders and dispersed them under machine gun guard. The miners subsequently organized a more patriotic union, the United Mine Workers of America. On account of its agreements and contacts throughout the United States, this union so encumbered itself that it could not free itself from the coal barons' bonds and oppose such united strength. ...

A NEW ERA—A NEW UNION

The miners in Colorado became convinced that the coal barons were able to be broken and therefore undertook to organize a more revolutionary union, the Industrial Workers of the World. When the current strike broke out, we barely had 2,000 members in the IWW, although more than 10,000 miners went out on strike! The coal barons thought that we were only a small group and that by arresting us they could smash the strike. But they were greatly mistaken. When they arrested one person, two others took his place and meetings continued to occur.

Mass pickets of 500 to 1,000 people each kept watch in front of the mines. Men, women, and children all took their turns on the picket lines. Mass arrests followed in Las Animas and Huerfano counties. The jails were full. New arrestees in groups of 50, 100, and 150 people each were led in through the front door, while their predecessors were released through the back one.

The county and municipal jails lacked space, so that several hundred people were detained in the courthouse. The judges released everyone, except the active [IWW] members, organizers, speakers, secretaries, and committee members. They were held without bail and not allowed to communicate with anyone. If any of them had a friend who wanted to post bail for them, it was not accepted. After being imprisoned for thirty days in one county without bail, the prisoners were transferred for another thirty-day period to other counties [in Colorado]. ... [The families of these prisoners] did not know where they were being held, if they were alive, or if they had been murdered somewhere by the brutal state police, militia, or the [coal] companies' hatchet men. [I] was arrested five times during the four-month strike. ...

AIRPLANES WITH MACHINE GUNS

We had a mass public meeting at the grave in Ludlow, where in 1913 thirteen people—women and children—were burned alive by Rockefeller's thugs. More than 1,500 people turned out for this gathering led by the undersigned. We had a gorgeous day—a beautiful blue sky without a cloud in it. More than 200 cars came from northern Colorado, 60 from Fremont County, 300 from Walsenburg, 80 from Aguilar, and 100 from Trinidad. All the strikers' cars formed a ten-mile-long procession.

Before the meeting commenced four airplanes buzzed in the air overhead. For the next two hours they flew over us with machine guns ready to fire into the crowd at a moment's notice. The noise of the airplane motors and the whir of their propellers ... created such a terrible din that the speakers could not be heard. As a result, I directed that we should all sing "Solidarity Forever," "Red Flag," "The Marseillaise" and other revolutionary songs, which rang out for the whole two hours. Finally the planes headed off in a northerly direction, probably for Denver, in order to report to the governor of the state.

After the planes departed, I briefly addressed the crowd in English and said more or less the following:

> This mass meeting has been called by the IWW. For the first time in the history of Colorado, coal miners from the southern and northern parts of the state have the opportunity to fight together for improved working conditions and better wages.

⚓ ⚓ ⚓

The union is now planning to organize immediately the agricultural workers in Colorado (ACWIU No. 110 of the IWW). Some 790 high school students have also formed union affiliates in the whole district, which the union has supplied with booklets and all the materials they require. These are the children of the proletariat who will become good unionists ahead of time.

This is the way the unionists fight and struggle who are organized under the IWW banner in Colorado. Here our work proceeds quickly and efficiently. This is only because the Communists do not have fertile soil for themselves. As always, the IWW General Defense Committee and the American Civil Liberties Union directed our legal defense.

⚓ ⚓ ⚓

Our first executive committee was arrested and unjustly detained. Nevertheless, we immediately created a second committee. When I was freed on bail, I was asked to join this second, seven-man committee. We were in constant danger because most of the time we had to travel at night on union business. Our union attorney, Fred Caldwell of Denver, sent me to Walsenburg, Aguilar, and Trinidad to gather our witnesses and examine them prior to the hearings.

I arrived at the courtroom [in Walsenburg] to hear the case of a certain widow who had accused the State Insurance Commission of not paying what was owed her. I barely had entered the courtroom when I was illegally arrested. I was only told that I did not have my bond with me and the state police chief had ordered me held pending a personal investigation.

Three days later the commission came to Walsenburg and at its request I was freed for the period of the hearings. "Only after they are over will we decide what to do with you," I was told as I left.

Witnesses from Las Animas and Huerfano counties were arrested at night, after which each of them was "kidnapped" and taken to isolated spots in New Mexico and Texas or to uninhabited parts of Oklahoma where these unfortunate individuals stumbled around for several days in search of food and a shady place, not knowing where they were. Others were thrown into large bags used for shipping rice, tied up, and taken by car to the snow-covered mountains. There the bags were thrown into a ditch and kicked in a cruel manner until those inside them lost consciousness. Afterwards these poor souls were left to their own fate as fodder for the wolves and coyotes.

One black miner testified before the commission that he was taken by car to a secluded spot and, under threat of being shot, was warned that if he returned to Walsenburg he would be hanged from a telephone pole and pumped full of holes. During the courtroom testimony a state police squad was present. Some of the witnesses were arrested immediately following their testimony because the police said they had warrants for them. In one room they filled out the warrants and served them in another.

        🐜 🐜 🐜

The capitalists and the police did everything in their power to destroy our solidarity. Twice they broke up the Polish Hall [IWW headquarters] in Walsenburg. It was so bombarded that not a single window was left in place. The hall in Trinidad was completely destroyed. The police, militia, machine guns, planes, army tanks, quarantine, deportation, malnutrition in jail, thousands of arrests—all of this could not break our solidarity. The capitalists then thought up another tactic: they would starve us into submission. They have more than five thousand scabs who work full time, but the owners don't want to give us work. The blacklist is already in use. When we ask the bosses for work, they order us to go sing "Solidarity Forever" and accordingly make fun of us. Our struggle must go on until we drive out all of the scabs. Our women and children have nothing to eat. This week we passed out a dollar [to each of the strikers], but this is all we had.

Workers! Hold meetings and social functions everywhere and collect money for the strikers in Colorado! We are fighting against the greatest power on earth, the uncrowned king, John D. Rockefeller. His assistant acknowledged that on account of the IWW, Rockefeller has lost $10 million and other smaller coal magnates have also lost the same amount. ...

In 1926 the Colorado Fuel and Iron Company had a clear profit of $2 million while for the first four months of 1927 it was $1 million! The raise for which we are striking would give the miners $3 million to $4 million per year. However, the capitalists prefer to lose $20 million for the four months of our strike than to pay the miners the $3 million to $4 million a year for their backbreaking labor. ... Our oppressors are ruining themselves through their own stinginess.

Workers of the world unite! Join the one great union, the IWW! Send us financial help, because bread will win this strike for us in Colorado. Do not let the companies break our spirit through hunger! Our struggle is your struggle! Away with Rockefeller! Send us what you can ...

BURIED UNSUNG

Zeese Papanikolas

THEY LIVED ABOVE THE TOWN'S one drugstore in rented rooms. The rooms were almost empty. A few pots and pans, thin beds, a few Greek newspapers. It was not poverty. It was simply a kind of austerity born out of a lifetime of habit. And what would they spend money for anyway, these two old men, in Oak Creek, Colorado? For these were men who pressed very lightly on the world. Their rooms had a look of being somehow improvised, temporary, as if at any minute one of these old bachelors could stuff a few shirts into a suitcase and disappear down the canyon with no mark of his passing left behind. Barba John Tsanakatsis, with his round peasant face, his sporty cap and marvelous laugh, went to Las Vegas toward the end of October to get warm. Old Mr. Papadakis stuck it out through the winter, a few miles up the road from the ski resort with its bars and restaurants and new plywood chalets for those comfortable enough to play with the season. In Mr. Papadakis' room there was one obvious center. It was not the bed or the table or the gas stove, but a steamer trunk. He opened it for me, showed me its elaborate compartments, its pressers for trousers and suits. He had bought it in the '30s for his first trip back to Crete.

"He used to have some new suitcases," Barba John said, winking slyly, "for the airplane. The best."

"I give them up," Mr. Papadakis said. "They were light, you know. Special made for the airplane. There was something about them. I just didn't like them." The few possessions in Barba John's room had been tumbled about in a genial disorder. Mr. Papadakis kept his room immaculate. He was a few years older than Barba John, a slender man with a white mustache. He held himself straight. When he spoke English, the words had a tart Cretan twang to them. That afternoon Barba John and I had driven down the canyon looking for him. We found him a few miles out of town where the remains of the mines stuck out of the brush and scrub oak, a rusted coal car, the stump of the tipple, here and there the black smudge of a dump. He was gathering chokecherries to make into wine. He was eighty-five years old.

We sat in his room drinking the sweet homemade wine and he was telling me what he knew of the man I was searching for.

". . . There was not too many of us speaking very much then. Louis, he didn't speak very much neither, but good enough to get by. But there was not too many to take the speakers' stand and speak and all that. Louis, he done pretty well. He got the appointment around Denver. I don't know who appointed him."

"Did you know him before?"

Artists Unknown, "The Colonel Investigates the Humboldt," from Beyond the Mississippi by Albert D. Richardson, 1867.

"I seen him, but I didn't know too much about him. A young, nice, pretty good man, that's all I can say."

"So anyway, he was sort of your spokesman?"

"Yes. More like he give us the dope and mix with the higher-ups, you know, and talk things over."

Barba John laughed and pushed back his cap and adjusted his thick glasses to look at the photograph I handed him. "Yes, yes, yes," Barba John said with his devilish chuckle, "here he is. Sure I knew Louis. Had a little coffeehouse in Denver."

"That was on Market Street?"

"Yeah, Market Street."

"What kind of place was it?"

"A coffeehouse. Like them coffeehouses. Maybe you seen them coffeehouses. Have you? Chairs, you know, couple of tables. Serve coffee, little *ouzo*, stuff like that …"

"No *ouzo*," Mr. Papadakis interrupted. It was important to him for things to be accurate.

"Sometimes," Barba John went on, "sometimes they have a dance, you know. Let them play the *laouto* … Have that two, three times …"

OUT OF THE DEPTHS

Barron B. Beshoar

MORE THAN FOUR DECADES HAVE passed since the memorable Colorado coal strike of 1913–1914, an industrial struggle that left an indelible imprint on the civilized world. Labor and capital have come to grips on many occasions since those historic years, but, except for isolated instances which were little more than repeat performances, the differences have not been so broad in scope or so far reaching in their consequences. It was on the field of Ludlow, where the blood of strikers, their women and children, was shed by a subsidized soldiery, that labor established its right to share in such basic American principles as those of religious and political liberty, free speech and free assembly, and economic freedom. The 1913–1914 strike was not a purely Colorado matter as the state was merely the testing ground for two divergent principles of life. On the one hand, firmly entrenched and in full power and strength, were those who held to the theory that all benefits properly trickle down from above, and on the other were those who devotedly maintained the democratic proposition that men and women who toil with their backs and hands are entitled to share in the fruits of their productive labor.

Colorado was the testing ground for several reasons. The great corporations of the East seized control of the natural resources of the state during its early, formative years. They invested their surpluses in the isolated holdings as business conditions warranted and they sought through crafty political arts a perpetuation of their absentee landlordism without regard for the desires of the people or the welfare of their own employees. That their policies and methods, which reached such full flower in Colorado, were both unbusinesslike and unmoral, has been demonstrated time and again in the years since 1913. It is a sad commentary on human intelligence and decency to record that it took a bloody war to expose the errors in all of their hideous implications and institute corrective measures, just as it required a war between the states to settle the slavery and federal questions.

Any story of the 1913–1914 strike must, of necessity, be the story of John R. Lawson who was the outstanding labor leader of the day. There were others who outranked him in the United Mine Workers of America, but none who equaled him in strike leadership or in the love and respect of the Colorado coal miners. He stood for the best in the union movement and has remained through the years a personification of honest, intelligent and capable leadership. While many of his colleagues, who held positions of trust and importance, sold themselves to the enemy or sought glory and personal power at the expense of the miners, John Lawson remained faithful to an ideal and devoted himself exclusively to the welfare of those who placed themselves under his care. His story and that of the strike are inseparably interwoven, so much so that the one cannot be told without the other. Much credit is due the United Mine Workers of America as an organization for the work it did in Colorado in 1913–1914. It spent much treasure, effort and blood in a glorious crusade, but John Lawson remains an outstanding figure. To him, both as a representative of the United Mine Workers and as an individual, the coal miners and labor generally owe the greatest measure of gratitude, respect and honor.

The record shows that the 1913–1914 strike was lost by the United Mine Workers, but in reality it was won. It is true that the great strike was brought to an end by the organization before its objectives were achieved, but public opinion, which had been aroused as never before or since in an industrial dispute, battered down the gates of the coal operators and in the end the miners and citizens of Colorado were the victors. It is fair to say that the citizens of the state shared in the victory because through it they were freed from a political domination that was as close to absolutism as anything ever attempted in a nation founded on such documents as the U.S. Constitution and the Bill of Rights.

If the account seems biased in favor of labor in general and the coal miners in particular, the reader is asked to remember that it deals with a period in our industrial history when the gun, the club and the fist were often the sole methods of management-labor communication. Certainly the Colorado record of that decade is clear and sustaining insofar as labor is concerned; it has been substantiated, not once but many times by courts of record and the earnest findings of impartial and honest investigators.

The material contained herein is not fiction. It is factual. Perhaps at times the coal operators and their henchmen will appear too devilish and the coal miners too angelic. Obviously neither side had a monopoly on honesty and morals, and just as obviously each camp had its share of dishonesty and greed, of lust and evil. However, the opposing principles that motivated the coal operators and the miners give an implication to the story of 1913–1914 that is inescapable in any honest presentation.

Many of the coal operators believed their system was fundamental and necessary. They were sincere in their fear that union organization would spell the end of business enterprise and industrial freedom of the type cherished by boards of directors. Their psychology was not unlike that of the ruling class of a monarchy or a kingdom of a century ago. Most of them had appropriated or inherited their wealth and believed it well within the realm of possibility for any deserving man to do likewise. It is charitable to believe that few of those who sat on the boards of the powerful coal corporations had any understanding of the lives and problems of their workers.

If the mine guards and detectives, the mercenaries who served as the Gestapo of the coal districts appear to be scoundrels who sold themselves and their fellowmen for a few corporation dollars, the author will consider them adequately presented.

In preparing this volume [Beshoar's], the author had the generous assistance of many men and women who lived through the hectic days of 1913–1914 and knew their events at first hand. I am forever indebted to my own father, Dr. Ben B. Beshoar, who served as the United Mine Workers physician in Trinidad and Las Animas County during those turbulent and dangerous days. I have a vague, small boy recollection of riding in the back seat of a touring car while he drove, without lights, up the river at night to see a sick miner. And above Trinidad the night sky was filled with the white beams of search lights sweeping restlessly back and forth, seeking out striking miners, seeking out the young doctor at the wheel of his Overland car, seeking out the little boy in the back seat, the little boy who knew from his father's face that those hard lights were to be feared, but was completely unaware that behind those luminous eyes were Rockefeller machine guns that could and would spit death if the lights caught our movement on the bumpy road. And I have other recollections, some dim, some sharp, of cavalrymen with gleaming sabres herding the people along Main and Commercial streets in Trinidad, of militiamen searching our house for guns and dumping the contents of bureau drawers on the floor while my mother watched them with loathing and contempt, of miners with red handkerchiefs around their necks and rifles in their hands who hailed my father with jovial but foreign-sounding cries that sounded like "Hello Doc Bee-shoo."

In another scene, way back in the chambers of memory, I see my Uncle John sitting in the laboratory of his dental office in Trinidad, patiently instructing an Austrian miner, who spoke little English, in how to shoot out a CF&I searchlight with the beautiful hammerless Savage rifle he was graciously lending to the cause.

And I have an immeasurable debt to John R. Lawson for his assistance though I must say his innate sense of modesty made him a reluctant and oftentimes unwilling witness to the events of 1913–1914 where John Lawson was directly concerned. One of the things in life that I cherish most was a close personal relationship with John and Olive Lawson. The Lawsons exemplified such virtues as love of freedom, love of fellow man, love of decency and love for one another. I think of them always with affection and admiration and respect. The world could well use many more Lawsons.

Lester Vavian, "Miner's House," n.d.

SECTION X

THE UNDERSIDE

ROUGHING IT

Mark Twain

REALLY AND TRULY, TWO THIRDS of the talk of drivers and conductors had been about this man Slade, ever since the day before we reached Julesburg. In order that the eastern reader may have a clear conception of what a Rocky Mountain desperado is, in his highest state of development, I will reduce all this mass of overland gossip to one straightforward narrative, and present it in the following shape:

Slade was born in Illinois, of good parentage. At about twenty-six years of age he killed a man in a quarrel and fled the country. At St. Joseph, Missouri, he joined one of the early California-bound emigrant trains, and was given the post of train-master. One day on the plains he had an angry dispute with one of his wagon-drivers, and both drew their revolvers. But the driver was the quicker artist, and had his weapon cocked first. So Slade said it was a pity to waste life on so small a matter, and proposed that the pistols be thrown on the ground and the quarrel settled by a fist-fight. The unsuspecting driver agreed, and threw down his pistol—whereupon Slade laughed at his simplicity, and shot him dead!

He made his escape, and lived a wild life for awhile, dividing his time between fighting Indians and avoiding an Illinois sheriff, who had been sent to arrest him for his first murder. It is said that in one Indian battle he killed three savages with his own hand, and afterward cut their ears off and sent them, with his compliments, to the chief of the tribe.

Slade soon gained a name for fearless resolution, and this was sufficient merit to procure for him the important post of overland division-agent at Julesburg, in place of Mr. Jules, removed. For some time previously, the company's horses had been frequently stolen, and the coaches delayed, by gangs of outlaws, who were wont to laugh at the idea of any man's having the temerity to resent such outrages. Slade resented them promptly. The outlaws soon found that the new agent was a man who did not fear anything that breathed the breath of life. He made short work of all offenders. The result was that delays ceased, the company's property was let alone, and no matter what happened or who suffered, Slade's coaches went through, every time! True, in order to bring about this wholesome change, Slade had to kill several men—some say three, others say four, and others six—but the world was the richer for their loss. The first prominent difficulty he had was with the ex-agent Jules, who bore the reputation of being a reckless and desperate man himself. Jules hated Slade for supplanting him, and a good fair occasion for a fight was all he was waiting for. By and by Slade dared to employ a man whom Jules had once discharged. Next, Slade seized a team of stage-horses which he accused Jules of having driven off and hidden somewhere for his own use. War was declared, and for a day or two the two men walked warily about the streets, seeking each other, Jules armed with a double-barreled shot gun, and Slade with his history-creating revolver. Finally, as Slade stepped into a store, Jules poured the contents of his gun into him from behind the door. Slade was plucky, and Jules got several bad pistol wounds in return. Then both men fell, and were carried to their respective lodgings, both swearing that better aim should do deadlier work next time. Both were bed-ridden a long time, but Jules got on his feet first, and gathering his possessions together, packed them on a couple of mules, and fled to the Rocky Mountains to gather strength in safety against the day of reckoning. For many months he was not seen or heard of, and was gradually dropped out of the remembrance of all save Slade himself. But Slade was not the man to forget him. On the contrary, common report said that Slade kept a reward standing for his capture, dead or alive!

After awhile, seeing that Slade's energetic administration had restored peace and order to one of the worst divisions of the road, the overland stage company transferred him to the Rocky Ridge division in the Rocky Mountains, to see if he could perform a like miracle there. It was the very paradise of outlaws and desperadoes. ...

         🐜 🐜 🐜

Slade took up his residence sweetly and peacefully in the midst of this hive of horse-thieves and assassins, and the very first time one of them aired his insolent swaggerings in his presence he shot him dead! He began a raid on the outlaws, and in a singularly short space of time he had completely stopped their depredations on the stage stock, recovered a large number of stolen horses, killed several of the worst desperadoes of the district, and gained such a dread ascendancy over the rest that they respected him, admired him, feared him, obeyed him! He wrought the same marvelous change in the ways of the community that had marked his administration at Overland City. ...

         🐜 🐜 🐜

In the fulness of time Slade's myrmidons captured his ancient enemy Jules, whom they found in a well-chosen hiding-place in the remote fastnesses of the mountains, gaining a precarious livelihood with his rifle. They brought him to Rocky Ridge, bound hand and foot, and deposited him in the middle of the cattle-yard with his back against a post. It is said that the pleasure that lit Slade's face when he heard of it was something fearful to contemplate. He examined his enemy to see that he was securely tied, and then went to bed, content to wait till morning before enjoying the luxury of killing him. Jules spent the night in the cattle-yard, and it is a region where warm nights are never known. In the morning Slade practised on him with his revolver, nipping the flesh here and there, and occasionally clipping off a finger, while Jules begged him to kill him outright and put him out of his misery. Finally Slade reloaded, and walking up close to his victim, made some characteristic remarks and then dispatched him. The body lay there half a day, nobody venturing to touch it without orders, and then Slade detailed a party and assisted at the burial himself. But he first cut off the dead man's ears and put them in his vest pocket, where he carried them for some time with great satisfaction. That is the story as I have frequently heard it told and seen it in print in California newspapers. It is doubtless correct in all essential particulars.

🐾 🐾 🐾

In due time we rattled up to a stage-station, and sat down to breakfast with a half-savage, half-civilized company of armed and bearded mountaineers, ranchmen and station employees. The most gentlemanly-appearing, quiet and affable officer we had yet found along the road in the Overland Company's service was the person who sat at the head of the table, at my elbow. Never youth stared and shivered as I did when I heard them call him SLADE!

Here was romance, and I sitting face to face with it!—looking upon it—touching it—hobnobbing with it, as it were! Here, right by my side, was the actual ogre who, in fights and brawls and various ways, *had taken the lives of twenty-six human beings*, or all men lied about him! I suppose I was the proudest stripling that ever traveled to see strange lands and wonderful people.

He was so friendly and so gentle-spoken that I warmed to him in spite of his awful history. It was hardly possible to realize that this pleasant person was the pitiless scourge of the outlaws, the raw-head-and-bloody-bones the nursing mothers of the mountains terrified their children with. And to this day I can remember nothing remarkable about Slade except that his face was rather broad across the cheek bones, and that the cheek bones were low and the lips peculiarly thin and straight. But that was enough to leave something of an effect upon me, for since then I seldom see a face possessing those characteristics without fancying that the owner of it is a dangerous man.

The coffee ran out. At least it was reduced to one tin-cupful, and Slade was about to take it when he saw that my cup was empty. He politely offered to fill it, but although I wanted it, I politely declined. I was afraid he had not killed anybody that morning, and might be needing diversion. But still with firm politeness he insisted on filling my cup, and said I had traveled all night and better deserved it than he—and while he talked he placidly poured the fluid, to the last drop. I thanked him and drank it, but it gave me no comfort, for I could not feel sure that he would not be sorry, presently, that he had given it away, and proceed to kill me to distract his thoughts from the loss. But nothing of the kind occurred. We left him with only twenty-six dead people to account for, and I felt a tranquil satisfaction in the thought that in so judiciously taking care of No. 1 at that breakfast-table I had pleasantly escaped being No. 27. Slade came out to the coach and saw us off, first ordering certain rearrangements of the mail-bags for our comfort, and then we took leave of him, satisfied that we should hear of him again, some day, and wondering in what connection.

THE KNIFE AND GUN CLUB

Eugene Richards

I GO TO SLEEP REMEMBERING what it was like when I was last there—the smells, the noises, the wild eyes, the blood—and wake up when it's still dark. Wrapping myself in a blanket, I go out onto the motel balcony. Denver General is only a few blocks away, a top-heavy building on a narrow base, much taller than the structures around it. From here I can't see the emergency room, which is on the ground floor, but there are lights on in a dozen windows, and higher up, a blinking red tower spikes the sky. I imagine the elevator running up and down from the operating room and hear a siren, but it's only the cold, rough wind.

The wind is bringing in some snow. It's falling like powdered milk onto the streets, blotting out the city. My blanket is getting wet, and my head. Now Denver General vanishes, lost in the swirling whiteness. I lean out over the rail trying to see and for a moment have the feeling that the world is truly changing, that I won't be able to find my way back to that place.

Once that would have been a great relief. I hated hospitals. My wife, Dorothea, spent years in and out of a cancer hospital. She died in a hospital. I came to DG the first time because I needed work, any work. A magazine assigned me to report on what goes on in a "typical" emergency room. So I began to take photographs, though the painful memories came in a continuous stream. There was no protection from them. I saw cuts, burns, broken limbs, heart attacks, and then, what's inside the human body. When a man's chest was cracked, I saw his heart floating in the pool of blood like a drowned puppy.

But now and then someone who surely would have died lived, and there were children who stopped crying and old people who could go back home. There were also peaceful moments when I talked one-on-one with doctors, nurses, and paramedics. I made friends, and my sorrow and fear grew into curiosity. Instead of watching the practice of medicine from a distance I began to move closer. Then closer. There were still whole days I wanted to run away, but there were others when I was wholly convinced I wanted to be a paramedic or a health aide. I was acquiring a knowledge. When my magazine assignment was up and I had to go home, I knew I wouldn't stay away. My own momentum wouldn't let me.

I arrive before 6:00—it's still dark and a few flakes of snow are still falling—and crawl in. Car Sixty-nine is an ugly beast. The floor is orange tile, as is the door. It has a white ceiling and nine dome lights, six that are working, and a fixed leather bench patched with electrician's tape to cover the needle holes. Its foam cushion has to have hosts of crud inside it from the used-up syringes that have been stuck there. The wagon area itself is maybe ten feet by five-and-a-half feet with just under five feet headroom. An open hatchway connects the cab to the wagon. Directly in front of the seat, the third rider's seat, is the stretcher with a metal frame and legs with rollers that drop when released. And on top of that is a clean white sheet.

Joe Parks logs in. I'd hug him, rather than just say, "Hello, I'm back," but he obviously woke up from an angry bed this morning. "Me and Tricia are fighting again. Goddamn." Heavyset, shaggy-haired, he moves slowly over the car, counting the medicines and stocking bandages, while Larry speeds. Larry Trump, who looks exactly like Buffalo Bill, tests the two-way radio, the siren, the strobes, tunes the portable to country-western, and we are gone.

"This is KAZY Radio. It is Monday again. Monday's the day for survivors, so hang in there. It's six-fifteen in Denver, the Mile High City. ..."

Out the back window of the ambulance, the city is just beginning to open up. I can see the downtown for a second, the Rocky Mountains, a flash of sunlight. Onto Speer Boulevard, with Joe and Larry settling down, quieting down, when we get our first call, a Code 10, and are pulled back from the music and everything we'd been thinking. The siren! My heart jumps up, touching my throat. Suddenly everything is centered and howling. The waves of sound go out. Suddenly everything is clear. Running hot is brutal, fast, life-giving, and I'll never get tired of it. I'll never get tired of it.

HANDS UP

General David J. Cook

THE MURDER OF AUGUST GALLINGER, *alias* "Cheap John," created a sensation in Denver in the latter part of the year 1866, which for a long while engaged the public attention. Mr. Gallinger kept a small store on the corner of Twelfth and Blake streets, and lived alone over the store in a small room. He had been a member of the Third Colorado regiment, enlisted for a hundred days, and had taken part in the Sand Creek fight. He was quite popular, and although a street peddler, he did a thriving

Alexander Brownlie, "[Street in] Georgetown, Colorado," n.d.

business. He lived in plain style, and was supposed by some to be a miser. This impression it was which led to his murder.

The assault occurred on the night of December 15th, 1866. Gen. Cook had been elected city marshal of Denver for the first time a few months previous. On the night of the occurrence he was passing across the Blake-Street bridge from Denver to West Denver, accompanied by another officer. They were walking leisurely along, when they heard something fall, creating a loud noise. Cook immediately formed the conclusion that something wrong had happened, and he and his companion started in the direction of the point from which the noise had come, and it appeared to be in John's house. There was no one below, hence the officers rushed up stairs. It was about nine o'clock in the evening, and as there were no artificial lights in the house, they found the place quite dark. As they went up the front steps they thought they heard someone descending the rear steps, but as they at that time did not know what had happened, they passed on into John's room, and did not pursue the party who was leaving the house.

Reaching Mr. Gallinger's room, their ears were greeted by moans from a man sitting on a lounge. Gen. Cook went up to where the man—who proved to be Gallinger—sat, and assisted him to his feet, demanding to know what had occurred and how it had all come about. He found Gallinger covered with blood, and when the officer pulled him up, the poor fellow clutched the lapel of Cook's coat with his bloody hands. The blood was flowing from a deep wound four inches long in the head. When questioned, John replied in German, and was evidently demented. But it did not require any speech to explain that murder had been attempted. The wound was of a nature that precluded the possibility of suicide; and, besides, the instrument with which it had been inflicted was nowhere to be seen. It was evident from the appearance of the wound that it had been made with a hatchet, the murderer coming upon the victim while sitting, and striking with the edge of the tool. Dr. F. J. Bancroft was summoned. Upon examination he found that the skull had been seriously fractured, and pronounced the wound necessarily fatal. It may as well be stated here, as elsewhere, that the doctor's prediction was verified, and that the old man died a week afterwards. He was never conscious after the night of the assault, and hence could throw no light whatever upon the affair.

Leaving the wounded man in care of others, Gen. Cook immediately began a search for the murderer. He found the tracks of a man leading out from the rear of the building, and made an exact measurement of them. He also found a woman who stated that she had seen a man go out of the building at the rear at about the time of the attack, but she had not been able to get a good look at him on account of the darkness, and thought she would be unable to recognize him.

Here was a dilemma. A crime had been committed only a few minutes before, but the criminal seemed to have escaped as effectually as if he had had a month's start of the officers. But Cook is not the man to lose time in hesitation. He spent the night in searching for some clue which would lead to the detection of the villain, whoever he might be.

He learned enough during the night to decide him in a determination to raid a house which stood near by. This house was occupied by several persons, all of them of loose character. Among others who occupied it was a worthless individual named George Corman, who was the "solid man" of another inmate of the dwelling, a low prostitute called Mrs. Foster. The fellow did not work for a living, but depended upon the earnings of this woman for support. He was known to be none too good to steal, and it was believed that he would commit murder if there was hope of reward. Cook knew enough about this man to lead him to believe that the chances were good for his being the murderer of Cheap John. He decided to investigate, at any rate. Accordingly in company with H. B. Haskell, then a special officer in Denver, he repaired to the Corman residence early in the morning succeeding the murderous assault. He found the front of the building occupied by Corman and his woman, while in the rear premises resided a Mrs. Mary Kerwin with her family.

The officers decided to investigate while the inmates of the house were still asleep. They entered the yard by a back entrance, and as they came up to the door found a hatchet lying upon the ground thoroughly besmeared with blood. Here was certainly a pointer—the first important one found—and it bid fair to lead to speedy results. The officers felt that they had made a big discovery, and without further ado walked into the house, where they met Mrs. Kerwin, of whom they demanded to know the name of the owner of the hatchet. Her reply was that it was the property of Corman.

Corman and the Foster woman were next approached. They did not deny the ownership of the hatchet.

"Where did this blood come from?" demanded Cook.

The woman became the spokesman. "I killed a chicken last night," she said, "and cut its head off with the hatchet."

"Chicken! chicken!" replied Cook. "Chickens are worth a dollar and a half apiece in this country now, and I know you can't afford chickens. Sowbelly is good enough for you."

The woman replied that she put on style occasionally herself.

When Cook asked where the feathers were, she declared that they had been thrown into the privy vault, while the bones had been burned in the stove.

A close search of the vault and of the ashes in the stove failed to reveal any trace of the remains of the alleged chicken. Here were other strong pointers. The arrest of Corman was decided upon. There seemed to be a pretty fair case against him already developed, and Mr. Cook had confidence in finding a great deal more testimony. Consequently he took Corman into custody and locked him up.

George Hopkins was then, as he now is, an officer in Denver, and he was called upon to aid in working up the case. He was sent to see Mrs. Kerwin and to ascertain, if possible, whether she did not know more about it than had so far been developed. Gen. Cook, himself, believed that she could tell the entire story if she would. In this case, as in most others, he hit the nail square on the head. The woman knew a great deal, and Hopkins was able to prevail upon her to tell her story. Her revelation was startling enough.

Mrs. Kerwin's sleeping apartments adjoined those of Corman and Mrs. Foster, and there was only a thin board partition between the two rooms, there being many cracks in the boards. On the night of the assault she had heard Corman come in. She had already retired, and was supposed by him and the Foster woman to be asleep, though she was not. He had appeared to be considerably flurried and had said to Mrs. Foster:

"Well, I hit the d———d old Jew, and I hit him hard; but I did not get anything—not a cent. The officers came so quick that I couldn't move a wheel, and had to run like the devil to get away."

As may be supposed, this disclosure had aroused the curiosity of the listening woman. She was now wide awake, and was determined to hear all that was to be said. She put her ear to an open crack, and then heard the man tell his woman how he had come upon the Jew and struck him with his hatchet. This he had no sooner done than John clutched him, the blood spurting out of his fresh wound and covering his shirt. The garment, he said, was then bloody. An examination by the two, which Mrs. Kerwin witnessed, confirmed his statement. It was then decided between them that the tell-tale garment must be disposed of. Corman accordingly took the shirt off, and they stowed it away in a cooking vessel which they found in the room, which Corman took to the back yard and buried, returning and going to bed.

The officers having this story in their possession, began to look for the hidden shirt. A snow had fallen in the early morning after it had been buried, and they were compelled to look over almost the entire yard for it before uncovering it; but they at last came upon the hidden article. It was found snugly buried some eight inches below the surface, and when brought out it was discovered to be pretty well bespattered with the crimson fluid.

Thus this case was worked up by Gen. Cook. He had not rested until he had probed the mystery to its foundation. It would seem that there could have hardly been the least chance for Corman to escape the gallows. Strange as it may appear to the reader, he not only was not hanged, but he was allowed to go scot free.

There was then but one term of the District Court held each year in Denver, and it came in January. The trial of Corman came on in January, 1867. The crime was then fresh in the minds of the people, and the proceedings were watched with very great interest. The jurors who sat in the case were H. M. Goodrich, W. S. Peabody, Eli Daugherty, R. S. Permar, Edward Bates, L. M. Sprague, C. M. Birdsall, Watson Holyer, W. S. Hurd, W. H. Levain, Robert Tait, and Dwight S. Thompson. The people were represented by Hon. V. D. Markham, then prosecuting attorney, while Messrs. M. Benedict, G. W. Chamberlain and———Bostwick appeared for the defense. The case was ably presented on both sides, the defense relying principally upon impeaching the testimony of Mrs. Kerwin, who was the most important witness for the prosecution. They succeeded in making such an impression upon the mind of one of the jurors as to cause him to hold out for acquittal against the other eleven, who favored a verdict of murder in the first degree, the penalty for which would have been hanging. The obstinacy of this one man resulted in the bringing in of a report of disagreement by the jury. The case was thus continued until the next term of court. By the time this term convened, Mrs. Kerwin had died and Mr. Haskell had left the city, and their testimony could not be obtained. Hence the case was dismissed, and the murderer of Cheap John became a free man in 1868.

When Corman was turned out of jail, he found Denver a very disagreeable place of residence, as everybody believed him guilty of murder. He went to Georgetown, where he soon became known as one of the worst sots of the town, earning a scanty living by scrubbing out bar-rooms. Even his woman deserted him.

Gen. Cook saw him in Georgetown in 1874, and asked why he did not tell all about the murder of Cheap John.

"If I should do so," he replied, "they couldn't prove it on me."

Poor fellow! he met with a worse fate than death on the scaffold. There was in those days an unused tunnel in the side of a mountain near Georgetown, extending in about a hundred feet. The people of the town were startled one quiet afternoon by a report of an explosion coming from the direction of this tunnel, which seemed to them to be loud enough for the bursting loose of a volcano. Almost the whole city was shocked.

The temporary bewilderment having subsided, an investigating committee was organized to explore the tunnel. They went in with lights, and soon discovered to their dismay that there was fresh flesh sticking to some of the rocks of the wall. Other pieces of flesh, and some clothing and fragments of bones were found scattered about. There was enough of the clothes left to identify them as those of old Corman. He had gone into the tunnel—for what purpose no one will probably ever know—and had found a five-pound can of nitro-glycerine lying on the ground, and had evidently picked it up to examine it, and, finding that it was nothing that he wanted, had thrown it down, creating the explosion which had shocked the town, and which tore his carcass into shreds.

People said it was Fate that did it. Who knows?

And this is the end of the story which began eight or nine years before, with Gen. Cook's hearing a strange noise while crossing the Cherry Creek bridge. Strange, isn't it, how all these scoundrels meet their just deserts? There are other laws than those which the courts deal with, and superior to them. One of these prescribes punishment for the murderer. It always comes sooner or later.

STRIP SEARCH

Rex Burns

WAGER STEERED THE WHITE sedan through the tangle of heavy traffic near the state capitol and its oval of dimly lit trees and paths. The area was now known as Sod Circle because of the male prostitutes who strolled these paths to pose and smile at the cruising cars. A monument to Colorful Colorado and the equality and majesty of the laws Wager was sworn to uphold. He turned onto East Colfax, one of the few corners of the city that still held life after dark, and joined the slowly moving cars nosing down the tunnel of neon and pin spots that made headlights unnecessary. Colfax Avenue was one of the longest sex strips in the country. The west end went four miles toward the mountains and was dotted with drive-in restaurants, a plentiful scattering of bars, and a line of motels that did business by the hour rather than by the night. It was mostly the teenie's drag strip. The east end was called adult—adult films, adult bookstores, adult arcades, adult live shows. It went across the prairie in the direction of Kansas, leaving Denver around mile eight, and then staggering on as far again before fading into the bug-spattered neon of all-night truck stops and cut-rate gas stations with their scratched and scarred "adult dispensers" on the grime-streaked walls of men's rooms.

At this, the lower end of the strip, a short walk from the capitol, the Cinnamon Club's glowing pink-and-green sign hung out over a sidewalk crowded with night people. The car glided past a Laundromat, half-filled at one-thirty in the morning with customers hunching their shoulders against one another. Across the street, a dark-colored van sat in the unlit parking lot of a small group of closed shops. Around the van half-a-dozen men of various ages clustered wearing the street uniform of the dope world: tattered fatigue jackets, Levi's, hats of several styles, vests. One, standing at the open door, carefully counted out his money while the driver, glancing anxiously at Wager's unmarked car, snapped his fingers.

"You recognize that dude?"

Axton craned his neck. "No. New pusher in town."

Wager tried to see the plates on the van, but they had been bent and smeared with dirt; besides, it was an item for Vice and Narcotics. If they had the time, if they had the manpower, if they had the interest, Vice and Narcotics might set the dealer up for a buy-and-bust. Had Wager and Axton swung around to arrest them for what was plainly a rolling dope market, the money and the dope would disappear into the vehicle, and so would the case—in some kind of constitutional infringement. It wasn't enough anymore to witness a crime in progress; you had to get a warrant to investigate a homicide if it was on private property. There was a lot of talk about some pendulum swinging back toward law enforcement, but Wager hadn't seen it yet.

He pulled into a yellow zone near the corner, half-aware of the cautious eyes slanting their way from the strolling crowd. Their car caused a subtle undertow among the people walking or standing and talking, or alone and watching the action along the street. A teenaged whore in white shorts turned away abruptly to wander toward the other end of the block, her legs awkwardly thin and bony on tall sandals. From the shadowy landing of a stairway leading up to the cheap apartments above the stores, a figure withdrew into the darkness. Wager and Axton locked the car's doors and walked toward the glare of light. Along the curb, eyes slid away from them, and a grimy pair of panhandlers eased out of their path.

The Cinnamon Club advertised its shows as Sweet-n-Spicy. A glass case at the brightly lit entry showed a fly-specked collection of nude girls standing at the edge of a stage, smiling regally down at the camera. At the top, near the center, stood one who looked like Annette Sheldon; it was hard to tell, though, because the stiff poses and the harsh light made them all look alike, except for the various hairstyles.

"Let's get some culture," said Max.

THE CASE OF ALFERD PACKER

Paul H. Gantt

LARRY DOLAN WAS THE FIRST MAN uptown from the courthouse after sentence had been passed. He hurried to his favorite resting place, the saloon.

"Well, boys, it's all over. Packer t'hang!"

Pressed for particulars by the *habitués* of the saloon, Larry took an appropriate attitude before his motley audience and delivered his version of the sentence:

The Judge says:

"Stan' up, yah voracious man eating son of a bitch, stand up!"

Then, pointing his trembling fingers at Packer, so raging mad he was, says he:

"They was sivin Dimmicrats in Hinsdale County, and ye eat five of them, G– – d– – ye!

"I sintins ye t'be hanged by the neck until ye're dead, dead, DEAD, as a warnin' ag'in reducin' the Dimmycratic population of th' state."

In this distorted form the "judgment" against Packer spread like wildfire over the West and became known all over the United States. It does great injustice to Judge Melville B. Gerry, a man of the highest type, a Southern gentleman of the old school from Macon, Georgia, a jurist of great learning and knowledge of the law.

THE BEAST

Ben B. Lindsey and Harvey J. O'Higgins

ONE WINTER AFTERNOON, AFTER I had been listening for days to one of these cases—if I remember rightly, it concerned the ownership of some musty old mortgaged furniture that had been stored in a warehouse and was claimed by the mortgagee on the mortgage and by the warehouseman on a storage lien—the Assistant District Attorney interrupted the proceedings to ask me if I would not dispose of a larceny case that would not take two minutes. I was willing. He brought in a boy, whom I shall call "Tony Costello," and arraigned him before the court. The Clerk read the indictment; a railroad detective gave his testimony; the boy was accused of stealing coal from the tracks, and he had no defence. Frightened and silent, he stood looking from me to the jury, from the jury to the attorney, and from the attorney back to me—big-eyed and trembling—a helpless infant, trying to follow in our faces what was going on. The case was clear. There was nothing for me to do under the law but to find him guilty and sentence him to a term in the State Reform School. I did it—and prepared to go back to the affair of the second-hand furniture.

There had been sitting at the back of the courtroom an old woman with a shawl on her head, huddled up like a squaw, wooden-faced, and incredibly wrinkled. She waddled down the aisle toward the bench, while papers of commitment were being made out against the boy, and began to talk to the court interpreter in an excited gabble which I did not understand. I signed to the counsel for the warehouseman to proceed with his case; he rose—and he was greeted with the most soul-piercing scream of agony that I ever heard from a human throat. The old woman stood there, clutching her shawl to her breast, her toothless mouth open, her face as contorted as if she were being torn limb from limb, shrieking horribly. She threw her hands up to her head, grasped her poor, thin gray hair, and pulled it, yelling, with protruding eyes, like a madwoman. When the bailiff of the court caught hold of her to take her from the room, she broke away from him and ran to the wall and beat her head against it, as if she would batter the court house down on us all and bury our injustice under the ruins. They dragged her out into the hall, but through the closed door I could still hear her shrieking—shrieking terribly. I adjourned the court and retreated to my chambers, very much shaken and unnerved; but I still heard her, in the hall, wailing and sobbing, and every now and then screaming as if her heart was being torn out of her.

I did not know what to do. I thought I had no power, under the law, to do anything but what I *had* done. The boy was guilty. The law required that I should sentence him. The mother might scream herself dumb, but I was unable to help her.

She continued to scream. Two reporters, attracted by the uproar, came to ask me if I could not do something for her. I telephoned the District Attorney and asked him whether I could not change my order against the boy—make it a suspended sentence—and let me look into the case myself. He was doubtful—as I was—about my right to do such a thing, but I accepted the responsibility of the act and he consented to it. After what seemed an hour to me—during which I could still hear the miserable woman wailing—the boy was returned to her and she was quieted.

Then I took the first step toward the founding of the Juvenile Court of Denver. I got an officer who knew Tony, and I went with him, at night, to the boy's home in the Italian quarter of North Denver. I need not describe the miserable conditions in which I found the Costellos living—in two rooms, in a filthy shack, with the father sick in bed, and the whole family struggling against starvation. I talked with Tony, and found him not a criminal, not a bad boy, but merely a boy. He had seen that his father and his mother and the baby were suffering from cold, and he had brought home fuel from the railroad tracks to keep them warm. I gave him a little lecture on the necessity of obeying the laws, and put him "on probation." The mother kissed my hands. The neighbours came in to salute me and to rejoice with the Costellos. I left them. But I carried away with me what must have been something of their view of my court and my absurd handling of their boy; and I began to think over this business of punishing infants as if they were adults and of maiming young lives by trying to make the gristle of their unformed characters carry the weight of our iron laws and heavy penalties.

GOING TO MEET A MAN

William M. King

As THE HOUR DREW CLOSER STILL, "People poured over the adjacent western bluffs on which were seated singly and in groups hundreds of [persons]" who had come out for the show. Not even the trees in the creek or along its banks were spared, as many men and boys nested in their branches for an elevated view of the proceedings. "The branches were black with swarming human beings, and the most prominent personage among them was an old gray-haired man, whose position was the envy of all observers." Throughout the crowd were many blacks, leading one paper to comment that "The colored people are largely represented, especially the female portion, and many seemed to regard the day and the event as peculiarly their own." The *Rocky Mountain News* wrote of an "old aunty" who said she was a friend of Andy Green, "but who also claimed that he ought to be hanged, and if nobody else would hang him she would herself." Earlier on, she had gone to the jail but was refused permission to see him. After several unsuccessful attempts to get inside the jail, "she sat down in the yard and gave herself up to meditation and song." In a low-pitched key, rocking back and forth with her hands locked about her knees, she chanted,

> Brudder, yo' troubbles will soon be over.
> Brudder, yo' troubbles will soon be over.
> Brudder, yo' troubbles will soon be over.
> And I'll meet you bye and bye.

Every so often a loud howl would escape her lips announcing a rite de passage from the disparate periods of black history. And yet, the *News* continued, she had been eager to arrive at the place of execution. Finding a spot near the barrier rope surrounding the gallows, she defended her fief with ferocious tenacity. "A small white boy crossed 'aunty's' path and she immediately grew wrathy. She descended like a cyclone on the boy, who was badly scared, and proceeded to mop the earth with him. After she had swept up several bushels of sand in her neighborhood and tossed the boy headforemost into the crowd she sat down complacently and fanned herself." After the boy was rescued, wrote a *Tribune-Republican* reporter at the scene, the crowd quieted again, having been provoked by the incident.

Measured in hours, Andrew Green's last day had actually begun the previous morning, on Monday, 26 July 1886. In a composition written especially for the *News* and sanctioned by the Reverend Gray, whom the paper said "Green followed with lamb-like obedience in his last moments," Green told the public how his final hours had been spent. First there had been religious services led by the Reverend Gray and others, which had lasted until 12:30 P.M. and then resumed at about 2:30 that afternoon. These continued, interspersed with visits from numerous folk, until almost midnight. A reporter from the *Tribune-Republican* wrote that "[Green's visitors'] departure seemed not to affect him. His face was wreathed in smiles as he lightly trod the corridor in front of his cell chatting good humoredly with the guards. This manner was continued until daybreak. His last night on earth had been a sleepless one for Andy Green."

Was he mad? Afraid and afraid to show it? A posturing fool? Who can truthfully say what was the state of Green's mind as his last hours passed away? Some indication of what he was feeling might be found in his farewell poem, published in the *Rocky Mountain News* on the day of his death:

> My name 'tis Andrew Green, that name I'll never deny,
>   I left my aged parents in sorrow for to cry;
> Little did they think that this should be my doom,
>   To die upon the gallows, all in my youth and bloom.

My parents nursed me tenderly, as you can plainly see,
　　And always gave me good advice to shun bad company;
To leave off night walking and shun bad company,
　　Else state prison or the gallows my doom would surely be.

But bad company and liquor was all of my delight
　　All of my companions invited me out at night
Said if I commit a murder hung I never shall be
　　Take warning boys take warning take warning from me.

Me and my companions went out here not very far
　　I had to kill the driver in my object to rob the car
Then I drew the fatal pop and shot him to the heart
　　Leaving his dear little wife a protector from her to part.

Afterwards I was compelled to run to make my escape,
　　But Providence was above me: alas! it was too late!

Now I am a prisoner and this to be my doom—
　　To die upon the gallows, all in my youth and bloom.

The day of my execution the people will draw nigh,
　　My father will come from the East to take his last view of me

He'll weep and fall into my arms and bitterly will cry:
　　"Dear son, my darling boy, this day you are doomed to die."

THE SPIDER MAN CASE

Gene Lowall

YOU COULD HAVE SCORCHED a piece of toast against the sun-seared shingles of surrounding roofs. It was July, 1942. A hot July, if ever there was. Gossamer heat-devils danced along the spine of the sharp-gabled roof. The roof, a high-barred "A" with a tiny ventilator leering like a droopy eye at the peak, topped a modest bungalow on the far side of West Moncrieff Place.

On the hither side, behind a tall hedge of lilac, two men crouched.

🐜 🐜 🐜

They were dicks. And one of them was saying, around a half a nickel's worth of gum, "A helluva way, if you ask me, to earn the taxpayers their money's worth—playing peek-a-boo with a spook."

🐜 🐜 🐜

The hole commanded an excellent view of the bungalow across the street. It was a substantial little house. The elms in front of it looked old enough to have voted for Taft, and were. The house looked long-lived-in. It should have. The elms had been saplings when Phil Peters and his bride moved in, half a century before, when the house was new.

Phil Peters had died the previous October. This was July.

He died in a downstairs bedroom in that sturdy, long-lived-in little house. When they found him, he had more than a dozen wounds in his skull—wounds delivered by a bludgeoner who, in the opinion of the dicks at the time, must have been a giant or twins or both to have done such a ghastly job of it. And blood-crazy.

He must have been a ghostly giant, too, the dicks concluded. He vanished without a trace, and all windows and doors of the bungalow were securely locked, from the inside.

🐜 🐜 🐜

It was the smaller dick who, from the corner of his eye, caught a fleeting glimpse of a hobgoblin face momentarily in the aperture between the curtains.

🐜 🐜 🐜

The face at the window had vanished as they tumbled from the hedge. Two brawny shoulders hit the door simultaneously and it collapsed. The men flattened themselves against the wall of the small entry hall into which their charge had carried them. Each pulled a gun. Each felt a little silly, too, and a little cold at the nape of the neck and in the guts.

🐜 🐜 🐜

The small dick was in the lead as they bounded up the stairs. He arrived at the top landing in time to see a closet door swinging slowly shut across the room. He reached it in a leap and wrenched it open.

In the murk within, he saw two bare feet kicking violently. Above the feet were the lower ends of what appeared to be the most ragged pair of trousers in the world.

The cop made a flying grab for a pants-leg. It ripped off rottenly in his hand.

Feet and legs were vanishing in quick kicks through a tiny niche in the ceiling of the closet. Dropping his gun, he grabbed one dangling foot with both hands and hung on. The closet was so small none could get in to assist him, although a half-dozen burly figures by then were swarming into the room at the head of the stairs.

The clinging cop gave a hearty wrench at the ankle in his grasp. It touched off a throaty, thoroughly unghostly yell of pain in the attic above the closet.

"Let go and I'll come down," a sepulchral voice moaned. "You've got me."

Five minutes later, a scarecrow of a man, his clothing in tatters and insufferably filthy, his feet bare and his hair a noisome tangle, lay outstretched on the bedroom floor.

He was unconscious. He had fainted as the struggling dick in the closet had withdrawn him like a cork from the hole in the ceiling.

It was a hole not quite three times the size of a cigar-box lid. It was fitted with a ply-board cover adjustable from above—a board that looked like a casual patch on the ceiling of the closet.

A heavy-set man on the up-grade side of middle age squatted beside the inert figure on the floor. He was square-built in shoulder and jaw. He wore neatly tailored, unobtrusive clothes. He looked like a successful football coach at a small and prosperous college. But he wasn't. He was Jim Childers, veteran captain of dicks in the Denver Police Department.

"Get a doctor and an ambulance," Childers was saying. "This man is barely alive. Looks like starvation to me."

The dick who had tussled with the ghostly one in the reeking closet meanwhile had re-entered the cubbyhole and was attempting to chin himself through the tiny opening in the ceiling. The overpowering animal stench was such that he couldn't have made it even had the hole been big enough to admit his shoulders.

A saw was brought and the hole was enlarged. Then Detective Fred Zarnow, small, wiry and agile, volunteered to scramble up into the attic.

The heat beneath the scorching shingles was terrific. The place smelled like a charnel house. A small incandescent bulb, hanging from a twisted wire, gleamed wanly in the murk. The attic cubby-hole was but a few sizes larger than a coffin.

On hands and knees, with a handkerchief over his face, Zarnow crawled to the center of the tiny chamber. Directly beneath the pallid globe was a heap of filthy, ragged bedding. The bed itself, bridging the bare joists with blobs of hardened plaster curling up through the laths below it, was an old ironing board, supplemented with broken pieces of a cheap suitcase at the head and foot. Tattered magazines lay among the rumpled bedding. In the dark corners of the cubicle hung festoons of spider webs. They veiled the most revolting discovery of all—a collection of open jars and tin cans brimming with excrement.

Zarnow climbed down, gagging.

"A man would have to be a spider to stand it long up there," he sputtered.

DENVER

John Dunning

THEY CALL THIS SKID ROW: a ten-block area of lower downtown, where fifty-year-old flophouses that had once been grand hotels stood crumbling in the sun. In newspaper lingo, the lowers. You can find the same street in Chicago or San Francisco, the liquor stores with plate windows barred against the night, the fifty-cent rooms, the pawnshops, the whorehouses. Here, men fought for the food they ate, for the cheap wine they drank, for the right to sleep out of the snow, on a roach-infested piece of floor that someone else had paid for. They came to Denver under trains, riding the rods in during the warm months of July and August. They camped in tree groves near the railroad yards, leaving behind piles of bottles and bean cans. Some of them left with the first snow. Those who stayed looked for shelter inside, in the hotels along the lowers. They camped under dark staircases, sat through the night four-deep in shower stalls, flopped and slept wherever there was a bare space. There were men who would kill for a bottle of watered whiskey.

It was a savage place, a place where a whore walking alone was fair game, not for her flesh but for what she had in her purse. Where glass is broken in the night and men scuffle in a deadly dance behind a neighborhood bar. Where the answer is quick and the scream is brief, as though life itself isn't worth the effort.

A savage world, the world of the lowers. The new world of Tom Hastings.

People called him Hasty down here. He sat alone in the dark, the bottle clutched tight in his fist. It was still half-full, the first good whiskey he had had in a week. Between then and now there had been plenty of bad. He knew some of it had been made with denatured alcohol. After a while you reached the point where, just by putting a drop on your tongue, you could tell good whiskey from bad. Little it mattered: You always drank it anyway, and hoped tomorrow's would be better. In the old days he had heard some bad stories of whiskey poisoning, and was almost afraid to drink out of any bottle without a label. People said you could go blind. There were newspaper stories of whole parties being poisoned on bootleg gin. Now he drank anything that had even the suggestion of alcohol. After that first greedy gulp, it didn't matter what it was. If it was good whiskey, you appreciated it all the more. If it was bad, as the old saying about sex went, it was still pretty good.

He was staying at the Silvercliff, a ramshackle place in the heart of the lowers. It was owned by a Japanese-Hawaiian family named Taketa, and was managed by the eldest son, Jon. Taketa had been his best source of human interest material when he'd been covering the lowers for the *Post* years ago. Taketa ran a store across from the Silvercliff, which had decayed year by year until it was now the city's worst flophouse. The Silvercliff had gotten so bad that even Taketa didn't go there. He had given Tom an old army cot and permission to use one of the rooms, and in return Tom collected his weekly rents. Three dollars a week, payable in advance. He dunned those who paid late, threw out those who didn't pay at all. Once a room was bought and paid for, what they did with it was none of his business. They could sleep twelve to a room for all he cared, as long as somebody was responsible for the rent next Friday. He knew Taketa didn't care either. Two or three times a week, to help keep him on his feet, Taketa gave him a dinner of old bread and thin stew.

Taketa liked to drink too. He was lively as hell for a Jap. Tom had never met an Oriental quite like Taketa. Usually they were such solemn bastards. But Taketa was cheerful and full of interesting talk. He had a fierce loyalty to his family. Talking about it made Tom think of *his* family. He looked at Taketa's telephone and thought about trying the old man's estate, just to see if they were there. He thought about Golden, and the night Paul had gotten Havana on his wireless, and he'd think, *Jesus, I really should call, let the kids at least know their old man's alive.* He would do that. Pull himself together, starting tomorrow morning. Wash up and go back to Capitol Hill, see if Georgeann had saved any of his things. Put on some clothes and catch the trolley for west Denver. Eat dinner tomorrow night with Anna and David. Take a week and dry out, never touch another goddamn drop as long as he lived. When he felt good about himself again, he'd put on his best coat and hat, tie his tie, slip into his good boots, and take himself a little walk downtown. Confidence was what counted in this game. Walk into the *Post* and give Bonfils one chance to hire him back, and if he didn't know a good thing when it walked right up to him, so be it. There were three other papers in this town, and half a dozen press agencies. But that afternoon he'd seen Malloy, passing the alley behind the hotel, and he knew it wasn't that simple. And now, looking up at Taketa's smiling face, he said, "Christ, Jon, I really need a drink." And Taketa poured generously from his bottle of good Canadian bourbon, because it had been a good day for him. Hie daughter had gotten married off and was off his hands forever. When Tom left, Taketa gave him the bottle.

He had been sitting on the floor of his room, nursing it for two hours.

He heard a noise outside his door, the sound of several men walking. Whoever it was had stopped just outside his door. His groping fingers found the cork, pushing it into the bottle, and tucked the bottle behind him in a corner. He felt around on the floor until he found his stick.

It was heavy, cut from a green elm tree. He always slept with it close by and had never had to use it. For perhaps a minute he heard nothing. Then came a soft knock on his door. He didn't move, hardly breathed. Again the knock, this time louder. One man spoke in Spanish and the doorknob turned. He heard the click of a tool, a jimmy against wood, and he got to his feet slowly as the wood split and the door swung in.

Three of them stood in the dim hallway. He had never seen any of them. The one nearest the door peered in, then moved inside.

"That's far enough, pilgrim," Tom said.

"Just a little whiskey, friend." The voice had a soft texture, lulling, and a slight Mexican accent. The three of them came in and began to fan out in the dark.

"I said that's far enough."

"Just a drink from your bottle. One drink and we'll go away."

"Not too likely, Mexican."

It was over in less than a minute. The three men backed him into the corner. The bottle crouched between his legs like a frightened child. He heard the snap of a switchblade, saw the gleam, and met the man as he lunged. He swung the stick at the black face, feeling the crunch as it smashed the nose flat. The man dropped at his feet and Tom finished him off with a kick in the ribs. It was like letting the air out of a balloon.

The others hung back, suddenly wary. Tom pushed the fallen one with his foot. "Get him out of here. Come on, pick him up before I give you a taste of it too. Next time watch whose room you break into."

THE SHINING

Stephen King

THE ROCK WALL FELL AWAY on their right, disclosing a slash valley that seemed to go down forever, lined a dark green with Rocky Mountain pine and spruce. The pines fell away to gray cliffs of rock that dropped for hundreds of feet before smoothing out. She saw a waterfall spilling over one of them, the early afternoon sun sparkling in it like a golden fish snared in a blue net. They were beautiful mountains but they were hard. She did not think they would forgive many mistakes. An unhappy foreboding rose in her throat. Further west in the Sierra Nevada the Donner Party had become snowbound and had resorted to cannibalism to stay alive. The mountains did not forgive many mistakes.

With a punch of the clutch and a jerk, Jack shifted down to first gear and they labored upward, the bug's engine thumping gamely.

"You know," she said, "I don't think we've seen five cars since we came through Sidewinder. And one of them was the hotel limousine."

Jack nodded. "It goes right to Stapleton Airport in Denver. There's already some icy patches up beyond the hotel, Watson says, and they're forecasting more snow for tomorrow up higher. Anybody going through the mountains now wants to be on one of the main roads, just in case. That goddam Ullman better still be up there. I guess he will be."

"You're sure the larder is fully stocked?" she asked, still thinking of the Donners.

Original promotional brochure, the Stanley Hotel, Estes Park, Colorado, n.d.

"He said so. He wanted Hallorann to go over it with you. Hallorann's the cook."

"Oh," she said faintly, looking at the speedometer. It had dropped from fifteen to ten miles an hour.

"There's the top," Jack said, pointing three hundred yards ahead. "There's a scenic turnout and you can see the Overlook from there. I'm going to pull off the road and give the bug a chance to rest." He craned over his shoulder at Danny, who was sitting on a pile of blankets. "What do you think, doc? We might see some deer. Or caribou."

"Sure, Dad."

The VW labored up and up. The speedometer dropped to just above the five-mile-an-hour hashmark and was beginning to hitch when Jack pulled off the road

("What's that sign, Mommy?" "SCENIC TURNOUT," she read dutifully.)

and stepped on the emergency brake and let the VW run in neutral.

"Come on," he said, and got out.

They walked to the guardrail together.

"That's it," Jack said, and pointed at eleven o'clock.

For Wendy, it was discovering truth in a cliché: her breath was taken away. For a moment she was unable to breathe at all; the view had knocked the wind from her. They were standing near the top of one peak. Across from them—who knew how far?—an even taller mountain reared into the sky, its jagged tip only a silhouette that was now nimbused by the sun, which was beginning its decline. The whole valley floor was spread out below them, the slopes that they had climbed in the laboring bug falling away with such dizzying suddenness that she knew to look down there for too long would bring on nausea and eventual vomiting. The imagination seemed to spring to full life in the clear air, beyond the rein of reason, and to look was to helplessly see one's self plunging down and down and down, sky and slopes changing places in slow cartwheels, the scream drifting from your mouth like a lazy balloon as your hair and your dress billowed out ...

She jerked her gaze away from the drop almost by force and followed Jack's finger. She could see the highway clinging to the side of this cathedral spire, switching back on itself but always tending northwest, still climbing but at a more gentle angle. Further up, seemingly set directly into the slope itself, she saw the grimly clinging pines give way to a wide square of green lawn and standing in the middle of it, overlooking all this, the hotel. The Overlook. Seeing it, she found breath and voice again.

"Oh, Jack, it's gorgeous!"

"Yes, it is," he said. "Ullman says he thinks it's the single most beautiful location in America. I don't care much for him, but I think he might be ... Danny! Danny, are you all right?"

She looked around for him and her sudden fear for him blotted out everything else, stupendous or not. She darted toward him. He was holding onto the guardrail and looking up at the hotel, his face a pasty gray color. His eyes had the blank look of someone on the verge of fainting.

She knelt beside him and put steadying hands on his shoulders. "Danny, what's—"

Jack was beside her. "You okay, doc?" He gave Danny a brisk little shake and his eyes cleared.

"I'm okay, Daddy. I'm fine."

"What was it, Danny?" she asked. "Were you dizzy, honey?"

"No, I was just ... thinking. I'm sorry. I didn't mean to scare you." He looked at his parents, kneeling in front of him, and offered them a small puzzled smile. "Maybe it was the sun. The sun got in my eyes."

"We'll get you up to the hotel and give you a drink of water," Daddy said.

"Okay."

And in the bug, which moved upward more surely on the gentler grade, he kept looking out between them as the road unwound, affording occasional glimpses of the Overlook Hotel, its massive bank of westward-looking windows reflecting back the sun. It was the place he had seen in the midst of the blizzard, the dark and booming place where some hideously familiar figure sought him down long corridors carpeted with jungle. The place Tony had warned him against. It was here. It was here. Whatever Redrum was, it was here.

Artist unknown, "The Stanley Hotel," from Vanities *by Jack Heifner, n.d.*

SECTION XI

DIVERSE PEOPLES

HARVEY

Mary Chase

ACT TWO

SCENE TWO

🐀 🐀 🐀

ELWOOD. I am trying to be factual. I then introduced him to Harvey.

WILSON. To who?

KELLY. A white rabbit. Six feet tall.

WILSON. Six feet!

ELWOOD. Six feet one and a half!

WILSON. Okay—fool around with him, and the doctor is probably some place bleedin' to death in a ditch.

ELWOOD. If those were his plans for the evening he did not tell me.

SANDERSON. Go on, Dowd.

ELWOOD. Dr. Chumley sat down in the booth with us. I was sitting on the outside like this. (*Shows.*) Harvey was on the inside near the wall, and Dr. Chumley was seated directly across from Harvey where he could look at him.

WILSON (*crosses a step* R). That's right. Spend all night on the seatin' arrangements!

ELWOOD. Harvey then suggested that I buy him a drink. Knowing that he does not like to drink alone, I suggested to Dr. Chumley that we join him.

WILSON. And so?

ELWOOD. We joined him.

WILSON. Go on—go on.

ELWOOD. We joined him again.

WILSON. Then what?

ELWOOD. We kept right on joining him.

WILSON. Oh, skip all the joining.

ELWOOD. You are asking me to skip a large portion of the evening—

WILSON. Tell us what happened—come on—please—

ELWOOD. Dr. Chumley and Harvey got into a conversation—quietly at first. Later it became rather heated and Dr. Chumley raised his voice.

WILSON. Yeah—why?

ELWOOD. Harvey seemed to feel that Dr. Chumley should assume part of the financial responsibility of the joining, but Dr. Chumley didn't seem to want to do that.

KELLY (*it breaks out from her*). I can believe *that* part of it!

WILSON. Let him talk. See how far he'll go. This guy's got guts.

ELWOOD. I agreed to take the whole thing because I did not want any trouble. We go down to Charlie's quite often—Harvey and I—and the proprietor is a fine man with an interesting approach to life. Then the other matter came up.

WILSON. Cut the damned double-talk and get on with it!

ELWOOD. Mr. Wilson, you are a sincere type of person, but I must ask you not to use that language in the presence of Miss Kelly. (*He makes a short bow to her.*)

SANDERSON. You're right, Dowd, and we're sorry. You say—the other matter came up?

ELWOOD. There was a beautiful blonde woman—a Mrs. Smethills—and her escort seated in the booth across from us. Dr. Chumley went over to sit next to her, explaining to her that they had once met. In Chicago. Her escort escorted Dr. Chumley back to me and Harvey and tried to point out that it would be better for Dr. Chumley to mind his own affairs. Does he have any?

WILSON. Does he have any what?

ELWOOD. Does he have any affairs?

WILSON. How would I know?

KELLY. Please hurry, Mr. Dowd—we're all so worried.

ELWOOD. Dr. Chumley then urged Harvey to go with him over to Blondie's Chicken Inn. Harvey wanted to go to Eddie's instead. While they were arguing about it I went to the bar to order another drink, and when I came back they were gone.

WILSON. Where did they go? I mean where did the doctor go?

ELWOOD. I don't know—I had a date out here with Dr. Sanderson and Miss Kelly, and I came out to pick them up—hoping that later on we might run into Harvey and the doctor and make a party of it.

WILSON. So you satisfied? You got his story—(*Goes over to* ELWOOD, *fists clenched.*) O.K. You're lyin' and we know it!

ELWOOD. I never lie, Mr. Wilson.

WILSON. You've done somethin' with the doctor and I'm findin' out what it is—

SANDERSON (*moving after him*). Don't touch him, Wilson—

KELLY. Maybe he isn't lying, Wilson—

WILSON (*turning on them. Furiously*). That's all this guy is, a bunch of lies! You two don't believe this story he tells about the doctor sittin' there talkin' to a big white rabbit, do you?

KELLY. Maybe Dr. Chumley *did* go to Charlie's Place.

WILSON. And saw a big rabbit, I suppose.

ELWOOD. And why not? Harvey was there. At first the doctor seemed a little frightened of Harvey, but that gave way to admiration as the evening wore on— The evening wore on! That's a nice expression. With your permission I'll say it again. The evening wore on.

WILSON (*lunging at him*). With your permission I'm gonna knock your teeth down your throat!

ELWOOD (*not moving an inch*). Mr. Wilson—haven't you some old friends you can go play with? (SANDERSON *has grabbed* WILSON *and is struggling with him.*)

WILSON (*he is being held. Glares fiercely at* ELWOOD. KELLY *dials phone*). The nerve of this guy! He couldn't come out here with an ordinary case of D.T.'s. No. He has to come out with a six-foot rabbit.

ELWOOD (*rises—goes toward desk* L). Stimulating as all this is, I really must be getting downtown.

KELLY (*on phone*). Charlie's Place? Is Dr. Chumley anywhere around there? He was there with Mr. Dowd earlier in the evening. What? Well, don't bite my head off! (*Hangs up.*) My, that man was mad. He said Mr. Dowd was welcome any time, but his friend was not.

ELWOOD. That's Mr. McNulty the bartender. He thinks a lot of me. Now let's all go down and have a drink.

WILSON. Wait a minute—

KELLY. Mr. Dowd—(*Goes over to him.*)

ELWOOD. Yes, my dear—may I hold your hand?

KELLY. Yes—if you want to. (ELWOOD *does.*) Poor Mrs. Chumley is so worried. Something must have happened to the doctor. Won't you please try and remember something—something else that might help her? Please—

ELWOOD. For you I would do anything. I would almost be willing to live my life over again. Almost. But I've told it all.

KELLY. You're sure?

ELWOOD. Quite sure—but ask me again, anyway, won't you? I liked that warm tone you had in your voice just then.

SANDERSON (*without realizing he is saying it*). So did I. (*Looks at* KELLY.)

WILSON. Oh, nuts!

ELWOOD. What?

WILSON. Nuts!

ELWOOD. Oh! I must be going. I have things to do.

KELLY. Mr. Dowd, what is it you do?

ELWOOD (*sits, as* KELLY *sits* R. *of desk*). Harvey and I sit in the bars and we have a drink or two and play the jukebox. Soon the faces of the other people turn toward mine and smile. They are saying: "We don't know your name, Mister, but you're a lovely fellow." Harvey and I warm ourselves in all these golden moments. We have entered as strangers—soon we have friends. They come over. They sit with us. They drink with us. They talk to us. They tell about the big terrible things they have done. The big wonderful things they *will* do. Their hopes, their regrets, their loves, their hates. All very large because nobody ever brings anything small into a bar. Then I introduce them to Harvey. And he is bigger and grander than anything they offer me. When they leave, they leave impressed. The same people seldom come back—but that's envy, my dear. There's a little bit of envy in the best of us—too bad, isn't it?

SANDERSON *(leaning forward)*. How did you happen to call him Harvey?

ELWOOD. Harvey is his name.

SANDERSON. How do you know that?

ELWOOD. That was rather an interesting coincidence, Doctor. One night several years ago I was walking early in the evening along Fairfax Street—between 18th and 19th. You know that block?

SANDERSON. Yes, yes.

ELWOOD. I had just helped Ed Hickey into a taxi. Ed had been mixing his rye with his gin, and I felt he needed conveying. I started to walk down the street when I heard a voice saying: "Good evening, Mr. Dowd." I turned, and there was this great white rabbit leaning against a lamp-post. Well, I thought nothing of that, because when you have lived in a town as long as I have lived in this one, you get used to the fact that everybody knows your name. Naturally, I went over to chat with him. He said to me: "Ed Hickey is a little spiffed this evening, or could I be mistaken?" Well, of course he was not mistaken. I think the world and all of Ed, but he was spiffed. Well, anyway, we stood there and talked, and finally I said—"You have the advantage of me. You know my name and I don't know yours." Right back at me he said: "What name do you like?" Well, I didn't even have to think a minute: Harvey has always been my favorite name. So I said, "Harvey," and this is the interesting part of the whole thing. He said—"What a coincidence! My name happens to be Harvey."

SANDERSON *(crossing above desk)*. What was your father's name, Dowd?

ELWOOD. John. John Frederick.

SANDERSON. Dowd, when you were a child you had a playmate, didn't you? Someone you were very fond of—with whom you spent many happy, carefree hours?

ELWOOD. Oh, yes, Doctor. Didn't you?

SANDERSON. What was his name?

ELWOOD. Verne. Verne McElhinney. Did you ever know the McElhinneys, Doctor?

SANDERSON. No.

ELWOOD. Too bad. There were a lot of them, and they circulated. Wonderful people.

SANDERSON. Think carefully, Dowd. Wasn't there someone, somewhere, sometime, whom you knew—by the name of Harvey? Didn't you ever know anybody by that name?

ELWOOD. No, Doctor. No one. Maybe that's why I always had such hopes for it.

SANDERSON. Come on, Wilson, we'll take Mr. Dowd upstairs now.

WILSON. I'm taking him nowhere. You've made this your show—now run it. Lettin' him sit here—forgettin' all about Dr. Chumley! O.K. It's your show—you run it.

SANDERSON. Come on, Dowd—(*Pause. Putting out his hand.*) Come on, Elwood—

ELWOOD (*rises*). Very well, Lyman. (SANDERSON *and* KELLY *take him to door.*) But I'm afraid I won't be able to visit with you for long. I have promised Harvey I will take him to the floor-show. (*They exit* U.C. WILSON *is alone. Sits at desk, looks at his watch.*)

WILSON. Oh, boy! (*Puts head in arms on desk.* DR. CHUMLEY *enters* L. WILSON *does not see him until he gets almost* C. *stage.*)

WILSON (*jumping up, going to him*). Dr. Chumley—Are you all right?

CHUMLEY. All right? Of course I'm all right. I'm being followed. Lock that door.

WILSON (*goes to door* L*., locks it.*) Who's following you?

CHUMLEY. None of your business. (*Exits into office* R., *locks door behind him.*) (WILSON *stands a moment perplexed, then shrugs shoulders, turns off lights and exits* U.C. *The stage is dimly lit. Then from door* L. *comes the rattle of the doorknob. Door opens and shuts, and we hear locks opening and closing, and see light from hall on stage. The invisible Harvey has come in. There is a count of eight while he crosses the stage, then door of* CHUMLEY'S *office opens and closes, with sound of locks clicking. Harvey has gone in —and then—*

CURTAIN

THE LIFE AND LEGEND OF GENE FOWLER

H. Allen Smith

THERE WAS ALWAYS A POKER game in progress at the Press Club. It ran night and day, seemingly without recess, and there were some who said it had gone on without interruption since the siege of Vicksburg. Players arrived and sat in for a few hours and then departed, to be replaced by other players.

The Press Club was quartered in a downtown office building, then moved to another downtown office building, and finally settled in its own two-story structure across from the Denver Athletic Club. Legend out of the heroic age tells us that when the moving vans arrived at the second location six players were engaged at stud poker. They refused to get out of their chairs. They refused to abandon the table. After much yelling and cursing a compromise was reached. The movers picked up the chairs and table and carried them quickly out to the van. The players followed, carrying chips and cards and whiskey glasses, and the stud game continued inside the van while it rumbled through the streets en route to the club's new quarters.

A chief fixture at the club's poker table was Colonel Gideon B. McFall, an associate member. As a general rule press clubs in American cities take in press agents, advertising blokes, politicians, and other riffraff, charging them heavily for the privilege of belonging, and of *saying* they belong. If it were not for the dues of these non-journalists, few clubs would be able to survive.

Colonel Gideon B. McFall was one of the members who had no connection with newspapers or other periodicals. Little was known about his history. It was a sure thing that he could pay his immoderate club dues out of his poker winnings and have enough left over to buy Elitch Gardens *and* the Brown Palace. He often referred to himself as a southerner, raised on a great plantation in Mississippi. Someone once investigated this julepy claim and established the fact that the colonel had his origin on a pig farm near Ottumwa, Iowa.

As long as anyone could remember, Colonel McFall had been banker of the Press Club poker game. He looked more like a banker than an Iowa farm boy and Gene Fowler said he had one of the two finest heads of silvery hair in the city— the other belonged to the County Coroner. Almost everybody on every newspaper in town owed the colonel money.

On a starless Saturday night in December the two most inept poker players west of St. Louis, Fowler and Lee Casey, made their way to the Press Club bent upon losing their paychecks to Colonel McFall or anyone else who might be around. They found the poker game overcrowded and even the colonel had withdrawn temporarily to stretch his legs and take on a ham-and-cheese sandwich. While Colonel McFall chewed at his supper he stood with Fowler, Casey, and police reporter Jack Carberry.

"There is a smell of snow in the air," said the colonel, "and I have a great idea. Let us repair to my little cottage in Park Hill, where I have an adequate supply of drinkin' whiskey and a large stack of firewood. The hell with frivoling away an entire night at the gaming table in this sordid den when we can settle down to a long evening of pleasant talk."

Fowler, Casey, and Carberry agreed with the stipulation that they be permitted to purchase a spare case of Wilson's whiskey, and the colonel, with his customary high-flown Dixieland style, ordered a horse-drawn cab. No plebeian streetcars for gentlemen when McFall was host.

The brougham had no more than got started up Seventeenth Street when snowflakes the size of potato chips began to swirl upon it and a few blocks farther on it became almost impossible to see through the storm. Then a faint halloo sounded in the night and a ghostly figure came groping through the snow. The figure turned out to be Charlie Carson, foreman of the *News* stereotype room. He stumbled his way up to the door of the carriage, peered within, recognized the occupants, and cried out: "You fellas on your way to a whorehouse?"

They hauled him in out of the storm, and he announced firmly that he was going home to his wife with his paycheck intact, and just because it was a Saturday night by God he wasn't going to no hookshop nor neither was he going to throw his hard-earned money away on drinking and gambling. "You fellas got a drink with you?" he asked, though he really didn't need one.

At the colonel's cottage Charlie resumed work on the Wilson's while the others were divesting themselves of their outer garments. He was soon asleep.

The colonel got into his red velvet carpet slippers, stirred up the fire, and then while reaching for his pipe tobacco his hand by accident fell upon a deck of playing cards.

"Egad!" he exclaimed. "This smacks of Kismet! Oh, well, why not? Just a little sociable hand or two by way of preliminary—then the good talk."

There would be no good talk

They played all night and up to noon the next day, and after that they began playing in relays, taking catnaps and partaking of snorts. Lee Casey, a worrier, discovered that the snow was up to the window tops and the doors could not be opened. He made telephone contact with the *News* and was told that Denver was in the grip of the worst blizzard since the second year of the Pony Express. Following which the lines went down and the little group of hardy and heroic souls played on in utter isolation from the world.

Early on the third morning the firewood ran out. The whiskey supply was still ample. The players donned overcoats and hats and continued the game, but after a while Fowler made mention of the cold. He got up and inspected two wooden chairs that stood against the back wall. He broke the chairs into pieces and put them on the dying fire. From time to time more furniture was broken up and fed to the flames, and then books and old newspapers—anything that would burn. By the next day the Donner Party of Park Hill was down to the oaken table in the middle of the room and the four chairs around it. These were shattered and tossed into the fireplace, but the game did not end. Colonel McFall, Fowler, Casey, and Carberry stretched themselves on the carpet and continued with stud and draw. Charlie Carson woke up long enough to crawl closer to the fire and then resumed his sleep.

Early on Thursday morning the Fire Department clawed its way through the snowbanks and rescued all hands. The booze was gone, there was no food in the house, and the poker players were tired. Before departing the cottage Colonel McFall totted up the reckoning. For the first time in recorded history the silver-haired cavalier from Ottumwa was a heavy loser.

"Pay up!" cried the others, proud of their achievement.

"Hold!" protested McFall. "You lads have forgotten something."

He quickly penciled out an inventory of those possessions that had been burned in the fireplace. He calculated the fair market value of furniture, books, clothing, and carpeting, then prorated the damage three ways. And he made it stick.

Recalling those fine days and nights when he worked for the *Rocky Mountain News*, Fowler said:

"It seemed that I never could have lived anywhere else in my youth but in that untamed town. I have to laugh at my own naïveté, for I had thought that the mass behavior of Denver, shortly after the century dawned, was the norm for the entire world. Both my great joys and supposedly great sorrows came from this childlike credo when I finally pranced along the avenues of New York and the Left Bank of Paris. Of course, I now know that a man who dares laugh or pursues his own simplicities is bound to be kicked to death. This does not deter me."

TIMBERLINE

Gene Fowler

MRS. BROWN WAS THIRTY-NINE YEARS old when she left Liverpool for New York on the *Titanic's* maiden voyage. Instead of a girlish slimness, she now was ruggedly and generously fleshed. Nevertheless, she still bubbled with a seldom-varying vitality.

She sang in the ship's concert and was popular with the traveling notables despite her growing eccentricities. She amused some and terrified others with pistol-feats, one of which consisted of tossing five oranges or grapefruits over the rail and puncturing each one before it reached the surface of the sea.

Although she spent great sums on clothes, she no longer paid attention to their detail or how she wore them. And, when she traveled, comfort, and not a desire to appear *chic*, was her primary consideration.

So, when Molly decided to take a few turns of the deck before retiring, she came from her cabin prepared for battle with the night sea air. She had on extra-heavy woolies, with bloomers bought in Switzerland (her favorite kind), two jersey petticoats, a plaid cashmere dress down to the heels of her English calfskin boots, a sportsman's cap, tied on with a woolen scarf, knotted in toothache style beneath her chin, golf stockings presented by a seventy-year-old admirer, the Duke Charlot of France, a muff of Russian sables, in which she absent-mindedly had left her Colt's automatic pistol—and over these frost-defying garments she wore a sixty-thousand-dollar chinchilla opera cloak!

If anyone was prepared for Arctic gales, Mrs. Brown was that person. She was not, however, prepared for a collision with an iceberg.

In fact, she was on the point of sending a deck steward below with her cumbersome pistol when the crash came.

In the history of that tragedy, her name appears as one who knew no fear. She did much to calm the women and children. Perhaps she was overzealous, for it is recorded that she refused to enter a lifeboat until all other women and their young ones had been cared for, and that crew members literally had to throw her into a boat.

Once in the boat, however, she didn't wait for approval—she seized command. There were only five men aboard, and about twenty women and children.

"Start rowing," she told the men, "and head the bow into the sea."

Keeping an eye on the rowers, she began removing her clothes. Her chinchilla coat she treated as though it were a blanket worth a few dollars. She used it to cover three small and shivering children. One by one she divested herself of heroic woolens. She "rationed" her garments to the women who were the oldest or most frail. It was said she presented a fantastic sight in the light of flares, half standing among the terrified passengers, stripped down to her corset, the beloved Swiss bloomers, the Duke of Charlot's golf stockings and her stout shoes.

One of the rowers seemed on the verge of collapse. "My heart," he said.

"God damn your heart!" said The Unsinkable Mrs. Brown. "Work those oars."

She herself now took an oar and began to row. She chose a position in the bow, where she could watch her crew. Her pistol was lashed to her waist with a rope.

The heart-troubled rower now gasped and almost lost his oar. "My heart," he said. "It's getting worse!"

The Unsinkable one roared: "Keep rowing or I'll blow your guts out and throw you overboard! Take your choice."

The man—who really *did* have a fatty condition of the heart—kept rowing. Mrs. Brown sprouted big blisters on her hands. But she didn't quit. Then her palms began to bleed. She cut strips from her Swiss bloomers and taped her hands. She kept rowing. And swearing.

At times, when the morale of her passengers was at its lowest, she would sing.

"The God damned critics say I can't sing," she howled. "Well, just listen to this ..."

And she sang from various operas.

"We'll have an Italian opera now," she said at one time. "Just let anyone say it's no good."

She kept rowing.

And so did the others. They knew she *would* throw anyone overboard who dared quit, exhaustion or no exhaustion.

She told stories. She gave a history of the Little Johnny. She told of the time she hid three hundred thousand dollars in a camp stove, and how it went up the flue.

"How much is three hundred thousand dollars?" she asked. "I'll tell you. It's nothing. Some of you people—the guy here with the heart trouble that I'm curing with oars—are rich. I'm rich. What in hell of it? What are your riches or mine doing for us this minute? And you can't wear the Social Register for water wings, can you? Keep rowing, you sons of bitches, or I'll toss you all overboard!"

When they were picked up at sea, and everyone was praising Mrs. Brown, she was asked:

"How did you manage it?"

"Just typical Brown luck," she replied. "I'm unsinkable."

And ever afterward she was known as "The Unsinkable Mrs. Brown."

A PARADISE FOR DYSPEPTICS AND CONSUMPTIVES

William H. Buchtel

I AM IN LOVE WITH COLORADO. Believing that I may thereby save many lives, and add to the happiness of thousands of my fellow-beings, I requested an eminent physician in Denver to write a careful description of its climate and its effects upon invalids. That description I here publish for the benefit of mankind. It fully coincides with my own personal observation: P.T.B. [P.T. Barnum]

THE CLIMATE OF COLORADO

The limited sources of information, to people East, on the climate of Colorado, has prompted the collation of some of its strong claims for consideration by the invalid from diseases of the lungs, bronchial tubes and digestive organs.

This climate is proverbial for its mildness; the average temperature of the region about Denver is from 50 to 55 degrees; the mercury rarely indicates below zero, even in the coldest weather, and seldom exceeds 80 degrees in the warmest. Damp, chilly days, or hot, sultry nights, are unknown. Snow seldom remains on the ground longer than twenty-four hours, the Winters being usually very mild. There is no "rainy season" in any portion of Colorado; the absence of clouds, the year round, is remarkable; the clear sky and warm, genial sunshine, are seldom hidden. The purity and dryness of the atmosphere are unsurpassed, possessing a large degree of electricity, consequent upon altitude; entirely free from humidity, wonderfully clear and exhilerating. Malarious or poisonous exhalations never burden this pure air. Decomposition of animal matter takes place so slowly that the noxious gases engendered pass away imperceptibly. We have warm days and cool nights, there not being half a dozen nights in a season when a pair of blankets are in any degree uncomfortable. There is no such thing known as "damp night air;"

although the air is cool, it is perfectly dry, and one may sleep with doors and windows wide open, Summer and Winter, without once "taking cold."

There are not a score of days, in any year, in which invalids may not sit out of doors, ride or walk, forenoon or afternoon, with comfort and pleasure. Add to this, the fact already cited, that the nights are always cool, insuring plenty of restful and refreshing sleep, and two of the most essential conditions for the restoration of shattered and nervous systems and broken constitutions have been secured.

For most forms of disease, the increased activity imposed on the respiratory organs, by residence in high altitudes, is a direct and constant benefit. Nothing is better for a dyspeptic, or a sufferer from hepatic disorder, or general torpor, than to make him breathe. Increase his respiration from sixteen to twenty-four per minute, and you give him a new experience. His blood circulates with increased rapidity, and is much more perfectly aerated; his appetite is increased, digestion and assimilation promptly responding to the increased demand and increased action. The bed of the Platte River, at Denver, is a lineal mile higher above the sea level than New-York or Philadelphia. Here, one must breathe both more fully and more rapidly. The result is a permanent increase of the breathing capacity, the formation of tubercle never taking place in lungs expanded with this rarified air.

The results of these climatological conditions are an extremely healthful and invigorating atmosphere, peculiarly beautiful and enjoyable; as a whole the most equable and desirable of any portion of the Western Hemisphere.

Probably one-half of the present population of Colorado are reconstructed invalids. Some came with intractable dyspepsia; some with asthma or bronchitis; others had commenced "bleeding at the lungs," or were confirmed victims of "consumption." Many came too late to be benefitted. On the other hand, thousands, whose cases were considered hopeless, have here found permanent relief. This is especially true of asthmatics. For this class of patients the atmosphere of Colorado is almost a certain panacea.

Consumptives, *in the first stage*, may come to Colorado with the assurance that whatever climate, natural hygienic surroundings, pure air and water, good food, grand scenery, and perpetual sunshine can do for an invalid, here awaits them.

Whatever will aid the consumptive will aid the dyspeptic, for the consumptive is first a dyspeptic; and, in fatal cases, always *starves to death*. In patients afflicted with bronchitis the results are very flattering, scarcely a case but is rapidly relieved. For all of scrofulous habit there is no better climate than that of Colorado. Chronic invalids are, almost always, benefitted by a mere change of regimen. If the change be made from the humdrum of the Eastern home, to the fresh and novel life of a mountain country, with its more substantial bread, more virile, blood-invigorating beef, its tempting mountain trout, and juicy wild meat, the benefits will be multiplied. Patients in the second and third stages of consumption, and those suffering from certain forms of heart disease, are more *injured* than benefitted by a removal to localities much more elevated than the one to which they have become accustomed.

That eminent English physician, Dr. Chambers, gives this very sensible rule respecting the choice of climate: "In choosing a home for your consumptive, do not mind the average height of the thermometer or its variations; do not trouble yourself about the mean rain-fall; do not be scientific at all, but find out, from somebody's journal, how many days were fine enough to go out, forenoon and afternoon, that is the test you require, and by that you may be confidently guided."

Judged by this standard, Colorado is one of the most favored spots on the face of the civilized globe for a consumptive's refuge.

Prospect Villa, Denver, February, 1873.

AT THE END OF THE SANTA FE TRAIL

Sister Blandina Segale

GOOD FRIDAY, 1873.—Sisters Marcella, Fidelis, and myself went up the mountainside—to see the *Penitentes* make the "Way to Calvary." About one hundred took part in it. They walked in twos, faces covered, backs bared. Each had several branches of long bruised cacti, with which they lashed their backs as they slowly ascended the spur. At each lash they said, *"Yo penitente pecador"* (I, a repentant sinner). When the one dragging the cross reached the summit of the spur, some of the *Penitentes* helped to raise the cross he alone had dragged. It seemed impossible for any one man to have accomplished such an act, but we saw him do it. We were several miles from Trinidad and wanted to reach our convent home before the lighter of our globe threw his golden rays to warn us that he soon would retire.

Easter Sunday, 1873.—I must tell you what information I received concerning the *Penitentes*. The Way of the Cross, of course, was taught the natives by the good Franciscans; so also penance was preached to them. When the Franciscans were obliged to leave the Southwest, it naturally fell to the stronger-minded and piously inclined to perpetuate what had been taught them, but in this teaching each leader followed his own idea; hence, we find that whilst the members of some lodges are perfectly docile to the teachings of the Church, other lodges have not the least conception of the correct spirit of Catholicity, though they consider themselves good Catholics.

The *Penitentes* in this vicinity do not even make their Easter duty. They do not scruple to abstract cattle from another man's ranch on the Easter Monday, after having scourged themselves on Good Friday and called themselves "Repentant sinners." This reminds one of the private interpretation of the Bible. The *Penitentes* interpret the teaching of the Franciscans in their own way. The initiation to these lodges varies also. Here is one form: —Ridges are made from neck to waist-line with sharp stones. By privilege I was allowed to visit one of their lodges—it was literally bespattered with blood—side, walls, and ceiling, too—yet the members of the lodge I visited are adroit pilferers of any branded domestic animals seen on the plains. These same members never approach the Sacraments.

Easter week—Here is a tragedy which took place this week. An elderly lady and gentleman—Americans—residing a few miles from Trinidad, were found murdered in their home. Suspicion at once pointed to the natives as the perpetrators of the horrible deed. Small groups of men were sent out to capture the murderers. One posse trailed four Mexicans, and because they would not acknowledge the deed, were hanged on the first tree to which they came. Afterwards the corpses were huddled into a wagon, brought to Trinidad in triumph and thrown into an old vacant adobe hut, twelve feet from the graveyard near the Convent. Can you imagine how we felt! Two days later the real murderers were captured and confessed the crime. They were outlawed Americans!

BITS OF TRAVEL AT HOME

H. H. (Helen Hunt Jackson)

WALSENBURG IS AN OLD MEXICAN town. There are perhaps fifty houses in it, and more than half of these are the true Mexican mud huts,—mud floor, mud wall, mud roof: if there had been any way of baking mud till you could see through it, they would have had mud windows as well. As there was not, they compromised on windows, and have but one to a room, and many rooms without a window at all. These houses are not as uncomfortable as one would suppose, and by no means as ugly. The baked mud is of a good color, and the gaudy Roman Catholic prints and effigies and shrines with which the walls are often adorned stand out well on the rich brown. The mud floors are hard, and for the most part clean and smooth. Gay blankets and shawls are thrown down upon them in the better class of houses; chairs are rare. The houses remind one more of bee-hives than of any thing else, they do so swarm at their one small entrance; women and girls are there by dozens and scores, all wearing bright shawls thrown over their heads in an indescribably graceful way. Even toddlers of six and seven have their brilliant shawls thrown over their heads and trailing in the dust behind; I am not sure that they are not born in them. The little boys are not so much clothed; in fact, many of them are not clothed at all. The most irresistible one I saw wore a short white shirt reaching perhaps one-third of the way to his knees; over this, for purposes of decoration, he had put a heavy woollen jacket much too big for him; thus arrayed he strutted up and down with as pompous an air as if he were a king in state robes; but the jacket was heavy: he could not endure it long; presently he shook one arm free of its sleeve, then the other, and then in a moment more dropped the garment in a crumpled pile on the ground, and with an exultant fling of his thin brown legs raced away, his shirt blowing back like a scanty wisp tied round his waist. His mother sat on the ground leaning against the wall of her house, nursing her baby and laughing till all her teeth showed like a row of white piano keys on her shining brown skin. I stopped and praised her baby; she spoke no English, but she understood the praise of the baby's eyes. By a gesture she summoned the hero of the shirt, said to him a single word, and in a second more he had sprung into the house, reappeared with a wooden chair, and placed it for me with a shy grace. Then he darted away sidewise, like a dragon-fly.

All the women's voices were low and sweet; their eyes were as dark and soft as the eyes of deer, and their unfailing courtesy was touching. An old woman, one of the oldest in the town, took me over her house, from room to room, and stood by with a gratified smile while I looked eagerly at every thing. The landlord's daughter, who had accompanied me, had mentioned to her that I was a stranger and had never before seen a Mexican town. When I took leave of her I said through my interpreter, "I am greatly obliged to you for showing me your house."

With rapid gestures and shrugs of the shoulders she poured forth sentence after sentence, all the while looking into my face with smiles and taking my hand in hers.

"What does she say?" I asked.

"She says," replied my guide, "that her poor house is not worth looking at, and she is the one who is obliged that so beautiful a lady should enter it." And this was a poverty-stricken old woman in a single garment of tattered calico, living in a mud hut, without a chair or a bed!

COUSIN JACK (OR ENGLISH) PASTIES

Ladies of Monte Vista

FOR CRUST, TWO AND ONE-HALF cups flour, three-fourths cup chopped suet, pinch of salt and about one tablespoon lard mixed with the other ingredients to form a dough like ordinary pie crust. Roll out one-half inch thick and the size of a dinner plate, on half of this place a layer of sliced onion (one small onion) or turnip, a good layer of sliced raw tomato, and on top a layer of small pieces of raw meat (beef or pork), one pound for two pastries, sprinkle with pepper, salt and bits of butter; fold the other half of the crust over this and crimp the edges as in a turnover.

—Mrs. Parmenter

THE WETHERILLS OF THE MESA VERDE

Benjamin Alfred Wetherill

I CANNOT TELL HOW WE GRADUATED from ranching to archaeology and I do not know why we were the first to annex it as our principal work.

Our first knowledge of the existence of the cliff dwellings was not in finding the buildings all at once, but through a gradual step-up from the abundance of ruins scattered everywhere. In almost the entire distance through the Mancos Cañon and its tributary cañons are found evidence of ruined dwellings of ancient peoples. All over the Mancos Valley and the cliffs surrounding it was evidence of what was once an immense population. Fragments of oddly colored pieces of crockery with strange markings, often of fine geometrical designs of angles and squares; chips of flint or obsidian; arrow points, some tiny and others larger; and stone axes were found everywhere. In plowing, we were always turning up broken crockery and stones of not ordinary shapes and sizes in the fields. Occasionally, too, we came upon large flat stones hollowed on one side and decided they were made to pound [grind] corn or seeds on. They are the same as modern Indians use and are called *metates*.

Our curiosity grew and grew as we dug into the mounds on the ranch, trying to find entire vessels of the unknown people. We were unsuccessful, but we did not give up, for we knew we had evidence of a very different people and had a desire to see where they were in history. I do not remember when we found our first piece of pottery, or if it was given to us. If we asked any of the old timers what the mounds and pottery represented, they would say it was just some old Aztec stuff and could be found almost anywhere in the Southwest. We received pamphlets and books along these lines, but all the knowledge we gained by them was nil. The mounds, or buildings, when spoken of, were passed by as Aztec ruins, although it was hard to see where there was any connecting link whatever, although it probably came from an Aztec superstition saying that they came from the north. Other claims were that they were just the ancient villages of the Moquis, or the Zunis, whose villages are to the south of the Mesa Verde. But all of those village Indians were always village people and never scattered out in little patches of individual houses such as were found in the valley and on the mesas everywhere.

So, we kept on with the job of looking for anything that could help us explain to ourselves the job we had undertaken.

🐜 🐜 🐜

Mostly we worked during the winters, carrying supplies and equipment up cliffs, across cañons, over ridges and mesa tops; through mud and in snow.

(Summers we had to work on the farm from early to late just to keep the home fires burning and the inner man fit.) Because there were no roads and very poor trails, everything taken in or out was, by necessity, carried by pack horses. They had to be left in the cañons miles away while we scouted with a mighty few provisions and our equipment rolled up in compact form to make back packs. Many a day we went over and around slippery cliffs, always looking for the places of the ancient people. When a likely place showed up, we camped and brought up the pack animals and horses. Even then there was much carrying on foot and swinging around by ropes to reach certain points. Sometimes we came down on ropes from above; sometimes we roped a projecting piece of timber; sometimes we made high tripods and extended them even higher with timbers. In camp, it was necessary at times to dig shallow holes in the ground, fill them with piñon branches, put the blankets over, and then crowd the dirt close around the edges so as to be able to get warm enough to sleep.

Artist unknown, "Cliff Dwellings" from The Crest of the Continent *by Ernest Ingersoll, 1885.*

🐾 🐾 🐾

Some time after I sighted the Cliff Palace, Richard and Charles [Mason] were riding the mesa top to locate water holes and cattle signs and came into view of the great ruin from across the cañon. Remembering what I had told them, they were half-prepared for the immensity of the vision but then, as later, the feeling struck them that the eerie sight could not be a reality. The cattle got away, but the amazement at seeing a miniature city spread out before them never did.

When they excitedly brought the story home, we all returned immediately to begin on this new project. For a number of years after that, everything else was of minor importance to us.

The ruin was quite accessible, not much over one hundred fifty feet from the top of the mesa to the ground floor of the ruin. A hundred yards up the cañon, there was a stone stairway, through a crevice in the rocks, which led down to the level of the cave, and it was easy to follow the cliff around right into the house.

Things were arranged in the rooms as if the people might just have been out visiting somewhere. Perfect specimens of pottery sat on the floors and other convenient locations; stone implements and household equipment were where the housewives had last used the articles; evidence of children playing house even as children do now; estufas where the men congregated, leaving the ancient ashes of altar fires long dead. There was no indication of violence toward the people themselves, but the greater part of the immense buildings had been pulled apart and the timbers in the roofs and floor removed.

We wondered about the possibility of the Spaniards, in their constant search for hidden gold, being responsible for the depredations. It had not been done by pothunters because the things that would have interested them were untouched. Nor were they destroyed by fire, for the walls still standing were not smoked up. The timbers had plainly been taken out and carried away, leaving the walls standing. Neither was there any evidence of battle, for the "mummies" indicated death occurred in the routine manner. They were not really mummies, but just the dried-up remains of a people without a name.

        🐾 🐾 🐾

As preliminary surveys and excavations were made, the dust of centuries filled the rooms and rose in thick clouds at every movement. We swallowed dirt and dust and dried-up Cliff Dwellers until we could almost read their hieroglyphics on the walls of the caverns and mud-smeared rooms and estufas.

As the work went along we could let our imaginations run riot, thinking of the people who had been there and were now gone. With the proper spirit of romance, you can gradually allow the mood of the Mesa Verde to take possession and let the silence speak and the mind's eye bring back to life and being the people whose book of life is forever closed. We could almost see them around us. We could watch them at work in the fields, with the dogs barking and the turkeys calling; the men coming in from work; women busy at their looms or grinding corn for the midday meal; the children playing near. The mother loved them the same as moderns do and the effort to bring them up right was a full duty, too. She made them toys and baskets and things and she looked after them both day and night until they were big enough and strong enough to handle bow or stone knife or axe. To be sure, the children were human things and got their usual spankings when impressions of their little hands were pressed in the mortar or for the mud balls they threw on the ceiling of the cave. Many are stuck there, even now. With so much just as the people left it, it is almost impossible to reconcile ourselves to the mental awakening of finding nothing but silent walls before us.

WAH-TO-YAH AND THE TAOS TRAIL

Lewis H. Garrard

THE MORNING CAME, AND WE were somewhat occupied in trading, but robes were scarce, the buffalo hair not being in prime order.

We were invited to Gray Eyes' lodge, to a feast, early in the day. Sitting down, after shaking hands, a wooden bowl of choice pieces of fat meat was set before us. We used our own knives and fingers. Gray Eyes has two wives and twelve children, two of whom—fine-looking boys of fifteen and thirteen summers, respectively—were in the lodge; their father's eye beamed on them fondly when he spoke of their killing buffalo from horseback with bow and arrow. The eldest had an open, frank countenance—the reverse of his father, whose features plainly showed duplicity, and his small gray eyes—hence his cognomen—twinkled replete with rascality, for which he is noted.

It is Indian custom that whatever is set before the guest belongs to him; and he is expected to take what he does not eat home with him; so we stuck our knives in some of Gray Eyes' fat slices when the pipe was finished.

Smith's son Jack took a crying fit one cold night, much to the annoyance of four or five chiefs, who had come to our lodge to talk and smoke. In vain did the mother shake and scold him with the severest Cheyenne words, until Smith, provoked beyond endurance, took the squalling youngster in hands; he "shu-ed," and shouted, and swore, but Jack had gone too far to be easily pacified. He then sent for a bucket of water from the river, and poured cupful after cupful on Jack, who stamped, and screamed, and bit, in his puny rage. Notwithstanding the icy stream slowly descended until the bucket was emptied, another was sent for, and again and again the cup was replenished and emptied on the blubbering youth. At last, exhausted with exertion and completely cooled down, he received the remaining water in silence, and, with a few words of admonition, was delivered over to his mother, in whose arms he stifled his sobs, until his heart-breaking grief and cares were drowned in sleep. What a devilish mixture Indian and American blood is!

The Indians never chastise a boy, as they think his spirit would be broken and cowed down, and, instead of a warrior, he would be a squaw—a harsh epithet, indicative of cowardice—and they resort to any method but infliction of blows to subdue a refractory scion.

Jack has three names: that of Jack, so called by the whites, and two Indian ones—Wo-pe-kon-ne and O-toz-vout-si—the former meaning "White Eyes"—a nickname—the latter, his proper title—"Buck Deer."

For pastime, I began a glossary of the Cheyenne tongue, to facilitate its acquirement; the visitors, thinking me a queer customer (mah-son-ne—"a fool"—

as they were pleased to denominate me and my vocabularic efforts), replied willingly to my inquiries of "*Ten-o-wast?*"—"What is it?"—at the same time pointing to any object whose name I wished to know. I wrote their answers according to the pronunciation. The squaws of our lodge gave me words, purposely, not easily articulated or written; my attempts at correct enunciation were greeted with lively sallies of laughter. Our conversation was carried on in broken, very broken, sentences; and, I must say, the part that they too ably sustained was not of the most refined character. No person so young as myself had ever visited the Cheyennes, and the gentle fair seemed glad to meet one divested of the trader's assumed consequence.

The visits of the Indians were divided between Mr. Bent's lodge and our own; but we saw as many as we wished, for our coffee and sugar cost us a dollar a pound. To secure the good will and robes of the sensitive men, we had to offer our dear-bought Java at meal time—the period of the greatest congregation. Still, their company was acceptable, as their manners, conversation, and pipes were agreeable.

So complete and comprehensive is their mode of communication by signs that they can understand each other without a word being said, and with more facility than with the lips.

Frederic Remington, "A Monte Game at the Southern Ute Agency, a.k.a. Mexican Monte," from Collier's Weekly, *April 20, 1901.*

I had a small box, in which were shirts, tobacco, a backgammon board, and a few books; one of them from Harper's series of the Family Library, on the heavenly bodies. The plates were incomprehensible to the natives; and, with all my efforts, I could but imperfectly make myself understood, even on most commonplace matters. Some of the chiefs, having seen this book, would not be put off without an answer to their queries; and it brought all my ingenuity into play to make suitable similes between the plates and things within their knowledge; consequently, great perversion of Dick's celestial geography took place.

A chief, named Mah-ke-o-nih, or the "Big Wolf," professedly took a great liking to me. We went, by his invitation, one day, to a feast, guided by his youngest son, where we found Mah-ke-o-nih in a small lodge. After the customary salutations, we sat down to a bowl of dried stewed pumpkin, with a horn spoon sticking in it, from which we partook by turns. The spoon was a curiosity in its way— manufactured from the horn of a Rocky Mountain sheep and holding at least a pint. The childish hint, "take a spoon pig," would not help the matter much if these kind were in use.

The meaning of *feast* (a term much in vogue with the traders) is anything set before one, by invitation, be it much or little, rare or common.

Mah-ke-o-nih was in mourning for the loss of a near relative; and, to show the outward customary signs of grief, he lived in a small lodge. He is now old; but, in younger days, the name of Mah-ke-o-nih was well known as that of a brave, and, in later years, as a fearless warrior of unspotted fame. Now he is honored and respected for his Indian virtues.

I gave him a bent piece of hickory, from an ox yoke, with which to make a bow. As hard wood is scarce, and as the chief knew that I had been offered, several times, a robe for it, he was much pleased by my preference; and, in return, gave me his title. After this circumstance I was known among the Cheyennes as Mah-ke-o-nih—sometimes as Veheo-kiss, or the "Young Whiteman."

In this village were more than a hundred dogs—from the large half-wolf down to the smallest specimen. Often, during the night, they broke forth in a prolonged howl, with the accompanying music of hundreds of prowling wolves making a most dissonant, unearthly noise. And such a fuss! Everyone ceased talking until the Voices of the Night were hushed. In our lodge were three huge curs and four cross feists; and, whenever the signal for a general bewailing was given by some superannuated mother of many canine generations, out, pellmell, tore our loud-mouthed curs and the snarling squawpets to join the doggish revelry.

The love of gaming seems inherent in our very natures; as a proof of this, it was ever a favorite amusement with the Cheyennes and other Indians long ere they became acquainted with the whites. Their game, however, is simple, though not the less injurious in its effects. It is played by the young men and women; who, sitting in a circle, and with a rocking to-and-fro motion of the body, accompanied by a low, quiet chant, increased in vigor as the game progresses, hold a bit of wood, cherrystone, or anything small in the hand; and after a series of dexterous shiftings, so as to deceive, hold them out, while the singing stops, for the players to bet in which hand is the stone. So soon as they say, the object is shown; the fortunate ones sweep the stakes; the stone is given to the next, in order of rotation, the chant again strikes up—other trinkets are put up, and the betting recommences. They laugh and get much excited over their primitive game; and, often, an unlucky maiden rises from her amusement without the numerous bracelets, rings, and beads with which she came gayly decked to the meeting lodge.

This morning was one of November's most genial days. About ten o'clock, I walked out and sat on a dry cottonwood log to admire the rural and domestic scene. The grass was green in many places—the majestic cottonwoods, not yet entirely robbed of their foliage, upreared their imposing trunks, while the branches gracefully overhung the clean, wind-swept grass.

The yellow, cone-shaped lodges looked like so many pyramids. Near them were industrious squaws; bringing, by dint of constant exertion, buffalo skins down to the required thinness by means of the dubber, which, as it struck the hard and dry robe, sounded like the escapement of steam from a small pipe. The valley was partly locked in by a low range of hills, on whose sides numerous bands of gay-colored horses were luxuriating on the fine, nutritious verdure. Around the lodges troops of boys were shooting at marks, with bow and arrow, or tumbling on the grass in childish sport. Dignified chiefs walked with stately step and erect heads to grave council or taciturn smoke.

I sat long—collecting and embodying the thoughts and actions of the past four months, summing up the whole, with a glance at my then present situation. My companions were rough men—used to the hardships of a mountaineer's life—whose manners are blunt, and whose speech is rude—men driven to the western wilds with embittered feelings—with better natures shattered—with hopes blasted—to seek, in the dangers of the warpath, fierce excitement and banishment of care. The winter snow wreaths drift over them unheeded, and the night wind, howling around their lonely camp, is heard with calm indifference. Yet these aliens from society, these strangers to the refinements of civilized life, who will tear off a bloody scalp with even grim smiles of satisfaction, are fine fellows, full of fun, and often kind and obliging.

EARLY DAYS ON THE WESTERN SLOPE OF COLORADO

Sidney Jocknick

IN THE YEAR 1881 OURAY PAID his last visit to Washington. He took his wife, Chipeta, with him. She was in those days a remarkably handsome woman. Ouray was very much devoted to her. They remained a month in Washington and had frequent interviews with the President and with the Secretary of the Interior, Carl Schurz. Of the impressions which Mr. Schurz received of Ouray I will here quote from his "Private Memoirs:"

"Ouray and Chipeta often visited me at my home and they always conducted themselves with perfect propriety. They observed the various belongings of the drawing room with keen but decorous interest, and were especially attracted by a large crystal chandelier which was suspended from the ceiling. They wished to know where such a chandelier could be bought, and what it would cost; it would be such an ornament to their home.

"In official conversation his talk was quite different from that of the ordinary Indian chief. He spoke like a man of a high order of intelligence and of larger views who had risen above the prejudices and aversions of his race, and expressed his thoughts in language clear and precise, entirely unburdened by the figures of speech and superfluities commonly current in Indian talk.

"He had evidently pondered much over the condition and future of the Indians of North America and expressed his mature conclusions with the simple eloquence of a statesman.

"He comprehended perfectly the utter hopelessness of the struggle of the Indians against the progress of civilization. He saw clearly that nothing was left to them but to accommodate themselves to civilized ways or perish. He admitted that it was very hard to make his people understand this; that so long as they did not fully appreciate it, they should, as much as possible, be kept out of harm's way; that it was the duty of influential chiefs to co-operate with the Government to make the transition as little dangerous and painful as possible; that he, therefore, recognized the necessity of removing the Utes from Colorado, hard as the parting from their old haunts might be, and that he depended on me to bring about that removal under conditions favorable to his people.

"Ouray was by far the brightest Indian I have ever met.

"After the conclusion of our negotiations which resulted in the restoration of peace, and in the eventual removal of the Utes to a reservation in Utah, Ouray returned to his Western home. Soon after he fell ill and died. Then something of a very touching nature happened.

"Some time after Ouray's death I received from a government agent on the Ute reservation a letter which Ouray's widow, Chipeta, had dictated to him. In it she told me that I had been her departed husband's best friend. He had said so. I had also done much to save his people from grave disaster, and was therefore their best friend. She wished to give a memory of her husband as a present the things he valued most. Would I accept the present?

"I thereupon wrote the agent asking him to inform himself whether my accepting a present would have a good effect with the Utes, and also whether my acceptance were thought advisable, whether it would be the proper thing on my part to send a present in return, and if so, what should it be.

"A few weeks afterward I received a box containing the clothes Ouray had worn while negotiating the treaty with me in Washington, and in addition, his tobacco pouch and an old powder horn which he used in his younger days.

"This was Chipeta's present. It was accompanied by a letter from the agent, giving me from Chipeta this message: If I accepted the present, to keep it while I lived and for my children it would be regarded by Chipeta and her people as a proof of true friendship on my part, and they would esteem that friendship very highly. But if I made a present in return it would be understood by them as signifying that I did not value their friendship much and simply wished to get rid of an obligation and be quits with them, and this would make them sad. Chipeta, therefore, hoped I would accept the present and let our friendship stand.

"It will be admitted that greater delicacy is seldom met with, even in the most refined society. It must be added, however, that this was an exceptional case. Ordinarily an Indian when he makes a present to a white man expects one in return and his equanimity is by no means disturbed when that which he received is much more valuable than that which he has given. Nor does he differ very much in this from a majority of the civilized race.

"What I wish to show is that the noble savage with chivalrous impulses and fine sentiments, as he occasionally appears in romance, should not be regarded as a mere figment of the imagination. He has existed, and no doubt he exists even now. It should, indeed, be remembered that the same superior Indians are at the same time in many respects not above the barbarous habits and the ways of thinking of their tribes."

WAIT UNTIL SPRING, BANDINI

John Fante

HE CAME ALONG, KICKING THE deep snow. Here was a disgusted man. His name was Svevo Bandini, and he lived three blocks down that street. He was cold and there were holes in his shoes. That morning he had patched the holes on the inside with pieces of cardboard from a macaroni box. The macaroni in that box was not paid for. He had thought of that as he placed the cardboard inside of his shoes.

He hated the snow. He was a bricklayer, and the snow froze the mortar between the brick he laid. He was on his way home, but what was the sense in going home? When he was a boy in Italy, in Abruzzi, he hated the snow too. No sunshine, no work. He was in America now, in the town of Rocklin, Colorado. He had just been in the Imperial Poolhall. In Italy there were mountains, too, like those white mountains a few miles west of him. The mountains were a huge white dress dropped plumb-like to the earth. Twenty years before, when he was twenty years old, he had starved for a full week in the folds of that savage white dress. He had been building a fireplace in a mountain lodge. It was dangerous up there in the winter. He had said the devil with the danger, because he was only twenty then, and he had a girl in Rocklin, and he needed money. But the roof of the lodge had caved beneath the suffocating snow.

It harassed him always, that beautiful snow. He could never understand why he didn't go to California. Yet he stayed in Colorado, in the deep snow, because it was too late now. The beautiful white snow was like the beautiful white wife of Svevo Bandini, so white, so fertile, lying in a white bed in a house up the street. 456 Walnut Street, Rocklin, Colorado.

Svevo Bandini's eyes watered in the cold air. They were brown, they were soft, they were a woman's eyes. At birth he had stolen them from his mother—for after the birth of Svevo Bandini, his mother was never quite the same, always ill, always with sickly eyes after his birth, and then she died and it was Svevo's turn to carry soft brown eyes.

A hundred and fifty pounds was the weight of Svevo Bandini, and he had a son named Arturo who loved to touch his round shoulders and feel for the snakes inside. He was a fine man, Svevo Bandini, all muscles, and he had a wife named Maria who had only to think of the muscle in his loins and her body and her mind melted like the spring snows. She was so white, that Maria, and looking at her was seeing her through a film of olive oil.

Dio cane. Dio cane. It means God is a dog, and Svevo Bandini was saying it to the snow. Why did Svevo lose ten dollars in a poker game tonight at the Imperial Poolhall? He was such a poor man, and he had three children, and the macaroni was not paid, nor was the house in which the three children and the macaroni were kept. God is a dog.

Svevo Bandini had a wife who never said: give me money for food for the children, but he had a wife with large black eyes, sickly bright from love, and those eyes had a way about them, a sly way of peering into his mouth, into his cars, into his stomach, and into his pockets. Those eyes were so clever in a sad way, for they always knew when the Imperial Poolhall had done a good business. Such eyes for a wife! They saw all he was and all he hoped to be, but they never saw his soul.

That was an odd thing, because Maria Bandini was a woman who looked upon all the living and the dead as souls. Maria knew what a soul was. A soul was an immortal thing she knew about. A soul was an immortal thing she would not argue about. A soul was an immortal thing. Well, whatever it was, a soul was immortal.

THUNDER IN THE ROCKIES

Bill Hosokawa

SINCE THE UNORTHODOX PLAYS SUCH a large part in *Post* history, perhaps it was natural that when honors began coming to the paper the scenario should be somewhat improbable. Take, for instance, the matter of the *Post*'s two Pulitzer Prize winners.

In May of 1964 it was announced that Paul Conrad had won the Pulitzer for editorial cartooning in the *Post* during 1963. But by then he was no longer in Denver. Four months earlier he had been hired away by the Los Angeles *Times*. If this seems to indicate the *Post*'s inability to recognize—and retain—talent, witness what followed next.

As Conrad's successor Hoyt picked Pat Oliphant, a young Australian who had never lived in the United States. Three years later Oliphant's political cartoons won a second Pulitzer for the *Post*.

It was something of an accident that Conrad came to work for the *Post* at all. In February of 1950 Paul and his identical twin, Jim, who had studied commercial art, were graduated from the University of Iowa. Paul had done some editorial cartoons for the school paper and he sent samples with a job application to a number of editors. The replies were not encouraging. The *Denver Post* said it would be happy to have Paul drop in for an interview if he happened to be in the neighborhood. Iowa winters being what they are, the brothers headed south with their sample books, visiting newspapers along the way. By the time they reached Florida they had just about exhausted both money and job prospects. The brothers flipped a coin and Paul won. Then he sent a telegram to the *Post* saying he was on his way. Managing editor Ed Dooley wired back: No JOBS OPEN, DON'T COME NOW.

Paul tore up the reply. With their pooled funds Paul bought a one-way ticket to Denver while Jim started for home. When Paul showed up at the *Post* Dooley asked if he hadn't received the telegram. "What telegram?" Paul said. Ed Hoyt, by then editorial-page editor, was impressed by Conrad's work. Palmer Hoyt at the time was trying to replace an editorial cartoonist who wasn't working out. "We'll put you to work for six months or so as a retouch artist," Hoyt said. "Ever operate an airbrush?"

"Hell," Conrad said, "any artist can handle an airbrush." But he had never learned to use one, and never became good at it. "So, for the first half year at the *Post*," Conrad recalls, "I was painting brassieres on photographs of native girls that Wally Taber was sending back from his African safari, and retouching the offensive equipment off pictures of prize bulls." Jim eventually made it to Denver, where he is a successful advertising artist.

Paul Conrad is tall and angular, a fey character who moves with all the vigor of an Anglo-Saxon Stepin Fetchit. When life pleases him, which is often, he reacts with high-pitched laughter. At his drawing board Conrad wields his pen like a stiletto dipped in vitriol; after work his greatest pleasure is his Little League baseball team. One of Conrad's best-remembered pranks at the *Post* nearly backfired. To celebrate the elderly Betty Craig's birthday, Conrad and Stanton Peckham, now the book editor, bought a cake, and studded it with candles. They lured Betty out of her office and lit the candles. But Betty had vanished. Before they could find her the candles had fused into a blazing pyre that incinerated the cake and nearly set the room afire.

Early in 1964 the Los Angeles *Times*, in the process of rebuilding its staff, invited Conrad to come out for an interview. He was offered about one hundred dollars more per week than he was getting at the *Post*, plus very favorable terms through the Times-Mirror Syndicate when his contract with the Register & Tribune Syndicate expired. Conrad was not enthusiastic about moving to Los Angeles. He would have remained if the *Post* could have come close to the *Times* offer. But there was no counter offer. He was told it was against *Post* policy to engage in a bidding contest. The *Post*, however, continues to buy Conrad's syndicated cartoons and uses them frequently.

Pat Oliphant, then twenty-nine years old, was working as political cartoonist for the Adelaide *Advertiser* when he read in *Time* magazine about Conrad's move. The *Advertiser* had sent Oliphant around the world a few years earlier to broaden his understanding. Oliphant fell in love with the United States and was looking for a way to return as a permanent resident.

Oliphant's application for the job was among more than fifty received by the *Post*. Mort Stern, then editor of the editorial page, sifted through the various samples but kept returning to Oliphant's. What excited him was the freshness of Oliphant's ideas, his humor, the boldness of his strokes. With some misgivings, because Oliphant was a stranger to the American scene, Stern told Hoyt the Australian was his first choice. To Stern's surprise Hoyt told him to hire Oliphant. Presently Oliphant received a letter offering him the job at two hundred dollars per week, which was fifty dollars above the Guild scale. Oliphant paid the transportation to Denver for himself, his wife, and two children.

"It took a lot of courage for the *Post* to hire me," Oliphant says. "They knew nothing about me. Nobody in America was using my style."

Slim and affable, Oliphant was able to fit in smoothly despite minor idiosyncrasies like eschewing meat. He arrived in the middle of the 1964 Presidential campaign and delighted Stern with his quick grasp of the issues. Oliphant describes his style as a distillation of more than twenty different influences, mostly European and Australian. A little penguin named Punk, who makes pithy remarks and enables Oliphant to inject a second statement, is his special trademark. Within a year the Times-Mirror Syndicate began distribution of his cartoons. (Conrad was still with the Register & Tribune Syndicate.) Oliphant's work appears in some 260 newspapers— more than any other political cartoonist—and at least a half-dozen American artists have paid him the ultimate tribute of adopting a style similar to his.

Early in 1975 Oliphant, too, left the *Post* but not Denver. He joined the staff of the Washington *Star* with a contract that enables him to live in Denver much of the time. His syndicated cartoons, like Conrad's, continue to appear in the *Post*.

SECOND BANANA

Dottie Lamm

FOR ALL THOSE SPOUSES MARRIED to Top Bananas in politics, art, medicine, business, academia, or life in general—

> The attention going to him did not threaten me. What did threaten me was that I was not doing anything. I didn't like being Mrs. Charlton Heston. I was Lydia Clark.
>
> Lydia Clark Heston

ANXIETY LURKING IN "SECOND BANANA"

By everyone's measure, the weekend was a happy one—packed snow, bright sunny weather, two children who acted as if their parents not only existed, but somehow were salvageable human beings.

V.I.P. day at Beaver Creek, a new Colorado ski area officially opened, featured in *Sports Illustrated,* and praised by all. From a former U.S. president to the newest and youngest ski operator, all cogs in the wheel of the area's success congratulated each other with smiles. Smiles. Chatter. More smiles. Jokes. A weekend of public and private acclaim. No booing. No family traumas. Not even a marginal inconvenience.

After each descent from the chair at the top of the mountain, the small groups gathered to exchange stories and vignettes. The snow crackled as the skiers stamped their fiberglass, their wood, and their metal on its polished surface. Poking their poles in the snow for emphasis, they shifted weight from side to side with a kind of stationary swagger. The anticipation of skiing combined with entrepreneurial success created a "macho" aura and demeanor, even in the women.

A good weekend. A great weekend! A weekend I wouldn't have missed. Why, then, the Monday morning blues? Why the exhaustion? The quiet depression? Why the feeling of relief to be home, as if the weekend had been a colossal burden instead of a darned good vacation?

I run to my office as if to embrace its musty clutter. I wrestle, I muse, I reflect, I try to work on an article regarding fashion which somehow feels lifeless, trivial. Good, however, just to be here. Calmer after working, I reflect again on the past 48 hours.

Why was all the smiling, the constant attention so debilitating? Aren't I proud of my husband's success? Yes. Can't I see that I have at least some part of it? Yes. Am I resentful? Sometimes. But isn't he considerate? Usually. Then aren't I just "grousing" unnecessarily? Maybe.

"Second banana." The phrase pops into my consciousness unexpectedly. Second banana. First encountered in a speech by actress Linda Lavin, the term encompasses the stilted passivity syndrome which can suddenly engulf the spouses of notable achievers.

For second bananas, so much time seems to be spent in limbo—waiting, smiling, waiting. A 20-minute wait after the speeches. A 5-minute wait for pictures. At least 10 minutes of socializing after each ride on the lift, foot stamping at the chill when the sun slips behind a cloud.

The governor comes in for lunch. Pictures. Waiting. Lunch. Talk. More waiting. Sunny ski minutes slip away. The family is dancing on a string of the father's position. The children have skied away on their own by mid-morning with my encouragement. But I remain, caught in the middle.

Caught in the middle—sniffing out the social expectations of others as I sniff in the exhilarating air. Would I cause concern or resentment if I skied off alone? Would I even be missed if I skied off a cliff?

Caught in the middle of a three-person chairlift for three long rides between people who talk over my head about issues of only peripheral interest to me. Caught in the middle. I hurry my daughter out of the ladies' room. "The governor is waiting," says the State Patrol driver pointedly, hovering over us as we exit. Big deal, I think, but I say nothing.

In time spent waiting, perhaps only one full ski run was lost. Did it really matter? Not much. The day was pleasant enough to stand and enjoy the view. And a full day of "public relations" on skis can hardly be considered a hardship compared with how most people in the world spend their workdays!

But "second-bananaing" becomes debilitating in any setting when it seems as if it will go on endlessly. By Monday morning, the retreat to the world of words that I alone weave and the attention to letters from readers directed just to me is a welcome respite.

And I wonder about all other spouses married to strong attention-getting others, who not only create their own wavelengths but also find that three-fourths of the world moves with them. How do those spouses survive if they don't have some escape, some activity which is theirs alone?

The weekend. What do I wish could have been different? I smile as I write all of this out of my system. Nothing specific, really. Nothing at all. But a general wish, yes, I do have one.

I wish that someday for some whole 24-hour period, all the "top bananas" of the world would walk in the shoes and feel the psychic vibrations of the "second bananas." Just for a day.

CHAMPION OF THE GREAT AMERICAN FAMILY

Congresswoman Patricia Schroeder

WITHOUT FAIL, EVERY YEAR, SOME organization has a new idea for a cookbook and asks me to contribute a favorite recipe. I have to laugh because I really don't prepare meals beyond the hunt-and-gather stage. My "cookbook" consists of a list of the phone numbers of every carry-out restaurant within a fifteen-minute radius of my house. When people insist on a recipe, here's the one I send for breakfast: "Find a bowl. If it's on the floor, wash it because the dog was probably using it last. Find a box of cereal, preferably sugar-coated so you won't have to find the sugar. Find the milk but check the spoil date before pouring. Then assemble."

🐾 🐾 🐾

When I first ran for Congress in 1972, as I have said, the chances for a successful Democratic candidacy in Denver did not look too good. Nationally, Richard Nixon was on his way to burying George McGovern in what was, at that time, the largest landslide victory in presidential election history.

In Denver, the prospects for a Democrat's winning the city's seat in Congress were so dim that no one wanted to run. Mike McKevitt, a popular Republican district attorney, had won the seat in 1970 after a bitter Democratic primary in which an antiwar challenger defeated the ten-term incumbent, thereby splitting the Democratic party. Worse, the 1971 redistricting had shifted a chunk of Democratic neighborhoods into an adjoining suburban district, thus improving McKevitt's chances.

A group of young, liberal Democrats, including my husband, caucused through the spring of 1972 to try to recruit a candidate. After a lot of discussion back and forth, the talk turned to running a woman. In the old days, there were two ways for a woman to run for Congress: as the widow of an incumbent or as challenger in a hopeless race. Scenario number two was how I was chosen to run.

Jim stayed out late one night and came home just as I was getting into bed. "Guess whose name came up as a candidate for Congress," he said.

"I don't know."

"Guess."

"I don't know," I said, slightly irritated.

Jim said, "Yours."

I stared at him blankly.

"Somebody's got to run in this one, Pat. And none of the men want to go for it. Larry Wright [a friend and a prominent Colorado Democrat] said, 'Let's run someone a little different. How about your wife, Jim?' "

"What did you say?" I asked.

" 'How about *your* wife?' "

I did end up running, but throughout the primary and the general race, I continued working at my part-time jobs teaching law, as hearing officer for Colorado's state personnel system, and as a volunteer counselor for Planned Parenthood. I spent little time wondering what life as a congresswoman would be like. There didn't seem to be much point. The one trip we made to Washington to raise money and support from the Democratic National Committee had been fruitless. I wanted to run a campaign on the issues—the Vietnam War, housing, the environment, children, the elderly. The DNC didn't think I would win that way—or any way—and they sent us home empty-handed.

So we raised money the same way we organized, at the grass roots. We had thousands of campaign posters printed on bright-colored paper because we "got a deal." It turned out that the bright colors were almost as controversial as the posters themselves. Few candidates defy the unspoken rule that campaign literature be printed in red, white, and blue, and that it show the candidate in front of the Capitol dome, with his family and the dog. (Republicans would always insert a horseback shot in their brochures, and the Democrats a bike-riding scene, to show their love of the outdoors.) Not only was the color of our paper unorthodox, my face didn't appear on any of my posters. Instead, one poster showed a field of tombstones in Arlington Cemetery with the headline "Yes, some American troops have already been withdrawn from Vietnam." Another had a picture of a young Hispanic child with the caption "This radical troublemaker wants something from you. Hope."

I discovered early in that first campaign that I enjoyed talking to people one-on-one, and I did a lot of it. Because they thought victory was a sure thing, the local Republican party kept my opponent in Washington for all but the last month of the campaign. That gave me a great head start. I began to relax and enjoy myself, whether I was going from door to door, from living room to living room, or from community center to community center.

Maybe I was good at campaigning because when I was a child, my family moved around a lot. Between the time I was born in Portland, Oregon, and my graduation from high school in Des Moines, Iowa, we had moved from Kansas City, Missouri, to North Platte, Nebraska, to Sioux City, Iowa, to Dallas, Texas, to Hamilton, Ohio. Starting at three, whenever we moved I had to find kids to play with in the new neighborhood, so as soon as the moving truck pulled away, I would line up my toys on the sidewalk and sit down next to them. It worked. The toys were like flypaper! I made friends almost at once.

Although I became an adept campaigner, I was so busy juggling campaign, part-time jobs, and family that I was taken by surprise when, on election day in November 1972, I won 52 percent of the vote. I wasn't expecting the victory and I certainly wasn't ready for what this would mean for me or my family. Jim wisecracked, "Well, you can't call a press conference now and say, 'I was only kidding.' "

BRIDEY MURPHY AND THE SKEPTICS

William J. Barker

I WAS THE FIRST WRITER TO PUT Bridey Murphy's name in print. To date I am the only reporter who has made an exhaustive search for evidence that the elusive lady existed ... and I've traveled over ten thousand miles in doing so.

When I first heard about the eldritch colleen I had no idea she would become an enduring topic of controversy and speculation around the world.

At the time I was columnist and feature writer for the Denver *Post*'s Sunday magazine, *Empire*. One summer afternoon in 1953, my brother-in-law, Robert S.

Gast, then an attorney in Pueblo, Colorado, suggested there might be an article in a lifelong friend and neighbor of his, a business executive named Morey Bernstein.

Bernstein, Bob told me, was a widely respected young man of wealth, board member of four of Pueblo's leading firms—and that after hours he was a skilled hypnotist.

Bernstein, it seemed, had made an intensive study of hypnosis for ten years, and was an "amateur" only in the sense that he donated his talent in this little-understood science to the city's medical men when requested to do so, always refusing payment.

"He hypnotized one local gal who, when she was in a trance, talked as if she'd lived a hundred years ago," Bob Gast said. "Wouldn't that make a story for you?" As *Time* magazine quoted me later, "Said Reporter Barker, 'Hell, yes!' "

Truthfully I wasn't all that enthusiastic. The thing sounded like some sort of hoax, but I had a newsman's interest in the weird and sensational, knowing Sunday readers love yarns about mind reading, unidentified flying objects, fortunetelling and the like.

My attitude therefore was that of a skeptic as I requested permission of the *Post* editors to do the story. They, in turn, were reluctant to give me a go-ahead. Their qualified consent, a reflection of Publisher Palmer Hoyt's ethical credo, summed up in this fashion: You may write the article only if (1) we can be satisfied that the persons involved are completely honest, (2) this is not some money-making stunt, (3) the reporting is objective and the newspaper does not endorse the phenomenon, and (4) you witness Bernstein's subject, Ruth Simmons, speaking as the long-dead Bridget Murphy under hypnosis.

Almost a year passed before I met Morey Bernstein in Pueblo. He was much involved in developing a New York investment firm at the time, and only occasionally visited his Colorado home.

Ironically, he was as hesitant to have me write about the Bridey case as my editors had been. An amiable, outgoing man who slightly resembles Frank Sinatra, Morey said, "I'm afraid you newspaper guys would make a circus out of this thing."

In the end, he was kind enough to let me hear the six tape recordings he'd made with Ruth Simmons speaking in trance as Bridey Murphy a hundred years back.

As I listened for hours to the recordings, I couldn't help but be surprised. Either I was hearing the voice of a consummate actress under the guidance of an adept director who'd written a masterly script—or this was truly spontaneous—genuinely what it sounded to be—evidence of a fantastic memory released through hypnosis.

I learned that the trances all had been conducted under close observation by witnesses with reputations for integrity beyond question in Pueblo, and later I interviewed them in detail. All are prominent executives and they with their wives to this day will swear there was no remote possibility that the Bridey Murphy phenomenon could have been fraudulent.

I continued to plead with Bernstein for the privilege of printing the story for the *Denver Post* readers, and finally he consented. I'm sure he never would have done so if I hadn't played heavily on his long friendship for my brother-in-law, Bob Gast.

Now I was in business! We made a date for a weekend interview.

I showed up at Bernstein's Pueblo home with my wife, Lydia Barker, and Orin A. Sealy, *Empire* magazine photographer. "Now," I told Morey, "please get Ruth Simmons over here and hypnotize her, so we can see her perform as Bridey."

He shook his head unhappily. "I'd like nothing better, but she has obliged me six times now, and she and her husband, Rex, frankly don't enjoy these sessions." The Simmonses, as I was to verify for myself, were an outgoing couple, interested in a good ball game, an evening of bridge, or a dancing party at the country club. Hypnotic experiments were not their idea of a pleasant pastime. The sessions had been especially upsetting for Rex. He was always uneasy at his wife's speaking in the voice of a stranger—and a not-too-attractive stranger at that.

Still I importuned for just one more Bridey trance. I told Bernstein, "My editors have said I must see this with my own eyes, or they won't accept the story."

Again Morey shook his head. Finally he said with resignation, "Well, I'll phone Ruth and ask her to do it. But I very much doubt she'll agree. On top of everything else, they have a horror of publicity."

I promised to keep their real names secret, and never to divulge their home address or that of Rex's place of business. Though the press later did publish these specifics, in this book we have gone back to concealing this information to insure the privacy of the persons involved.

Bernstein called the Simmonses' number. The conversation was brief. After he'd hung up, he said, "Well, that settles it. Ruth is expecting a child. While I know hypnosis wouldn't affect the birth in the slightest, if so much as a freckle were out of line on the baby, hypnosis would be blamed. No, I'm afraid your story is out."

"All right then," I said. "Hypnotize *me*. Send *me* back through time and space. My bosses'll accept that."

Bernstein looked at me dubiously. He told me that certain high-strung, inquisitive types make poor subjects. Prosecuting attorneys, hypnotists, and nosy reporters, for instance.

"These are analytical people who become so interested in the means used to hypnotize them they unconsciously refuse to relax and take hypnotic suggestion," he said. "However, we'll give it a try."

We went out and ate a steak dinner. Bernstein urged me to stuff myself ("I want you good and sleepy"), and afterward we retired to Bob Gast's residence.

In the quiet, paneled library of the old brownstone house were Mr. and Mrs. Morey Bernstein; Sealy, the photographer; Ann and Bob Gast; my wife Lydia and I. I stretched out in a big easy chair, my feet elevated on an overstuffed stool.

"While Bill is drowsing there," Bernstein said to the others, "I'd like to test the rest of you as a group for hypnotic susceptibility."

In the first test, which involved each person clasping his own fingers atop his head while Morey droned on and on about "muscular control," it suddenly became evident that Lydia's fingers had become locked and she couldn't pull them apart.

The others had no difficulty in parting their hands and there was Lyd, keenly and conspicuously embarrassed.

Morey with a word assured her that she could release her entwined fingers, and immediately she did so with a great gasp of relief.

(I, of course, was now sitting up, my own instructions to doze forgotten. Indeed, I never *did* become hypnotized by Morey.)

Lydia had never seen hypnosis demonstrated anywhere, and announced she had no intention of becoming a subject. We all urged her to try a second susceptibility test, and she gave in, not too happily .

Once again—though wide awake—she demonstrated that she was a "natural" at taking suggestion. On the third test, she amazed us all by going into a deep trance though not told to do so! Morey himself, despite his years of experience, admitted that this was an exceptional reaction.

"Now here's the situation," he said, smiling. "Ethically I can't ask Lydia to answer any questions because I didn't really have her permission to hypnotize her in the first place. However, I can suggest to her that she recall incidents from her earliest childhood ... and later from a former lifetime. I'll request that she raise a finger when each such memory occurs to her, and I'll assure her that she'll be able to recall these things aloud when I awaken her *but only if she wishes*."

And that's what he did. He took her through what is called an age regression. She raised a finger each time he asked her to remember a scene from her kiddie days. Then he requested her to slide back through the ages till she had a glimpse of something she'd seen "the last time she'd lived on earth."

Lyd raised her finger at this suggestion in a stronger gesture than she'd given during the entire session. Shortly thereafter, Morey awakened her. She seemed a bit dreamy, but proceeded to tell us of the childhood memories evoked during her trance.

🐿 🐿 🐿

All right—what did I think about this? First, I knew that Lydia has a horror of melodrama, dislikes being the center of attention, and is the most honest person of my acquaintance. She'd had no private conversation with Bernstein, whom we'd met only once before. She had no reason to fake anything.

She hated being hypnotized. It scared her. She said simply, "I don't want to remember who I might have been."

Photographer Sealy, quick to see opportunity, had shot a sequence of pictures of my wife during the brief session. Sealy and I returned to the *Denver Post* with the photos and the story of Lydia's convincing reaction in Bernstein's hypnotic demonstration.

The *Post* editors knew Lyd to be completely trustworthy. As it worked out, they were much more ready to accept her performance as proof there was no fakery where the Pueblo hypnotist was involved than if I'd reported witnessing Ruth Simmons, a stranger, in a trance.

In short, I was given a go-ahead on the Bridey story at last.

With Morey's generous aid, I prepared a three-part account of his hypnotic experiences. These, titled *The Strange Search for Bridey Murphy*, appeared in *Empire* magazine September 12, 19, and 26, 1954—the first printing anywhere of the intriguing tale.

The public reaction was all but overwhelming. The great majority of readers, surprisingly, accepted the implication that Bridey was evidence that man lives many lives. However, there were an articulate few who attacked the reincarnation idea. It outraged the religious beliefs of some, and seemed as philosophy "just too good to be true" in the minds of others.

It interested me to note that among those who took opposite sides on the reincarnation issue there were people who used identical quotations from the Bible to justify their arguments. An often-cited scriptural passage was the one that begins, "In my Father's house there are many mansions." It was employed by some to substantiate the reincarnation theory and by others to discredit it.

January 1, 1956, saw the first publication of Morey's book, *The Search for Bridey Murphy*, and its national newspaper syndication shortly thereafter.

Morey phoned me from New York to say he was dissatisfied with the limited research on Bridey which had been done in Ireland by hired investigators for his book. We both had speculated many times during the seventeen months since the printing of my *Post* articles about what Irish researchers might verify to furnish material of interest for the final chapter. ...

The check-up on Ruth Simmons' Hibernian incarnation had been directed largely by correspondence between the American publishers and a handful of individuals in Old Erin—a law solicitor, librarians and a couple of others who were not professional "snoopers." None of them was shown the Bernstein manuscript, the feeling being that the reincarnation implications might prejudice them against the assignment.

Morey in his phone call said he believed only a surface job of validating Bridey's recollections had been done. Would *I* go to Ireland and take an educated crack at tracing the elusive Miss Murphy? I told him I liked the idea and would ask my bosses for the assignment.

🐜 🐜 🐜

Four days later, I was able to advise Bernstein that Palmer Hoyt, editor and publisher of the *Denver Post*, had ordered me to Ireland for three weeks to conduct the only really intensive hunt for "Bridey evidence" which has been made right up to the present.

The *Post*, first publication of any sort to carry the Bridey story, thus scored another first on March 11, 1956, with a nineteen-thousand-word report of my Irish adventure titled *The Truth About Bridey Murphy*. It appeared as a special twelve-page supplement, later widely reprinted in U.S. and Canadian dailies.

In all this, I had functioned as an impartial reporter. In all that I had written about Bridey I'd editorialized neither for nor against her. In something like diary style, I told of the sources I'd consulted in Ireland, the scholars I'd interviewed, and the records I'd checked. I told without bias of the things she said that couldn't be proved, and of the things which could.

I didn't take sides. I left the decision up to the jury, the readers.

But after my Irish findings were published, I found that other writers didn't want to play that way. Slanted articles blossomed all over the place, purporting to give the "inside facts" about Bridey Murphy. Inevitably the debunking, scoffing line was exploited. And the incredible aspect of so many of these "exposés" was the apparent willingness to substitute so-called experts' *opinions* for researchers' *provable findings*. Even *Life* magazine erred in this direction, though it termed Morey "a businessman of impeccable reputation and honesty." (*Life*'s Herbert Brean wrote of the original book, "There are few who can go through its 256 pages without being shaken or impressed or at least made agitatedly voluble.")

It was vital in certain camps to destroy Bridey, because Bridey symbolized reincarnation. And reincarnation in much of our dogmatic Western world is, to use the old damning word of the Inquisition, anathema.

Who were (and are) in the ranks of the debunkers? Interestingly enough, a number of types who don't think much of each *other* either.

Some psychiatrists (not all!) and some psychologists (with brilliant exceptions) basically do not believe in any kind of a Hereafter, much less a Heretofore.

Several persons of various religious persuasions do not acknowledge any Hereafter other than Heaven, Purgatory, and Hell—and in many dogmas the middle stage, Purgatory, is missing.

One religion, interestingly enough, okays Bridey's reincarnation—that's all right—but it is *hypnosis* that's unacceptable!

Many spiritualist groups who evoke ghostly voices via the use of mediums were violently anti-Bridey: Probably because they reason that if there's reincarnation, and the soul returns to live on earth again, there's bound to be a shortage of spirits left to speak through seers and to tap tables and animate ouija boards.

And inevitably there are my old colleagues in the newspaper, magazine, radio, and television reporting business. To them, exposé stories are not only a must—they're traditional. A good exposé will sell almost as many copies of a tabloid as the original story (being exploded) did.

Some fascinating attacks were made on *The Search for Bridey Murphy*. In the last chapter of the book you have in hand [Bernstein's], you'll find the outstanding "hatchet jobs" reviewed.

🐜 🐜 🐜

No cheating now. No fair looking back there yet.

Your next assignment: Read *The Search for Bridey Murphy!*

LIMERICKS

Eugene Field

A darling young fellow named Day
Prints the *Solid Muldoon* at Ouray;
    When folks pay their back dues,
    He's as mild as you choose,
When they don't, there's the devil to pay.

A certain young lady at Golden
Once sought her best beau to embolden
    By observing, "Don't you
    Think one chair's 'nuff f'r two?"
And now when he calls, she is holden.

Now what in the world shall we dioux
With the bloody and murderous Sioux
    Who sometime ago
    Took his arrow and bow
And raised such a hellabelioux?

A beautiful belle of Del Norte
Is reckoned disdainful and horty,
    Because during the day
    She says, "Boys keep away,"
But she yums in the gloaming like forty!

A beautiful young man at Saguache
Once courted the charming Miss Sauche,
    But when she was wed
    To another he said,
"My life is a horrible bauche."

In Leadville a certain girl's bonnet
Has four yards of ostrich plumes on it,
    While her sister, poor thing,
    Wears a red rooster wing,
And that is the cause of this sonnet.

SECTION XII

QUEEN CITY OF THE PLAINS

ON THE ROAD

Jack Kerouac

THE BUS STATION WAS CROWDED to the doors. All kinds of people were waiting for buses or just standing around; there were a lot of Indians, who watched everything with their stony eyes. The girl disengaged herself from my talk and joined the sailor and the others. Slim was dozing on a bench. I sat down. The floors of bus stations were the same all over the country, always covered with butts and spit and they give a feeling of sadness that only bus stations have. For a moment it was no different from being in Newark, except for the great hugeness outside that I loved so much. I rued the way I had broken up the purity of my entire trip, not saving every dime, and dawdling and not really making time, fooling around with this sullen girl and spending all my money. It made me sick. I hadn't slept in so long I got too tired to curse and fuss and went off to sleep; I curled up on the seat with my canvas bag for a pillow, and slept till eight o'clock in the morning among the dreamy murmurs and noises of the station and of hundreds of people passing.

I woke up with a big headache. Slim was gone—to Montana, I guess. I went outside. And there in the blue air I saw for the first time, far off, the great snowy tops of the Rocky Mountains. I took a deep breath. I had to get to Denver at once. First I ate a breakfast, a modest one of toast and coffee and one egg, and then I cut out of town to the highway. The Wild West festival was still going on; there was a rodeo, and the whooping and jumping were about to start all over again. I left it behind me. I wanted to see my gang in Denver. I crossed a railroad overpass and и ал lи сl а Iиии li оf аlие lои whеie, iwо liiglиисiо furked off, both for Denver. I took the one nearest the mountains so I could look at them, and pointed myself that way. I got a ride right off from a young fellow from Connecticut who was driving around the country in his jalopy, painting; he was the son of an editor in the East. He talked and talked; I was sick from drinking and from the altitude. At one point I almost had to stick my head out the window. But by the time he let me off at Longmont, Colorado, I was feeling normal again and had even started telling him about the state of my own travels. He wished me luck.

It was beautiful in Longmont. Under a tremendous old tree was a bed of green lawn-grass belonging to a gas station. I asked the attendant if I could sleep there, and he said sure; so I stretched out a wool shirt, laid my face flat on it, with an elbow out, and with one eye cocked at the snowy Rockies in the hot sun for just a moment. I fell asleep for two delicious hours, the only discomfort being an occasional Colorado ant. And here I am in Colorado! I kept thinking gleefully. Damn! damn! damn! I'm making it! And after a refreshing sleep filled with cobwebby dreams of my past life in the East I got up, washed in the station men's room, and strode off, fit and slick as a fiddle, and got me a rich thick milkshake at the roadhouse to put some freeze in my hot, tormented stomach.

Incidentally, a very beautiful Colorado gal shook me that cream; she was all smiles too; I was grateful, it made up for last night. I said to myself, Wow! What'll *Denver* be like! I got on that hot road, and off I went in a brand-new car driven by a Denver businessman of about thirty-five. He went seventy. I tingled all over; I counted minutes and subtracted miles. Just ahead, over the rolling wheatfields all golden beneath the distant snows of Estes, I'd be seeing old Denver at last. I pictured myself in a Denver bar that night, with all the gang, and in their eyes I would be strange and ragged and like the Prophet who has walked across the land to bring the dark Word, and the only Word I had was "Wow!" The man and I had a long, warm conversation about our respective schemes in life, and before I knew it we were going over the wholesale fruitmarkets outside Denver; there were smoke-stacks, smoke, railyards, red-brick buildings, and the distant downtown graystone buildings, and here I was in Denver. He let me off at Larimer Street, I stumbled along with the most wicked grin of joy in the world, among the old bums and beat cowboys of Larimer Street.

COLORADO

William MacLeod Raine

AS THEY CROSSED THE BRIDGE INTO Denver, the two men could look down Cherry Creek to the Platte. Hundreds of tents and covered wagons lined the banks of both streams. In the darkness, these could not be seen, but scores of camp fires gleamed among the cottonwoods. The population was a continuously shifting one. Many immigrants arrived each day, and many left for the diggings at the gold camps. Another wave of travel beat back from the hills. It was made up of dissatisfied miners who had sold their tools and superfluous provisions and were heading back for "the States." The two men sauntered up F Street and along Larimer. They were in no hurry, and the life outside was as interesting as that inside the gambling halls and saloons which offered the only amusement in the town.

The thoroughfares surged with humanity. On either side of the road were one-story frame buildings devoted to games of chance. Some of these resorts were more pretentious, notably the Criterion and Denver Hall.

Into the latter, Tom and his companion drifted. The dirt floor had been well sprinkled to keep down the dust from hundreds of moving feet. A long bar ran part way down one side of the room. This was lined with customers drinking and smoking. Hundreds of roughly dressed men moved to and fro, wandering from one gaming table to another. Others sat steadily in one place, intent on the game before them, whether it war faro, roulette, Mexican monte, or poker.

One group stood in front of a man on a box behind a raised table. The patter of his sing-song monologue came to Tom, and he recognized the voice before he caught sight of Mose Wilson's bearded face.

"Here y'are, gents. This ace of hearts is the winning card. Watch it. Keep yore eye on it as I shuffle. Here it is now—now here. I lay all three cards face down on the table. Which one is it? Point it out the first time, an' I lose, you win. Right here it is, see. Now watch again." He shuffled the three cards once more. "I take no bets from paupers, children, or cripples. The ace of hearts, gents. A square game. The hand is quicker than the eye. Tha's my proposition. The ace of hearts, gents. If you pick it first time you win. Who'll go me twenty?"

A man shuffled forward. "Go you once," he growled.

Tom, on the outskirts of the group, stood on tiptoe. The man was Buck Comstock. He was, Tom guessed at once, a capper. Comstock slapped down a twenty-dollar gold piece, and the three-card-monte man covered it with another. The capper picked the ace, pocketed the money, and swaggered through the crowd boasting how easy it had been.

"My friend, you won. You're a stranger to me, but no hard feelings. Next time I'll win—maybe. Who else wants easy money?" asked Wilson.

He continued to deal the cards. One interested tenderfoot edged a little closer. The dealer marked him for his prey without ever letting his eyes rest on him. The patter ran on without ceasing.

Tom watched the tenderfoot and could almost read his thoughts. This game looks simple. The dealer has, evidently without noticing it, turned up slightly one corner of the ace. Now is the time to bet. The tenderfoot tosses out a gold piece. He points to the card with the raised corner, but alas! it is not the ace. Puzzled and chagrined, he retreats, aware that somehow he had been tricked and that the hand is quicker than the eye.

THE "REAL DENVER" IS GONE FOREVER

Gene Amole

COWTOWN

THE HEADLINE ON WILLIAM GALLO'S Sunday *News'* story about downtown architecture asked, "Where is the real Denver?"

He talked to architects and critics about our downtown. They agreed that our skyscrapers ignore Denver's individuality. Almost identical structures can be found in Houston, San Francisco, New York, Chicago.

Absolutely true. We have traded our soul to the devil for the big time. Denver has been lusting after the big time since I can remember.

Lester Vavian, "Broadway (Denver)," c. 1920.

We apologized for being an "overgrown cowtown" by proclaiming, "We are a mile closer to the sun," or, "We have the largest whatever between Kansas City and the West Coast."

But we were just kidding ourselves. We really wanted those cookie-cutter tall buildings, freeways, suburbs and all the other superficial accouterments of the big time. We wanted to look like New York, San Francisco and Chicago. Well, we got our big time, and the devil claimed our soul. Perhaps the most important question is, "What was the real Denver?"

We have always had imitative architecture. Our cherished D&F Tower is a copy of St. Mark's campanile in Venice. The old Windsor Hotel was supposed to look like Windsor Castle. And our post office is a poor replica of a Roman bath house.

If there is anything traditional about us, it is that we have coveted other architectural styles. In our pursuit of the big time, we never really made the effort to create an appropriate style for our climate, our terrain, our people.

Our lost "real Denver" had less to do with structures than it did with the consequences of making the big time. We had to give up our small time, our overgrown cowtown.

The Loop at 15th and Arapahoe is gone. It was the Denver Tramway Co. Terminal where the old trolleys turned around, and where, as Elwood and Max Brooks advertised, "working people can bank on a transfer at the Central Bank & Trust Co."

We lost an important part of downtown when the Home Public Market closed. Remember the rich smells of warm bread, pickled herring, fresh ground coffee? The butchers walked on sawdust behind the counters. Produce gleamed like rows of jewels. There was clatter, loud talk, cash registers jingling. It closed when the *Denver Post* moved there from its "bucket of blood" plant on Champa Street.

We were ashamed of gaudy old Curtis Street with its Empress, Isis and Rialto theaters. But didn't those coney islands and fried onions smell great in Sam's No. 3? Hardly anyone remembers Hop Alley. And not many will admit remembering the old Ace High bawdy house.

We gave up Keables' sandwich shops, the Tabor Grand, the Oxford Hotel coffee shop, Harry Bramer's, the Mozart Bar, Pell's Oyster House, McVittie's, the Blue Parrot Inn, the Golden Eagle, Boggio's, the Navarre, the Shirley Savoy, the Albany and the Mizpah Arch.

That Denver is gone. Forever.

February 22, 1983

CHINATOWN

Emil Habdank Dunikowski

WE DEPARTED MANITOU LATE AT NIGHT and, having been awakened after a short sleep by the warm rays of the sun, we left our train. We immediately found ourselves in the heart of downtown Denver, a fascinating young giant which has developed in the most amazing way. In 1859 the first "blockhouse" was built here; in 1870 the town still numbered only 4,700 inhabitants; in 1880 35,628; and at present [1891] the population has exceeded 150,000.

Denver is the Queen [City] of the Great Plains, the Empress of the Rockies! We found ourselves on a flat upland. The mountains are far behind us—undoubtedly they have already disappeared. ... No ... they have not! For to the west one sees a magnificent picture unfolding before him! Resembling a great, jagged blue wall, the Front Range lays some fifteen kilometers behind the city. From this mountain belt our eyes can encompass a section at least 240 kilometers long. Numerous peaks covered here and there with white patches of snow shoot up high into the air; we can clearly make out Long's Peak ... Gray's Peak ... Mt. Evans ... Pike's Peak, and many others.

Artist unknown, "A Group of Celestials" from Beyond the Mississippi *by Albert D. Richardson, 1867.*

Satiated with the view of the mountains, we began to walk about the city. It is exceptionally beautiful. Expensive homes, wide streets, many shade trees and gardens, excellent water, marvelous air—one can easily envy the Denverites. Of all the larger American cities, Denver has the lowest mortality rate. ... ten per every thousand inhabitants. In view of this, we children of the Old World are indeed less fortunate in the mortality rate of our cities, which annually lose some thirty-odd people per thousand inhabitants.

On all the more important [Denver] streets we see electric trams. The illumination [i.e. street lights] are also electric—the same as in Detroit—that is, a whole wreath of lamps on a high steel pole. The homes, however tasteless, are magnificent and expensive. Above all, one is struck by the variety and beauty of the building materials, all of which are obtained from within Colorado and primarily in the vicinity of Denver itself. One of the most beautiful and most frequently used building materials, especially for large public edifices, is glossy riolitic tuff stippled black by biotite, which comes from the tertiary areas south of the city.

The most beautiful public buildings in Denver are the State Capitol located at the highest point in the city, affording a magnificent view of the surrounding area, the County Courthouse, and the University. At every step one can see that the city is very young—all the trees, primarily plane-trees and maples, obviously have been recently planted, since none of them is more than thirty years old. Everywhere one sees construction, the laying of pavement and of pipelines—in a word, a young giant is growing up before our eyes. Some 250,000 shade trees already have been planted so that [the reader] can imagine how beautiful it looks. The water here is extremely good, so it is therefore not surprising that the general health [of the population] is excellent. Several years ago while exploring for a seam of coal near Denver, they even reached water which burst forth like an artesian well at a depth of 175 to 1,200 feet.

🪰 🪰 🪰

As soon as the electric lights came on in the city, we went with a policeman to the local Chinese quarter. After San Francisco this is the largest Chinatown in the United States. The children of Heaven have set up things here just as in their own country and have managed to cleverly circumvent local municipal laws. Since the Chinese do not like wide streets, in the middle of the blocks belonging to them, that is, where buildings themselves should stand, they have arranged things in their own way creating something resembling a miniature town within a larger city.

Narrow little streets, dark passageways, breakneck stairs and hiding places in which an individual would get hopelessly lost without a guide—this, in essence, is the dwelling place of the Chinese. Our policeman leads the way, occasionally lighting wax matches en route, and we follow him with great interest. We visit the Chinese stores offering for sale thousands of the most varied kinds of items whose identity and usefulness are known only [to the Chinese]. Naturally our "collectors" of curios buy whole piles [of them] with the policeman serving as an intermediary in the bargaining process.

From the stores we went to the Chinese restaurants and tea parlors. What an unpleasant smell, what strange dishes do the Sons of the Heavenly Kingdom eat with chopsticks—and so elegantly that they don't drop a single grain of rice! Our Chinese host invited us to a banquet at which we sampled some kind of dish made from worms' ganglion or trotters and we had enough.

Nearby were alcoves with gaming tables. In front of the slant-eyed banker lay piles of Chinese coins in small denominations. Around him gamblers play with such concentration and enthusiasm, which is hard to imagine unless seen for yourself.

MEMORIES OF "BUFFALO BILL"

John B. Crosby

FOR SOME REASON, ALTHOUGH I was born and raised in the city, I've always had an affinity for nature and the open country. The history of the Old West has always been one of my consuming passions and *"Buffalo Bill" Cody* my boyhood hero.

We lived only a few blocks from the Sells-Floto Circus winter quarters at West 27th and Hazel Court. And since Buffalo Bill's Wild West Show, in connection with the circus, was housed there too, I used to spend a lot of time nosing around the grounds. The buildings had formerly been used as a foundry for the manufacture of heating stoves. The adjoining vacant ground became an area where the big canvas tents could be spread out and repaired by sail makers during the off season. The heavy circus wagons were rebuilt and painted and the bleacher seating refurbished after the wear and tear of a long summer on the road.

The old foundry buildings, surrounded by a high wooden fence, housed the circus animals: lions, tigers, elephants, camels and a big cage of monkeys. I can remember being chased out one time because we had been loading our water pistols at the watering trough and squirting them at the monkeys, which made them go crazy, screeching and racing around the cage. In the early spring the elephants were walked around Sloans and Coopers lakes to toughen their feet for the summer tour. Whenever possible we kids would tag along. The trainers, or elephant men, on occasion would pull us up in front of them to ride for a block or two, legs clamped tightly behind the elephant's ears.

The lions and tigers were put through their acts in a big circular cage that was erected in the quarter's yard. Over on Hayward Place, about a block from our home, a troop of aerialists had rigging erected in the backyard and practiced their flying trapeze act daily.

The big thrill was seeing Buffalo Bill in his show-time regalia: fringed white buckskin clothing, gauntlet gloves and jacket decorated in colorful Indian bead work, soft, thigh high black leather boots and topped off with a big white frontiersman's hat. Sunday afternoons, a few weeks before the circus went on the road, the grounds were open for visitors, for a fee as I recall of 15 cents. Sometimes I couldn't come up with the fee so I'd wait at the side of the line for a family with several children and walk in with them. I was in seventh heaven when I could shake hands with the old scout.

A few years later, to make spending money, I delivered flowers for Ben Boldt, the neighboring florist, going by street car. On one occasion there was a plant to deliver to Cody's home on Lafayette Street. After making my delivery I lingered on the front porch. The front window curtains were open and I could see the old scout, his snow white hair falling in a cascade onto a black shawl drawn over his shoulders, sitting in an old fashioned rocker before the warmth of the fireplace. He was a pretty sick man then. A few days later he was dead.

His wish was that he be buried at Colorow Point, named for an old Indian chief friend, on Lookout Mountain, overlooking the plains he loved so well. It was several months before the crypt, blasted out of the granite on Lookout, at the head of the Lariat Trail, was completed. On the day of the interment my close friend, Ransom Prose, and I rode our bicycles to Golden, leaving them at the Armory building— according to *Believe It or Not, Ripley*, the largest cobblestone structure in the world. Built with boulders from nearby Clear Creek in 1913, the building still stands and is listed in the National Registry, a designated landmark.

From Golden we hiked up the funicular railroad track to the grave site and, as we were passing the casket to pay our respects, a photographer from the *Denver Post* snapped a picture and it was included in that evening's edition of the *Post*, a copy of which I still treasure. On a trip to Cody, Wyoming a few years later I was surprised and pleased to see that same edition displayed there—two young boys in knee pants and overalls paying a final tribute to the world famous old man; our boyhood hero in fringed buckskins.

DENVER'S LARIMER STREET

Thomas J. Noel

On September 14, 1958, a Mexican family arrived in Denver with their life savings of $500. Gonzalo G. Silva brought his wife and nine children. They liked the vacant one-story hall at 2010 Larimer. From 1920 to 1947 it had been the jewelry store of H. T. Osumi. Then William Katchen and his son had operated a jewelry and clothing shop there.

"We thought that $500 would be plenty to open a restaurant," recalled Manuel Silva. "But Public Service wanted a $350 deposit and the phone company wanted $35. And in this part of town it is hard to get credit. So we just sat here with no heat, light or phone.

"Finally Mariano Galindo of La Popular next door came over and asked us what was happening. Then he borrowed $300 from the St. Cajetan Credit Union and gave it to us. Tomas Molino of Molino Foods also loaned us money. So we opened the Monterey House #1 here and within a year we paid Mariano and Tomas back."

The Silvas served only Mexican food and made nearly everything from scratch. Gonzalo Silva prospered and decided to retire to Mexico. His son Manuel took over the restaurant in 1974. "Mexican people from all over come down here," Manuel reports. "They come from Greeley, Fort Lupton and Pueblo because this block has everything they need and everybody speaks Spanish—even the Jews and Italians.

"Mexican people also come because they can sell their chiles, peppers, onions, tomatoes, tamales and tortillas to the little stores here. I buy from them. They bring in produce that is twice as good and half as cheap as Safeway." Manuel can be found cooking in back or cashiering in front of the century-old building six days a week. "I will stay here," Manuel promises, "where we got our start." "You'd be surprised," says Manuel, "but Larimer Street is one of the safest in Denver. Too many witnesses here. Some break-ins but no hold-up-hands much.

"I keep peace here. Juke box cause fights, so I have no more juke box. Once when I close a man tells me, 'hold up hands.' He stick gun in my face. But his hand shake so much I get nervous. So I tell him, 'Give me gun.' He did. I let him go. He came back eight days later for the gun.

"On Larimer we have the craziest hold-up-hands. A guy make hold-up at Hunchie's Bar. Have everybody lie on floor. Then the guy emptying garbage comes in and bangs down a trash can. The noise frightened the robber and he dropped his gun. They grabbed him, beat the shit out of him and made him call the cops on himself.

"Another time at the bakery, two robbers see paddy wagon and two cops out front. But they think it is bakery truck and that the cops are delivery men. So they went to jail in the bread truck."

WASHINGTON McCLINTOCK'S BLOCK.
Corner Larimer and 16th Streets.
DENVER, COL.

Artist unknown, "Washington McClintok's Block," from History of the City of Denver, Arapahoe County, and Colorado, *1880.*

MY LARIMER STREET: PAST AND GONE

Harold Woods

Thursday P.M. 4:25 Mr. Harold Woods:

Dear Friend:

I JUST HAD RETURNED FROM a 5 cent cup of coffee at the U.S. Drug where Mamie sent me for a dog book Clover Leaf. If she don't start hitting a winner pretty soon You'll have to see what you can do about her rent as we'll all be sleeping in under the bridge. Well I was in hopes you might drop around today. I had quite an experience the other A.M. With some good looking square and what she asked me to do will not be permitted to be explained through Uncle Sam's mail even though he did up the ante a penny and besides it might be opened by the wrong person should you decided to take the day off. I told her to talk to old Tom the Cashier as for my part I'd stick to Cabbage after all there is a slight Variation unless the cabbage is left to rot in the Patch. I saw the galloping Swede (Smittys old buddy) they both used to have the same gal. You must have seen her around about 7 ft. tall. I went up to see Smitty once about 4 yrs. ago and swede was snoring on one side of the bed and Smitty on the other big skinny June was in the middle clutching a big bottle full of "sweet Lucy" all knocked out with her dirty feet protruding a good 10 inches over the foot of the mattress. I couldn't wake none of them so I helped myself to Junes Jug and made a quiet but hasty exit taking along the bottle as in my drinking days I sent Swede to make a run and he got his room numbers mixed and brought the wine in to his old lady and me ready to die and my last buck. So I didn't steal the jug I just collected what I had coming. About an hour later I was beyond any knowledge of what transpired of yeah I shook the swedes pants down and found my 35 cents Change and a half buck and a dime. I left the dime and took the 4 bits as a gentlemans agreement as a precautionary measure for any future occasion I might have to be silly enough to trust the swede on another errand of mercy.

June came pounding at my door. The Swede and Smitty were still asleep and she needed a drink. She had forgotten about having the Jug in bed and pulled out a buck and it was 5:30 A.M. and she said she'd give me a buck for the half bottle of wine I had on my dresser so I poured myself a stiff water glass full gulped it down coughed and sneezed and dam near heaved and said between Burps, "What was it now You said June" I don't hear so good in the A.M. at such an early hour. She said I'll give You 6 bits now for the rest of Your Jug. "No dice June I Just paid two for it full from a bootlegger down on the street I'll take a buck for the 3/5 thats left or you don't drink. Shes Crooked too I suppose rolled Smitty for the frog skin she

A. E. Mathew, lithograph of Larimer Street (1860–1867).

had. Any way Junes thirst for the grappo over powered her peneuryism and she reluctantly handed me my fee leaving me with the total sum of $1.60 $1.40 for 2 Jugs at .70 per Copy and a pkg. of Domino Cigarettes with the extra 20 cents 18 cents per pk. Stamps were 2 cents in the city then so that killed my purse and put me right back in my sad but daily expected financial Status once more I was staying at Franks then and had but to ask Murdock or any one for that matter and prove I had a jug and was welcome as the prodigal Son or did You hear about him. I heard it once. Well I went to murdocks room and Lo and behold what did I run into? 4 guys sleeping on the floor and full Jugs and half Jugs all over the floor and all passed out but Murdock who said Hey Lion I pounded on Your door but You didn't answer. You was in the John I guess. Sit down and help Yourself as You aren't drunk and I'm hungry and Will send You with a buck to the owl to get me a bowl of Oysters. I said "come up with the buck before I get my nose in any more of that panther P or the oysters may well have stayed in the sea.

So I got the oysters and made that Greek give me a recpt as I didn't think Murdock would believe the price 91 cents Boy he must have rolled every sheep herder on the floor. I told you once Mr. Woods that Im not a petty thief fur that stealing from each other seemed to be the only way You could be a member of that benevolent Society of Jack rollers. Even stoled my leather Jacket once. But Wait I'm going past the horse in my sulky. First things first. While getting the oysters some guy approached me I asked him if I could be of any service as I had no hat nor coat on as usual and he said where can I get a jug for 2.00? Now there was 1 full gallon and seven and a half quarts in Murdocks room so I asked Murdock for a quart to take to my room. He was pleased With the oysters and always was my good friend since I always helped him up and down the stairs he said hell yes take one but don't go home Yet as one of these guys got 320.00 in the office and a good old ex-con friend of mine. He will give me 50 and we'll run these other 3 bums out when they come too and have a hell of a party. A bird in the hand is worth two in the bush so I told Murdock I'll play it safe and take mine now Case the guy who bought it all came to and Changed his mind about his promise. Boy luck was sure with me Murdock copped out to beating the guy for $20.00. He'd have let one of the prostitutes take it any way and, Murdock needed it worse. He'd let any friend share his room and poor boy sandwiches. I hurried out with the bottle not to my room but back to the owl Cafe where the hay hand waited itching to give me the duce for the merchandise I had stuffed under my shirt. I sat down with him to complete the transaction in the booth and in walked two cops. I thought the guy fixed a plant for me, but every thing so far was legal. The stamp was intact on the Jug, and no evidence of an illegal sale but it turned out they Just went to the back booth for free Coffee black and believe it or not one of them pulled out a silver flask like a Cigarrette Case and they made a couple Coffee Royals. I slid the Jug under the table and he handed me the 2.00 I shook hands and took of for Murdocks as I was getting dry all over again what with all the business transactions and running around. I opened Murdocks door and Woodsie I'm a sober man now I hate the suff but Just as I entered the room I don't know what made me glance under Murdocks bed but there in plain sight was a five spot and I waited a while before Murdock spoke and when he did it was sweet music. Like I said I was the best friend he had up there who was like the 3 proverbial monkeys and him being a loser himself Went for me any way he says you stay here Leo and if the guy dont miss these 4, $5.00 bills I'll give You one. Wow! I had to pinch my self here was more money than I'd seen since I paid the Jap my rent. Well me and Murdock lowered the boom on that gallon Jug we took it down about 3 inches I guess and murdock decided that it being near 7 A.M. We would go down to Denvers oldest for a can of cold beer as the wine was hot He wasnt too drunk nor was I. He said throw my pants to me. My mind had to do double action before he got up and spied the 5 under the bed so I threw him his pants right over his fact at the same time doing a double take with my free hand and sweeping up the five from its resting place. I now had 9.00 in my kick and prospects of 5.00 more if the chump Murdock had didn't get wise. Murdock woke up the 3 other bums and told them to grab a bottle and get lost as he was going out. Those fellows wanted to stay till the big money man woke up but Murdock could be tough when I was there and these guys were in no physical shape to argue so they took off. Murdock told them that he let them sleep there and his pal furnished the drinks and gave them each $1.00 for breakfast and now they had a Jug what more did they expect and to get lost quick. Now that I have no further desire to drink again and pray God it never returns, some of my experiences are enough to write a book like Jack London. Maybe I will some day. Its better for You to read all this so when it gets too dull You can discard it and not feel embarrassed as I can't see You like as if I told it to You and You'd get up and go. As soon as they went Murdock woke up the financier of the spree and told the guy the beer joints was open and they had plenty of wine. The guy never remembered having any money left so took a couple drinks from the gal. Jug and layed across the bed. All of a sudden he said gee I spent a lot I got to draw 40 or 50 from Frank. I'll be back. While he was gone Murdock true to his word gave me the 5 and another bottle there was 7 all together and the 1/2 gal. I took it to my room and didn't go back as I was afraid Murdock might roll him again when he passed out and some one might lay the blame one me. I had 14.00 a jug of wine and already 3 sheets in the wind so I let well enough alone I'll finish this when I see you. Woodsie I'd hate to live that life over I was only free from pain when I was drunk. But no more ever.

Mr. Woods:

I just came up from the floor. I didn't get hurt. (Thank God) Woodsie! I am all alone with my spells. This is something, they can't do any thing about, Even the Mayo Clinic.

Daniel P. Webster The Boy who wrote the "Dictionary was an epileptic. He was well educated. I'm sorry Mr. Woods; I hate like hell to make you feel bad. I only hope you feel better. To heck with me. I'll get by one way or another

Good nite now.

DOWNTOWN DENVER IN THE 1920s

Forrest Hall Johnson

DOWNTOWN DENVER IN THE 1920S, and for a while before, was more or less a wide open town. Almost every drug store had a slot machine, a punch-board and a "26" dice game at the cigar counter. Many of the hotels from Larimer to Welton Street were of a dubious reputation, and Ladies of the Evening were pretty much tolerated by the authorities. Professional pool hustlers, cold-deck artists and dice sharpies were plentiful, and prohibition being in effect bootlegging was big business—a quart of bath tub gin, with a genuine counterfeit label, bringing $16.00.

The legitimate theater was in ascendancy in Denver until the opening [of] Harry Lubelski's Novelty at 1632 Curtis in 1903, which became Denver's first electrically lighted movie house. A Variety Show with two very popular black-face comedians, vaudeville, and short two-reel movies were offered here—with great success. After the Princess opened in 1909 showing the first six-reelers, more and more theaters were built on Curtis, and by World War I vaudeville and movies had taken over.

In 1915, when on a visit to Denver, Thomas Edison reportedly said that Curtis was "the best-lighted street in the world," between 15th and 18th. At night it was almost as bright as day—so bright in fact, that no city street lights were ever used.

Every theater lobby was a dazzling place, jammed with waiting patrons. Marquees were ablaze with travelling electric words and signs. Blinking and intermittent spot and floodlights were on every business establishment and surplus World War I carbon arc anti-aircraft searchlights roamed the sky.

Going north, on the west side of Curtis, were the Tabor, America, Empress, Colonial, Palace, Plaza and Paris (later the Rivoli). The Rialto, Princess (later the Victory), Strand (later the State), the Beautiful Isis, with Franz Rath, that master improvisor, at the Wurlitzer organ, the Iris (later the Gem), and the Riant, were on the opposite side. I played silent picture organ at most of them. Only three are not torn down. (1967).

In between the theaters were cotton-candy, cherry cider and root beer stands, self-photo booths, song-plugger offices, Chinese restaurants, freak side shows, pig-ear sandwich wagons, pool halls, pitch men and taxi-dance halls with their bleached and painted dime-a-dance girls.

A group of them waited inside the entrance behind a velvet rope, and the customer picked the one he wanted. She collected a ticket from him for every two-minute dance, and at closing time received ten cents for every other ticket she had.

L. C. McClure, Night View of Downtown Denver, 1915.

THE WPA GUIDE TO 1930s COLORADO

Works Projects Administration

DENVER (5,280 ALT., 287,861 POP.), "Queen City of the Plains," the State's capital and largest community, radiates a wide influence throughout the Rocky Mountain region as a commercial, financial, and tourist center. Here a mile above the sea, on fifty-eight square miles of high plains at the junction of Cherry Creek and the South Platte, lives almost a third of all Coloradoans. Eastward, and to the north and south, stretch the tawny plains as far as the eye can see. Some twelve miles to the west abruptly rise the brown and green foothills of the Rockies: beyond them towers the snow-capped Front Range, visible on clear days from Pikes Peak on the south to Longs Peak on the north, a distance of 150 miles.

In the older section of the city, close to the creek and river, lies the wholesale district with rough brick-paved streets, faded brick buildings, and dingy rooming houses. The business and shopping district, its skyline dominated by a department store observation tower and a fifteen-story office building, is laid out at a 45-degree angle to the streets of the residential areas, no doubt because the founders wisely fitted it into the angle formed by the South Platte and Cherry Creek.

Many of the downtown thoroughfares have their distinguishing features. Larimer Street serves roughly as a dividing line between the older and newer business districts. Denver's Broadway when the old Windsor Hotel was in its glory, it is today a down-at-the-heels street of shabby brick and granite structures housing innumerable pawnshops, saloons, second-hand stores, upstairs hotels, and employment offices. Along its uneven sandstone sidewalks congregate cowmen, miners, and ranchers in from the hills and prairies, and derelicts from the four points of the compass. Just off Sixteenth Street, its faded lettering still discernible high on the facade, stands the brick structure that housed the noted Delmonico's of the West, which often served banquets at $100 a plate, with beaver-tail soup as the specialty. Northeastward along the street live Orientals, Spanish-Americans, and Negroes; jogging southwestward across Cherry Creek, Larimer Street looks down from a broad viaduct upon a maze of railroad sidings, junk yards, and the Platte before merging with West Colfax.

Along Sixteenth Street stand the large department and chain stores, smart shops, and larger motion picture houses. For a stretch of two blocks Curtis Street until recently blazed as the local Rialto and the most brightly lighted thoroughfare in the West, but has declined to a midway of small picture theaters, shooting galleries, penny arcades, soft drink and sandwich shops. Seventeenth Street, known as the Wall Street of the West, runs a short course from the Union Station to Broadway. Here, between Curtis Street and Broadway, are the large banks and brokerage firms of the "17th Street Crowd," many of whom are descended from pioneers. Along the street also are travel bureaus, bus stations, railroad ticket offices, headquarters of sightseeing companies, and a plethora of curio shops. Broadway, the principal north-south thoroughfare and the route of two U.S. highways, extends southward from lofty hotels and gleaming cocktail lounges to split the broad lawns of the Capitol and the Civic Center and become neon-lighted Automobile Row.

East of the Civic Center, in the old Capitol Hill residential section, ornate sandstone dwellings have long since been abandoned by their wealthy builders and converted into rooming and boarding houses. Their "mounting blocks" along the curbing and their cast-iron curb hitching posts in the form of jockeys have gone the way of their stables. Many of the houses have been torn down to be replaced by apartment buildings and small hotels. The better residential sections today lie in the Cherry Hills and Country Club districts, and east of City Park.

North of Capitol Hill live the majority of the city's 7,000 Negroes, employed for the most part as laborers and domestic servants. The settlement has two weekly papers, seventeen churches, and a motion picture theater. Nearby is the Spanish-American settlement, with its small stores, restaurants serving native dishes, recreational centers, newspapers, and the Teatro Mexicala, which presents Mexican-made films. Residents here hold to their Latin characteristics and colorful fiestas. Spanish is the common tongue and most shop-window signs are in that language. Many of the 15,000 inhabitants of this area leave the city during summer to work in the beet fields.

Jewish people early settled along West Colfax Avenue west of the Platte. Their kosher restaurants, poultry stores, and shops line the streets in this section, and they have their own newspapers and motion picture houses. The Jews have contributed much to the development of Denver; through their efforts the first large, free, non-sectarian tubercular hospital in the United States was established here in 1899.

The highlands north across the Platte from the business district have a large Italian population, which has retained many Old World customs, including gay feast days and the use of community ovens for the weekly baking of bread. The small well-scrubbed houses of other groups—Poles, German-Russians, and Austrians—cluster around Globeville in extreme north-central Denver, where a smelter, railroad yards, stock yards, packing plants, and pipe and clay manufactories provide employment for the majority of the residents. Like the Spanish-Americans, many of these families migrate to the beet fields in summer. The Globeville district has eight churches but no theater.

The State's transportation system pivots upon Denver. Seven major railroad lines have their terminals here; more than sixty passenger trains enter and leave the Union Station daily during summer; it has been estimated that 4,000,000 travelers pass through the station annually, while an average of thirty interstate busses roll in and out of the many terminals every twenty-four hours. Four main highways converge here, and the majority of tourists visiting the State pass through the city and usually remain a few days before scattering to the many mountain resorts.

Denver's greatest asset is its summer climate and its proximity to beautiful mountain playgrounds. With country-wide motor travel there came into existence a large number of small hotels, furnished cottages and apartments, auto camps, and sight-seeing companies with fleets of busses. This commerce from June through August constitutes one of the city's chief sources of revenue. During these months the streets are thronged with cars from every State in the Union; visitors in gay sports attire, in khaki, in overalls, throng the shopping centers and hotels, and tax to capacity the parking lots in the heart of the city. Restaurants hang out signs to welcome tourists, with the invitation: "Come in as you are." Booklets, maps, and racks of picture postcards are everywhere displayed. Shop windows are filled with Indian silver jewelry, beads and blankets, ore specimens, playtime clothes, and hunting, fishing, and camping equipment. Newcomers from the East exclaim over silver dollars given them in change for paper bills, and usually carry away several newly minted "cart wheels" as souvenirs. But vacationing and outings are not alone for tourists. With dozens of mountain resorts, lakes, trout streams, and camp grounds within a few hours' drive, Denverites pour out of the city on every summer weekend and holiday.

Denver's forty municipal parks contain almost 2,000 acres, and the city, one of the first in the United States to establish a chain of mountain parks, has twenty-five natural playgrounds, many with camping facilities; these embrace more than 121,000 acres scattered through the Front Range and adjoining mountains, all easily accessible by improved highways.

The character of the city has been influenced by the establishment of more Federal Government offices here than in any city but Washington, D.C. Denver is proud of being known as "the western Capital." Four large Federal buildings house the activities of more than sixty-four Federal units; others, chiefly of an emergency nature, are quartered in downtown office buildings. Among the more important are the national office of the Supervisor of Surveys; the regional offices of the Forest Service, the Bureau of Public Roads, the Farm Security Administration, and the Veterans Bureau; and the field offices of the Bureau of Reclamation. Denver has one of three U.S. coinage mints, and near by is an Army post, an Army hospital, and an air corps technical school.

With its dry air and its sunshine Denver continues to attract health-seekers, although in diminishing numbers, and some health institutions have been closed since the World War. The city has nine large hospitals, two of which are tax-supported. Several large sanatoriums, specializing in the treatment of respiratory diseases, have attained prominence for their laboratory experiments and clinical care—among others, the $4,000,000 Fitzsimons General Hospital established by the Federal Government in 1918.

The first settlers did not build for permanency as few expected to remain. Their houses, stores, and offices were flimsy structures, and few erected before 1870 still stand. The city's architecture records the stages of its growth. The weathered stone office buildings, churches, and clubs still standing in the business district date from the 1880's, as do the brick and sandstone houses in the once-fashionable residential sections. Massive government structures of granite and marble, neo-classic memorials, the increasing use of tile and glass brick in the business area, and the Romanesque design of public school buildings mark the trend since the World War. The better new houses, usually of brick or stucco, are in Georgian Colonial Tudor, and variations of Mediterranean design.

Since 1886 fire ordinances have restricted Denver buildings to masonry construction and moderate height, and constant rebuilding imparts a new, bright aspect to the city. Wide, straight, shaded streets, many parks, and rows of trim brick houses with well-tended lawns and flower gardens create a cool and spacious pattern. The thousands of oaks, maples, elms, and poplars that border residential streets and shade the parks, and all of the lilacs, snowballs, roses, bridalwreath, and shrubbery that ornament front lawns, represent an incalculable amount of patient care and labor, for the city was built on desolate hills and bluffs, with only a scattering of cottonwoods and willows along the watercourses. Denver has changed vastly since Isabella Bird, English journalist, recorded her impression of it in 1872: "I looked down where the great braggart city lay spread out, brown and treeless, upon a brown and treeless plain which seemed to nourish nothing but wormwood and Spanish bayonet. ... I saw a great sand-storm which in a few minutes covered the city, blotting it out of sight with a dense brown cloud."

Water is and always has been a precious commodity here. The supply from the eleven great mountain reservoirs, some more than 100 miles distant, depends wholly upon snowfall; the heavier the snow on the ranges, the greater is Denver's rejoicing. Novel to many is the sight of householders lovingly sprinkling their lawns and shrubbery both mornings and evenings. No newspaper reports are scanned more attentively than the edicts of the Denver Water Board governing the hours of irrigation. Residents pay a flat rate based upon the number of outlets on their property; automobile owners pay an additional 50¢ quarterly.

No one man or group of men was solely responsible for the founding and development of Denver, which, in a sense, just "growed," like Topsy. It was not the first white settlement in Colorado. The site was and still is well away from the main overland routes of commerce. Other towns were nearer the gold and silver strikes, or were in more prosperous agricultural districts. Yet, in spite of this, Denver has thrived from the start. One after another, boom towns challenged its supremacy in the Territory and then in the State; one after another, they were outdistanced; Colorado City, Silver Cliff, and Golden were serious rivals in the race to become the State capital, but eventually Denver triumphed.

THE INTERIOR CASTLE

Jean Stafford

MRS. FAWCETT AND HER ELDER daughters, on their way West from Rachel's commencement, met Ralph and Molly late in June in Denver. As in former years when only their mother had been with the children, they stayed at the Brown Palace hotel. While Leah and Rachel and Mrs. Fawcett were shopping and Molly was at the Museum of Natural History, Ralph sat in the lobby where one looked up past gallery after gallery to a fretted dome, and he imagined the days of the gold and silver harvest when towns sprang up in the mountains to exist for a few opulent years and then to be abandoned. The train that took them to the Bar K passed through several of these ghost towns: the sagging, rotten, tall Victorian houses, windowless and with the porches maimed, still wore traces of their original elegance, and there was something deeply mournful in the sight of a cupola whose gingerbread remained intact but which listed like a hat on a drunk man's head. Patches of gilt still clung to the pillars of the boarded-up opera houses; the saloons and gambling dens, as haggard as death itself, still wore their flush names: The Golden Horn, The Gold Nugget, The Silver Dollar, The Silver Moon. The mouths of old mines yawned blackly beside the pyramids of ore. Grass grew in the streets, all the houses were tenantless, and even the trees looked dead.

The Brown Palace had been part of those days, and while it was as flamboyant as ever with its profusion of marble, of tall rubber plants, of gilt-framed mirrors and of frescoes, it failed to recall the life of the Eldorado as clearly as did the derelict opera houses. It seemed like any hotel in Los Angeles, and the businessmen who sat in the modern leather lounge chairs, smoking good cigars, were pale-faced and stout, not Westerners. Only occasionally did ranchers, unmistakable by their gait and their hewn faces under tall buff hats, amble through the lobby like restless dogs; uneasy in their city clothes they picked the chairs behind the rubber plants so that they would not be seen. The others, the buyers and the sugar merchants, were often in the company of women who were too young to be their wives and Ralph, against his will, was pleased by this just as he was pleased that his mother and Leah and Rachel were the objects of admiring, libidinous stares when they came into the dining room.

THE LILIES OF THE FIELD

William E. Barrett

THE CITY WAS TRAFFIC-CHOKED and noisy, and its lights were bright. The heat of summer rested on it like a cloud without rain, but a man could wet his throat with cold beer in the daytime and mingle with his own kind at night, eating and drinking whatever he found. He could listen to loud, rhythmic sound from juke boxes and dance with women and laugh at jokes. He could look into the eyes of women and see himself there, feeling pride in his manhood. He could stand big in his body with gray fog in his mind and hear his own blood running in his veins. He could go to the Baptist church on Sunday and sing hymns that his mother and his father sang before he was born, weeping a little because he had been a sinner all week. He could leave the church with all the sin washed out of him, feeling clean.

Homer Smith loved all of it, the standing tall and the falling down. Most of all, he liked the speech of men and women like himself, and the humor of them. A man heard no funny stories from people of another language who could not speak English well, and he could tell no funny stories. Humor belonged to the language that a man knew. He liked companionship and his room in the boardinghouse, and the bathroom down the hall where he could bathe in a tub instead of showering himself from a bucket. He liked the hard feel of pavement under his feet, the odor of cooking food that floated out of strange windows and doorways, the children who were in constant motion around him. He liked the sirens of police, fire, and hospital vehicles, the bright exteriors of taverns and the twilight dimness within. This was the city.

The nuns and a town named Piedras and the Livingston Construction Company belonged to a hazy dream, as unreal as incidents in the life of another man. He never sat down deliberately to think about them and such stray memories as floated in and out of his mind did not disturb him. His life in the Army was gone, too, to be recalled only through conscious effort and not worth that. He lived in what he had, and with what he had, finding life good.

His money ran low in ten days and he went to work for a wrecking company. His first job was with a crew that was wrecking a carbarn no longer used by the tramway company. It was heavy, dirty, dangerous work, with much steel to handle and grime over everything. The next job, by comparison, was easy. A half-block of houses had to come down to create a blank which could be converted into a parking lot. They were small and old, low-rent houses, known in the South as row houses but in the West as terraces; houses all alike, built together wall to wall. Everything that could be stripped by hand was stripped, then a crane, with a big metal ball, knocked the walls down. The job took three days.

On the third day, Homer was sorting through the salvage, stacking the theoretically usable doors, window frames and fixtures. There were sinks, basins, eight bathtubs. He piled the bathtubs, then stood looking at them, hearing in his mind a high, clear call as compelling as a coyote's cry to the moon.

"Those girls need a bathtub," he said.

It was the first time he had consciously thought about the nuns and they were suddenly alive in his mind. He had seen them hauling buckets of water from the well in the evening, many buckets, and he had seen how crude everything was about the house. Gus Ritter, that old German farmer, had been a tight-fisted man. He didn't improve a place except where it paid him.

The foreman was a big man, almost as big as Homer was. Homer sought him out. "How's to buy one of those tubs?" he said.

"Sure enough? You want your own personal tub, boy?"

"How much?"

"You could steal it and nobody would care. That kind is no good. You got some way to haul it?"

"Yes."

"Okay. Give me two bucks to keep it honest."

Homer gave him the two dollars. He saw the bills go into the foreman's pocket and he knew that the company would never see those bills. That didn't matter. He'd bought what he wanted at the price asked. The bathtubs were high and narrow, standing on dragon feet. He picked the best one of them. It wouldn't go into the station wagon so he upended it on the top, the feet pointing skyward, lashing it in place with rope. The bathroom windows had been removed intact, small windows of red, yellow, and green glass in diamond pattern. He bought two of them from the foreman for a dollar each and, with the purchase, a vision returned, haunting him.

He drew his pay at the end of the day and headed for the hills.

It was afternoon on Friday when he drove into familiar territory. He stayed on the highway when it looped around North Fork. The crops were prospering under a bright sun; potatoes, wheat, barley, lettuce, cauliflower. The hazy blue mountains were on his right. Within a few miles the fields on his left became bleak, sage, and greasewood, sprinkled with a few indomitable flowers of blue, yellow, and pink. A hawk floated low, gliding on motionless wings, and a rabbit scurried across the road.

Homer drove over a small bridge and the stream below it was a thin trickle. He turned to his right on a rutted road and the nuns were in the field, working on their variegated crop, fighting for their growing stuff against weeds and voracious insects and the parched dryness of the soil. It was good to see them again, but he did not slow down nor look in their direction. He was not certain of his reception and he was willing to defer it. He parked in his accustomed spot and sat looking at his unfinished church.

Nobody had disturbed it and no one had brought bricks with which to complete it. It had a desolate look; one wall built as high as a man's shoulder, the others low; the chimney pointing upward like the skeleton finger of a giant. There was an untidy scattering of rubble on the ground. Homer got the scoop shovel from the barn toolroom and started shoveling. He cleared the area and dug a hole with his spade into which he tumbled the debris.

The bell rang and he straightened. Old Mother never rang the bell for the nuns because they knew when to come for meals. That bell was for him. He laid the spade aside, carried his bucket to the well, washed his hands and walked into the house. They were waiting for him, standing in their places at the table, just as if he had never been away. He bowed his head while they prayed. When he looked up after the "Amen" they were all looking at him happily. Nobody said anything but they were glad that he was home. A man felt a thing like that. Nobody had to say anything.

There was an omelet and coarse bread, but there were vegetables, too, fresh vegetables. The farm was starting to pay off.

They resumed the English lessons after supper and Homer's ear was sharper because he had been away. They were doing better with the language but he could hear the soft echo of South Carolina coming back to him when they spoke.

Better than a phonograph accent, he thought. Used to be you could hear the turntable going around when they spoke anything in English.

He did not unveil the bathtub until after breakfast the next day. He drove the station wagon close to the house and eased the tub down from the top. He called old Mother out to see it. Sisters Gertrud and Albertine came with her. He made an awkward gesture toward the tub, not naming it. After all, these were girls who built a high fence around the privy.

"A present," he said.

He was facing Mother Maria Marthe. Her eyes squinted as though she found the sun too bright. "*Das ist gut,* Schmidt," she said, "*Das ist gut.*"

She said something in German to the two nuns and went hurriedly into the house. Homer did not have to explain to her that he needed a place in which to install the tub. When she returned, she led him to a pantry off the kitchen. This was the deepest penetration that he had made into the nuns' quarters. He had not even known that the pantry existed.

"Here," she said.

It was a small room but that was her problem. He hauled the tub in and set it on its feet. He had taken some pipe as a necessary accessory to the tub and he had bought a secondhand blowtorch in the city. He cut a hole in the floor where it met the wall and angled the pipe through it, attaching it to the drain pipe of the tub and soldering it in place. He put the rubber plug in the drain and the tub was in business. He dug a trench outside the house to run the water off. They would still have to haul water because he couldn't give them a pump and a plumbing job, but this was something. He felt good about it.

WEST SIDE STORY RELIVED

Michael Jay Zelinger

MY MEMORIES ARE NOT your memories.

I remember waking to the sounds of blasting in the mountains somewhere west of Golden, or to the crowing of our rooster and all the answering roosters across the creek in Barnum, and always the pealing of the bells at St. Anthony's.

I remember cutting through the vacant lots to Colfax School and stopping to chew the stems of sand lilies or attacking the insides of a prickly cactus and spitting fuzz all the way to school. I remember fantasizing about the mansions on Stuart Street and wondering about the School of Mines students who were eternally surveying West Colfax. I hope they finally got it right.

I remember the day our teachers had us line West Colfax as the Queen of Rumania's entourage rolled by to the mountains, and I remember many other times watching the gypsies in their beige touring cars fill up West Colfax for many blocks.

I remember swimming in Cooper's Lake before it was joined to Sloans and ice skating on Sloans when it was cold enough (No, the winters were not as cold as some old-timers claim).

I remember the No. 61 streetcar on the viaduct from which you could watch naked brown-skinned boys swimming in the muddy Platte, and I remember taking the No. 84 interurban with my mother to Bloomfield Park to buy a flapping carp which would try desperately to escape from the newspaper it was wrapped in.

I remember my father cranking the Chevy and keeping me out of the way in case the crank slipped, and then when he did get it going, getting stuck on the muddy Quitman Street hill. I remember the West Side Center where the missionaries taught sewing and hymns. It wasn't necessary for my parents to forbid me to attend because one budding missionary had stolen the miniature papoose I had gotten at Buffalo Bill's grave.

I remember the promenade on Rosh Hashanah to all the synagogues on the way to the Platte in our best itchy woolen dresses and the burrs in our silk stockings with which we were rewarded.

I remember the green fence around the Florence Crittenden Home for unwed mothers, and I remember that when we came back from the mountains, our first stop was the Colorado Ice and Storage Company where my father picked up a block of ice for our icebox.

And you, if you are younger, may remember the same landmarks, but they evoke different memories.

You remember the annual Rosh Hashanah street parties on Raleigh Street in the '50s. You remember that, in the best tradition, Halloween was celebrated for two days.

You remember the installation of officers at Lake Junior High when the Lady of the Lake dubbed you with a real sword. You remember Sloans Lake and feeding the ducks, particularly before Pesach. You remember the miniature golf course, the drive-in movies, and the radio station on Sheridan Boulevard, not far from the trap-shooting range where my friends and I engaged in play-acting on the concrete "stage" where there were no guns or clay pigeons around.

All of our memories of West Colfax fit into a larger framework that forms the history of a street that was at the same time, a Jewish *shtetl* and a small American town.

RAISE THE TITANIC!

Clive Cussler

UNITED'S EARLY FLIGHT TOUCHED down at Denver's Stapleton Airfield at eight in the morning. Mel Donner passed quickly through the baggage claim and settled behind the wheel of an Avis Plymouth for the fifteen-minute drive to 400 West Colfax Avenue and the *Rocky Mountain News*. As he followed the west-bound traffic, his gaze alternated between the windshield and a street map stretched open beside him on the front seat.

He had never been in Denver before, and he was mildly surprised to see a pall of smog hanging over the city. He expected to be confronted with the dirty brown and gray cloud over places like Los Angeles and New York, but Denver had always conjured up visions in his mind of a city cleansed by crystal clean air, nestled under the protective shadow of Purple Mountain Majesties. Even these were a disappointment; Denver sat naked on the edge of the great plains, at least twenty-five miles from the nearest foothills.

He parked the car and found his way to the newspaper's library. The girl behind the counter peered back at him through tear-shaped glasses and smiled an uneven-toothed, friendly smile.

"Can I help you?"

"Do you have an issue of your paper dated November 17, 1911?"

"Oh my, that does go back." She twisted her lips. "I can give you a photocopy, but the original issues are at the State Historical Society."

"I only need to see page three."

"If you care to wait, it'll take about fifteen minutes to track down the film of November 17, 1911, and run the page you want through the copy machine."

"Thank you. By the way, would you happen to have a business directory for Colorado?"

"We certainly do." She reached under the counter and laid a booklet on the smudged plastic top.

Donner sat down to study the directory as the girl disappeared to search out his request. There was no listing of a Guthrie and Sons Foundry in Pueblo. He thumbed to the T's. Nothing there either for the Thor Forge and Ironworks of Denver. It was almost too much to expect, he reasoned, for two firms still to be in business after nearly eight decades.

The fifteen minutes came and went, and the girl hadn't returned, so he idly leafed through the directory to pass the time. With the exception of Kodak, Martin Marietta, and Gates Rubber, there were very few companies he'd heard of. Then suddenly he stiffened. Under the J listings his eyes picked out a Jensen and Thor Metal Fabricators in Denver. He tore out the page, stuffed it in his pocket, and tossed the booklet back on the counter.

"Here you are, sir," the girl said. "That'll be fifty cents."

Donner paid and quickly scanned the headline in the upper-right corner of the old newsprint's reproduction. The article covered a mine disaster.

"Is it what you were looking for?" the girl asked.

"It will have to do," he said as he walked away.

DESPERADO

Grace Lichtenstein

I should hate even to spend a week there. The sight of those glories [the mountains] so near and yet out of reach would make me nearly crazy.
—Isabella Bird,
writing of Denver, in
A Lady's Life in the Rocky Mountains

A YEAR AFTER MY ARRIVAL in Colorado, during an interview, I asked Henry John Deutschendorf, also known as John Denver, why he had ever named himself after such a boring city. "Why, because I liked the mountains," he replied innocently.

Ah, how myths grow. As it is, John Denver (both his name and his music) must be held a tiny bit responsible for Denver-the-city's currently inflated reputation.

Not that there is anything terribly wrong with Denver. It compares favorably with many places. Omaha, for instance. But there is a popular image of Denver—of Colorado as a whole—as a paradise of towering peaks and stoned freaks. Outsiders flock there prepared to find blond folk-singers in flower-embroidered shirts greeting their Greyhound bus, eagles soaring over Colfax Avenue and streets paved with wildflowers. "Rocky Mountain High" to the contrary, Denver, like half of Colorado, is an extension of the Midwest, an Omaha with a mountain backdrop. Its original nickname was "Queen City of the Plains." That's what it still is—the most important supply, labor, and transportation center for a fan-shaped region that spreads along the Continental Divide north to the Canadian border, south to Mexico, and east toward Kansas City, Omaha, and Minneapolis. The first foothills of the Rockies are some twenty miles from downtown Denver and they are not very impressive. The first real mountains are more than thirty-five miles west. Salt Lake is a far more spectacular city, its mountains rising precipitously in its east backyard. Denver's kinship with the flat, dry, dust-choking plains is attested to by the fact that, with the exception of a few isolated cottonwoods by the banks of the South Platte River or Cherry Creek, every tree in town had to be planted. What the Denver area looked like to Major Stephen H. Long in 1820, when he surveyed the territory for the U.S. government, was summed up by his phrase "the Great American Desert." In terms of aridity Denver is still practically desert, greened only by the pumping of 186 million gallons of water into the city each day, much of it from mountain reservoirs on the other side of the Continental Divide.

I tried to like Denver, I really did. I patronized its third-rate symphony orchestra, its second-rate football team, its Disneyland fairy-castle monstrosity of an art museum. I appreciated its crisp climate, until one day I looked out the window and couldn't find the mountains because the smog was so thick. The radio announced there was an air pollution alert in effect; the general idea was to breathe as little as possible. (Denver is among the most polluted cities in the country.) There were some interesting people, but the majority walked, talked, and thought slower than the ones I was used to. "Have a nice day" or "far out" was no substitute for conversation. My feelings surfaced one Sunday afternoon when I went to see the Denver Bears baseball team. It was an amusing game, if you liked midgets playing second base. Like the Bears, Denver was just triple-A. East Coast snob that I was, I preferred the big leagues.

"Little-*d*," I called it.

Leon Loughridge, untitled, n.d.

"WELL, JOHN, I GUESS WE'VE TAKEN YOU ALIVE"

John Coit

Dec. 7, 1984

WHEN CPL. DONALD GILLETT, the Denver County deputy known as the best boot man in the business, walked up to the side of my 1974 Pontiac Le Mans Sport Coupe, I knew the jig was up.

I was caught.

He had a smile on his face as wide as Kansas.

"Well, John," he said, "I guess we've taken you alive."

One of the problems with being a big mouth is it doesn't go well with a scofflaw.

As you may remember, reporter Kevin Flynn did a Sunday spread on the 4,000 or so who are on Denver's boot list, including the names of the worst violators.

I came in 119th with something like $334 worth of delinquent tickets for parking violations and for having no emissions sticker.

Flynn asked for a comment, which wasn't hard, because we sit next to each other in the city room.

They'll never take me alive, I had said.

When I read that in the paper, I knew they'd get me. It was just a matter of time and so it became a game.

I parked in those hard-to-find private lots rather than on the street, tried to drive only at night and learned to duck down side streets whenever I saw the patrol trucks lurking.

The tickets had come in a flurry between June and late September, and it seemed that every time I parked I got one.

When Flynn told me how much I'd managed to accrue in four months, I figured the cost benefit.

I bought the coupe on East Colfax Avenue when I got into town in August of 1983. It cost me $890 plus tax. With normal wear and tear and devaluation, the car was worth about as much as the tickets.

And of course I'd saved a bit by not feeding parking meters.

I needed to buy time to think about it.

Anyway, this whole deal of being a petty parking ticket criminal was beginning to cause a lot of fear and loathing.

I knew I should take care of these tickets. The Cherry Creek Jedi Master who gives me advice said that if I didn't learn to put the brakes on my infantile rebellion against authority, somebody would do it for me, including the sheriff's department.

Especially the sheriff's department.

Anyway, Deputy Gillett, known as Old Eagle Eye around the department for being able to spot license plate numbers, was so nice about immobilizing my car that it seemed downright unfriendly to kill myself over it.

He nailed me on the roll, too. I was almost to the paper, moving down Tremont a few days ago, and as luck would have it I had legal plates, registration, proof of insurance and the emissions sticker in place.

I hoped they'd never notice. But suddenly there were the flashing red lights and siren, and two sheriff's trucks—not one—and I knew these boys meant business.

Look, I said. Fun is fun. Why don't I just mosey on over to the courthouse and pay up and let's be reasonable about the boot.

Gillett said he'd check.

He came back and said no way.

I walked down to the paper and made a statement.

Busted, I said.

My editor, always interested in full disclosure, never looked up from his desk: "Go pay it. Then write it."

Well, here's the deal: If you don't pay your tickets and get booted, they won't let you write a check. You have to get cash.

I thought about just letting the county have the car, but then what?

I went to the referee, a very harried, very nice man who works in Room 109 of the City and County Building.

I copped.

I couldn't help it, I said

Not enough, he said.

Uh, I was insane.

OK, he said. He took a C-note off the bill. I still had to pay the rest, and for the boot, too. Cash.

This meant I had to go to the bank, get the cash and come back.

I thought about getting $297 worth of pennies. But why press it? And besides, everybody was being so nice.

Cashier Ravi Chopra took the money as I counted it. I tried to explain to him what had happened. He was too busy.

Then I went into the parking division office. Margaret Miller, another kind person, called the boot police and told them to get it off the car.

"Now, don't you feel better?" she said.

Yes, ma'am, I answered.

Back in the office, I called Mountain Bell and asked: Can I pay my phone bill on Tuesday?

The woman on the other end asked how come.

Had to get a boot off my car and now I'm broke, I said.

She laughed: "I thought they weren't going to take you alive."

Yeah, well it sounded good when Dillinger said it.

How 'bout it, can we cut a deal?

She said fine, and paused: "But if you aren't in here by Tuesday afternoon, we aren't going to cut you any slack either."

OK, OK. I've learned my lesson.

DENVER'S CAPITOL HILL

Phil Goodstein

CELEBRATION WAS A KEYNOTE of the hippie culture. "Do it!" "Perform!" "Enjoy!" "Let others see what you have!" were constant refrains of the gatherings held by the hippies from coast to coast. The result was numerous community festivals where hippie artists displayed their wares and anybody who wanted to sing or dance had the chance for an audience.

The first such gathering in Denver was the city's inaugural "be-in" in City Park on September 24, 1967 on the lawn west of the Museum of Natural History. Periodically thereafter, the hippies staged comparable festivals in the city's parks. In 1970, Denver Free University took the lead in sponsoring a series of community free festivals in association with St. Andrew's Abbey. (The latter, located near the northwest corner of 20th and Sherman, was then the major hippie church and crashpad in town.) Though never well organized or publicized, these events were the first real people's fairs of Capitol Hill.

These experiences formed the background when the Capitol Hill Coordinating Committee for Community Services (CHCCCS) met in the winter/spring of 1972. The committee was an ad hoc group of service providers, concerned church people, the Capitol Hill Police Storefront and neighborhood activists who gathered informally every month or so for a brown bag luncheon. There they sought [to] exchange ideas, share experiences and discuss how they could improve their relations with Capitol Hill as a whole.

One idea stemming from their meetings was that a community celebration would be the ideal means to reinforce Capitol Hill's identity, let neighborhood craftspeople display their wares and performers play their music. Not only would it allow the residents to feel good about themselves, but it would attract others into the area and would be an open statement of Capitol Hill's vitality.

With office space provided by the newly opened police storefront at 1031

Colfax, backers of the proposed celebration recruited volunteers. The PTA of Morey Junior High School agreed to help sponsor the affair. St. John's Cathedral similarly expressed its support and, with the American Lutheran Church, provided $1,500 seed money for the festival. Since this was to be a gathering of neighborhood residents, "People's Fair" was the natural title that was given to the first such gathering, held on a Saturday in May 1972 on the asphalt playground at Morey Junior High.

The affair was a success. No sooner was the first People's Fair history than there was a general commitment that it should be repeated the next year. Once more, it was a volunteer effort, only this time larger, drawing more people and using the St. John's Cathedral grounds along Clarkson in addition to the Morey lot. The same was true with the 1974 fair. Now booths expanded to the St. John's parking lot while Clarkson Street was closed for the fair. More than 7,500 attended that year's celebration.

As it grew, the People's Fair faced a crisis: it was getting out of control from its original sponsors. Neither the police storefront nor the CHCCCS had the resources or desire to adopt the fair as its permanent project. Nor were volunteer efforts alone sufficient to keep the festival going while poor financial management had left the fair in the red.

In light of these problems, the sponsors of the People's Fair approached CHUN [Capital Hill United Neighborhoods] in 1975. The fair's existing resources were turned over to the neighborhood group. CHUN was then a low-budget operation that wasn't sure it wanted the People's Fair or how to handle it. With the fair's future murky, Denver Free University stepped in to rescue the celebration.

DFU's John Hand was lent to the fair for three months in the spring of 1975 to coordinate that year's festival, DFU footing the bill for Hand's salary. Thanks to this effort and the success of the 1975 fair, $2,800 in seed money was raised for the continued existence of the fair. This money was turned over to CHUN with the promise that CHUN would be responsible for the fair in the future which was to be run by a paid organizer.

Here a second People's Fair problem was apparent. By 1975, the Morey location would no longer do. Crowds of upward of 10,000 attended that year's celebration, straining the existing facilities. Even more problematic was the physical nature of the Morey setting on an asphalt lot that became extremely hot and uncomfortable on a sunny May day. Obviously, the People's Fair needed a larger and better home.

The logical choice for the People's Fair was Cheesman Park. With this in mind, CHUN activists joined with newly elected Capitol Hill city councilwoman Cathy Donohue (herself an early activist in both the Capitol Hill Congress and in CHUN) and approached Denver Mayor William McNichols, an old Capitol Hill boy who had attended Morey and East High.

The mayor was not at all sympathetic. If anything, he looked at CHUN as an organization, and the People's Fair as a celebration, as somehow suspect, as alien influences that detracted from the growth and continued expansion of the city as a whole. Were the city to give the People's Fair permission to stage its festival in Cheesman Park, McNichols feared, it would simply be opening the city's parks to profiteers and hucksters. If one group were allowed to sell goods in the parks for a profit, then the city would be forced to allow any and every group to stage such festivals in the city's parks, so destroying them as open spaces for peaceful relaxation. Consequently, McNichols vetoed the Cheesman Park proposal.

Donohue then suggested the Civic Center as home for the fair. If anything, it would be preferable to Cheesman Park, she believed, since there were no surrounding residents who would be disturbed by the fair, while it was the natural role of the Civic Center to host such celebrations. Nothing came of this since the Civic Center was also under the reins of the city's Department of Parks and Recreation.

Then the Denver Public Schools were approached. They agreed that the People's Fair could use the Esplanade in front of East High School (which is technically part of City Park). Consequently, the People's Fair moved to East in 1976, marking a new chapter in the history of the festival.

The late 1970s were a period of unrestrained growth for the People's Fair. The festival expanded to two days in 1978 and each year it got bigger, virtually doubling in size from one fair to the next. Money started rolling in to CHUN from the fair, especially from beer sales. While volunteer efforts still formed the core of the fair, a paid organizer became a prominent CHUN employee. That organization, in turn, was transformed from a shoestring operation that had frequently operated out of the president's home to a group complete with an office, sizable budget and paid staff. Furthermore, CHUN even became something of a philanthropic organization thanks to the profits generated by the People's Fair; it gave grants to community groups and worthy causes from the proceeds of each year's fair.

Not everybody was happy with this or the changing nature of the People's Fair. Disgruntled individuals weren't sure growth was good for the festival. They pointed out the celebration was increasingly losing its Capitol Hill orientation, while a bland, indistinct sameness was coming to mark the art and craft goods displayed at the fair.

Nor was the music related to a people's celebration. Opposed to the early fairs marked by acoustic music, neighborhood songs, open stages and informal performances by DFU song, dance and theater classes, by the late 1970s the fair was almost something of a rock festival. Auditions were staged long before the fair while three stages were set up around East High. They were complete with powerful amplification equipment that drowned out any attempts at folk music or performances of baroque chamber pieces by recorder players.

Similarly, policing the People's Fair became a problem. The issue was that numerous street artists descended upon the fair to perform their stunts without the authorization of the organizers. CHUN did not like the presence of these entertainers nor that of leafleteers who figured the fair was a great time to make their causes known. The result was something of a crackdown on unauthorized people at the festival, a development, critics charged, totally unworthy of a "people's" fair.

By the mid-1980s, the East High facilities were becoming strained. Over 200,000 people were then descending on Capitol Hill for the fair, many of them suburbanites who would not otherwise come to the neighborhood. Nor were conditions at East High that good. With massive crowds, movement around and through the fair was often hampered. Parking headaches ensued, along with complaints of nearby residents that the People's Fair did not serve the neighborhood; rather, it had become nothing more than a crass money-making affair of a self-appointed group of do-gooders who were wrecking one section of Capitol Hill each year for a weekend in the name of saving it. The conclusion at the end of the 1986 fair was that it was again time for the People's Fair to seek a new home.

By this time, conditions in the city government had changed. Federico Peña was mayor. His administration's goal was to do anything and everything to boost fancy retail sales in Denver. Toward this end, food festivals were increasingly encouraged by the city. Most notable was how the city's historic Festival of Mountain and Plain—Denver's fall version of the Mardi Gras in the 1890s—was reincarnated in 1983 as a festival of consumption and eating in a place called "Civic Center Park."

The last term was a creation of the city and boosters at that time. After neglecting the city's famed Civic Center for years, planners and individuals ignorant of what the Civic Center was all about rediscovered this area directly west of Capitol Hill. Not knowing that the Civic Center was by definition a park, they gave it this new redundant title of "Civic Center Park."

That's where the People's Fair moved in 1987. Despite the fact that the history of the Civic Center in that year's People's Fair program clearly stated that there was no such thing as "Civic Center Park," the official poster of the People's Fair noted it was being held in that fictitious location.

More than this, the relocation of the People's Fair in the Civic Center rather than in Cheesman Park or City Park was significant. It marked the end of the People's Fair as a Capitol Hill celebration since the People's Fair had now become totally indistinct and inseparable from other festivals held in and around the city. This trend was reinforced in 1988 when the People's Fair was staged in June so that people would buy more beer in the hotter weather.

Nonetheless, the People's Fair was a Capitol Hill success story. It was indicative of how Capitol Hill was transformed in the 1970s from a struggling neighborhood into one that was taking the form of a vibrant urban center. As the 1980s approached, many were sure that the community was on the verge of a renaissance. But problems continued to haunt parts of the area, particularly the section north of Colfax.

THE SETTING

Jim Carrier

IT RAINED HARD THIS AFTERNOON WITH thunder and lightning and sharp gusts of wind that broke off leaves and a small branch from the elm in my front yard.

The tree shouldn't miss the branch. It is in stately shape, big around, tall and spread at the top in the classic arch that made elms such a favorite for shade at the turn of the century. I do not know its age precisely, but I reckon it was planted at about the same time as the silver maple next to it. Their gnarled trunks are roughly the same girth and the house they shade, my house, was built in 1907.

The two trees stand by the street, one on either side of the sidewalk, and spread their shadows and detritus like aging royalty. I don't mind cleaning up after them.

Their arthritic underground knees push the young sidewalk between them, buckling it at the seams, exposing the earth, and creating a catch for debris that falls and blows in. Grass and weeds have invaded those seams: bluegrass from the yard, an errant dandelion, creeping pigweed.

The crack also is a gate to a tiny kingdom that came alive before today's rain stopped. As I watched through a window shade, a robin bounced along the sidewalk's edge, pulling worms that had crawled up for air. A flicker joined it, digging a hole with its beak, flinging wet leaves and tufts of grass and nibbling at ants that had colonized the crack. The flicker shoved its beak deep inside the seam to probe for food. The rain had brought out a feast for these birds, aided by trees planted by humans and a concrete sidewalk that, despite all its intended imperviousness, has been unable to suppress the persistence of nature.

This little tableau of urban wildlife probably was occurring everywhere in the Denver metropolitan area. After 125 years of "civilizing" this landscape, we have failed to run out the wildlife. They have taken root just as we have—in many cases *because* we have.

The flicker, for example, is a woodpecker that lives around trees. It makes no distinction between a natural forest and trees planted by homeowners. The fox squirrel that runs along power lines behind the house must avoid predators as urbane as house cats, but predators the cats are nonetheless. And the magpie that chatters from the alley scavenges there, perhaps finding better pickings than in its normal place in the wild.

The urban setting, from older neighborhoods like mine to the suburbs that creep across the prairie and foothills of the Front Range, eradicates much native habitat. But it also creates pockets for wildlife, sometimes by design, often without intention.

The habitat varies just as neighborhoods do. From what I know of the natural world, that means that the wildlife varies, too. If my sidewalk could be a feeder for birds, imagine what a city park must hold—or a boulevard bordered by flowers, a restaurant's dumpster, the Highline Canal, Cherry Creek Reservoir. In an expanse as wide as the Denver metropolitan area, the possibilities are exciting.

I opened the door to my front yard, quietly stepped around the busy birds and set out to see what the city had to offer.

The old trees still dripped and the sidewalk carried a rivulet of water toward the corner of my property. It ran past a neighbor's wall. On the street side manicured bluegrass lay, uniform and lifeless, like a mat around the lot. Inside the wall a lilac bush spread like a tree, hard against a spruce and two aspen. I could hear birds deep in the bush.

The next yard contained a catalpa, looking equatorial with its broad leaves and snaky seedpods. Across the street two young oaks grew vigorously. And where the water ran off the sidewalk and disappeared into the corner storm drain two old cedars stood like sentinels.

I walked past a red maple, a Russian thistle, a plum tree, a blue spruce, a locust—an exotic forest. The wind that followed the storm shook the rain from their crowns with a wet whoosh. I could have been in a woodland anywhere. When I stepped onto Speer Boulevard, the noise of cars startled me.

Two men in black Lycra whizzed past, their heads down, pedaling bikes hard. They disappeared down a ramp. I followed and found Cherry Creek running between concrete banks. It was noticeably cooler, perhaps by 10 degrees, along the creek. The air was moist, and beneath the viaduct nearly dank.

Water from the storm drain gushed out of a pipe in the concrete and fell onto the rocks below. A small pool swirled with leaves and worms washed down from my street. In the murk, two small goldfish darted at my reflection. In the mud around the rocks there were dog tracks, sneaker tracks, and the tiny sharp paw marks of a fox squirrel. Overhead, swallows darted through the shadows, chasing airborne bugs. One lit on a mud nest stuck to a concrete beam and the screams of three chicks erupted, their black-and-beige bodies nearly overflowing their gray house. The mud had been scooped from the creek bottom beneath the viaduct and its humming traffic.

I had been drawn to this waterway just as the wildlife had been. The stream ran wedged between the walls of a flood barricade, and, for the most part, below the street, out of sight and mind of city folks. Yet it still provided the essentials for life: food, water and shelter.

But barely. Where I stood, the creek bed was shorn of nearly all shrubbery. The grass had been cut along the bike path. The water in the creek ran shallow across a smooth sand bottom. Except for some minnows stirring in a tiny eddy and skitterbugs rowing on the surface tension, the creek looked pretty sterile.

Just upstream, though, where a fence blocked my path I could see the banks thicken with life. A big aspen tree had fallen in disarray. A bird nest sat near the top of another aspen. I slipped around the fence, into a thicket of willows. Their roots were exposed along the banks, holding the soil. This was fox, skunk and raccoon country. I pushed through the saplings along what looked like a game trail running parallel to the creek.

Suddenly the thicket ended at a lawn. The grass was sheared like a crewcut. Funny-looking blobs lay on the grass where long slices were cut in the sod. I had found the fifth tee of the Denver Country Club.

The club, 200 acres of luxurious open space in the middle of the city, also marked a change in habitat on Cherry Creek. Downstream, the creek lay between flood barricades as it ran through the city. Its banks were clipped regularly. There was little life there. Upstream, the creek went wild. Willows clogged the banks; shady cottonwoods loomed over the water. There was less erosion, and much more wildlife.

Muskrats live on the country club grounds. So do rabbits and owls. In the 1970s, a den of red foxes got some local publicity. Within a week, someone had shot them, to the extreme consternation of club members. Occasionally mule deer and elk drift in from upstream, according to Mike Fiddelke, the club's general manager. When animals show up on the fairway, they are allowed to play through.

In the midst of the fastidious grooming Cherry Creek's flora is allowed to grow natural. The weeds and willows are thick as dog hair. The cottonwoods are huge. Wild asparagus and prickly lettuce spring up, and Rocky Mountain bee plants hold water from rainstorms in tiny cups formed by the leaves and stem. It is heaven for wildlife. The tall grasses provide shelter; the weeds produce many seeds. An intricate food chain thrives in the thicket: seeds, butterfly larvae, grasshoppers, rodents.

Beaver so far have stayed off country club property, but their gnawings are visible just up Cherry Creek, across University Boulevard, and in the shadow of a new shopping center. Freed of its concrete banks, the creek here looks like the country.

As I poked around in it, a downy woodpecker flew over the head of a construction worker eating lunch and disappeared into a hole in an old cottonwood. Both beings were here for the same reason, I suspect. Both found in the streambed a bit of respite.

In an unlikely place for wildlife, creatures had found a niche. In an unlikely place for a wildlife lesson, I had found one. The greater the neglect, it seemed, the greater the habitat. A vacant lot gone to weeds could support more life than a perfect lawn. And open space gave wildlife room to roam, to hunt, to hide, to nest. The duffers on the back nine were just another hazard.

Cherry Creek had become for me the artery to the heart of urban wildlife. Following it, I found the heart of the city, too.

Denver was founded along Cherry Creek at the spot where it flows into the South Platte River. In 1860 the confluence was a flat watering hole surrounded by short-grass prairie.

Cherry Creek, flowing from the southeast, drained a land that, with only 14 inches of rain a year, baked in the summer. Buffalo grazed, pronghorn gamboled, and both drank at the river's edge. The water spilled over the banks when thunderstorms from the mountains drenched the grasslands. The South Platte River, running northeast, drained the creeks of the Front Range, flooding in spring and later flowing sluggishly, the consistency of molasses.

Outside the watercourses, the confluence was a dry old place in the rain shadow of the mountains, which stripped most of the moisture from the westerly weather systems. The earliest drawings of Denver show a landscape dominated by the two streams with a few cottonwoods along the banks. A lone cabin began the settlement. In one drawing an owl sits beside a prairie dog town. A deer head is mounted over the cabin's door.

Denver grew as a supply and trade community for both the mining in the mountains and agriculture on the plains. In a broad sense, the city is ideally located for wildlife, on the "edge" between the geographic features. Within 30 miles of Denver, the land rises 8,000 feet, creating moist forests, meadows and alpine tundra. The uplift is cut by deep ravines that flow with snowmelt most of the year. Such variety creates a rich array of wildlife, almost 400 species of fish, amphibians and reptiles, birds and mammals.

As Denver grew in the 1800s, the order that only humans bring began to invade the landscape. Streets were laid out in a grid. Bridges leaped Cherry Creek. Homes began their march along the streets. And in front of them, in picketlike rows, new trees were planted. It was the beginning of the urban forest. By the turn of the century, when the trees along my street were planted, the confluence of Cherry Creek and the Platte River could no longer be seen in city pictures. It had been hidden among the rising structures of the Queen City of the Plains. More visible were the trees rising above the homes.

But the water was not forgotten. The city fathers had learned to bend it to their will. As early as 1867 City Ditch was flowing away from the South Platte to water yards, gardens and trees. Where the ditch ran, according to the contours of the ground, Denver's first parks were built: Washington and City Parks as water parks, with large lakes at the center. As the city spread in all directions, so did the waterways. Reservoirs were created along the many streams that flowed into the Platte to save the waters of the spring floods for the rest of the year.

Every suburb that surrounded Denver built reservoirs and ditches. Every mountain community that began creeping up the foothills built elaborate water and flood control systems.

An incredible array of waterways was created. Largely lost in the grid of buildings and streets, and missing from most modern maps of the city, these waterways still serve the original purpose: the creation of an oasis on a semi-arid plain.

The new oasis was not lost on wildlife. The urban forest became home to dozens of bird species not found on the short-grass prairie. Mammals normally confined to the edges of the mountain forests ventured into the suburbs. Nonnative fish and reptiles found their niches, too. Eastern birds like the blue jay moved westward along the rivers and found homes in Denver. The fox squirrel moved in. Houses weren't complete without house mice. And raccoons, which rarely existed in the foothills 50 years ago, began exploring the alleys.

As the city grew, a number of species disappeared, unable to cope with civilization. Buffalo was one. Pronghorn was another, relegated to remnant prairie to the east. That process continues today. A pronghorn herd grazes where a new airport will be built, and its members will no doubt be victims of "progress." Pronghorn are what biologists consider "specialists," limited to a narrow lifestyle.

The urban species tended to be "generalists," capable of adapting to or coping with a variety of conditions and habitat. The coyote is a prime example of a species capable of coexisting with civilization.

The hundreds of species of wildlife found in the Denver area today all have one thing in common: the need for food, water and shelter. Where that exists, they have established themselves. The Colorado Division of Wildlife estimates that 85 percent of the wildlife in the urban landscape lives along the waterways.

Over the course of a summer I made several random searches for wildlife in the metropolitan area, and I was constantly surprised by the variety and vigor of the creatures. Despite our best efforts to pave the Front Range, they have found places to live.

• At the city's birthplace, Confluence Park, a waddle of young mallards paddled up Cherry Creek, feeding on submerged plants. Swallows flicked the air along Speer Boulevard and under the Fifteenth Avenue bridge. A doublecrested cormorant flew up the Platte toward Mile High Stadium. There were carp, channel catfish and sunfish in the water. A flock of pigeons peeled away and headed across a railroad yard in search of their adopted home, the warehouse district. A flock of 18 white pelicans swirled in formation over the confluence and headed north. A jet roared above them; a fire engine wailed. But cicadas buzzed just as loudly in a cottonwood.

• At the Division of Wildlife office, stuck in an industrialized section on north Broadway, red foxes and mule deer could be seen along with almost constant tractor-trailer traffic. Just to the north of the office, Clear Creek flows toward the South Platte beneath Interstate 25. Now, whenever I hurtle by at 65 mph, I watch for the trees along it and imagine the life in its shade.

• At the Denver Tech Center, I saw burrowing owls in prairie dog towns on land that is set aside as open space. Voles fed on lawns in the reflection of shiny glass buildings. Hawks wheeled against the skyline. In a white petunia flower bed near the entrance to an office building, a cottontail nibbled at something. Butterflies were everywhere. A shrike sat on barbed wire fence that surrounded the reservoir. To the credit of its developers, the Tech Center has dedicated open space that wildlife has adopted. But there is a big difference between the mowed "open space" with scattered trees seen around many buildings and parks and the unkempt, rather abandoned areas of fields and hedgerows that wildlife need.

• Within yards of the Aurora Mall, prairie dogs are active on land owned by Prudential Insurance Company. On the outskirts of Aurora, where townhomes end and the prairie resumes, sloughs full of cattails, bullrushes and sedges have been allowed to grow between housing developments in foresighted planning. In them, I flushed a red-winged blackbird, peeping frogs by the score and a vesper sparrow.

• In Littleton, a young girl startled me by picking crawdads from an artificially created waterway that channeled runoff from the blacktop streets. She fished among the rocks placed there by a contractor, on a waterfall of concrete and netting and PVC pipe, and pulled from the waterway specimens of one of nature's scavengers.

• A steady flow of news stories from the Front Range reports on urban animals so common that some of them have become pests: beaver on Bear Creek, jackrabbits at Stapleton Airport, deer in Boulder's backyards. There are foxes in Crown Hill Cemetery, night-herons in City Park, pheasants at Chatfield Reservoir, bald eagles at Barr Lake. If further proof is needed, consider this: fishing, hunting and trapping still are allowed in places on the urbanized Front Range.

The concrete jungle is not much for supporting wildlife. It's not a very pleasant place for people either. Malls, for example, do not support much wildlife, except for the occasional house sparrow picking at French fries dropped in the parking lot.

But within and around that jungle there are soft spots and wet spots—habitat. In Denver, humans have taken a confluence surrounded by a desert and made it shadier in summer, warmer in winter, and considerably wetter. It has become a comfortable home for millions of people.

One can decry the growth and development of a spreading Front Range, the loss of prime prairie, riparian and foothills habitat, the draining of mountain waters to slake our thirst. The examples of our blundering, ignorant ways are enormous.

Protest is not the purpose of this book. Rather, it is to celebrate nature's ability to compensate for our blunders, and to applaud efforts by some people to take our kindred creatures into account. But most of all it is to notice, and to stand in awe at, the bird in the stoplight, the fox in the cloverleaf, the beaver—bless its nuisance hide—on the golf course. These wild animals remind us every day that we are part of the natural world. They connect us to the earth. In doing so, they civilize the city.

"The Unsinkable Molly Brown" by Meredith Willson, sheet music, 1960.

BEA-U-TI-FUL PEOPLE OF DENVER

Meredith Willson

Bea-u-ti-ful People of Denver,
Bea-u-ti-ful People of Denver.
Willowy ladies,
Billowy gowns,
Avenues, buildings and parks.
I ate fish off of a silver plate,
Brown's hotel gave me the four bit rate.
I saw lamps lighting the street each
    night.
Not one drunk offered to fight!

Bea-u-ti-ful People of Denver,
Bea-u-ti-ful People of Denver.
Whipperty gentlemen,
Flipperty talk,
Nightingales, peacocks and larks. (To
    eat!)
No one laughs ev'ryone smiles instead,
Don't say "Back house" say "The shed."
One horse rigs don't get around no
    more
Six matched greys wait at your door!

Bea-u-ti-ful People of Denver,
Bea-u-ti-ful People of Denver.
Never a dog fight,
Never a brawl,
Never a knife or a gun.
Ev'ry girl carries her gloves in hand,
Sunday night there is a concert band.
Men may smoke under the silv'ry moon.
No one spits without a spittoon.

Bea-u-ti-ful People of Denver,
Bea-u-ti-ful People of Denver.
Aren't any gussies,
Floozies or hussies,
Never a girl with a bun.
They won't hang even an old horse thief,
Ev'ry man carries a handkerchief.
Holds you loose during the minuets.
Just in case somebody sweats.

Bea-u-ti-ful People of Denver.
Bea-u-ti-ful People of Denver.
Here I come to stay!

PERMISSIONS

Every attempt has been made to secure permission for the reprinting of material in The Colorado Book. *Enquiries may be addressed to Fulcrum Publishing, Golden, Colorado.*

AUTHORS

ARTISTS

Cover—William Henry Jackson, "Heart of the Rockies," photograph, color lithography by Detroit Publishing Company. Courtesy of the Denver Public Library, Western History Collection.

Frontispiece—George Elbert Burr, "Mount of the Holy Cross," n.d., etching. Collection of Dick and Mary Bowman.

Page 15—John Frederick Kensett, "In the Heart of the Rockies [Bergen Park]," 1870, oil on paper, 10" x 14". Courtesy of Kennedy Galleries, Inc., New York. Art in private collection.

Page 31—John Casilear, "The Rockies from near Greeley, Colorado," 1881, oil, 24" x 46". Courtesy of Harmsen's Western American Collection, Denver, Colorado.

Page 42—Artist unknown, "Seven Views in Denver, Colorado, 1859," from *Beyond the Mississippi, from the Great River to the Great Ocean: Life and Adventure of the Plains, Mountains and Pacific Coast* by Albert D. Richardson, (New York: Bliss & Company, 1867). Courtesy of Denver Public Library, Western History Collection.

Page 46—Artist unknown, "Busted, By Thunder!," from *Beyond the Mississippi, from the Great River to the Great Ocean: Life and Adventure of the Plains, Mountains and Pacific Coast* by Albert D. Richardson (New York: Bliss & Company, 1867). Courtesy of the Denver Public Library, Western History Collection.

Page 49—Artist unknown, "Return of Pike's Peakers," from *Beyond the Mississippi, from the Great River to the Great Ocean: Life and Adventure of the Plains, Mountains and Pacific Coast* by Albert D. Richardson (New York: Bliss & Company, 1867). Courtesy of the Denver Public Library, Western History Collection.

Page 61—Mary Elizabeth Michael Achey, "Soldier's Camp on the Arkansas River, Colorado (1862)," drawing, pencil on paper, 10" x 16". Courtesy of the Seattle Historical Society, Seattle, Washington.

Page 63—Charles Craig (1846–1931), "Utes, Winter Camp," n.d., oil on canvas. Collection of the Sangre de Cristo Arts and Conference Center.

Page 88—Artist unknown, narrow-gauge train through the Rockies, wood cut.

Page 95—Charles Partridge Adams, "Golden Hour of the Rockies," n.d., oil on canvas. Collection of the Sangre de Cristo Arts and Conference Center.

Page 99—Thomas Worthington Whittredge, "In the Rockies [Bergen Park, Colorado]," 1870, oil, 14 1/2" x 10". Courtesy of Harmsen's Western American Collection, Denver, Colorado.

Page 110—A. Howard Brodie, "Jack Dempsey," from *The Life and Legend of Gene Fowler* by H. Allen Smith, (New York: William Morrow and Co., 1977).

Page 113—Jenne Magafan, "Country Dance," c. 1941, lithograph, 11" x 14". Collection of Ethel Magafan.

Page 119—Frank Mechau, "Wild Horse Race," oil on canvas, 40" x 100". Courtesy of the Auschutz Collection.

Page 129—Artist unknown, "Cutting Out," from *New Colorado and The Santa Fe Trail* by A.A. Hayes, Jr., A M, (New York: Harper and Brothers, Franklin Square, 1880). Courtesy of the Denver Public Library, Western History Collection.

Page 141—Artist unknown, "Gregory Gold Diggings, Colorado, May 1855," from *Beyond the Mississippi, from the Great River to the Great Ocean: Life and Adventure of the Plains, Mountains and Pacific Coast* by Albert D. Richardson (New York: Bliss & Company, 1867). Courtesy of the Denver Public Library, Western History Collection.

Page 151—Artist unknown, "A Mining-Camp Court-House," from *The West from a Car-Window* by Richard Harding Davis (New York: Harper and Brothers, 1892). Courtesy of the Denver Public Library, Western History Collection.

Page 155—Artist unknown, "Down the Shaft," from *Beyond the Mississippi, from the Great River to the Great Ocean: Life and Adventure of the Plains, Mountains and Pacific Coast* by Albert D. Richardson (New York: Bliss & Company, 1867). Courtesy of the Denver Public Library, Western History Collection.

Page 158—Doris Lee, "Eagle's Rest, Cripple Creek," c. 1938, lithograph, 9 3/4" x 14 1/4". Collection of Elizabeth E. Wilder.

Page 162—Artist unknown, "When Cripple Creek District Towns Were Wide Open," from *Yellow Gold of Cripple Creek: Romances and Anecdotes of the Mines, Mining Men and Mining Fortunes* by Harry J. Newton (Denver: Nelson Publishing Company, 1928). Courtesy of the Denver Public Library, Western History Collection.

Page 167—*The La Jara Cook Book*, n.d., published by The Sewing Circle of La Jara.

Page 172—Muriel Sibell Wolle, "Teller House, Central City," n.d., sketch. Courtesy of Sandra Atchinson Dallas.

Page 174—Promotional brochure for the Tabor Grand Opera House, 1881. Courtesy of the Denver Public Library, Western History Collection.

Page 175—Artist unknown, "Horace Tabor," from *History of the City of Denver, Arapahoe County, and Colorado* (Chicago: O.L. Baskin & Co., Historical Publishers, 1880). Courtesy of the Denver Public Library, Western History Collection.

Page 178—Artist Unknown, "Mining Camp in Colorado" from *The West From a Car-Window,* by Richard Harding Davis, (New York: Harper and Brothers, 1892). Courtesy of the Denver Public Library, Western History Collection.

Page 180—C. Waldo Love, "Baby Doe Tabor," 1935, oil on canvas, 24" x 30". Collection of Colorado Historical Society.

Page 184—Original cast list for the New York production of "The Ballad of Baby Doe," 1958. Courtesy of the Colorado Historical Society.

Page 196—Charles Partridge Adams, "Pikes Peak," n.d., watercolor, 4 3/4" x 6 7/8". Private collection, printed with permission.

Page 197—Lyman Byxbe, "Autumn," n.d. The Liz Miller Collection, printed with permission.

Page 200—Titian Ramsay Peale, "Rocky Mountain ... from a Sketch by S ...," n.d., oil, 7 1/4" x 13". Courtesy of Joslyn Art Museum, Omaha, Nebraska.

Page 207—Artist unknown, "Climbing Pikes Peak," from *Beyond the Mississippi, from the Great River to the Great Ocean: Life and Adventure of the Plains, Mountains and Pacific Coast* by Albert D. Richardson (New York: Bliss & Company, 1867). Courtesy of the Denver Public Library, Western History Collection.

Page 210—"Pike's Peak Gallop," n.d., sheet music. Courtesy of Colorado Historical Society.

Page 212—William Henry Jackson, untitled, circa 1890, photograph enhanced through color lithography. Courtesy of the Denver Public Library, Western History Collection.

Page 217—Adolph Arthur Dehn, "Fishing—Colorado," 1945 or 1946, etching. Private collection, printed with permission.

Page 224—Max Beerbohm, caricature of Oscar Wilde on his lecture tour through America in 1882. Courtesy of Denver Public Library, Western History Collection.

Page 227—John Harrison Mills, portrait of Mary Elitch, n.d., oil on canvas. Courtesy of the Colorado Historical Society.

Page 234,—Promotional brochure for the California Zephyr, n.d. Courtesy of Denver Public Library, Western History Collection.

Page 244—William Sanderson, untitled, n.d., sketch. Courtesy of Connie Wallick.

Page 254—Artist unknown, "Surprise Attack on a Hostile Indian Camp," from *I Stand By Sand Creek: A Defense of Colonel John M. Chivington and the Third Colorado Cavalry* by William R. Dunn, Lt. Colonel. (The Old Army Press, 1985).

Page 260—Eliza Greatorex, "View from South Pueblo," from *Summer Etchings in Colorado* by Eliza Greatorex (New York: G.P. Putnam's Sons, 1873). Courtesy of Denver Public Library, Western History Collection.

Page 261—Eliza Greatorex, "Old Pueblo," from *Summer Etchings in Colorado* by Eliza Greatorex (New York: G.P. Putnam's Sons, 1873). Courtesy of Denver Public Library, Western History Collection.

Page 266—Nadine Drummond, untitled, c. 1947, pencil drawing. Courtesy of Stanley L. Cuba.

Page 271—Artists unknown, "The Colonel Investigates the Humboldt,from *Beyond the Mississippi from the Great River to the Great Ocean: Life and Adventures of the Plains, Mountains and Pacific Coast* by Albert D. Richardson (new York: Bliss & Company, 1867). Courtesy of the Denver Public Library, Western History Collection.

Page 276—Lester Vavian, "Miner's House," n.d., sketch. Courtesy of Stanley L. Cuba.

Page 284—Alexander Brownlie, "[Street in] Georgetown, Colorado," n.d., watercolor, 9" x 6". Courtesy of the Denver Public Library, Western History Collection.

Page 300—Original promotional brochure for the Stanley Hotel, Estes Park, Colorado. Courtesy of the Stanley Hotel.

Page 302—Artist unknown, "Stanley Hotel," from *Vanities* by Jack Heifner. Courtesy of the Denver Public Library, Western History Collection.

Page 320—Artist unknown, "Cliff Dwellings" from *The Crest of the Continent: A record of a Summer's Ramble in the Rocky Mountain and Beyond* by Ernest Ingersoll (Chicago: R.R. Donnelley & Sons, 1885). Courtesy of the Denver Public Library, Western History Collection.

Page 323—Frederic Remington, "A Monte Game at the Southern Ute Agency, a.k.a. Mexican Monte," from *Collier's Weekly* [April 20, 1901]. Courtesy of the Frederic Remington Art Museum.

Page 348—Lester Vavian, "Broadway (Denver)," c. 1920, etching. Courtesy of Stanley L. Cuba.

Page 350—Artist unknown, "A group of Celestials," from *Beyond the Mississippi, from the Great River to the Great Ocean: Life and Adventure of the Plains, Mountains and Pacific Coast* by Albert D. Richardson (New York: Bliss & Company, 1867). Courtesy of the Denver Public Library, Western History Collection.

Page 354—Artist unknown, "Washington McClintock's Block," corner of Larimer and 16th Street, Denver, Colorado, from *History of the City of Denver, Arapahoe County, and Colorado*, (Chicago: O.L. Baskin & Co., Historical Publishers, 1880). Courtesy of the Denver Public Library, Western History Collection.

Page 356—A. E. Mathew, lithograph of Larimer Street (1860–1867). Courtesy of Denver Public Library, Western History Collection.

Page 359—L. C. McClure, "Night View of Downtown Denver," c. 1915, photograph. Courtesy of Denver Public Library, Western History Collection.

Page 371—Leon Loughridge, untitled, n.d., watercolor 12" x 16". Courtesy of Stanley L. Cuba.

Page 384—"The Unsinkable Molly Brown" by Meredith Willson, 1960, sheet music. Courtesy of Frank Music Corporation.

BIBLIOGRAPHY

Section I
The Centennial State

Chapman, Arthur. In the *Denver Republican*. December 3, 1911.

Ferril, Thomas Hornsby. *Anvil of Roses*. Boise, Idaho: Ahsahta Press, 1983.

Frost, Robert. "Dedication to Thomas Hornsby Ferril." In "Denver Memories of a Great Poet," by Robert L. Perkin. In the *Rocky Mountain News*, January 30, 1963.

Fynn, Arthur J. "Where the Columbines Grow." Denver: A. J. Fynn, 1911.

Gunther, John *Inside U.S.A.* New York. Harper and Brothers, 1947.

Michener, James A. *About Centennial: Some Notes on the Novel*. New York: Random House, 1974.

Scoggins, C. H. and Charles Avril. "Where the Silvery Colorado Wends Its Way." New York: Jerry Vogel Music Co., Inc., 1929.

Waters, Frank. *The Colorado*. New York: Rinehart and Co., 1946.

Section II
Discovering Colorado

Arnold, Sam'l P. *Eating Up the Santa Fe Trail*. Niwot: University Press of Colorado, 1990.

Clark, C. M. *A Trip to Pike's Peak & Notes by the Way with Numerous Illustrations: Being Descriptive of Incidents and Accidents that Attended the Pilgrimage of the Country through Kansas and Nebraska; Rocky Mountains; Mining Regions; Mining Operations, etc., etc.* Chicago: S.P. Round's Steam Book and Job Printing House, 1861.

Escalante, Francisco Silvestre Vélez de. *The Domínguez-Escalante Journal: Their Expedition through Colorado, Utah, Arizona, and New Mexico in 1776*. Translated by Fray Angelico Chavez. Edited by Ted J. Warner. Provo, Utah: Brigham Young University Press, 1976.

Field, Matt. *Matt Field on the Santa Fe Trail*. Edited by John E. Sunder. Norman: University of Oklahoma Press, 1960.

Fowler, Jacob. *The Journal of Jacob Fowler Narrating an Adventure from Arkansas through the Indian Territory, Oklahoma, Kansas, Colorado, and New Mexico to the Sources of the Rio Grande del Norte, 1821–22*. Edited by Elliott Coues. New York: F.P. Harper, 1898.

Frémont, John Charles. *A Report on an Exploration of the Country Lying between the Missouri River and the Rocky Mountains, on the Line of the Kansas and Great Platte Rivers*. 27th Cong., 3d Sess., 1843. S. Doc. 243.

Greeley, Horace. *An Overland Journey from New York to San Francisco in the Summer of 1859*. New York: C. M. Saxton, Barker and Co., 1860.

Jackson, William Henry. *Time Exposure: The Autobiography of William Henry Jackson.* New York: G. P. Putnam's Sons, 1940.

Larimer, William H.H.. *Reminiscences of General William Larimer and of His Son William H. H. Larimer: Two of the Founders of Denver City.* Lancaster, Pa: The New Era Printing Co., 1918.

Magoffin, Susan Shelby. *Down the Santa Fe Trail and into Mexico: The Diary of Susan Shelby Magoffin, 1846–1847.* Edited by Stella M. Drumm. New Haven: Yale University Press, 1926.

McGrew, A. O. In the *Omaha Times,* February 17, 1859.

Otero, Miguel Antonio. *My Life on the Frontier 1864–1882: Incidents and Characters of the Period when Kansas, Colorado and New Mexico were Passing through the Last of Their Wild and Romantic Years.* New York: The Press of the Pioneers, 1935.

Parkman, Francis. *The California and Oregon Trail.* New York: G. P. Putnam, 1849.

Simonin, Louis L. *The Rocky Mountain West in 1867.* Translated and annotated by Wilson O. Clough. Lincoln: University of Nebraska Press, 1966.

Taylor, Bayard. *Colorado: A Summer Trip.* New York: G. P. Putnam, 1867.

Ward, Artemus. *Artemus Ward: His Travels.* New York: Carleton, 1865.

Wislizenus, F. Adolphus *A Journey to the Rocky Mountains in the Year 1839.* St. Louis: Missouri Historical Society, 1912.

Section III
Shining Mountains

Beebe, Lucius, and Charles Clegg. *Narrow Gauge in the Rockies.* Berkeley, Calif.: Howell-North, 1958.

Bird, Isabella L. *A Lady's Life in the Rocky Mountains.* New York: G. P. Putnam, 1880.

Collins, Judy. *Trust Your Heart: An Autobiography.* Boston: Houghton Mifflin Co., 1987.

Denver, John, and Mike Taylor. "Rocky Mountain High." New York: Cherry Lane Music Publishing Co., Inc., 1972.

Hayes, Mary Eshbaugh. *Aspen Potpourri: A Collection of Aspen Recipes and Ideas.* Aspen, Colo.: Aspen Potpourri Publishers, 1968.

Lavender, David. *One Man's West.* Garden City, N.Y.: Doubleday, 1956.

Lindberg, Gene, and Blanche M. Tice. *In the Shadow of the Rockies.* Denver: Blanche M. Tice, 1931.

Lissy, David. *Colorado Ski!* Englewood, Colo.: Westcliffe Publishers, Inc., 1988.

McCall, C. W. "Wolf Creek Pass." New York: PolyGram Records, Inc., 1978.

Mills, Enos A. *The Spell of the Rockies.* New York: Houghton Mifflin Co., 1911.

Rogers, James Grafton. *My Rocky Mountain Valley.* Boulder, Colo.: Pruett Press, 1968.

Whitman, Walt. *Specimen Days in America.* London: Walter Scott Publishing Co., 1887.

Woolsey, Mary Hale, and Robert Sauer. "When It's Springtime in the Rockies." New York: Robbins Music Corp., 1951.

Zwinger, Ann. *Beyond the Aspen Grove.* Tucson: University of Arizona Press, 1988.

Section IV
Growing Up with Colorado

Black, Baxter. *A Rider, A Roper and a Heck'Uva Windmill Man.* Salinas, Calif.: Coyote Cowboy Company and Record Stockman Press, 1982.

Borland, Hal. *High, Wide and Lonesome.* Philadelphia: J. B. Lippincott Co., 1956.

Bowles, Samuel. *The Switzerland of America: A Summer Vacation in the Parks and Mountains of Colorado.* Springfield, Mass.: Samuel Bowles and Co., 1869.

Dempsey, Jack. *Round by Round: An Autobiography.* New York: McGraw-Hill Book Co., 1940.

Greenberg, Joanne. *Founder's Praise.* New York: Holt, Rinehart and Winston, 1976.

Miller, Nellie Burget. *The Sun Drops Red: Collected Poems of Nellie Burget Miller, Poet Laureate of Colorado.* Denver: Sage Books, 1947.

Moody, Ralph. *Little Britches.* New York: W. W. Norton and Co., 1962.

Sandoz, Mari. *The Cattlemen: From the Rio Grande across the Far Marias.* New York: Hastings House, 1958.

Sykes, Hope Williams. *Second Hoeing.* New York: Putnam, 1935.

Townshend, Richard Baxter. *A Tenderfoot in Colorado.* New York: Dodd, Mead and Co., 1923.

Williams, John. *Butcher's Crossing.* New York: The Macmillan Co., 1960.

Section V
Mining Towns

Backus, Harriet Fish. *Tomboy Bride.* Boulder, Colo.: Pruett Publishing Co., 1969.

Davis, Richard Harding. *The West from a Car Window.* New York: Harper and Brothers, 1892.

Dyer, John Lewis. *The Snow-Shoe Itinerant: An Autobiography of the Rev. John L. Dyer, Familiarly Known as "Father Dyer," of the Colorado Conference, Methodist Episcopal Church.* Cincinnati: Cranston and Stowe, 1890.

Ellis, Anne. *The Life of an Ordinary Woman.* Boston: Houghton Mifflin Co., 1929.

Field, Eugene. *A Little Book of Western Verse.* New York.: Charles Scribner's Sons, 1889.

Foote, Mary Hallock. *A Victorian Gentlewoman in the Far West: The Reminiscences of Mary Hallock Foote.* Edited by Rodman W. Paul. San Marino, Calif.: The Huntington Library, 1972.

Lee, Mabel Barbee. *Cripple Creek Days.* Garden City, N.Y.: Doubleday, 1958.

McLean, Evalyn Walsh. *Father Struck It Rich.* Boston: Little, Brown and Co., 1936.

Rich, Helen. *The Willow-Bender.* New York: Simon and Schuster, 1950.

Richardson, Albert D. *Beyond the Mississippi: From the Great River to the Great Ocean. Life and Adventure on the Prairies, Mountains, and Pacific Coast.* Hartford, Conn.: American Publishing Co., 1867.

Smythe, Pete. *Sweepin's from Smythe's General Store, with Somethin' for the Daily Battle of Life.* Littleton, Colo.: East Tincup Printery, 1987.

Street, Julian. *Abroad at Home: American Ramblings, Observations, and Adventures of Julian Street.* Garden City, N.Y.: Garden City Publishing Co., 1914.

Turnbull, Belle. *The Tenmile Range.* Iowa City: Prairie Press, 1957.

Warman, Cy. *Songs of Cy Warman.* Boston: Rand Avery Co., 1911.

Wolle, Muriel Sibell. *Stampede to Timberline: The Ghost Towns and Mining Camps of Colorado.* Boulder, Colo.: Muriel Sibell Wolle, 1949.

Section VI
The Tabors

Bancroft, Caroline. *Silver Queen: The Fabulous Story of Baby Doe Tabor.* Denver: Golden Press, Inc., 1950.

Dallas, Sandra. "Let's Remember the Real Caroline Bancroft." In the *Denver Post,* October 20, 1985.

Moore, Douglas, and John Latouche. *The Ballad of Baby Doe.* New York: Chappell and Co., Inc., 1956.

Smith, Duane A. *Horace Tabor: His Life and the Legend.* Boulder: Colorado Associated University Press, 1973.

Tabor, Mrs. H. A. W. "Cabin Life in Colorado." In *The Colorado Magazine,* 4 (March 1927): 71–75.

Tabor, Silver Dollar. *Star of Blood.* Denver: Silver Dollar Tabor, 1912.

Tabor, Silver Dollar. *Our President Roosevelt's Colorado Hunt.* Denver: Silver Dollar Tabor, 1908.

Section VII
Pikes Peak

Holmes, Julia Archibald. *A Bloomer Girl on Pikes Peak, 1858.* Edited by Agnes Wright Spring. Denver: Western History Department, Denver Public Library, 1949.

James, Edwin. *Account of an Expedition from Pittsburgh to the Rocky Mountains, Performed in the Years 1819 and '20, by Order of the Hon. J.C. Calhoun, Sec'y of War, under the Command of Major Stephen H. Long.* Philadelphia: H.C. Carey and I. Lea, 1822–23.

Kingsley, Rev. Charles. *South By West, or Winter in the Rocky Mountains and Spring in Mexico.* London: W. Isbister and Co., 1874.

Pike, Zebulon Montgomery. *An Account of Expeditions to the Sources of the Mississippi, and through the Western Parts of Louisiana, to the Sources of the*

Arkansaw, Kans, La Platte, and Pierre Jaun Rivers; Performed by the Order of the Government of the United States During the Years 1805, 1806, and 1807. Philadelphia.: C. and A. Conrad, 1810.

Unser, Bobby. "Introduction." In *Pikes Peak Is Unser Mountain: A History of the Pikes Peak Auto Hill Climb, 1916–1990,* by Stanley L. DeGeer. Albuquerque, N.M.: Peak Publishing Co., 1990.

Section VIII
Good Times

Datwoholet, Ralph J. *The Flick and I.* Smithtown, N.Y.: Exposition Press, 1981.

Dier, Caroline Lawrence *The Lady of the Gardens: Mary Elitch Long.* Hollywood: Hollycrofters, 1932.

Jackson, Carlton. *Hattie: The Life of Hattie McDaniel.* Lanham, Md.: Madison Books, 1990.

Martin, Russell. *The Color Orange: A Superbowl Season with the Denver Broncos.* New York: Henry Holt and Co., 1987.

Melrose, Frances. *Rocky Mountain Memories.* Denver: Denver Publishing Co., 1986.

Norton, Caroline Trask. *The Rocky Mountain Cookbook for High Altitude Cooking.* Denver: Caroline Trask Norton, 1903.

Parkhill, Forbes. *The Wildest of the West.* New York: Henry Holt and Co., 1951.

Sprague, Marshall. *Newport in the Rockies: The Life and Good Times of Colorado Springs.* Denver: Sage Books, 1961.

Thatcher, Joseph Addison. *A Colorado Outing.* Denver: Smith-Brooks Press, 1905.

White, Stephen. *Privileged Information.* New York: Viking, 1991.

Wilde, Oscar. *Impressions of America.* Sunderland, England: Keystone Press, 1906.

Zimmermann, Karl R. *CZ: The Story of the California Zephyr.* Starrucca, Pa.: Starrucca Valley Publications, 1972.

Section IX
Hard Times

Beshoar, Barron B. *Out of the Depths: The Story of John R. Lawson, a Labor Leader.* Denver: The Colorado Labor Historical Committee of the Denver Trades and Labor Assembly, 1942.

Fossett, Frank. *Colorado: Its Gold and Silver Mines, Farms and Stock Ranges, and Health and Pleasure Resorts.* New York: C.G. Crawford, Printer, 1879.

French, Emily. *Emily: The Diary of a Hard-Worked Woman.* Edited by Janet Lecompte. Lincoln: University of Nebraska Press, 1987.

Greatorex, Eliza. *Summer Etchings in Colorado.* New York: G. P. Putnam's Sons, 1873.

Hamil, Harold. *Colorado without Mountains.* Kansas City, Mo.: The Lowell Press, 1976.

Hyde, George E. *Life of George Bent: Written from His Letters*. Edited by Savoie Lottinville. Norman: University of Oklahoma Press, 1968.

Papanikolas, Zeese. *Buried Unsung: Louis Tikas and the Ludlow Massacre*. Salt Lake City: University of Utah Press, 1982.

Różański, Emil. "History of the Miners' Strike in Colorado." In *Essays and Monographs in Colorado History* 7(1987): 73–80.

Sanford, Mollie Dorsey. *Mollie: The Journal of Mollie Dorsey Sanford in Nebraska and Colorado Territories, 1857–1866*. Lincoln: University of Nebraska Press, 1959.

Sinclair, Upton. *King Coal*. New York: The MacMillan Co., 1917.

Section X
The Underside

Burns, Rex. *Strip Search*. New York: The Viking Press, 1984.

Cook, General David J. *Hands Up; or, Twenty Years of Detective Life in the Mountains and on the Plains*. Denver: Republican Publishing Co., 1882.

Dunning, John. *Denver*. New York: Times Books, 1980.

Gantt, Paul H. *The Case of Alferd Packer, the Man-Eater*. Denver: University of Denver Press, 1952.

King, Stephen. *The Shining*. Garden City, N.Y.: Doubleday, 1977.

King, William M. *Going to Meet a Man: Denver's Last Legal Public Execution, 27 July 1886*. Niwot: University Press of Colorado, 1990.

Lindsey, Ben B., and Harvey J. O'Higgins. *The Beast*. New York: Doubleday, Page and Co., 1910.

Lowall, Gene. "The Spider Man Case." In *Denver Murders*. Edited by Lee Casey. New York: Duell, Sloan and Pearce, 1946.

Richards, Eugene. *The Knife and Gun Club*. New York: The Atlantic Monthly Press, 1989.

Twain, Mark. *Roughing It*. Hartford, Conn.: American Publishing Co., 1872.

Section XI
Diverse Peoples

Barker, William J. "Bridey Murphy and the Skeptics." In *The Search for Bridey Murphy,* by Morey Bernstein, with new material by William J. Barker. Garden City, N.Y.: Doubleday, 1965.

Buchtel, William H. "A Paradise for Dyspeptics and Consumptives, 1873." Western History Department, Denver Public Library.

Chase, Mary. *Harvey*. New York: Dramatists Play Service, 1944.

Fante, John. *Wait Until Spring, Bandini*. New York: Stackpole Sons, 1938.

Field, Eugene. *The Little Book of Tribune Verse*. New York: Grosset and Dunlap, 1901.

Fowler, Gene. *Timber Line: A Story of Bonfils and Tammen*. New York: Blue Ribbon Books, 1933.

Garrard, Lewis H. *Wah-To-Yah and The Taos Trail: Or Prairie Travel and Scalp Dances, with a Look at Los Rancheros from Muleback and the Rocky Mountain Campfire*. Cincinnati: H. W. Derby and Co., 1850.

H.H. (Helen Hunt Jackson). *Bits of Travel at Home*. Boston: Roberts Brothers, 1878.

Hosokawa, Bill. *Thunder in the Rockies: The Incredible Denver Post*. New York: William Morrow and Co., Inc., 1976.

Jocknick, Sidney. *Early Days on the Western Slope of Colorado*. Denver: The Carson-Harper Co., 1913.

Lamm, Dottie. *Second Banana*. Boulder, Colo.: Johnson Books, 1983.

Schroeder, Patricia. *Champion of the Great American Family*. New York: Random House, 1989.

Segale, Sister Blandina. *At the End of the Santa Fe Trail*. Milwaukee: The Bruce Publishing Co., 1948.

Smith, H. Allen. *The Life and Legend of Gene Fowler*. New York: William Morrow and Co., 1977.

Wetherill, Benjamin Alfred. *The Wetherills of the Mesa Verde: The Autobiography of Benjamin Alfred Wetherill*. Edited and annotated by Maurine S. Fletcher. Rutherford, N.J.: Fairleigh Dickinson University Presses, 1977.

Section XII
Queen City of the Plains

Amole, Gene. *Morning*. Denver: Denver Publishing Co., 1983.

Barrett, William E. *The Lilies of the Field*. Garden City, N.Y.: Doubleday, 1962.

Carrier, Jim. "The Setting." In *Close to Home: Colorado's Urban Wildlife*. Denver: Denver Museum of Natural History, 1990.

Coit, John. *John Coit: Collection of His Most Popular Columns from the Rocky Mountain News*. Edited by Dave Butler. Denver: Denver Publishing Co., 1986.

Crosby, John B. *Looking Back*. Denver: Logos, Ltd., 1983.

Cussler, Clive. *Raise the Titanic!* New York: The Viking Press, 1976.

Dunikowski, Emil Habdank. "Across the Rocky Mountains in Colorado." In *Essays and Monographs in Colorado History 5* (1987): 27–39.

Goodstein, Phil. *Denver's Capitol Hill*. Denver: Life Publications, 1988.

Johnson, Forrest Hall. *Denver's Old Theater Row: The Story of Curtis Street and Its Glamorous Show Business*. Denver: Gem Publications/Bill Lay Litho, Printers, 1970.

Kerouac, Jack. *On the Road*. New York: Viking Press, 1957.

Lichtenstein, Grace. *Desperado*. New York: The Dial Press, 1977.

Noel, Thomas J. *Denver's Larimer Street: Main Street, Skid Row and Urban Renaissance*. Denver: Historic Denver, 1981.

Raine, William MacLeod. *Colorado*. Garden City, N. Y.: Doubleday, Doran and Co., 1928.

Stafford, Jean. *The Interior Castle*. New York: Harcourt, Brace and Co., 1953.

Willson, Meredith. "Bea-u-ti-ful People of Denver." From the score of *The Unsinkable Molly Brown*. New York: Frank Music Corp., 1960.

Woods, Harold. *My Larimer Street: Past and Gone, 1943–1973*. Winona, Minn.: Ironwood Press, Inc., 1986.

Writers' Program of the Work Projects Administration. *Colorado: A Guide to the Highest State*. New York: Hastings House, 1941.

Zelinger, Michael Jay. *West Side Story Relived: A Collection of Individual Life Histories and Photographs Chronicling Life in the Jewish West Side of Denver Over the Past 100 Years*. Denver: West Side Reunion Committee, 1987.

INDEX OF AUTHORS

INDEX OF ARTISTS

INDEX

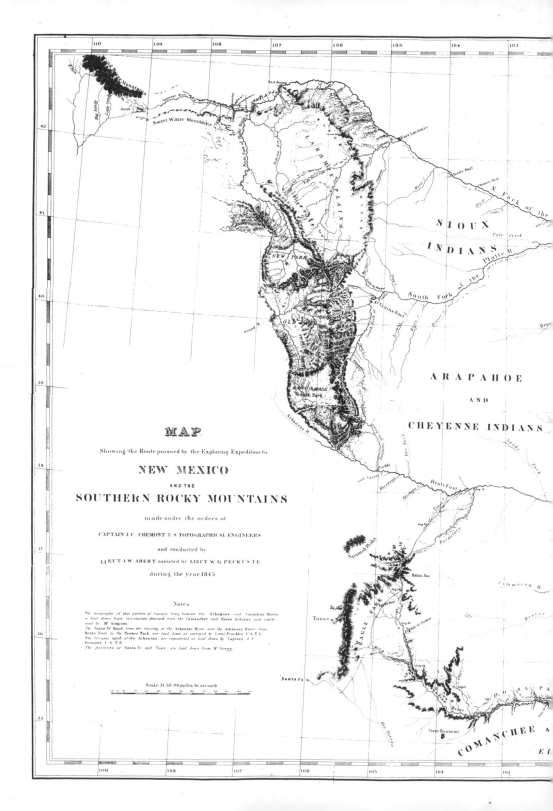

MAP

Showing the Route pursued by the Exploring Expedition to

NEW MEXICO

AND THE

SOUTHERN ROCKY MOUNTAINS

made under the orders of

CAPTAIN J. C. FREMONT U S TOPOGRAPHICAL ENGINEERS

and conducted by

LIEUT. J. W. ABERT, assisted by LIEUT. W. G. PECK U S T E

during the year 1845

Notes

The topography of that portion of Country lying between the Arkansas and Canadian Rivers
is laid down from information obtained from the Comanche and Kiowa Indians and continued by Mr Simpson.
The Santa Fe Road, from the crossing of the Arkansas River and the Arkansas River, from
Bents Fort to the Pawnee Rock are laid down as surveyed by Lieut. Franklin U.S T.E.
The Streams north of the Arkansas are represented as laid down by Captain J. C.
Fremont, U.S T.E.
The positions of Santa Fe and Taos are laid down from Mr Gregg.

Scale 31.56.99 miles to an inch